DANGER FORWARD

The Story of the First Division In World War II

UNITED STATES ARMY

WORLD WAR II

BY

H. R. KNICKERBOCKER, JACK THOMPSON
JACK BELDEN, DON WHITEHEAD
A. J. LIEBLING, MARK WATSON
CY PETERMAN, IRIS CARPENTER
COL. R. E. DUPUY, DREW MIDDLETON AND FORMER
OFFICERS OF THE DIVISION

WITH INTRODUCTION BY HANSON BALDWIN

SOCIETY OF THE FIRST DIVISION
WASHINGTON, D. C.

PUBLISHED BY
ALBERT LOVE ENTERPRISES, ATLANTA, GEORGIA

Printed and Bound by FOOTE AND DAVIES, INC., *Atlanta, Georgia*

Printing Statement:

Due to the very old age and scarcity of this book,
many of the pages may be hard to read due to the
blurring of the original text, possible missing pages,
missing text and other issues beyond our control.

Because this is such an important and rare work, we
believe it is best to reproduce this book regardless of
its original condition.

Thank you for your understanding.

*This book is dedicated to our
4325 comrades who gave
their lives for their country*

FOREWORD

IN presenting this history to men of the First Division, The History Committee feels a word of explanation is due the many subscribers who have so patiently awaited its publication. Difficulties of a not insurmountable, but rather of a time consuming nature have constantly attended this work. It is earnestly hoped that the product will not only justify the time and effort spent but will also justify the patience of those who have so long awaited its completion.

Throughout the war commanders and staffs appreciated the importance of building a "history file". Maintenance of these files was commendably executed, but in the course of the Division's travels these files necessarily had to be stored and subsequently shipped to the United States. There, operational records became part of a vast War Department Historical file in the Pentagon whereas administrative records were assembled in St. Louis. Naturally it has taken time to assemble authentic data—an impossible task but for the complete cooperation of the Historical Division, War Department Special Staff. Fortunately records are most adequate for a detailed military study of First Division operations should some historian desire to undertake such a work. This book, less pretentious in scope, attempts primarily to recount the story of where the First Division went and what it did. The imagination and the memory of its veteran readers will supply those important personal details. Secondarily this book is a story, largely written by recognized masters of the art of story telling, and should therefore be entertaining to soldier and civilian alike.

To our contributing correspondents we of the Division owe our deepest gratitude. Scattered at wars end all over the world, they responded nobly to the call for help. They have generously given their time and talents. The pleasure you men of The First Division derive from reading their chapters will be their sole reward.

If an attempt were made to acknowledge credit due the many individuals in service who have furthered this work, the roster would be too space consuming for publication. No one individual can be credited with complete editorship. Because of the intense interest in this project on the part of Lt. Gen. C. R. Huebner, actual work was begun in 1945. Lt. Col. E. Van V. Sutherland was detailed to Washington to commence the work. Military considerations forced his assignment to other duties and he was replaced by Capt. T. E. Bennett whose work in locating and assembling records, recording data and drafting chapters of "The Record" was invaluable.

Lt. Col. R. F. Evans is due the greatest individual credit. It was he who organized the outline of the book, made the publishing arrangements, secured the help of the correspondents, and accomplished all those tasks which made it possible for the committee to take over a task already well along toward completion. Assignment on foreign service required his relinquishing supervision to Col. R. W. Porter Jr. and, in turn to Col. S. B. Mason.

Maj. Gen. W. G. Wyman has supplied a drive, deftly combined with tact, which has pushed this work to conclusion. He has labored at proof reading drafts, he has handled voluminous correspondence, but most of all he has supplied encouragement and backing when needed. Maj. Gen. F. W. Milburn as commander and representative of the present Division overseas has been most cooperative in pledging financial as well as moral support.

To the authors of chapters of "The Record", much appreciation is due for their contribution. Col. Mason wrote "The Record" on Algeria and on St. Lo.-Mortain. Col. Porter, assisted by Major Don Kellett, wrote Tunicia. Capt. Bennett furnished the basic drafts for other chapters together with extractions from previous Division publications. Capt. C. D. Baylis, USMC (Ret.) was commissioned by the committee to compose, type, edit, assemble and otherwise prepare all manuscripts for the publisher. To Capt. Baylis is due credit for "The Record" on "The Last Kilometer", and for the tedious research necessary for compilation of the "Supplement".

Other officers have helped, among them Col. Seitz, Col. Curtis, Lt. Col. Beck, Lt. Col. Grant and Lt. Col. Rippert whose assistance in proof reading the galleys was of inestimable value in hastening the date of publication.

And last, the title. All units from battalion to supreme headquarters are assigned code names, principally for simplicity of designation in communications. That assigned the First Division was "Danger" for its Division Headquarters. Its forward, or operating headquarters in the field was therefore "Danger Forward" to distinguish it from "Danger Rear", the administrative headquarters. During the battle of El Guettar, Don Whitehead, returning from a front line trip where he had undergone the usual Stukka bombing, came into the forward command post just in time to undergo another bombing. At the entrance to the command post, Don noted a sign on the roadside, arrow pointing toward a grove of date palms and beneath the arrow the words "Danger Forward". In a harrassed sort of way, Don remarked that if he lived through the show he was certainly going to write a book with the title "Danger Forward". Well, here it is, Don. The Division has written *your* book—but not as ably as you have written *our* Omaha Beach.

Washington, D. C.
4 June 1948

The History Committee
Washington, D. C. Branch
Society of the First Division
S. B. Mason
Col., U. S. Army
Chairman

CONTENTS

INTRODUCTION: *By Hanson W. Baldwin.*

THE FIGHTING FIRST

by

HANSON BALDWIN

THE FIRST DIVISION has no monopoly of courage. Its men are human, its generals fallible. It has had its share of panic and disaster, funk and fright. It has known defeat; it has suffered frustration. It was but one of eighty-nine divisions of the United States Army that fought the good fight in World War II, only a part of the team that scaled the ramparts of glory to bring down into the dust the ambitions of Hitler and the pretensions of Japan.

But it has the magic of its name—*The Red One; the Fighting First*. It wears the armor of history and carries the shield of tradition. It is a symbol—of legitimate pride in past achievements, of a democracy's martial determination. It is a fitting representative of the American Army, and there can be no higher praise.

I have known the First Division in peace and war for almost twenty years. I have seen it, in the dull days of garrison duty before the war, split up into small elements, understrength, neglected. I saw it after Kasserine—bloody but unbowed, fighting over the cold djebels and through the steep wadis of North Africa across a land where the ancient legions had kept the Pax Romana with the sword. I saw it in Normandy, upon that bitter beach now forever famed, and I saw it in the hedgerows, where the sunken roads of France were death traps and the pastoral landscape was gouged and torn by war.

Then—and now, as the First stands *en guarde* in Germany in the difficult duties of occupation—there was, to me, one quality above all others which distinguished this division and set it apart beyond all others. It was—and is—a consciousness of tradition. To those who have never soldiered this may seem a trivial characteristic. But it is the backbone of military morale. A unit has esprit when it believes it is the "best damned squad in the best damned platoon in the best damned company in the best damned battalion in the best damned regiment in the best damned division in the whole goddam army". And it gets this esprit from leadership and from a sense of obligation to history.

The First Division has this quality highly. Like the cadet at West Point, with the "long grey line" of those who have gone before beside him, the First does not march alone. Its battle rings and streamers attest its past; its ghostly veterans of St. Mihiel, of the Meuse-Argonne, of El Guettar, of Sicily and Normandy, of Belgium and the Rhine tramp beside the living. Nor is their presence an insensate thing. Almost, the First Division has become—apart and aside from the men who make it—a living entity, a distinct personality with a past, a present and a future. For its officers have taken care to see that this is so, to preserve and strengthen this sense of tradition, to impress upon its new recruits a pride of unit and an understanding—which once absorbed can never be forgotten—of the duties of the living to the dead. To some, this may seem a heavy burden—this sense of obligation to history, this maintenance of the high standards of a brave past—but to the soldier it can be a steadying influence in time of trouble.

He is sustained, too,—the soldier of the Fighting First—by another obligation, the obligation to his comrades. Some psychologists say that one of the dominant factors that keeps men to their guns even in the worst hell of battle is their fear of showing fear. But this is at best a negative explanation of a positive action; many soldiers perform deeds above and beyond the call of duty to help their "buddies". In few units, I think, is this sense of obligation to comrades, this spiritual development of the idea of a fighting team, carried to greater and more successful heights than the First Division.

The First has been blessed through most of its career by leaders who understood the importance of tradition and the twin obligations each good soldier owes—to his unit, past and present, and to his "buddies". Terry Allen and Huebner understood it—and their predecessors in the days between the two wars when it was harder to keep alive a sense of history and to pass on the torch of the past to the future. The First's officers still understand it; in a sense this book represents part of this understanding, by preserving for the future the deeds of the past.

* * * * *

Approximately 50,000 men of whom 4,325 died in battle, served in the First Division in World War II; throughout its history a quarter million to half a million Americans must at one time or another have served in its units. This book is specially for them —the men of the Red One, the Fighting First—but it is a book, too, for Americans, for it chronicles deeds that are now warp and woof of American history, and it interprets—through the eyes of the First Division—the combat narrative of the struggle against Germany in World War II.

The "First was first" has long been an axiom in the Army—a somewhat irritating one to men who did not wear the Red One as their shoulder patch. But it was true again in World War II. The First was among the first divisions to land in North Africa; its units waded out of a rolling, surging sea on to a bloody beach named Omaha, in June 1944, to crack Hitler's Atlantic Wall and from then until the battered remnants of the Wehrmacht dissolved into confusion, the First was always in the van of combat.

Few of its men served it continuously from Oran to the Elbe; the laws of chance were too greatly against them. The experiences recorded here are therefore the composit experiences of 50,000 men; collectively these experiences form part of the soul of the division.

It is difficult if not impossible to single out one action from another, for bullets have a catholic application no matter where they are fired, and blood and mud, boredom and hardship, courage and sacrifice, are part of every campaign.

Yet to the omniscient historian of the future, who will be able to survey his past.—our present,—with the bird's eye view of distance, several names must stand out on the escutcheon of battle. Kasserine—a lonely pass in the North African hills; Kasserine, an American defeat—but yet a place where some men stood and brave men died; Kasserine will live. So, too, will Troina, that hill town of Sicily, set upon its magnificent diadem of mountain; Troina, circled by vineyards raddled by the guns—Troina will live among the battle streamers and the traditions. So, too, will Omaha, that beach on the Bay of the Seine, where the dun-brown sea rolls briskly toward the cliffs and escarpments of Normandy. Omaha will live in proud tradition, for here the backbone of German resistance was forever broken; here the First was first. Omaha and Colleville, Balleroy and its ancient chateau, the shell-splintered trees of the Forest of Cerisy. St. Lo and the surging break-through; this shall live; St. Lo and the sweep across France. Aachen and the West-wall; the "iron shoulder" of the Bulge; St. Vith and Malmedy; the splintered pines and snow-mantled bodies of the slain in Hurtgen Forest—bloodiest of battles—these, too shall live. Then on to the Rhine, mother of German rivers, to and across it—deep into Germany; the First was first.

It will be long, indeed, before the sweeping ebb and flow of these actions find their epic historian. It may even be, like Culloden and Leipzig and Waterloo, that these great battles will someday be but place names on a map marked by the crossed swords of the geographer; to men of another generation, these names so visable to us, may be but half-forgotten memories of dim battles long ago. But even when the details are obscured and gone, even when all the veterans who long since fought them have passd on, there will remain to startle the emotions, quicken the heart and lighten the eye, the traditions that men live by, the traditions of the Fighting First Division—which with the blood and brawn and brains of its men has written across the ramparts of two continents an American Iliad.

◆　　◆　　◆

Chapter I

THE SITUATION

August 1942

THE true significance of America's participation in World War II came on August 14, 1942, with this rather cryptic "news flash" "General Dwight D. Eisenhower has this day been appointed Commander-in-Chief Allied Expeditionary Forces." Coincident with this appointment, General Eisenhower received a secret operational directive from the Combined Chiefs-of-Staff, which stated:—"The President of The United States and the Prime Minister of Great Britain have decided that combined military operations be directed against Africa as early as practicable, with a view of gaining, in conjunction with the Allied Forces in the Middle East, complete control of North Africa from the Atlantic Ocean to the Red Sea."

The decision of the Allied High Command called for an "all-out" movement to either drive the Axis back through the Mediterranean, or at least into smaller corridors, there to be dealt with in due time, as Allied forces grew in strength.

The conquest of North Africa envisaged the attainment of the ultimate objective in three stages: first—the establishment of firm and mutually supported lodgements in the area of Oran (Algiers), and Tunis (Tunisia), on the north coast, and of Casablanca (Morocco), on the west coast. Second—the use of these lodgements as bases to acquire compete control over all North Africa (French), and, if necessary, Spanish Morocco. Third—a thrust eastwards through the Libyan Desert, to take the Axis forces in the Western Desert, in the rear, and annihilate them.

Because of strict limitations in shipping and in naval support, including carriers, the latter two objectives — Morocco and the Libyan Desert were recognized as being "possibly beyond the realm of possibility on a long term basis." In anticipation of the enemy's plan that might rush him into Tunisia, where he might possibly forestall the Allied plans, the conclusions of Prime Minister Churchill are worthy of note:—"Well, if the enemy rushes into Tunisia—where is a better place to kill Germans?"

The strategic problem that faced the Allied High Command was greatly complicated by political considerations outside the scope of strictly military planning. The reactions of the neutral countries of Vichy France, and French North Africa, were clearly to have a vital bearing upon the course of the enemy's counter blows.

The first plan of the Allied High Command was to capture Casablanca in the initial stages as an opening for an auxiliary line of communications, with considerable forces held in readiness to seize Spanish Morocco, and hold it against German onslaught.

It was regarded as a certainty that the Axis would immediately occupy the whole of France, their aim being to forestall the Allies from any possible landing on the Mediterranean Coast, and above all, to attempt to gain control of the French Fleet. "What about the French Fleet?" brought to British hearts an echo of the anxious days of June, 1940.

It also seemed possible that the Axis would do all in its power to retain control of the Sicilian Channel, by seizing Tunis and Bizerte, before the Allies could reach these two important cities. The ability of the Allies to get there first depended on three things: the distance between the two cities and The Allies most easterly lodgement; upon the strength of the forces that could be made sufficiently mobile to act offensively over considerable distance; and upon the resistance, or lack of resistance, that might be offered by the French to the respective invasions.

It was therefore decided that the expedition to take North Africa should appear to be predominately American, and that the necessary contribution of the British Services should be played down in the initial stages. The assaults were to be "All-American", and no British troops were to be landed, for at least a week, in order that the President of The United States would have time to negotiate with the French.

Whether the French greeted the Allied forces as liberators, or resisted Allied invasion, apparent to them as a violation of their neutrality, it was clearly imperative that the Allies should make an impressive display of strength on initial invasions. Half measures would fail to inspire confidence on the one hand, or would encourage resistance on the other. However, there was a greater chance that Spain would maintain her neutrality if she knew that strong forces were at hand to counter any sign of hostility.

Thus the strategic concept of sweeping the Axis from North Africa and establishing Allied control from the Atlantic Ocean to the Red Sea, necessitated an operation on a scale of such magnitude that, once initiated, it would have to be followed through with all the forces and shipping that the situation demanded. It would be the major Allied operation of 1942 and 1943; a substitute for the expedition across the English Channel, originally planned for 1942, but abandoned in June of that year as "strategically unsound at that stage of the war."

The invasion of Africa was the first major United States operation in the war against Germany, World War II. The invasion just had to be successful; anything short of success would have a damaging effect upon the morale of all whose hopes had been buoyed by the entry of The United States into World War II.

In the first plan for the invasion of Africa, it was estimated that seven combat divisions would be adequate. Later it was estimated that twelve divisions would be needed.

The only U. S. Combat Division in the European Theater of Operations, as of August, 1942, was the First Infantry Division. This Division was ready to spearhead any invasion, on any continent, at any time.

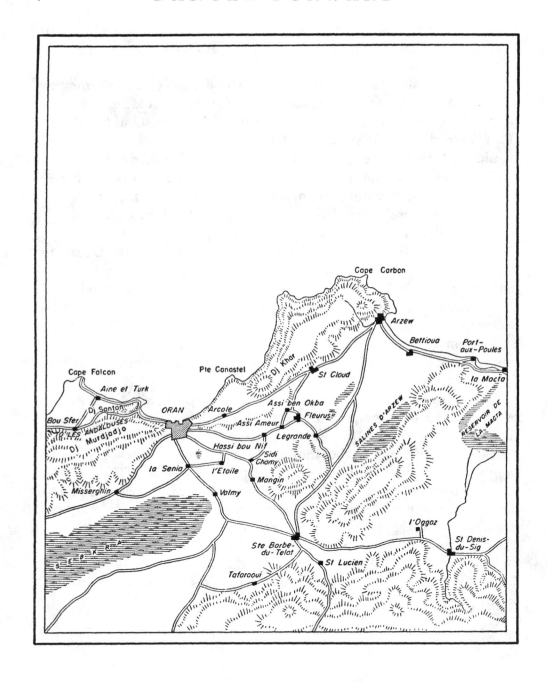

(November 8 to November 10, 1942)

The Record

TO MEN of the First Division there are foreign-place names which conjure up memories both pleasant and bitter. For instance, mere mention of the name Arzeu creates in the imagination that acrid, pungent odor for ever to be associated with the first sensory perception of the North African coast. Les Andalouses means wetness, and darkness and nervous expectancy. Djebel Murdjadjo seems synonymous with rocks, whining bullets, and a lofty view. St. Cloud means death, and shell-spattered buildings, and sullen unforgiving inhabitants. Ste. Barbe du Tlelat means a big white chateau set apart in a sea of mud. The name of each town and village brings a vivid memory. And Oran means a city—trolley tracks, the odor of automobiles burning alcohol, wine doped with a sort of hashish, chic French women and slovenly dressed men, dirty Arabs and dirty streets. Dilapidated and down at heel in 1942, confused and suspicious in November of that year, it emerged like Cinderella for an hour of acclaim, and at the stroke of twelve when the war moved on, it sank back into the obscurity of its dirty streets and its ragged Arabs.

To all the world, though it could not be apparent at the time, Oran, like Gettysburg or the Marne, symbolizes the high tide of an ideology whose destiny was written in the smoking ruins of Berlin. To the Allies of 1942, Oran is a milestone which marked the first offensive step toward final victory. Oran is an unforgettable memory of the first shock of battle, the first assault, the first objective taken in World War II by American troops in the European Theater. And to those men fortunate enough to return from the vicious fighting in Tunisia, Oran means bitter disappointment, for during the months between Ousseltia, El Guettar and Oued Tine, Oran had become populated with a new soldier, smartly dressed in fresh khaki with distinguishing insignia of the SOS, and feeling a curious jealousy toward the wool-clad combat soldier newly returned from the magnificent accomplishment of Rommel's defeat in Tunisia.

That the First Division was involved in the capture of Oran was not just a happenstance. Back before Pearl Harbor, the Division was perfecting its technique in both ground and amphibious work. One of the few Regular Army Divisions in a shrunken peacetime establishment, it was proudly displaying its heritage of six campaign stars won in World War I. Its major components had not lost their identity through the years of peace. Its standards were high; an obligation to its heritage was keenly felt by all.

When, in August of 1942 the First Division, less an advance detachment of one battalion of the 16th Infantry, moved from Indiantown Gap to the New York Port of Embarkation to board the Queen Mary, it was spearheading a mighty buildup in the European Theater in furtherance of the War Department's strategic decision to defeat Germany first, then finish off the Japanese. With the whole Division aboard ship, the Queen Mary silently slipped out of New York Harbor overnight the 1st-2nd of August.

On the 8th of August the Queen Mary entered the Clyde and majestically warped up to the docks of Gourock, Scotland, where waiting trains were prepared to carry the Division to its temporary home in England. This home, which the Division was to know less than two months, was a British Army cavalry post called Tidworth Barracks, built much on the order of a permanent garrison in the United States, and located near Salisbury, Wiltshire, approximately 50 miles southwest of London. There the advance detachment had everything well organized for the reception of the Division. Barracks and quarters were occupied, communications established, and training made more realistic by blackout and air raids, was begun in earnest.

This stay at Tidworth Barracks, served most admirably as a transition period for men of the Division. Back in the States the war had been far away. Auto tires and gasoline were being rationed, but in all other respects life among civilians were more or less normal. Here in England, however, one immediately sensed a difference.

Unreality had disappeared with the first blitz. Everybody was working. People went seriously about their necessary duties, with some spare time for play, but no heart for it. This nearness to war was impressive.

Perhaps through naivete, perhaps because of his vitality, the American soldier brought a new hope to England. There were not many American soldiers in England in the summer of 1942. Some air corps units had arrived but had not, at the time, flown any operational missions. Big headquarters, too, were being established, but on the whole, an American soldier on pass in London was not a common sight.

In appraising British attitude toward the Yanks, each man will have his own unalterable opinion. Yet on the whole, men of the First Division have often summarized this attitude by saying: "They were friendly and courteous, better hosts than we'd have been if British troops had been in our country." So the First Divisioner took his blackout, food shortages, crowded trains and busses, rationing, and hard training which he balanced off against widespread friendliness, passes to London, dates with ATS girls and excellent NAFFI shows. It all added up on the plus side for the American so morale was high.

The British, on the other hand, were giving a marvelous exhibition of their steadiness in the face of great adversity. From their viewpoint, things were a bit sticky. They had stalled off invasion in the Battle of Britain, but German air raids were still doing considerable damage to London and other important cities. U-boats were sinking ships the Allies could ill afford to lose. Convoys through the Mediterranean to Malta or Cairo took a beating from both U-boats and aircraft. Rommel was at the height of his success in the western desert, with the British Army pushed back a hundred miles inside the frontiers of Egypt. The Russian Ally wasn't doing so well either, having just lost the Kerch Peninsula and a large part of the food-producing Ukraine, while further north he was fighting desperately to keep the Germans out of Stalingrad. A platoon of First Division infantry making a daytime practice march near Tidworth Barracks was attacked by a lone German fighter-bomber. In the United States newspapers reported that an audacious German submarine had laid underwater mines across the entrance to Chesapeake Bay, blocking all sea traffic there for two days. Our own war with the Japs was not adding much encouragement either, with Bataan still a very fresh memory. Into this pessimistic atmosphere came the First Division bringing some hope of striking back in the near future — some promise of future events taking a turn for the better.

Routine was quickly established at Tidworth Barracks. There was no indication of any specific operational mission in the offing so activity again centered around combat training and re-equipping. So wide was the field of choice for possible operational use, one could hear in any discussion of future moves the names Dakar, Brittany Peninsula or Norway. It therefore came as somewhat of a shock to receive orders in mid-August to lay on plans for CT 18 to take Philippeville, which lies along the North African coast about halfway between Tunis and Algiers. At first sight, the proposed plan appeared quite risky. On second sight it looked worse, so that plan was discarded only to be superseded by another more impossible of accomplishment than the first. This latter envisaged a cross channel invasion by the First Division unassisted on either flank and with no follow-up reserves. A quick check of landing craft available in the United Kingdom proved shortages so acute this shore-to-shore amphibious operation hardly got beyond the academic discussion stage.

Then, on the 3rd of September the Division Commander, Major General Terry Allen, who had gone into London the night before for a command conference, telephoned his Chief of Staff, Colonel Dutch Cota, at Tidworth Barracks giving instructions that he (Colonel Cota) was to come to London at once and bring the G2, G3, and G4 along with him. The only information General Allen could give over the telephone was that an important staff conference was to be held there in London the next morning.

At 9:30 A.M. on the morning of September 4th, General Allen and his staff reported to Norfolk House (planning headquarters in London) as directed. It was at once apparent that something of major importance was about to transpire. The presence of so many senior officers — British and American — Army, Navy and Air — could only mean one thing — an offensive operation.

The conference, once under way, lasted until late afternoon. So far as the First Division was concerned, that day saw the evolution of the basic strategy and tactics which guided its successful attack on Oran.

In order to understand the action of the First Division in the Oran operation it is essential that one have some knowledge of the overall strategy being employed. Without going into details, suffice it to say that both the United States and British governments considered it politically as well as militarily desirable that offensive operations be undertaken somewhere in the European Theater before the end of the year. When approached from the military point of view successful invasion of the continent of Europe was discarded as being beyond Allied capabilities in 1942. Norway offered no possibilities for a decisive campaign. North Africa, on the other hand, did offer certain distinct advantages as a theater for operations. Politically, North Africa being a French colonial area would, or should, be fundamentally pro-ally. It could therefore be expected to offer no serious resistance to allied occupation. It might even renounce its Vichy allegiance and welcome the Allies without even a token resistance. The persistence of this thought in the minds of certain individuals is one of the more intriguing psychological aspects of the North African campaign.

But whether the French in North Africa resisted or not, there still existed a very real allied capability of establishing a firm foothold on the North African continent. Military advantages resulting therefrom are obvious. Bases from Casablanca to Cairo would give sorely needed protection to Mediterranean convoys, deprive the Axis of local agricultural products, threaten the "soft underbelly of Europe" and might even trap Rommel and his Afrika Korps. Once the Allies established these bases, an Axis effort to dislodge them could be made extremely costly in men, supplies and transportation. To the high command, it looked good. They gave the nod of approval on the strategic concept and operational plans were formulated.

"TORCH" was the code word given this operation. All operations in this war were given some such designation. There was "OVERLORD" for the Normandy invasion, "NEPTUNE" for the assault phase, "COBRA" for the St. Lo breakout, "HUSKY," "BOLERO," and countless more. These code words served no purpose of secrecy but did simplify references to the particular operation. So "TORCH" meant the operation which landed three task forces in North Africa on the 8th of November, 1942.

One of these three task forces was organized in and sailed from the United States. It struck near Casablanca and had as its mission the capture of Casablanca and surrounding territory. It was known as the Western Task Force.

The other two task forces were mounted in the United Kingdom, sailed in British ships from British ports and were known respectively as the Eastern Task Force and the Center Task Force. The former was largely a British contingent, landed near Algiers and had as its mission the capture of that town.

The Center Task Force, whose principal element was the First Division, landed near Oran and had that city as its final objective. Being on British ships, naval command was vested in a British Admiral, Troubridge, but ground forces, being American, were under the command of Major General Lloyd Fredendall, Commanding General, II Corps.

All three task forces were to make a simultaneous landing on designated beaches at 1:00 A.M. on November 8th. Making allowances for the difference in time zone, President Roosevelt was able to broadcast an announcement of the landings on the evening of November 7th, in the United States.

From September 4th, until all echelons of the Division were aboard ships, Norfolk House was a nerve center of constantly increasing activity. Many apparently loose ends had to be tied together in order to produce a complete and practical plan, worked out in the most minute detail while constantly straining to maintain that fine balance between effective secrecy and effective dissemination of sufficient information to permit intelligent cooperation. American Army personnel had to learn British Naval jargon, and vice versa. No firm list of available ships could be obtained. Almost daily some new unit was added to the troop list which required a refiguring of all personnel and cargo space. Every subordinate unit could prove, at least to its own satisfaction, that it was not being given a fair share of ship space. The number of landing craft available at destination was anybody's guess — it depended on receipt of craft from the United States and on shipyard engineers for the number of davits which could be installed on ships not yet in the yards.

Through this maze of intangibles the plan took form. Oran would be taken by a double pincer. The Division less Combat Team 26, would constitute the "Z" force, would land in and south of Arzeu and then drive inland to strike Oran from the east. CT 26 would constitute the "Y" force, would land in the vicinity of Les Andalouses, seize the western heights dominating Oran, then drive in toward the city from the west in coordination with the drive from the east. These two forces forming a main effort, or base of maneuver, were augmented by armored forces from the First Armored Division. Landing on Z beach behind the left flank unit of the First Division, the bulk of Combat Command B was to pass through the captured beachhead, swing south of the Z force and enter Oran from the southeast. A second armored column from this same Combat Command B would land to the westward of the First Division Y force, then swing in on Oran from the southwest.

Accurately timed to arrive previously at H-Hour, a paratroop battalion (2nd Battalion, 503rd Parachute Infantry), would drop on La Senia airport, just six kilometers south of Oran, for quick seizure of that airfield. It would then speed southward to take the second airfield in the Oran area, Tafaraoui, some fifteen kilometers away.

An important element of the grand strategy of the North African campaign was an extension eastward to Tunisia. Almost certainly the Germans would attempt to get there first, and they were better positioned to do so. Nevertheless, advantages of winning the race for Tunisia were sufficient to warrant the Allies making a try for it. Thus speed in capturing Oran became important as did securing its port facilities before demolition work could be effected. A task force under the code name "RESERVIST" was set up to accomplish this end. Made up of combat elements of the 6th Armored Infantry Battalion, and embarked on two converted destroyers, this force was scheduled to break its way into the inner harbor of Oran at H plus two hours, seize the docks, and prevent sabotage. Unfortunately the operation proved disastrous when attempted. The ships met a withering fire from port defenses, both went down, and few men survived the short engagement.

With this general plan of action in mind and with a full appreciation of the important influence of terrain on any military operation, it is well to examine the battlefield topography before proceeding to a more detailed discussion of the final plan as executed by the First Division.

In the first place there seems to be a general misconception of the geography and climate of the north coast of Africa. Romantic novels of the Beau Geste variety would have one visualize this country as a sandy desert populated by Arab warriors on prancing white horses with a sprinkling of French Foreign Legionnaires for color. Dissuasion from such a misconception is necessary if one is to accurately picture the country or properly associate its natural romantic attractiveness. The Mediterranean coast is definitely not a desert. An inland mountain range separates this coastal strip from the Sahara Desert giving the former a climate not unlike that of the south coast of continental Europe. All important cities, in fact all development of the country, is to be found in this fertile coastal strip. Hot and dry in summer, cool to cold and rainy in winter, Northern Algeria supports a mixed population of Arabs and French colonials who exploit its great agricultural potentialities. South of the mountains the Sahara Desert is pretty much as romantic novels picture it.

Oran, focal point of all converging attacks and principal objective of the First Division, lies amphitheatre-like in a break of the coastal mountains. Immediately on its western side Djebel Santon towers over the dock area and Djebel Murdjadjo rises some two thousand feet to completely dominate the city. On the southern side of the city, *i.e.,* the side away from the waterfront, the ground is rather flat and open. Some ten kilometers south of Oran is the Sebkra, one of those North African wet weather lakes which is in reality a shallow depression with no natural drainage. This one is about fifteen kilometers wide by forty kilometers long, is covered with a few inches of water in rainy weather and, as might be expected, the area is useless the year round. La Senia Airport lies between the Sebkra and the city.

The area southeast and east of the city is a practically treeless, gently rolling and open country used almost exclusively for grape farming. Fairly good hard surface roads criss-cross this farming section, with two main arterial routes leading generally eastward. The inland route passes through such familiar towns as Valmy, Ste. Barbe du Tlelat, St. Denis du Sig, Perregaux and thence eventually to Algiers. Approximately twenty-six kilometers from Oran out this inland route was situated the large military airdrome at Tafaroui. The second route leading northeastward out of Oran leads through such places as Assi Bou Nif, Fleurus, St. Cloud, and Renan, strikes the coast at Arzeu, then follows the coast through Mostaganem and on into Algiers.

Northeastward of Oran along the coastline the terrain becomes precipitous so that the point of land north of the highway from Oran to Arzeu is a mountainous mass rising some 2,000 feet at the high point. On the Oran end of these mountains Djebel Khar looks down on fortified Point Canastel and dominates at its midpoint the main road from St. Cloud to Oran. The eastern end of these mountains forms a rugged cape which separates the Bay of Oran from the Gulf of Arzeu — the latter a semi-circular body of water some 35 kilometers across and characterized by a sandy shoreline backed by low flat country inland. The town of Arzeu lies on the western edge of this gulf; Mostaganem is directly across on the eastern side. The highway around the shoreline is paralleled by a narrow-gauge railroad which turns inland at Arzeu and runs through St. Cloud and Fleurus to Oran.

Approximately 22 kilometers west of Oran, Cape Lindles and Cape Falcon form between them a small gulf which shelters the little village of Les Andalouses. A network of coastal roads serves the farming country and the small villages which lie between the shoreline and the dorsal range which rises immediately inland. The principal route connecting Les Andalouses with Oran runs first through Bou Sfer then through the narrow defile between Djebel Santon and Djebel Murdjadjo before emerging on the western side of the city. A second route important in this operation runs out to the point of Cape Falcon, where large coast defense guns were located, thence along the coast through Mers el Kebir and into Oran. In the flat base of Cape Falcon, the small village of Aine el Turk lies at the hub of several secondary farm roads. At Mers el Kebir the road passes through a rocky defile between Djebel Santon's precipitious north slope and the sea. No roads and few trails traverse the dorsal range which closely parallels the coast and occupies all the area between the sea shore and the previously described marshy area known as the Sebkra. Westward, the dorsal extends on down the coast. Its eastern terminus is the rugged Djebel Murdjadjo.

Looking down on Oran from the heights of Djebel Murdjadjo, one's perspective prods the imagination into evoking visions of the past. Oran had seen violence throughout its centuries of existence. Roman legions wrested it from Carthaginians and in turn lost it to Arab conquerors. Spain owned it a short while, then lost it to the Turks. Around 1830 the French took it from the Turks which more or less ended its days of violence until the British Fleet was forced to shell French Naval vessels at Mers el Kebir in 1940 to prevent their use by the Axis. The next conquerors of Oran wore steel helmets, miniature Stars and Stripes and RED ONES.

As a city Oran ranks second to Algiers in French North Africa with a pre-war population of some 200,000 inhabitants, three-fourths of them being European. As an objective of the First Division, Oran is passed back to history with the accompanying notation: "Mission accomplished, objective taken."

Returning to a more detailed consideration of the Division's tactical plan, it will be remembered that the main effort consisted of a double envelopment of Oran, one force coming in from the east and the other approaching from the west. The eastern arm of the double pincer, and somewhat the stronger of the two, was to land in Arzeu and on the beaches directly south thereof. From right (north) to left (south) the alignment of units was as follows:

The 1st Ranger Battalion, under Lieutenant Colonel Bill Darby, was to land half of its force right in Arzeu, the other half on narrow beaches just north of the town, seize the docks as a precaution against sabotage, sweep through the upper part of the town, join forces and capture or neutralize the seacoast defenses at North Battery and Fort de la Pointe. The importance of this latter mission was emphasized because large caliber guns in these fortifications would endanger the landing if still in enemy hands at daylight when observed fire would permit their more effective use.

On the left of the Rangers, and beginning just south of Arzeu, CT 18 was to land two Battalion Landing Teams abreast over Z Green Beach, the 3rd Battalion on the right with the mission of assisting the Rangers in the capture of Arzeu. The 1st Battalion on the left had the mission of driving inland to seize St. Cloud and Djebel Khar (on the Division Beachhead line), and being prepared to continue on order toward capture of the Division objective. The 2nd Battalion was to land in rear of the 1st and 3rd Battalions as CT Reserve, employable as directed by the CT commander, Colonel Frank U. Greer.

Next, leftward (southward) along the beach, CT 16 under command of Colonel Henry B. Cheadle, was to land with two Battalion Landing Teams abreast on Z White Beach. The 3rd Battalion on the right was to advance straight inland to seize and secure its portion of the Division Beachhead Line through Fleurus-Ferme St. Eloi, while assuring an open road for the passage of CC "B" 1st Armored Division. The 1st Battalion on the left was to rapidly clear its beaches for the subsequent landing of CC "B," then push south along the beach to La Macta and En Nekala, there to secure the left flank of the landing.

The above mentioned armored columns of CC "B" were to land on Z Red Beach under First Division command, pass through the 16th and through the Division Beachhead Line at which point command reverted, thence on into Oran on the southeast of the city.

The pincer arm from the west, Combat Team 26, was to land on Y Beach (vicinity Les Andalouses) with two battalions abreast. The 3rd Battalion on the left (east) had the mission of driving through Bou Sfer and on to the heights of Djebel Murdjadjo.

The 2nd Battalion on the right (west) was to protect the right flank of the landing with one company from the vicinity of El Ancor while the remainder of the Battalion pushed eastward along the left flank of the 3rd Battalion with the principal mission of clearing Aine el Turk and the coast defenses on Cape Falcon. The 1st Battalion landing in reserve would fulfill a normal reserve mission, generally following the 3rd Battalion unless ordered otherwise.

Colonel Alexander N. Stark, Jr., was in command of the Regiment (and Combat Team), but since this force was operating as a detached command until effective communication could be established ashore, Brigadier General Teddy Roosevelt, Assistant Division Commander, was placed in overall command of the "Y" force by the Division Commander, Major General Terry Allen.

Landing further westward down the coast at the village of Mersa Bou Zedjar, Force X (part of CC "B" 1st Armored Division), was to drive inland along the north side of the Senkra and strike Oran from the southwest.

Previous mention has been made that all landings were scheduled for 1:00 A.M., November 8th.

From the earliest inception of a plan for invasion of North Africa, the paramount enigma was probable French reaction to invasion. The high command tended toward optimism. Lower echelons, more intimately involved with execution of the plans, took a dim view of walking ashore to be immediately greeted as friends. As G2's unfolded the capabilities of the French defenders in the Oran area, it was readily apparent that the capture of Oran could be a bitterly contested operation. In the area, and capable of being put into action on the day of the landings, were no less than 5,500 French troops organized as infantry, mechanized cavalry, artillery and supporting elements. On the following day an additional 2,000 could be put into action, and by the end of five days approximately 12,000 men could be mustered to oppose our landings.

By the middle of October all echelons had completed their plans. In the six weeks devoted to this planning work, commanders and staffs down to and including battalion level had been drawn into the secret of the operation. Sincere efforts were made to limit knowledge of "TORCH" to just those whose duties required this top secret information, but it is surprising how many individuals this category includes. More surprising is the number of individuals who were not given the information. The only significance attaching to this observation is that plans had to be so minutely complete that no oversight would crop up during briefing aboard ships when secrecy was entirely lifted. Even the distribution of orders and maps became an enormous practical problem under these conditions.

Since only a small percentage of the Division was involved in the planning, training of the Division continued, with greater objectivity but with due caution not to divulge the objective. A final amphibious exercise, known as "MOSSTROOPER," was held in Scotland on October 18th after which all troops, staffs, commanders and attaches began final embarkation. Tidworth Barracks closed out, the London planning group folded, the administrative headquarters in Glasgow packed up, and all converged on the transports waiting in the Clyde.

Organization for transport loading logically paralleled the tactical employment of the units so loaded. In general there were three transport divisions, each having personnel and cargo ships assigned for loading in accordance with the overall plan. A natural grouping was effected by assigning each Combat Team to a transport division as a basic element. In chart form assignments were as follows, listing only basic infantry assault units to achieve brevity.

TRANSDIV. 18
(Combat Team 18)

SHIP: PRINCIPAL ASSAULT UNIT:

HMS. *Royal Ulsterman*)
HMS. *Ulster Monarch*)   1st Ranger Battalion.
HMS. *Royal Scotsman*)

HMS. *Reina del Pacifico*)   Division Headquarters; CT 18
                               Headquarters; 3rd Battalion, 18th
                               Infantry CT.

HMS. *Tegelberg*)   2nd Battalion, 18th Infantry CT.

HMS. *Ettrick*)   1st Battalion, 18th Infantry CT.

TRANSDIV. 16
(Combat Team 16)

HMS. *Warwick Castle*)   Division Artillery Headquarters;
                               CT 16th Infantry Headquarters;
                               3rd Battalion, 16th Infantry CT.

HMS. *Duchess of Bedford*)   1st Battalion, 16th Infantry CT; 2nd
                               Battalion, 16th Infantry CT.

TRANSDIV. 26
(Combat Team 26)

HMS. *Monarch of Bermuda*)   Assistant Division Commander;
                               Headquarters, Combat Team 26;
                               2nd Battalion, 26th Infantry CT.

HMS. *Glengyle*)   3rd Battalion, 26th Infantry CT.

HMS. *Llangibby Castle*)   1st Battalion, 26th Infantry CT.

In all, there were approximately fifty transports in the Center Task Force plus a British escort of some fifty naval vessels impressively led by the *Battleship HMS. Rodney*.

Drama attends every sailing, even in peacetime. Imagination takes hold, obscures reality, and whispers of romance and high adventure at the far end of an ocean voyage. Thus on the evening of October 26th, aboard the mightiest assault convoy yet assembled, thousands of men waited quietly for the feel of throbbing engines which would signal them on to high adventure — place unknown, time unknown. For hundreds of them that high adventure would be death on the field of battle. For other hundreds, high adventure would come in the form of painful wounds, or decorations, or failure, or merely survival to move on to other battlefields. At nine o'clock that evening a light, almost imperceptible, vibration ran through the ship. Another, and still another — until a steady pulsing of engines under full power signaled the start toward that high adventure.

The following morning, October 27th, found the convoy steaming westward, out of sight of land and experiencing typical First Division weather. On the water First Division weather is a high wind and a heavy sea. On land it is rain and mud. In the air it is overcast, operational for enemy planes but not for our own. Rough water was provoking its usual discomforts. Not until November 1st did the weather break advantageously. By that time the convoy had zig-zagged in a wide arc to warmer latitudes. A bright sun, a calm sea, and a total absence of enemy submarines combined to engender an atmosphere not unlike that of a pleasure cruise. War seemed very far away — until this first day of November, when secrecy was completely lifted on the forthcoming operation. From that day onward, right up to H-hour, intensive study of the "TORCH" plan occupied the waking hours of every officer and man. No longer was there danger of a torpedoed ship giving up the secret through some rescued soldier or sailor. D-Day was too close at hand for possible leakage of information to be acted on by the enemy. Now the job was to get down to facts; to study in detail the beaches, the terrain, in fact all parts of the plan so that its execution could be as flawless as was humanly possible.

Ensuing days brought little change in conditions until November 6th, when the convoy headed into the Mediterranean. After such careful briefing every one knew the convoy had to pass Gibraltar some time during that day in order to reach its destination. However, no landfall was made until darkness disclosed a glow in the sky on the port bow which was correctly taken to be the Spanish mainland whose non-belligerant cities had no need for blackout. At 10:00 P.M. a single light on the starboard beam marked Tangiers. On the port side Gibraltar was dark.

As the dawn light of November 7th brought land into sharper focus, the ship's rails were crowded with spectators. On the port quarter Gibraltar could still be faintly seen receding across the horizon while the Spanish coast to the east of Gibraltar was quite discernible even to the naked eye. On the starboard side, the point of land at Tangiers, where a light was seen the night before, had faded into the skyline. In a constantly changing pattern, the convoy formation was steaming due eastward, transports in three long columns in the center, heavier warships next outermost, and the tiny destroyers bobbing rapidly on the perimeter so distant the eye could barely distinguish their silhouettes. Anxious eyes looked skyward, momentarily expecting the appearance of enemy planes. Equally anxious eyes studied the chopping sea where every wave was imagined to be hiding an enemy submarine. As the day wore on anxiety tapered off to amazed incredulity that such an enormous convoy could traverse such limited waters without inviting a single attack. But a soldier can accept unseen danger just so long, and when it fails to materialize he accepts the situation and relaxes, while still retaining the sixth sense which will alert him in a flash should the danger suddenly materialize. Preparation for debarkation was complete. There was nothing to do now but wait for the order to form at boat stations for the assault on the beach.

No large military operation is properly conducted without a cover plan. Deceiving the enemy is not only sound military strategy leading to greater assurance of success, but it is also a problem of the first magnitude involving details of planning and execution no less difficult of coordination than the operation itself. Plausibility is its essential and fundamental characteristic. Absence of a major enemy effort against this gigantic North African convoy is lofty tribute to the careful thought and effort which went into the cover plan.

It would be naive to assume that such port filling concentrations of shipping could be assembled in English waters without coming to the attention of German intelligence. But it did make sense to assume they could be misled as to purpose and destination. Until the convoy steamed into the Mediterranean, there were so many logical places the convoy could go it was hardly worthwhile to resort to deception. But once in the Mediterranean it was imperative that Axis intelligence be led to believe the destination was the Eastern Mediterranean. If this belief could be fostered and subsequently supported by other bits of evidence, the enemy could be expected to strike at a time and place most advantageous to himself. The narrow passage between Sicily and Tunisia looked like the place. Axis submarines, bombers, fighters and surface craft could concentrate in this area where they already had bases, and could strike a disastrous blow to the unsuspecting convoy while most vulnerable. It also made sense to Axis intelligence that the convoy would go through this trap. British interests in Cyprus, in Turkey, Suez, Cairo, logically called for support by sea. General Montgomery, pushing westward across the desert, could certainly use supplies and reinforcements. Malta, just inside the bottleneck, was still bravely holding on only because British convoys took their losses and continued to supply its defenders. No. G2 could ignore the logic of the Eastern Mediterranean as a destination for this convoy.

So the German high command concentrated all available forces in the Sicilian channel area, then sat back gloatingly to wait for the convoy to steam into the trap.

As darkness swallowed up the convoy on the evening of November 7th, it was still steaming at 11½ knots toward Malta and destruction.

Soldiers leaning over the starboard rail in the increasing darkness could plainly see a bright glow on the horizon. Suddenly all the hours of briefing since the lifting of secrecy on the operation kaleidescoped into full realization of the correct answer to a question which needed no asking. Oran. And the lights were on. An individual surge of optimism was a first reaction. Surely if there was no blackout, the French were joyously awaiting our debarkation. What a celebration. The First Division would know what to do about that. Imagination being what it is, and individuals being what they are, these fanciful thoughts raced excitingly through every mind, bringing an unseen light to the eyes and a faint smile to bronzed features. A kindly darkness providentially substituted therefor a realistic comprehension of the explanation of why Oran was a blaze of light. The cover plan had worked.

Lest a watchful enemy submarine or reconnaissance plane pick up some significant change of direction in the convoy, all ships continued sailing eastward until they disappeared from view in the gathering darkness. Then, by individually executing a sharp turn to starboard, the convoy melted away into groups of ships steaming southward toward the African shore where they would drop anchor in their respective transport areas some five miles off the assigned beach.

Shortly before midnight all transports had come to rest and sailors were working feverishly in the darkness to get the landing craft lowered into the water. Passageways were crowded as assault teams groped their way into the boats. No sound could be heard on the beaches. Not a shot had been fired. The muffled roar of landing craft motors seemed loud enough in the oppressive still-

ness to wake the dead. As loaded landing craft assembled around
the transports, prepared to make a dash for the beach, time stood
still. Every individual listened intently for the first hostile shot
which would start the battle. Completely assembled boat groups
eased shoreward, motors still muffled at half speed. A thousand
yards from the beach throttles were opened wide and with a mighty
roar all landing craft surged toward the beach. Almost immediately, off on the right flank where the Rangers were assaulting
the Arzeu dock area, a stream of tracer bullets announced the
opening of the Battle of Oran. Ships clocks on the bridge of the
Reina showed precisely 12:55 o'clock.

On the right at Arzeu, the Ranger Battalion will be remembered as having the primary mission of capturing the seacoast
defenses at Fort de la Pointe and North Battery. Two companies
landed right in the dock area and quickly had complete control of
the docks. Then they pushed on through Arzeu to join with two
more companies which had landed two miles north of the town.
The combined force then proceeded to the capture of the seacoast
defenses. A prearranged Very light signal — green and amber —
denoting success in the neutralization of these naval guns was seen
at 2:00 A.M. The British naval commander on seeing this signal
heaved a sigh of relief, moved his flotilla two miles closer to shore,
and the Rangers went about the job of mopping up the town, picking up prisoners and securing all defenses of the town.

The 3rd Battalion, 18th Infantry (reinforced), landed on the
strand just south of the town, overcame scattered resistance, then
moved in on Arzeu from the south side to help the Rangers mop up
the town. By 9:00 A.M. the town was completely in American
hands and was comparatively quiet except for an occasional sniping shot from a disgruntled civilian. This, incidentally, was a
source of great irritation and no small danger to troops charged
with policing the newly taken town.

The 1st Battalion, 18th Infantry, had no difficulty on the beach
so proceeded directly to the attack on St. Cloud. The 2nd Bat-

talion, 18th Infantry (in reserve), when landed, followed in trace behind the 1st Battalion. At 9:00 A.M. the 1st Battalion was heavily engaged at St. Cloud where unexpected but determined opposition was causing an appreciable number of casualties. The 2nd Battalion was moving up to help the 1st Battalion.

On Z White beach Combat Team 16 landed its right battalion (the 3rd) without beach opposition and at once commenced its advance to Ferme St. Eloi against light and unorganized small arms opposition. On the left the 1st Battalion, 16th Infantry, found initially no opposition on the beach, cleared the beach, as per plan, for the landing of the armored column of CC "B," then fired its Very pistol signal — one white star — as notification to CC "B" to start its landings. The 1st Battalion then proceeded on its mission to the left flank. Against slight opposition it moved to La Macta, took this village against increased opposition, then detached one company to Porte Aux Poules and one company to En Nekala, both these latter villages being taken against minor opposition.

Command Posts of the two Combat Teams came ashore without incident except perhaps the amusing mishap to Combat Team 18's group. Portable loudspeakers with specially trained crews to man them were placed in several of the assault craft in anticipation of a possible friendly reception on the beach. When close enough to be heard, the crews were to broadcast in very "Americanized" French, "Do not fire — we are Americans — we are your friends." That scheme was abandoned on the initiative of the individual loudspeaker operators when rifle fire from the beach outranged their loudspeakers. But Colonel Greer, Combat Team 18's commander, had been given another means of giving notification of the presence of Americans. Against many protests he was ordered to carry a Coney Island type mortar, enormous and heavy, which would shoot a candy Easter-egg-shaped bomb about two hundred feet into the air where it would burst into a magnificent pyrotechnic display of the American flag in colors. Only Billy Rose could have conceived a more showy display or one more in keeping with the American tradition of "bigger and better." As might be expected, the Combat Team commander, with certain other matters of non-trivial importance on his mind, buck-passed the mortar job to a sergeant. About 3:00 A.M., when Combat Team 18's Command Post was ashore, when the fire fight on the south side of Arzeu was at its heaviest, and when Colonel Greer was most occupied tactically, the sergeant appeared and wanted to know if it was time to shoot the flag. The answer was approximately: "Yes, take it somewhere, away from here, and shoot it." A few minutes later and at a distance of less than fifty yards from the Command Post a mighty light blazed. Colorful sparks drifted slowly and majestically from the mortars spurting column of flame. The flag burst forth, exactly in accordance with the manufacturer's specifications. Then all hell broke loose. Bewildered French defenders who hitherto had no specific target in the darkness, now had one. Mortars, machineguns and rifles converged on the newly established aiming point while the Command Post personnel mashed their imprints on the hard ground. At the first slackening of fire, the Command Post "echeloned forward in mass."

Over on Y beach, west of Oran, landings were meeting no opposition on the beaches. Unfortunately, hydrographic charts had not disclosed a sand bar about fifty yards off shore which caused landing craft to ground with a short stretch of deep water ahead. Its only consequence was to delay by some twenty minutes the officially recorded time of touchdown and to make everyone uncomfortably wet.

The 2nd Battalion, on the right, detached Company G to El Ancor for flank and rear protection, then pushed on to secure Cape Falcon. Shore defenses in and around Cap Falcon were expected to cause trouble in the transport area when daylight permitted observed fire on the ships lying at anchor close by. All day of November 8th, Aine el Turk held out against the Battalion, while the seacoast guns north of the town alternated their fire from troops to ships. The Llnagibby Castle took a pounding all that day and part of the next. Just about dusk the Battalion succeeded in capturing Aine el Turk but were unable to overrun and silence the guns out Cap Falcon way.

The 3rd Battalion on the left, landed on Y White beach, moved without opposition through Les Andalouses, quickly captured Bou Sfer, then pushed on toward its first objective, Ferme Combier, which it reached about 7:40 A.M. There it was stopped by small arms fire from pillboxes and artillery fire from nearby Djebel Santon.

The 1st Battalion landed in Combat Team reserve and remained in assembly area near Bou Sfer throughout the day.

The Division Command Post opened at Tourville (in southern extremity of Arzeu at 7:45 A.M. Thus by 9:00 A.M. practically all personnel of the Division were ashore and functioning. Heavy equipment was not coming in so well. Very little artillery had ferried ashore. Vehicle ferrying was even worse. Communications were not functioning satisfactorily. During the remainder of the day every effort was made to speed up the shore delivery of heavy equipment but without too much success. That artillery which had come ashore was in action and was ably supporting the infantry. Probably the greatest handicap to operations was the shortage of transportation, which had the effect of slowing action to the speed of a man on foot.

As of midnight November 8th, the 1st and 2nd Battalions, 18th Infantry, were bogged down against St. Cloud and the remainder of the Combat Team, including the Rangers, generally in the vicinity of Arzeu. The 16th Infantry at midnight, November 8th, had its 1st Battalion successfully protecting the left flank along the La Macta-En Nekala line; the 3rd Battalion, in Le Grande, and the 2nd Battalion back in the beach area. Combat Team 26 had its 3rd Battalion on the heights of Djebel Murdjadjo about five kilometers west of Oran and halted by effective opposition. Its 2nd Battalion was in Aine el Turk and its 1st Battalion just east of Bou Sfer. Casualties had not been heavy for the day, but to newly shot over troops with no yardstick of experience by which to measure the severity of an action, these battlefield deaths had a sobering effect. Preparations were made and orders issued for the resumption of a more coordinated effort at daylight on the 9th.

St. Cloud was doing a most excellent job of delaying the First Division's advance on Oran. Situated about one-third the way on the most direct route from Arzeu to Oran and at the focal point of all roads in the general area, it was initially assigned to Combat Team

18 as an intermediate objective. Pre-landing intelligence gave no indication that it was garrisoned or even prepared for defense.

Coming up over a rise of ground west of Renan, one's first view of St. Cloud is completely unobstructed. No clumps of trees, no bushes, no heavy vegetation of any kind relieve the bareness of the little stone village sitting in the middle of a saucer-shaped depression. To the right, or north, the ground slopes gently uphill for a couple of kilometers, then abruptly rises to form the hill mass whose western extremity is Djebel Khar. Otherwise, the illusion of a village centered in a huge bowl is not dispelled. The entire inside of the bowl is agricultural land devoted to grape growing, and in November fields were almost barren due to a recent seasonal planting. Stone and brick houses solidly built along streets which meet at right angles offered unbeatable cover for a small arms fight. On the south side of the town a cemetery surrounded by a thick stone wall added to the defensive value of the position. Clear fields of fire extending at least 1,000 yards in all directions offered no vestige of cover for the attacking riflemen. The Arzeu-Oran narrow-gauge railroad ran through St. Cloud, its one shallow grade cut being beautifully enfiladed from the cemetery position. The village was an ideal strong point for a reverse slope position.

On the morning of November 9th, Combat Team 18 placed a 15-minute artillery concentration on the town, then, with its three battalions now up and in position, jumped off at 7:00 A.M. to take the town. The defenders fought viciously. Division men getting into the outskirts of the village were infiladed down the streets by expertly sited machineguns. Any individual movement within 700 yards of the village drew accurate rifle fire. The attack bogged down and in so doing had sucked all three battalions into a converging attack where the number of men in the attacking force was out of all proportion to the number of defenders. But maneuverability was lost and the attack failed.

The 3rd Battalion, 16th Infantry, was ordered to swing right to the base of Djebel Khar thereby completing the isolation of the village. Unfortunately this threat did not make the garrison surrender. Corps needled Division and Division pushed the Combat

Team commander.   Time was being lost, time which the Division could ill afford to lose.   By late morning the Combat Team commander was fretted into requesting all Division Artillery available, including the 155 mm Howitzers, for a thirty-minute concentrated shelling of the town at 1:00 P.M.   Tactically, that was the answer under the circumstances since all the infantry of the Combat Team had lost its maneuverability.   On the other hand, the village was full of women and children.   Already several had been killed by mortar fire during the early morning shelling.   Further destruction of civilian life and property in the village would embitter the French and cause much political hostility.   The Division Commander decided against the artillery concentration and ordered Combat Team 18 to leave one battalion as a containing force while the other two battalions withdrew sufficiently to regain mobility.   That accomplished, the Combat Team, less one battalion, was to bypass St. Cloud and press forward to the capture of Oran.   As a commentary on the St. Cloud action, the defenders were still doggedly holding out when the Oran High Command surrendered all French troops in the area. The village was the worst damaged of the campaign and an undercurrent of hostility subsequently felt in St. Cloud was non-existent elsewhere in the area.

A second fight developed the morning of November 9th on the extreme left flank. La Macta lies on the eastern side of a bridge over an unfordable gorge. To protect the highway and railroad bridge over the gorge, the 1st Battalion, 16th Infantry, had been given the mission of capturing La Macta. To do so had previously required a fight as the French garrison in La Macta did not see fit to voluntarily surrender the town.

On the morning of November 9th, a counter-attacking force moved in from the Mostaganem sector and, with artillery support, succeeded in crossing the stream above La Macta. They then attacked between Port Aux Poules and La Macta, threatening to isolate the garrison in the latter place. In this action meager communications and lack of transportation was keenly felt. Reinforcements were requested by the commanding officer of the 1st Battalion. The most readily available was a II Corps unit, the 1st Battalion, 19th Engineers, which was at once dispatched to Port Aux Poules, along with Battery C, 32nd Field Artillery. A British artillery observer with the 1st Battalion, 16th Infantry, considered the situation sufficiently serious to warrant a request for naval gunfire support. Before the latter could be made effective over the slow communication net, the counter-attack had been repulsed and the situation satisfactorily stabilized.

The 2nd Battalion and the 3rd Battalion, of Combat Team 16, continued their advance on Oran against a somewhat stiffening opposition.

Turning westward to review the progress of Combat Team 26, the 2nd Battalion, with the help of the 33rd Field Artillery Battalion, had a rough fight with the shore defenses north of Aine el Turk but succeeded in silencing these guns and capturing all the defensive positions on Cap Falcon.

Overnight of November 8-9, enemy foot troops had infiltrated the rocky hilltop in back of the 3rd Battalion and had cut its communications with Combat Team Headquarters. Engineer half-tracks had some exciting moments breaking through this infiltration to get ammunition and water up to the 3rd Battalion, but were unable to re-establish its communications to the rear. The plight of the 3rd Battalion remained unchanged until the 1st Battalion was sent in on the right. This re-established communications but did not succeed in pushing the advance on Oran against the determined and well positioned defenders of Oran's western heights.

As of midnight, November 9th, positions of all units were as follows:

The Rangers were in reserve in and around Arzeu.

The 1st Battalion, 18th Infantry, was containing St. Cloud.

The 2nd Battalion, 18th Infantry, having successfully bypassed St. Cloud on the south, was approximately six kilometers east of Arcole and moving toward Oran on its assigned route of advance.

The 3rd Battalion, 18th Infantry, had bypassed St. Cloud on the north and was occupying a position on the southeast slopes of Djebel Khar.

The 1st Battalion, 16th Infantry, had been relieved during the early evening by the 1st Battalion, 19th Engineers, and had moved to Fleurus where it was being held overnight in Combat Team Reserve.

The 2nd Battalion, 16th Infantry, was passing through Assi Bou Nif and containing its advance on Oran.

The 3rd Battalion, 16th Infantry, having been turned northward during the day to interpose itself between St. Cloud and Oran, was now on the Arcole road and was executing an order to advance via that route on Oran. At midnight it was well on the way with its leading elements on the outskirts of the city. As a result of inadequate communications, Division Headquarters did not have information that the 3rd Battalion was so far advanced. The picture as seen at Division placed the 2nd Battalion of the 18th Infantry on this main Arcole-Oran road with the 3rd Battalion of the 16th Infantry still off the road and in position on the southwest slopes of Djebel Khar. As a result of this lagging information, the 3rd Battalion, 16th Infantry, was ordered through its Combat Team commander to move south to the route of advance of Combat Team 16 where, under its own Combat Team commander, integrity of units would be preserved, thus making for a more orderly and coordinated attack the morning of November 10th.

Unfortunately the execution of this order necessitated a countermarch by the 3rd Battalion, 16th Infantry, which amounted to a flank movement in the face of the enemy. Artillery, mortar and small arms fire continually harassed this movement and it is to the everlasting credit of the Battalion that, by 6:00 A.M., it had accomplished its march without greater mishap.

On the western side of Oran, the 2nd and 3rd Battalions of the 26th Infantry were still engaged in a small arms fight against the pillbox occupants on the crest of Djebel Murdjadjo and were not making any progress.

The 2nd Battalion in the Aine el Turk-Cap Falcon area was reorganizing the captured battery positions while preparing to move eastward at first light.

The Division Command Post had been in Renan all day. Communications were getting somewhat better with the landing of

additional equipment, but a shortage of vehicles for this express purpose precluded the use of wire lines since they could be neither
installed nor maintained without truck transportation. Ammunition
was ashore in ample quantity, as was water and food. At about 9:30
P.M. the Corps G3 (Colonel Ferrenbaugh) visited the Command
Post at Renan bringing with him a message from General Fredendall, Commanding General Center Task Force (II Corps), to the
effect that the drive on Oran was going too slowly and that it was
imperative Oran be taken the next day. Harking back to the original
strategy, it will be remembered that if Oran and Algiers could be
taken quickly, there was a chance of moving to Tunisia before the
Germans could reinforce the small garrisons already there. Furthermore, a follow-up convoy of ships was due in on D-plus-5, just three
days hence, and lives could be saved if these plans satisfactorily
materialized. It was under these circumstances that General Allen
issued Field Order 3, as of 10:00 P.M., November 9, 1943, for the
coordinated attack on Oran to take place at 7:15 A.M. on November
10th. A paragraph in this order carried for the first time General
Allen's often repeated expression: "Nothing in Hell must delay or
stop the First Division."

The attack on November 10th was essentially a continuation of
the basic plan. St. Cloud's defenders were no longer causing delay.
Combat Teams were under better control with the 3rd Battalion, 16th
Infantry, back in its zone; the 1st Battalion, 16th Infantry, returned
from left flank beach protection, and the artillery all ashore and in
firing position. A steady and coordinated push on all fronts made
itself felt most effectively. Enemy resistance dwindled rapidly. By
8:00 A.M. forces converging on Oran were meeting little more than
sniper fire from the outskirts of the city. At 10:00 A.M. fighting was
over. Combat Team 18, coming in through Arcole, had its leading
Battalion (2nd Battalion) in the city limits at 10:00 A.M. but Combat Team 16, moving via its more southerly route, had the leading
elements of both the 1st and 2nd Battalions inside the city by
8:30 A.M. Combat Team 26 had successfully occupied the heights
of Djebel Murdjadjo and at 10:00 A.M. was in a position to descend
on Oran with full force. The Division Command Post had made

two rapid moves during the morning, first to Fleurus at 3:00 A.M., then to Assi Bou Nif at 8:00 A.M. Just before noon it moved again to Ferme St. Jean le Baptiste from which position it could better control the final occupation of Oran and the subsequent disposition of troops.

No drama attended the fall of Oran. As armored and infantry columns moved into the city, sidewalks were crowded with civilian spectators. Perhaps there were some who harbored a bitterness toward their American captors but, taken as a whole, the populace was quite friendly. A significant number were sufficiently lavish in their display of welcome to satisfy the most dour of soldiers. Veterans looking back on this Oran scene after such experiences as the sweep around Paris, entry into Mons, Charleroi and Liege must sense that some invisible hand was restraining the natural impulsiveness of the French people on this November day. They were too formal — too polite. They were not being French, at least not that newly liberated kind who were seeing the end of loathsome oppression. What they *were* seeing was reprisal. Possibly the Americans wouldn't stay. Surely there would not be bombing raids — a sobering enough thought for anyone. And the French were hungry.

Little by little the Axis Armistice Commission had squeezed them economically. Soap and olive oil and sugar and coffee — all these things they wanted, but most of all they wanted to know who stood for what. Would their traitorous politicians be put back in power? Which of their many political factions would get the nod of approval from the Allies? Without the shock of battle to dull their senses, these questions vitally affecting their future were certain to impinge on their consciousness in one huge unanswerable question: "What next?" The Allies had set up no precedent which would point to an answer. This was a first — the first step on a long road to Axis defeat. Then, too, there was the ever-present possibility that the Axis might come back and throw out these invaders. The practical mind of the Frenchman cautioned: "Wait. Let's be neither black nor white until we see which color best serves our interests."

Such thoughts were not troubling the victorious Americans. They, too, were bewildered, uncertain of the next move politically, but that, as usual, was someone else's worry. Their immediate task was to carry out the detailed plans for the occupation of the city. The Corps Commander entered the city shortly before noon on November 10th, and received the surrender of General Boisseau, commanding general of all French forces in the Oran area. Orders went out to all forces, French and Americans, that, as of twelve noon, an armistice was in effect. All firing was to cease, French soldiers taken prisoner, some 1,400 of them, were to be returned to the French barracks in Oran and order was to be preserved.

The Division issued Field Order No. 4 designating an assembly area for troops, detailed a policing force for the city of Oran, then proceeded with the business of reorganization. Ste. Barbe du Tlelat was chosen as a Command Post because of its central location within the Division sector of responsibility. Movement thereto took place on November 11th. Combat Team 16 placed its Command Post at St. Louis, Combat Team 18 at L'Oggaz, and Combat Team 26 at Misserghin. Division Artillery Headquarters was adjacent to Ste. Barbe du Tlelat. Service units were interspersed throughout the area. The division mission now became one of security and patrol work in an area so large as to far exceed the capability of one division should organized opposition develop. Already the operation had cost the Division 94 killed in action, 73 seriously wounded, 178 slightly wounded and 73 missing — a total of 416, which eloquently controverts any statements that Oran was taken against "token opposition." But for a most efficient medical service the killed in action would have been more than 94. The medical service of the Division was most ably backed by the 48th Surgical Hospital which came in early, one detachment of 8 officers, 20 enlisted men and 6 nurses having come in with the assault elements of Combat Team 26.

In late November, Oran was rainy. Cold winds blew over bare fields which the homefolks pictured as hot sandy deserts. The first letters finally began to trickle to and from the States. Mud sloshed in the streets and tracked into the few buildings being used as billets. Tentage served as an only shelter for most of the division — pup tents at that. But men of the Division were hardened to a rough life. They took what *was* as a situation which would probably get worse before it got better. A taste of battle had made them veterans — wise veterans, fortunately, who knew that there were harder battles ahead. They were proud veterans, shock troops, soldiers who knew the FIRST was an assault division which would always, as General Teddy Roosevelt expressed it — "March to the sound of the guns."

While the folks back home were singing "Silent Night" on Christmas Eve, 1942, wearers of the Big Red One were killing and being killed in a bitter engagement in far-off Tunisia. Their mission was not too difficult. Their sacrifice was not too great.

◆ ◆ ◆

ALGERIA

As I Saw It

by

H. R. KNICKERBOCKER

YEARS LATER I asked Terry Allen what had been the high point of the war for him. He said it was the landing at Oran. That landing was practically unopposed. It could not be compared with later battles of the First Division led by General Allen, either in danger or losses. Yet General Allen, smiling that leathery smile of his, nodded "Yes, nothing has ever equalled that night. There was something about it that never was repeated. It was the first time. That's what made it."

The first time. The first landing. The first amphibious operation. Historians of war and staff colleges had believed that overseas operations could not succeed because they never had succeeded. From the Spanish Armada to Dieppe, the record showed failure and often catastrophe.

No wonder then that the men who went on the first expedition to North Africa were filled with an excitement that never was to be repeated, not even at the infinitely more deadly Omaha Beach.

And no wonder that it was the First Division which of all American fighting units, was chosen to lead the first landing at Oran and the last at Omaha Beach. Why was the First Division distinguished by the reputation that "The United States Army consists of the First Division and ten million replacements?"

Not one out of a thousand of the members of the Division could have given more than the sketchiest account of the long record of its glory, but that did not prevent every man with the red "1" on his shoulder from believing himself a specially privileged person and from feeling that the possession of this insignia had made him a person different from the man he was before he became a member of the Division.

This I believe to be due to the power of the Myth. Webster says that a Myth differs from a legend in that Myth deals with beings conceived as having supernatural attributes while legend deals with human beings. It is therefore not of the legend, but of the Myth of the First Division that I speak.

What was the Myth? Merely this: that the First Division never retreats; the First Division always goes forward; the First Division always takes its objectives; the First Division is invincible. That is all, and that is everything. For the miraculous thing about the myth was that because the First Division believed it, it was true. The First Division did not have supernatural attributes. The personality of the Division was different from and greater than the sum of the personalities of all the men in the Division. The collective known as the First Division had qualities superior to the qualities of the most superior men in the Division.

We boarded the "Reina del Pacifico" towards dark the night of October 24, 1942, at Gourock, port of Glasgow, Scotland, and left her fifteen days later at six in the morning of November 8, at Arzeu Beach, Oran, Algiers, North Africa. Of the two thousand or more on board the ancient liner, only the most senior officers knew that the "Reina del Pacifico" was but one of some five hundred passenger ships, merchantmen and naval escort vessels putting out from other ports in the British Isles, and from America, and that, coming from two continents, all were to converge on three widely separated ports of a third continent, land a great army and take the initiative from Hitler for the first time in the war.

It was only eleven months since Pearl Harbor. The Germans were confident of victory. They were still attacking at Stalingrad. The British had not yet won the Battle of Egypt. The Nazi armies held Fortress Europe in what they believed impregnable strength. Hitler dismissed the great, soft, self-indulgent and wounded United States as negligible. From Pearl Harbor through Corregidor, America had had no victories, only defeats, retreats. That the pacifistic, pampered, plutocratic Americans who had allowed their Navy to be stricken from their hands, and who had no army or air force worth mentioning, could in eleven months organize a successful invasion of Nazi territory was improbable, thought Hitler. He was of course entirely correct. It was improbable.

On board the "Reina del Pacifico" seasick boys shivered in the cold winds under the lowering sky and wondered whither they were going. Some thought Norway, some the coast of France, some the Low Countries, and at all these points the Germans, cleverly deceived, kept many divisions. But we headed south.

Warm days, sunny skies and calming seas brought on deck swarms of soldiers to exercise the muscles they had hardened in twenty to thirty mile hikes in England. For the first time we could see the convoy and sense the dimensions of the operation. With binoculars, we counted eighty vessels, great and small liners, freighters and warships of every variety, circled by cruisers and destroyers and far away, hull-down on the horizon, the prodigious battleships and aircraft carriers. The force in sight was awe-inspiring. The infantry exclaimed, "God Almighty!" The Royal Navy murmured, "Isn't it stupendous!"

Only when we sighted the dark bulk of Gibraltar did the command consider it fit to put the Division in the picture. After Gibraltar there was not much chance of anyone guessing far wrong.

General Allen called his officers to the lounge of the old ship which for a generation had carried well-to-do passengers in the South American trade with California. Many a stimulating evening must have been had by the gentry in that pleasant social hall. Now it was the scene of the announcement of the way and the place and the hour when the listening young men would find out what they were like.

The General stood before a large map, most secret, top secret; nothing could be more secret than that map. And no man could have more authority with the Division than this one, who had taken it raw, trained it, molded it, and made it what it was to be.

"We are the Center Force. Oran is our objective. Another landing will be made at Casablanca; another landing at Algiers. The First Division will take this beach at Arzeu and this one at Les Andalouses." The General took a pointer from Colonel Robert Porter and laid its end at Arzeu, and then at Les Andalouses.

The men fixed their eyes on the map. That was where it was going to happen. In Arzeu and Les Andalouses they would find out. No young man in that room had ever known battle before and before this moment they had not known where they were going to know it. There was a long time to think, long enough for the General to drop the tip of his pointer and with the familiar smile say: "Now you know it!"

On the way out I asked Colonel Porter, the scholarly G-2, why we could not all have been told as soon as we put to sea, and he replied that if we had been torpeoded and men had been captured by the enemy it would have been best for them not to know. Colonel Porter took us below to G-2's secret rooms and led the way through the encyclopaedic information gathered by our military intelligence about the coast we were to visit. In its way it was as impressive as the size of the convoy. It contained photographic profiles of the coast, topographic maps showing individual houses, the location of every enemy formation, the names of their officers, the political character of the inhabitants, besides meteorological charts indicating the probable weather based on the experience of decades.

It seemed the weather would be perfect. The sun shone on

hundreds of men drilling, violently playing medicine ball and staring still entranced at the convoy as we passed into the Mediterranean and saw first the Spanish shore then the dim mysterious loom of Africa. The ship sang with activity. Boys polished bayonets and trench knives, oiled rifles and pistols and gaily wondered what made the sea so blue and what would the girls be like in Algeria.

Then the sea changed. Only a few hours before we were to land, the wind blew up to a stiff breeze, whitecaps appeared and in his last talk to us, Colonel Porter's lips were tight with seasickness and the thought of what our flat-bottomed landing craft would do in heavy waves.

The whistling and the laughter diminished and the chaplains were busy. It is true of landing operations as of trenches that the thought of God comes with the need of his protection. The cooks served the final dinner, sumptuous as a condemned man's, and as little appreciated. Colonel D'Alary Fechet and I sat down for a final game of chess, but it was poorly played.

As night fell, the sea subsided and by that time our ship coasted to a noiseless anchoring, the surface was as smooth as a lake. General Allen, Ken Downs and I circled the deck, not speaking. Silence and darkness enveloped us. In a blackout more complete than ever, we knew our ship existed by the feel of it, and we knew the ships of the convoy were there by the feel of them too. For awhile no one in the whole ship spoke aloud. Men walked softly.

Then we saw the lights far off. I touched the General on the arm.

"What are those lights?" I whispered.

"The shore," quietly answered the General.

And that is what Terry Allen meant when he told me years later in El Paso that the first night was the best of the war. That was the moment.

At that moment, with hardly a rattle of a block, the first landing craft touched water. We could see it swaying far below and men climbing into it.

This was H-hour.

But why were there lights on the enemy shore? Should we call it enemy? It was French. And we were going to help the French become free. But Hitler's noose was around France's neck, and until we destroyed Hitler, some Frenchmen would rather fight us than suffer the noose to be drawn tighter. So it was enemy shore, but were the lights there because they were not expecting us or were they there because it was a trap?

Actually some of them were lit by our friends on shore. We hoped to make more friends when we landed, and our propaganda weapons were as ingenious as any the Germans devised. We had prepared pyrotechnical set pieces representing the American flag to be discharged in the sky by the commander of the 18th Infantry as soon as he had cleared the trenches and taken the town of Arzeu. There were four such sets of fireworks, each of them capable of flinging the star-spangled banner a hundred feet across the sky in flames. I never heard what became of them.

Every effort was made to let the French know this was an American operation. Just before H-hour we were astonished to hear from the radio room that President Roosevelt was addressing the French people in French and telling them of our enterprise even before we had accomplished it. Our first airplane assaults on French positions were showers of leaflets in French and Arabic bearing from Roosevelt and Eisenhower the message: "We come to restore your liberty."

The most original of our devices was a set of loudspeakers carried with each first wave by the soldiers chosen for their distinct American accents in French. "Ne tirez pas! ne tirez pas!" they bawled. "We have come as your friends. We are here again on your side. Don't shoot. Down with the Boches. Down with the Macaroni. Vive la France." And then a great many more of "Ne tirez pas!" It must have been the first time in military history that a victorious attacking force cried "Don't shoot!" and it struck the First Division as the funniest thing so far in this campaign.

Fifteen minutes after midnight General Allen uttered his first exclamation as we saw from shore a white flare shoot into the sky. It was the signal that our first landing party was ashore unopposed.

A few minutes later another flare, this time red, told us the second landing party had succeeded.

We hurried to the large room where the second assault wave of troops were gathered to await their turn. "Boys," announced General Allen, "I think you'd like to know that our first assault wave landed and took up positions without opposition." Then, smiling, "I've just sent a signal to the French to put in their first team."

Now we could hear firing. The initial landing had been unopposed. It had taken the enemy by surprise, but the French Algerian army had not considered us friends. The knowledge of this fact, later to become clearer, spurred the impatience of our group which was to have left the ship at three o'clock in the morning. We burned with the irritability that comes of passionate curiosity and the desire to get over a danger. General Allen also felt the compulsion to get on shore to direct the fighting, but not even the Commanding General could get us embarked before six o'clock. It was nearly light when our landing craft came alongside.

There are several especially unpleasant moments about an amphibious operation. One of them is leaving the landing craft, but one of them is entering it. There were to board our craft General Allen, fourteen staff officers, ten non-coms, ten privates, and one non-combatant correspondent, thirty-five in all. Nearly every officer carried besides his automatic pistol either a tommygun, an automatic rifle or a carbine. Most of them had trench knives or commando daggers and some had hand-grenades. Each wore a steel helmet and carried a gasmask and musette bag with the scantiest toilet articles and three days' canned rations.

Altogether most officers carried a weight of over forty-five pounds. Under their other gear everyone wore a bulky naval lifesaver. My pack weighed fifty pounds of which twenty was my typewriter slung in a canvas sack and carried on my back with the musette bag balancing it in front. It was the unhappiest arrangement ever conceived by a reporter.

We had to board the first amphibious DANGER FORWARD from a deck fifteen feet above the LCA by a rope ladder which would have been difficult to descend carrying nothing. General Allen swung down like a gymnast. Luckily Lieutenant Colonel Murtagh had a cane with a curved handle which he used to pass down his stuff and mine. All hands were finally shoved in by Royal Navy officers and petty officers who ran the boat. We sat, or rather half-lay, on our backs spoonwise in each others' laps flat on the floor.

They were nested thus: On the starboard side, General Allen on Colonel Fechet on Lieutenant Dick Harris, on Colonel Robert Porter, on Colonel John Waters, on Captain Pickett, on Captain Ken Downs, on Sergeant Wells, on Private First Class Lewandowski, on Private Gronseth, on Private Cyplik, on Private Hutter; on the port side, Captain Barclay, Lieutenant Bessman, Major Gaskell, Sergeant Guillaume, Corporal Werkheiser, Private Patton, Private Simkovich, Private Hils, Private First-Class Michaud, Private Lewis, Sergeant Tramontano, Sergeant Joseph; in the middle, Captian Bennett, Sergeant Roger, Sergeant Spiegel, myself, T/5 Mims, Lieutenant Barber, Lieutenant Ahearn, Sergeant Harrington, Sergeant Kass and Private Kusick. Names worth recording, because with staff officers in another craft they constituted the central personnel of the first DANGER FORWARD.

I wonder how many of these men are still alive after those beach-heads and battles of the First Division. Most of us in the boat were friends. There was no conversation. The craft was semi-roofed with armorplate, so we could see nothing and could only inquire of the helmsman how far were the shots which sounded close. A few minutes after we left our ship an enemy mortar shell struck her and did little damage.

We could hear artillery and machineguns near enough to indicate the fight between our first assault waves and the enemy inland. In the direction of Oran flames flickered on the horizon and now and then something like sheet-lightning lit the sky. That, as we learned later, came from the two U. S. COAST GUARD cutters which rammed and broke the boom across Oran Harbor, where they were then blown up by point-blank enemy fire.

As the machineguns sounded closer, we assumed we were near-

ing shore, and presently the Navy sent smoke shells looping grace-
fully across at our right to lay a screen between us and enemy gunners
still holding out in a brick building on the side of the hill near the
town of Arzeu.

The screen worked. About 100 yards from shore our boatman
threw out an anchor to keep the LCA head-on to the beach, paid out
the rope and brought us in nose first, but the water was too shallow
for the gangplank to reach dry land. We stepped off in the surf just
over knee-high. This, the other moment which may be particularly
unpleasant, was too full of movement to leave time to think. Only
Colonel Porter remembered to shout a totally unnecessary reminder
to "Get off the beach." None of us had the remotest desire to linger
there.

As we staggered through the surf, swayed by the weight of
unwieldly packs, a group of British sailors, stripped to the waist,
came splashing through the water, gay as boys in swimming, and
helped us with heavy luggage. As though this were not enough to
shatter the illusion of gallantry, there appeared the astonishing sight
of Ray Kellogg, U. S. Navy, kneeling on the beach with a movie
camera, filming our landing.

The opposition was becoming successful farther on. The battle
for St. Cloud, the chief obstacle between us and Oran, was already
developing, but it was too far away for us to reach on foot. We concentrated on getting off the beach, which by now was cluttered with
broached LCA's, gasmasks, life belts and all the refuse of men in a
very great hurry. The sand was clinging, the walking difficult. One
of the worst things about a landing is that you stay up all night, can't
eat and just when you need strength the most there is the least of it.

Another hundred yards of sand took us to a ploughed field where
we picked up a Signal Corps line that led to the Command Post,
General Allen was just establishing in a tiny native schoolhouse.
This was the first DANGER FORWARD in this war.

I left my pack there and went out to look back at the beach where
men were still landing and would continue to land for many days.
I was watching this with Colonel Fred Butler when a tall, thin man

in the uniform of a Captain of the French Foreign Legion came up to me and addressed me in perfect American:

"I think you had better do something about the Arzeu Barracks; they are still occupied by Tunisian Fusiliers, and until they are cleared out of town, the town is not safe."

"Captain Hamilton!" I exclaimed.

The Legion officer looked at me, his cadaverous face lined by tropical fever broke into a smile, and he reached out his hand. "Knickerbocker, My God, I haven't seen you since Saigon."

Five years before I had met Captain Edgar Guerard Hamilton, the only American officer then in the Foreign Legion, in Saigon, Indo-China, where he had told me the story of his twenty-five years in the most romanticized military unit on earth. He had joined it after World War I. He now told me the war had caught him in Algeria and the Germans had kept him there as they knew he wanted to join the American army. From this moment he became an auxiliary of the First Division.

Colonel Butler was too business-minded to do more than nod at this unusual encounter. He wanted to know more about the Tunisians, and as soon as he learned the tactical situation, he rounded up three non-coms with a machinegun and automatic rifles as his task force, and with Kellogg, Hamilton and myself following, led the way to action.

The Arzeu Barracks were a few minutes from DANGER FORWARD. As we came to the edge of the drill-ground we saw a large white building surrounded by a high brown, adobe wall-slotted with rifle slits. "There's a battalion of Fusiliers in there," said Hamilton, "and the fact they aren't firing is a sign they are waiting for a good target. If you go across that drillground you are certain to be fired at."

"What do you expect in war?" inquired the lean, athletic, prematurely white-haired Colonel? "Come on."

We all followed the Colonel, and immediately the Captain was proved correct. A crackle of rifle fire broke from the barracks windows and dust spurted around us and the sound of bullets ricocheting brought to me a flash of memory of street fighting in Berlin years ago and the vision of a dead man in a doorway. Kellogg and I ran straight ahead for the cover of a stone wall that jutted out into the middle of the field, while Colonel Butler and Captain Hamilton dashed for a ditch which ran parallel to the wall of the barracks, and was about fifty yards from it.

Running from bullets is never funny when it happens. It is disgusting. It makes you feel ridiculous, especially because there is an irresistible urge to hunch your shoulders and try and make yourself smaller, and you think how silly that is but you do it anyway.

We reached the wall to find ourselves accompanied by a boy with a Garand rifle. His chest was heaving and his eyes glittered with excitement as he went on one knee, and panted: "Gee, do you know that a year ago back in Brooklyn I never would have believed I could do this." Whereupon he levelled his rifle, took aim and discharged three clips at the barracks windows. The muzzle of his rifle a few inches from our ears roared like artillery.

Colonel Butler, from the ditch, began shouting at First Division soldiers in a house across the drill-field to fire at the barracks and presently first one and then another soldier ran across the open field to the stone wall. They were completely exposed and the enemy fire ripped the earth around them. The last American to run across the field was carrying a machinegun and could not run fast. We held our breath as we saw him start and saw the bullets ploughing around him. Somebody yelled "Zig-zag," and he tried, but the weight of the machinegun was too much for him to do any zig-zagging. He gave up the idea, headed straight for the ditch, did not stop to crawl into it but pitched the machinegun in ahead of him and dived after it.

We of the stone wall made one more run and dive for the ditch, then we all crawled until we turned a corner and Colonel Butler, with a gesture reminiscent of "Come on, do you want to live forever!" led us to the shelter of the barracks wall. There our boys put their rifles through the slits and opened a pounding fire which lasted about two minutes, broke all barracks windows, and exhausted our ammunition.

When Colonel Butler and Kellogg had shot up their last forty-five clips, Captain Hamilton proposed that we go to the City Hall, twist the arm of the Mayor of Arzeu and see if he could not make the barracks surrender. Captain Hamilton was mildly amused by the whole battle, but said seriously that until we took or silenced the barracks, it would be impossible to move about Arzeu safely.

We reached the Hotel de Ville by a roundabout way, out of reach of the barracks, and found hundreds of excited villagers milling about. The mayor, Dr. Miguel Maille, received his first American visitors in great agitation. His jaw trembled until his teeth clicked like castanets as Colonel Butler in slow, clear French ordered him to telephone the barracks and give the Fusiliers, Butler's ultimatum: Surrender or be shelled to pieces.

The mayor made superhuman effort, forced his jaw to slow down, and with a burst of emotion exclaimed: "First, Mers el Kebir, then Dakar, then Madagascar, and now it's Oran! I protest!" It was interesting to hear for the first time a follower of Vichy parrot the German propaganda that all these actions were aggressions against France. Colonel Butler firmly repeated his order, and so steely were his blue eyes that the mayor reached for the telephone. His hands were shaking so badly that he had to use both of them to hold the receiver to his ear. He talked a long time, then turned to us: "The officer requests you come to the barracks and take his surrender."

That night in DANGER FORWARD, General Allen and his staff worked by the light of pocket flashlights dimmed with red tissue paper. Finally the General lay down on the best bed, a litter stained with fresh blood. I made a pillow of my shoes, stretched out on the stone floor and went to sleep like a rock falling into a well.

The voice of Colonel Porter woke me at dawn, Monday, November 9th. He was G-twoing the staff at the schoolroom blackboard on an easel. He ceased, the staff left, and the first DANGER FORWARD disappeared, to reappear miles inland in another schoolhouse at Renan.

There we found every effort concentrated on the capture or

reduction of St. Cloud, that pretty little Algerian village which looked so innocent and was so lethal. The French commanders of the Algerian mercenaries were vain young men who had never had a chance to fight the Germans and wanted to prove their military valour. Their method was to kill their friends, The Americans.

It did not seem unreasonable for the French to fight their liberators that to the normal battle anger of the Americans we added an intense indignation. Colonel Greer, of the 18th Infantry, decided to wipe out St. Cloud off the map. At his Command Post, near a winery, he told me he was going to put 1,500 shells on the town in thirty minutes, beginning at two o'clock. I went to fetch my field-glasses, rejoined Colonel Greer, and was surveying the town when General Allen drove up.

"No," said General Allen, "we are not going to bombard the town. We are going to bypass it. First, because I don't want to kill civilians and there are 4,000 of them there; second, regardless of sentiment, it would make a bad political impression; third, if we bombarded it, and yet failed to take it by attack, it would be disasterous; fourth, it would take too much ammunition; fifth, it is unnecessary because we can reach our objective, Oran, without it."

Colonel Greer was disappointed, but it was the decision which made a flawless success of the First Division's first military operation of the war. That night at the second DANGER FORWARD, I saw at work once more the General who first taught the First Division in this war to live up to the Magic Myth.

The schoolroom was lighted by one gasoline lantern swinging from a beam. General Allen sat under it, his figure in the dark. Around him stood his staff, their faces turned to the light, their bodies in the shadow. General Oliver, in Command of Tanks, and General Andrus, in Command of Division Artillery, stood facing General Allen. Colonel Ferrenbaugh, of the II Corps, representing General Fredendall, in overall Command of Center Task Force, towered at General Allen's elbow; the beloved "Dutch" Cota, Chief of Staff; the military intellectual, Colonel Porter, G-2; the popular Colonel "Stan" Mason, G-3; the poker-faced Colonel Eymer, G-4;

the self-effacing Major Revere, G-1; the General's Aides, Captain Downes and Lieutenant Dick Harris, all attended intently. On the floor, Captain Paul Gale, assistant G-2, and Lieutenant Joe Dawson, who later had a ridge named after him, in France, were asleep. Under the desks slept half a dozen soldiers. Sergeants Al Kosgaard and Trumantano, some other orderlies and clerks squatted between the standing officers.

The assault for Oran was ordered for tomorrow, Tuesday, November 10th. Topic of discussion was the time of attack. General Oliver said he would not be able to get his tanks ready to jump off before nine o'clock. Colonel Ferrenbaugh, pressing for II Corps, said the original jumpoff time was 5:00 A.M.; it ought to be made as near that time as possible. General Allen said the infantry was ready to jumpoff any time. Colonel Ferrenbaugh asked General Oliver if he couldn't have his tanks ready by 6:00 A.M. It was finally fixed that the infantry should jumpoff at 7:15, and the tanks at 7:30.

An orderly kneeled on the floor and stenotyped the battle order General Allen dictated. The operative sentence was "Nothing in Hell must delay or stop the attack." That sounds at best unorthodox, at worst commonplace, here, now, on paper, but it did not sound commonplace to the men in that room. From General Allen it became an imperative that they would have given their lives to obey.

An hour before midnight the conference broke up, and I had just gone to sleep on a wooden platform in the adjoining school room, when an orderly called me to Colonel Fechet, who said he had to carry the battle orders to the 18th and 16th Infantry Combat Teams and that General Allen had invited me to go along.

As I packed my typewriter and musette bag, Colonel Fechet suggested I carry a carbine. The fact that I carried it did not alter my status as a non-combatant. Colonel Fechet did not know that I did not know how to load it. It was strictly a morale weapon.

We started in a stinging, sleety rain, and an unrelenting wind, to find in a total blackout, between eleven and dawn, two commanders of regiments on the move along unknown roads through a battle area. Colonel Fechet sat in front with the driver. I sat behind with the carbine between my legs. The jeep had no cover.

When Colonel Fechet read the map he had to take off his steel helmet and hold it on the floor and slip the map and flashlight under it while the rain beat down on his head. Colonel Fechet was not a youngster. I think his feat that night led to his eventual command of the 16th Infantry.

"Remember the password," he said to the driver. "And when a sentry says Halt! stop quickly. Then the sentry will say "Heigh-Yo Silver!" and we will answer "Away!"

That was the immortal password of the First Division that memorable night. But when the first sentry cried out of impentrable darkness that shattering word "Halt!" Colonel Fechet for all his steel nerves, shouted as in one word "Heigh-Yo-Silver—Away!"

It was an incomparable password. What non-American could ever have thought of it or fathomed its meaning? We used it at night at least a hundred times, and always it was successful, which was a miracle, considering that the cold, lonesome, nerve-racked young American boys doing sentry duty in a battle area for the first time in their lives, were bound to be disposed to shoot first and ask questions afterwards.

Once we felt the password might fail when, going fast around a village corner, there came a blasting "Halt!" from the blackness and our driver, startled, stepped on the accelerator instead of the brake, and knocked over a traffic post. But the cry of the Lone Ranger saved us.

All this time flares were lighting the horizon and far away artillery made flashes in the dark while the chatter of machineguns was continuous. Sentries thinned out. One of them warned us not to go on, the enemy was machinegunning the crossroads ahead. Fechet exclaimed: "What's a little machinegunning?"

But, finally, Colonel Fechet conceded, "All right, I think we had better leave the jeep here and go up on foot." He asked me did I want to stay with the jeep or go along with him. I feebly replied I would go with him, and, taking my token carbine, stumbled alongside the Colonel up the rutted, slippery road. After a few yards, an officer materialized ghostlike out of the dark, and Colonel Fechet asked where Colonel Maxwell was. The officer replied that Colonel Maxwell was up the road about 100 yards. Colonel Fechet said that was sufficient, since it was his mission to establish where Colonel Maxwell was — one-third of his mission.

We turned around — this was 12:30 A.M. — and drove for two hours more through the blackout, with the same flares, cannonading, machinegunning and "Heigh-Yo-Silvering," the same rain, sleet and wind, until we struck the 18th Infantry, marching. Thereafter was a long stretch of empty road with no Americans, and it began to look as though we had run ahead of the troops. Colonel Fechet said we would carry on a few hundred yards. Suddenly we overtook the rear of the 16th Infantry.

There were two truckloads of French wounded, groaning in the dark. We pushed our way past several score of vehicles until we found the command car with Colonel Cheadle. Colonel Fechet said: "Colonel, I have important orders for you from the Commanding General." Colonel Cheadle got out. Colonel Fechet told Colonel Cheadle: "You will attack at 7:15; we are going to take Oran tomorrow."

Colonel Cheadle, very much surprised, got out, went to the side of the road and asked to see the written order. They spread out and I held my helmet over the flashlight while the two Colonels read the order and examined the map. Colonel Cheadle meanwhile had halted the regiment and ordered the 1st Battalion, which had overshot the crossroad, to turn around. He said that the boys were tired and had had no sleep for forty-eight hours, and nothing to eat.

Colonel Fechet said: "That makes no difference. You have got to attack with everything you've got. Those are the General's orders. See his last paragraph."

Colonel Cheadle carefully read the sentence: "Nothing in Hell must stop or delay this attack."

That ended two-thirds of Colonel Fechet's mission. It was about 3:00 A.M., and the rain had increased and the wind seemed colder

We drove, as it was clear we were to drive forever, back through the five-mile gap between the 16th and 18th Infantry Regiments, and upon passing the 18th Infantry, we turned into Colonel Greer's advanced Command Post and found him and his staff asleep in their jeeps and command cars.

Colonel Fechet waked Colonel Greer, gave him the order, then asked when he (Colonel Greer) was going to move, and didn't he think that if he was going to jumpoff at 7:15, there was little time left. It was then nearly 4:00 A.M.

Colonel Greer said: "I'll be there on time all right." Colonel Fechet asked Colonel Greer, again: "But if you are to be on time, does that mean you will move very soon?" Colonel Greer almost shouted: "If I am going to be on time, what do you think it means; doesn't it mean I am going to move very soon?" Colonel Fechet paused, then said: "Thank you," and started to move when Colonel Greer said: "Of course I'm moving soon."

Out of the dark, a young Major said: "The men haven't had any sleep at all, and only one can of rations to eat all day long; how can they attack in that condition?" Colonel Fechet, quietly, but furiously, said: "You will not talk that way; you will attack." The Major did not talk that way any more.

DANGER FORWARD had moved again while we were on this mission. We found it at Fleurus, for the third time in a schoolhouse, where Colonel Fechet reported to General Allen, who had been asleep on the floor, this time without even a litter. While General Allen and Colonel Fechet whispered together, I went over and woke Ray Kellogg to go with us.

It was 4:00 A.M. when we set out to meet Colonel Cheadle, and as daylight came we found the end of the 16th Infantry's column. We put our gear beside Colonel Cheadle. I lay on my back and went to sleep for an hour and when I woke found the 16th Infantry had established its Command Post all around us.

I lay there and listened to the officers talk. It was about an hour before jumpingoff time. One young Captain from the South was keen as a racehorse prancing at the barrier. Another was heavily pessimistic. He kept talking as though we were beaten already. He said the 3rd Battalion was only half-strength, the men tired to death, hadn't eaten in days." This talk was distressing. I said to Kellogg it made me feel as though we'd better give the whole thing up and go home before anybody got hurt. Through years of watching the war, I later realized that such griping frequently prefaces the acquisition of a Distinguished Service Cross.

I walked around among the troops digging individual trenches and found most of them talking nervously. Some did not mind showing it. Presently a jeep with two stars on it came whistling by. Major General Terry Allen, freshly shaved, boots shining, stepped out, his grin like a slit in a saddle. Instantly the tone of the Command Post took on the tone of the General's shave, shine, and grin.

General Terry Allen drove off. One of our field pieces swung into position beside our Command Post, and fired its first shot. Several young officers, mistaking the detonation for an enemy shell, flung themselves down, got up, dusted their trousers, and, with red faces, laughed at themselves. Our cannonading increased and at precisely 7:15 the first of the 16th Infantry's riflemen began to move in open formation across the fields towards a big farmhouse about 1,000 yards ahead on the left and another on the right of the road. It seemed a good time to cheer, but I never heard troops cheer in this war except at Cassino.

About forty minutes after the assault began we saw the first group of enemy prisoners, twenty native soldiers and four French officers, with hands in the air, being driven by one American soldier to the rear. It stimulated the Americans.

We hitched a ride in a Red Cross jeep and stopped at an advanced field dressing station where were about thirty of our wounded. I noticed that one young officer lay with his head on a musette bag out of which protruded a copy of Stephen Crane's "The Red Badge of Courage."

One of the medics paused in the midst of his heavy work to ask me if it were true that when you hear the sound of a shell "like that one," the shell has already passed and can't hit you, and that the shell that hits you is the one you don't hear. I told him I believed that was true and he knelt to ask a youngster who had just been brought in what was the matter with him. The boy said he had a bullet in his belly. The medic took out a packet of morphine and put a shot of it in the wounded boy's chest. The boy smiled and closed his eyes. It is true, that as a rule, there is no complaint from the wounded, and no sound, except from those alone on the battlefield who cry "Medic."

We started on foot up the road to Oran again when our old friend, Colonel Butler, came driving up stylishly in an amphibious jeep. We rode with him another mile but he and half a dozen other officers swiftly took to the ditch as shells from a smallbore cannon began screaming at this new target. They entered the ditch at almost the same second a shell punctured the jeep's radiator and shattered its engine.

The firing intensified. Between the contending batteries of artillery the noise was deafening. Machinegun bullets clipped the trees along the side of the ditch and filled it with gently falling leaves. But there was plenty of protection and I started to open a can of meat and beans when infantrymen jumped out of our ditch and out of the one across the road and began running across the fields. Kellogg looked up and shouted: "For Christ's sake, it's a bleeding big tank coming down the road. Get over here, quick."

I had been lying in an elbow of the ditch which would have been exposed to fire from any tank that might pass. In great haste I crawled into a part of the ditch where Kellogg, Butler and the others were, and we all tried to become as small as possible, when someone noticed a big white star on the tank. It was Lieutenant Colonel John Waters' tank, coming from Oran. It meant the end of the battle.

What had happened was that our tanks had burst into Oran, churned around and mortally injured the guts of the interior military defense, then burst out through the crust of enemy infantry. Four non-coms in the first American tank had entered Oran without knowing it, lost their way, ran over and destroyed two 75's, saw a road block which looked to them like a group of trucks, decided to smash through it, hit a solid concrete pillar which killed their tank engine and cut up the tankmen but did not prevent them from restarting their engine and getting back safely.

Then one tank column, under Lieutenant Colonel John Todd, hit Oran from one side and another column under command of Lieutenant Colonel Waters hit it from the other side, while young Lieutenant Arthur C. Edson had a field day guiding his light tank against an enemy convoy including thirty former overland busses. About 11:00 A.M. Todd's tank got to the Oran Fortress Le Pont Neuf, and there captured the French Commanding General, Boisseau. Meanwhile, Edson's tank had frightened everybody so badly that the mayor of Oran, without waiting for military authority, came out and under a white flag met the First Division officers and offered to surrender.

We came up at the moment and Colonel Fred Butler told us it had been arranged to march into the city precisely at noon. Tanks would precede the infantry as it was not certain what the reception would be. A few minutes before noon, Colonel Waters reappeared in his tank and invited Colonel Butler and Kellogg and me to ride into Oran. His would be the leading tank.

We climbed on top and started down the highway which had been the battlefield an hour before, but was empty now and quiet. Inside the tank Colonel Waters and his crew were distant from us as though on another planet, distant by inches of armor plate. We clung to the lurching vehicle and waited to see what sort of welcome Oran would give the First Division.

We need have had no anxiety. The 400,000 inhabitants of Oran went quite out of their minds with joy and shattered the air with "Vive America!" . . . "Vive les Etats Unis!" . . . "Vive la Liberte."

We left the tank and drove to Le Pont Neuf where in the turreted courtyard General Allen reported to General Lloyd R. Fredendall. The II Corps Commander received the salutes of the leaders of the battle units, Brigadier General Theodore Roosevelt, Jr., who had brilliantly led the 26th Infantry's attack on Los Anfalouses, Cheadle of the 16th, Colonel Johnny Bowen of the 26th

Infantry, and Colonel Greer of the 18th Infantry. The French General Boisseau and Admiral Rioult, presenting their formal surrender, were in spirits as high as ours. They, too, were freed.

It was "the end of the beginning" of the long and bloody and glorious road of the First Division through Tunis, Sicily, and France, to Germany and victory. Victory for what? The people of Oran cried "Vive la Liberte!" That is what the war was all about. The United States was well represented by the First Division.

CHAPTER II

T U N I S I A

(November 20, 1942, to May 8, 1943)

The Situation

AFTER the successful early landings in North Africa, the Allies rushed their meager forces east to seize the strategic key to the Central Mediterranean—Tunisia. They knew that final victory in North Africa depended upon Allied possession of Tunis and Bizerte.

While Montgomery's Eighth Army swept Rommel and his Africa Korps toward Northern Tunisia, the British, French and Americans in Western and Southern Tunisia were to be molded rapidly into the other jaw of the Allied pincers which finally would squeeze the Axis forces into a trap from which there was no escape— Cap Bon and Tunis.

The initial movements in the execution of this plan were made in October. The confusing pieces of the African jig-saw puzzle were being fitted into a soul testing but clear picture portraying an Allied victory. The British Eighth Army had started to drive west from El Alamein on October 24, 1942. On this same day a great convoy put to sea from American ports. In the next twenty-four hours two more convoys sailed from British ports. All were bound for North Africa. The objective of this Allied armada, as publicly announced by Churchill, was "to open a new front against Hitler and Hitlerism; to cleanse the shores of Africa from the stain of Nazi and Fascist tyranny; to open the Mediterranean to Allied sea power and thus effect the liberation of the peoples of Europe."

All Allied efforts now were concentrated on rapidly seizing Tunisia.

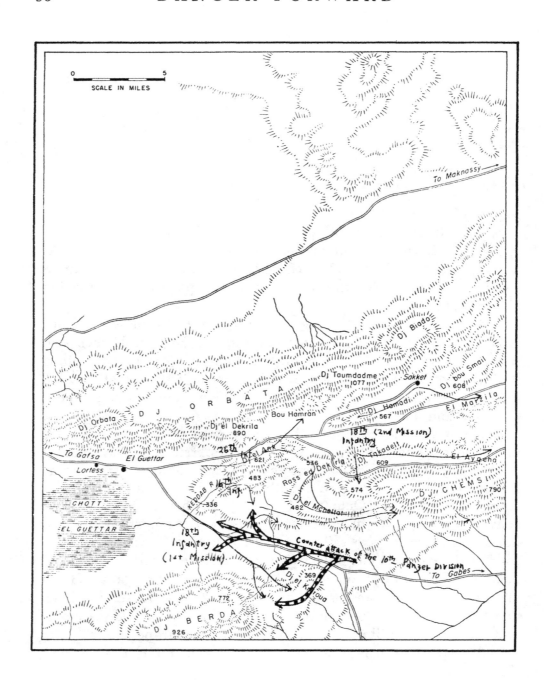

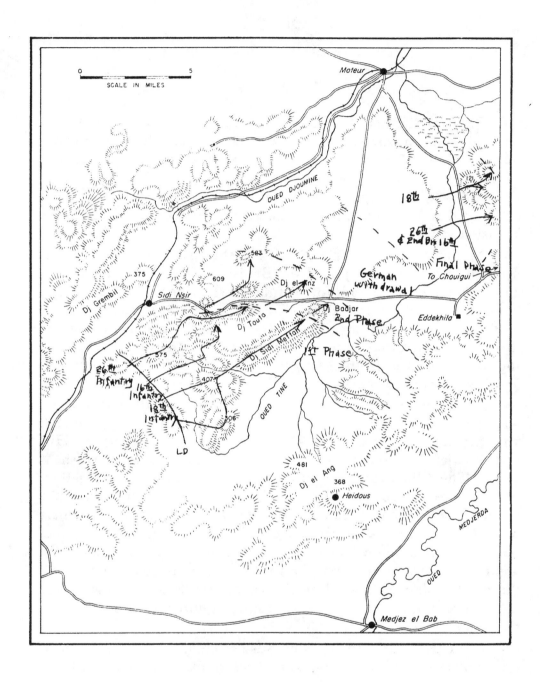

T U N I S I A

(November 20, 1942, to May 8, 1943)

The Record

HARDLY had the First Division regrouped and reorganized after the surrender of the French at Oran when the 3rd Battalion, 26th Infantry, was flown east to Youk les Bains. By November 25th they were outposting southern Tunisia and guarding the south and east approaches to the Atlas Mountains. Weird tales of isolated actions in a big, empty, desert country filtered back to the Division at Oran.

At about the same time, the 5th Field Artillery Battalion was ordered to Tunisia and joined the British V Corps and elements of an American armored task force of the First Armored Division. The battalion joined the British on November 23, 1942, and remained under British control until February 7, 1943. The heroic actions of this famous old battalion while supporting the British V Corps during this period was tempered by the loss of the battalion commander and his battery commanders.

In late November, the 18th Infantry Regimental Combat Team was alerted. It started east by trucks in early December. The 18th Infantry Regimental Combat Team made history at Longstop Hill and Medjez el Bab where they fought as part of the British V Corps. The Allied forces, in spite of their great sacrifice and gallantry, were so slowed down by logistics and winter weather that the Germans were able to stabilize the situation in northern Tunisia during the last week of December. As additional forces arrived, positions were developed on to the south of Pont du Faho through the Tunisian hills. German positions in general were selected to cover the coastal plain and to block Allied approach to the low, sunny coastal area with its fine highways leading southward through Gabes to Tripoli.

In January while the fighting was becoming stabilized in northern Tunisia, the rest of the 26th Infantry Regiment and the 33rd Field

Artillery Battalion were alerted and started east to join the II Corps in southern Tunisia. The II Corps with the 1st Armored and elements of the First Division, was to reinforce the French and secure the southern flank of the Allied position in the Tunisian hills.

After a short alert, the remainder of the Division was ordered into the General Reserve by Allied Force Headquarters on the 18th of January, 1943. The Division moved east and concentrated in the Guelma area, 60 miles east of Constantine, between the 18th and 24th of January, 1943.

The entire First Division was finally en route to Tunisia! However, the series of emergencies which confronted the Allied forces in Tunisia resulted in elements of the Division being committed to action over a wide area. The first week in February, Allied lists showed First Division units in action from Medjez el Bab in the north to Gafsa in the south, an air line distance of over 200 miles.

"My most serious concern in mid-January," wrote General Eisenhower, "was the French." Early in December General Giraud had volunteered to take over the critical high ridge which fronts the Tunisian coastal plain. This ridge, the massive eastern dorsal, begins about 15 miles south of Pont du Fahs and extends south to Pichon. Between this outer ridge on the eastern dorsal and the central dorsal lies the Ousseltia Valley. The valley is heavily eroded, cut up by seasonal streams. The enemy realized that the French forces who held this section were weak and utterly destitute of modern mobile combat and anti-tank weapons. On January 18th, Von Arnim attacked these French forces south of Pont du Fahs, using Tiger tanks. He broke through the French lines and moved down the Ousseltia Valley. He was stopped on January 24th by elements of II Corps which were rushed north from southern Tunisia. This force, Combat Command B, First Armored Division with the 26th Regimental Combat Team, less the 3rd Infantry Battalion, attached, stabilized the front after considerable fighting on the high ground east of Ousseltia.

On January 21st orders came from Allied Force Headquarters to concentrate the 16th Infantry in the Maktar area preparatory to taking over a part of the French Corps Sector from Combat Command B, First Armored Division. The same order placed the First Division (less the 18th and 26th Infantry) under the French XIX Corps. Contact was made with the elements of the First Armored Division and the 26th Infantry in the Ousseltia Valley, and the relief took place during the period January 27 to 30, 1943. During this period another attack came in on the French forces to the north of the sector where the First Division was going into the line. British troops were rushed to the central dorsal and the 1st Battalion, 16th Infantry, was moved behind the French and British troops to provide a reserve. This battalion was thrown into the fight to stop attacks by German mountain troops and fought splendidly in a 2-day action which ended with the withdrawal of the Germans from advanced positions around Robaa.

While the Germans were being defeated in the northern part of the French Corps Sector, the First Division was organizing its sector. The Division sector consisted of a 22-mile stretch of rough terrain stretching north from Pichon along the outer dorsal to a dominating hill mass just west of Kairouan, and then northwest across the floor of the Ousseltia Valley to connect with the French in the central dorsal.

The 15 days spent in the Ousseltia sector were quiet. During this period about 7,000 French troops were attached to the First Division. They were organized into the Conne Groupment and consisted of six battalions of infantry and a Tabour of Goums supported by a small groupment of artillery equipped with 75-mm guns and 65-mm howitzers and a few obsolete anti-tank weapons. Actions were limited to patrol encounters. The enemy had complete superiority in the air. On February 5th, the French XIX Corps for the 34th Infantry Division to relieve the Conne Groupment in the Pichon area. The relief was completed on the night of February 13-14, at which time the 34th Division took command of its elements in the area, and responsibility for the Pichon area. This order restated the mission of the First Division directing it to oppose all sudden thrusts from the north and prevent the enemy from seizing the Ousseltia Valley and threatening Pichon from the north or from advancing from the direction of Pichon on Maktar.

On February 14th the Germans launched a powerful attack on First Armored Division positions in the vicinity of Faid, about 80 miles south of the First Infantry Division sector. This attack was successful and the II Corps position in the Faid area was ruptured, exposing the flank of the XIX French Corps. The II Corps was caught off balance and over-extended by Rommel's forces and was defeated piecemeal. It was forced to fall back into the mountains east of Tebessa and reorganize. The 26th Infantry which had been detached from the Division, and was operating under II Corps, was involved in this operation. The 3rd Battalion, 26th Infantry, withdrew 50 miles from Gafsa and covered the southern approach to Tebessa. The balance of the 26th Infantry, together with the 19th Engineers, hastily organized a new position astride the Oued Hateb to defend the Kasserine Pass.

On February 16th the First Division issued a warning alerting the Division for movement from their advanced positions in the eastern dorsal to the central dorsal 15 miles to the west. The 34th Division was also alerted to withdraw from its exposed position at Pichon. Orders for the withdrawal were issued by the XIX Corps a few hours later.

The French XIX Corps was responsible for a large sector. Its communications facilities were sketchy and consisted principally of the existing local civilian telephone lines. Communications between the First Division and the Corps Headquarters was normally maintained through the radio set furnished by the Division liaison officer at Corps Headquarters. Consequently information and orders were sketchy. Illustrative of the situation are the messages taken from the Division G-3 Journals.

February 18, 1943. Allen to Koeltz: "Sector quiet. Withdrawal successful. Air activity negative. Weather cold and overcast. Last element 16th Infantry just coming into area. Complete evacuation not confirmed officially."

February 18, 1943. Koeltz to Allen: "This is a warning.

General Anderson has just issued a directive to Colonel Fechet's Regiment complete to go to Fredendall as soon as possible."

The Ousseltia Valley campaign was over! The First Division was moving to the Kasserine Pass to assist in restoring the Allied positions in southern Tunisia.

In spite of most disagreeable weather — winter rains and snow — the 16th Infantry was rapidly relieved by other elements of the French XIX Corps and sent east through Tebessa to assembly positions on the northwest slopes of Djebel Chambi — the highest point in Tunisia.

Other elements of the First Division rapidly followed the 16th Infantry south, and on February 20th the Division Forward Command Post was established at Bou Chebka. Liaison was established during the day with the French Constantine Division, and other troops in the area.

Meanwhile, II Corps forces, recoiling before the heavy German attacks launched on February 14th at Faid Pass, took up defensive positions on the hills covering routes leading west to Tebessa and north to Thala and Le Kef. Corridors into this position existed in the vicinity of Kasserine and Sbiba. German probing attacks were launched at both places on February 19, 1943.

The 18th Infantry Combat Team was placed in position to cover Sbiba and attached to the 34th Infantry Division. They repulsed enemy probing attacks in the vicinity of Sbiba on February 19th, inflicting heavy losses.

The Headquarters 26th Regimental Combat Team took over the forces in the Kasserine area, consisting of the 19th Engineer Regiment and the 1st Battalion, 26th Infantry, just as the enemy probing attack was launched there. The Germans discovered that the position was not a strong one on February 19th, and so renewed their attack on February 20th. By noon the right flank of the 19th Engineers had been pierced.

In spite of American and British armored and infantry reinforcements the Germans were able to widen the breach and our decimated forces were ordered to withdraw. On the night of February 20-21, British forces with the 1st Battalion, 26th Infantry, withdrew to the northwest up the valley of the Oued Hatab.

To assist in covering Tebessa, the 16th Infantry under First Division command were ordered to move east at daylight, February 21st, to establish contact on the right with elements of the Constantine Division north of Djebel Chambi, with elements of the First Armored Division on the left flank, to gain contact with the enemy, and to drive him back into Kasserine Pass. At daylight, leading elements of the 16th Infantry gained contact with German infantry elements and attacked. After considerable close fighting, the Gremans withdrew to the north only to find escape in that direction blocked by elements of the First Armored Division. Almost 300 Germans were taken by the First Armored Division as a result of this action by the 16th Infantry.

On the night of February 21-22, II Corps plans were changed. It was necessary to move the bulk of the 16th Infantry that night by truck over 40 miles of strange roads and install them in position to attack at daylight with Combat Command B, First Armored Division. The 16th Infantry arrived as scheduled, and reported to the Commander, Combat Command B, for orders. The attack was not launched due to the need for further reconnaissance. The attack was finally postponed until daylight, February 23rd. However, contact with the enemy was lost, and the dawn attack on February 23rd was in effect an approach march to the Kasserine Pass. Rommel had withdrawn his forces. Some days later, contact was regained with enemy forces in the vicinity of Gafsa, Maknassy, Faid and Pichon.

By the time the Germans had withdrawn from the Kasserine Pass, the First Division had organized its sector on Djebel Chambi and had taken command of all forces in the area. These forces were a heterogeneous lot. The principal combat elements were the French Constantine Division, the 1st Ranger Battalion and the 3rd Battalion, 26th Infantry.

By March 1st most of the Ninth Infantry Division had arrived from French Morocco. The First Division was ordered to turn over the Djebel Chambi sector to the Ninth Division and regroup northwest of Tebessa at Marsott. Here all of the elements of the First Division were assembled, rested and filled with replacements preparatory to further operations. Reorganization was badly needed, as there had been considerable casualties in some units. For example, there were 9 officers and 151 enlisted men killed, wounded or missing in action in the 26th Infantry (less the 2nd and 3rd Battalions). While elements of the Division had been in action continuously since late November, 1942, and all elements of the Division had been committed since the latter part of January, the First Division had not been fought as a team. It had been committed piecemeal by the British First Army to block or counter German moves.

After a ten day rest the Division received movement orders. For the first time in the Tunisian Campaign, the First Division was assembled as a unit. It was dispersed throughout the scrub forests surrounding Bou Chebka while monotonous early spring rains filtered through the sparse spring foliage and the shelter-halves of the troops. Time dragged by heavily. The troops knew that something big was in the wind, and fretted from the inactivity in the too-familiar mud. Finally the plan—"Operation WOP"—was made known. The Division was to capture and defend Gafsa, and secure bases for the British Eighth Army in the vicinity. The date selected by coincidence or sentimental whimsy was St. Patrick's Day, March 17, 1943.

The French garrison town of Gafsa lay some 50 miles south of Bou Chebka on the northern edge of the Sahara, and was a famous oasis along the ancient caravan route. Earlier in the year it had been occupied by units of the 26th Infantry, who had operated against Sened, Maknassy and Faid Pass from this base. Now it was occupied by an Italian garrison, having been given up without a fight when the II Corps line had been punctured at Faid Pass and Sidi Bou Zid. Rommel had withdrawn to the eastern range of the Grand Dorsal, and a vast and mysterious land stretched out from the First Division's mountain bivouac toward the southeast. The Italian garrison at Gafsa stood between the Division and Montgomery's Eighth Army which was hammering forward toward the Mareth Line.

During the night of March 16-17, the First Division moved by truck to assembly points outside of Gafsa. The move was rapid and cohesive. It was made along roads de-mined by the 1st Engineers, who had harvested over 2,000 Teller-mines. Once more American troops passed among the ancient Roman ruins of Thelepte and Feriana, and by 6:00 A.M. March 17th the entire Division was deployed in assembly areas and ready for the attack.

It is likely that "Operation WOP" was expected by the enemy, since the Engineers had been guarding the cleared areas and building roads for several days previously. Also, on the night of the assembly, mechanized patrols of attached Tank Destroyer units moved boldly along the paved highway to within a mile of the city's approaches, and shot it out with enemy outposts.

The position of Gafsa might be likened to that of a golf ball pinioned between the directly opposite points of two shoes. The 18th Infantry had approached the eastern shoe, and clamboring over the toe, just below the laces, were prepared to invest the town from the east. Two battalions of the 16th Infantry climbed the western shoe, and were maneuvering down the instep. A motorized task force from the 26th Infantry, led by Colonel "Johnny" Bowen, formerly one of the garrison commanders at Gafsa, had skirted the eastern mountain mass entirely and was moving upon the town from the southwest. A reserve of the 2nd Battalion, 16th Infantry, awaited a call to follow up in an assault from the flats of the north, if necessary. The 26th Infantry, less the 3rd Battalion, was in Division Reserve.

H-Hour was postponed from 6:00 A.M. to 10:00 A.M. to allow an air strike. Finally American planes appeared, glinting in the brilliant sunlight, followed by the great crash of bombs somewhere on the back side of the "golf ball," and the infantry pressed in under the comfortable barrage of the Division Artillery. "Long Tom" 155-mm rifles were ready to reach out behind the town's southeast exit, and to harass any retreat toward El Guettar.

Operation "WOP" proved to be a dry run. The enemy had abandoned the town, quite wisely, since it was indefensible. By

12:20 P.M. patrols of the 16th Infantry entered the town from the west and the 18th Infantry cut off the exit road at Lala. Natives, still quaking from the assault of the bombers and the artillery barrage, stated that the covering force of 1,200 Italians had withdrawn at 8:00 A.M. screened by the German 580th Reconnaissance Battalion. Through the corner of the town and the ancient fort, crumbled by the aerial bombardment, long files of infantry wearily threaded their way toward El Guettar in pursuit. The only American casualties quartermaster items, some troops having worn out trousers and shoes completely on the jagged mountain approaches. Chaplains, as they had predicted, held mass within the city in honor of St. Patrick.

Meanwhile, the Division's motorized patrols probed southeast toward El Guettar, in search of the Italian garrison whose inopportune withdrawal had made the day of the patron saint notable for little more than a large-scale maneuver expertly executed. That night torrential rains poured down, engulfing the troops who had bivouaced in the wadies outside the town, and miring those more exalted echelons who had chosen the famous "Garden of Allah" oasis for a resting place.

The situation of the town of Gafsa was eminently unsuited for defense of any kind, although the original French garrison had transformed a few small hills within the town into a veritable mass of futile trenches and tunnels. Since the untenanted mountains east and west of the town were too vast to organize defensively, General Allen decided that the best defense for the prospective Eighth Army railhead would be found further eastward. Early skirmishes in the region, previous to the arrival of the Afrika Korps in February, indicated that the enemy had organized a position of considerable natural strength astride the Gabes highway in the hills east of El Guettar. To the northeast the Maknassy Gap had also been occupied and offered a similar threat to Gafsa.

At 6:00 P.M., March 20th, the First Division received orders to attack east along the Gabes Road and secure the commanding positions east of El Guettar. Simultaneously a task force of the 60th Infantry (Ninth Division) and elements of the First Armored Division were moved toward the northeast gap near Maknassy.

Since March 17th elements of the Rangers and 1st Reconnaissance Troop had been in contact with Italian mechanized units near the great oasis of El Guettar, where an estimated 6,000 Italian troops, of the Centauro Armored Division, were in position. This unit had been one of the few Italian formations not sacrificed by Rommel in the Tripolitanian retreat.

The plan for the advance to the east from El Guettar placed the 18th Infantry south of the highway with the 26th Infantry to the north. A flanking maneuver by the 1st Ranger Battalion, supported by the Division Artillery and the heavy weapons of the 1st Engineers, was planned over the precipitous cliffs of the Djebel Orbata, a ridge north of the Gabes highway, which dominated the oasis of El Guettar and in spots reached the height of 3,500 feet.

By mid-morning of March 21st, the Italian position was effectively captured, the 26th Infantry and the Rangers securing the road fork east of El Guettar by occupying a knife-edged feature called Djebel El Ank (621) and advancing east along a narrow unimproved road called the Gumtree Road, toward the native village of Bou Hamran. The 18th Infantry followed the southern fork, the Gabes highway, sending the 3rd Battalion into the escarpment west of a horseshoe feature called Djebel Moheltat, and the 1st and 2nd Battalions toward a commanding feature to the south, Djebel Berda.

Fighting was limited to sharp, brief actions with the Italians. The Luftwaffe, however, bombed and strafed our advancing infantry incessantly, and savagely attacked the First Division Artillery.

As the attack had progressed the 3rd Battalion, 16th Infantry, as a precautionary measure was moved into a switch position east of the junction of the Gafsa Road and the Gumtree Road. The battalion dug in behind a minefield and astride the Gafsa Road. The ridge was deeply eroded by dry tributaries of the Oued el Kebir, and later proved a fortuitous sanctuary.

The 2nd Battalion, 16th Infantry, was entrucked at Gafsa, and made a night march into the oasis, where it was hidden among the deep-terraced gardens and walls. They awaited orders which would send them scurrying straight toward Gabes, once the 18th Infantry had secured the line Djebel Moheltat-Djebel el Kreroua. The 1st

Battalion, 16th Infantry, with its teammate, the 7th Field Artillery Battalion, remained as the garrison of Gafsa, puzzling over the strange French defenses and observing the erection of a forward fighter landing strip. Meanwhile, from the northeast, came news that the tank-infantry-artillery task force had fought through lightly-held Sened, entered Maknassy, and appeared capable of breaking into the coastal plain west of Sfax.

Early, during the morning hours of March 23rd, heavy small arms fire from the valley east of El Guettar could be heard in the Division Command Post in the oasis. The first light reports from the 18th Infantry and the 601st Tank Destroyer Battalion indicated that a vicious counter-attack was being made by the 10th Panzer Division.

As the morning fog burned off the plain, the Observation Post of the 18th Infantry Command Post on Hill 336 reported the valley swarming with German tanks, furiously duelling with the outgunned, but not outgamed, half-tracks of the 601st Tank Destroyer Battalion. Enemy infantry had passed through the Italian defenders facing the Division attack from Djebel Berda and the southern rim of Djebel Moheltat, and were pressing hard upon all three battalions of the 18th Infantry. Probing columns of German tanks and infantry had infiltrated behind the 18th beleaguered battalions, and overrun six field pieces each of the 5th and 32nd Field Artillery Battalions. The 3rd Battalion, 16th Infantry, was digging deeper into their switch position on the low ridge, from whence Observation Posts could see the valiant Division Artillerymen far to the front defending their gun positions with rifles and grenades. Along the highway, the German main tank group appeared ready to rush the small pass below Hill 336. Limping back through the covering minefield, just completed by the 1st Engineers, came a few remaining half-tracks of the 601st Tank Destroyer Battalion which had accounted for at least 10 Mark III and IV tanks, some artillery personnel and signalmen, and assorted unhappy foot soldiers.

The Germans had reacted rapidly to the Italian debacle. They had rushed into action from a reserve position near Kairouan a battle group of the 10th Panzer Division, heroes of the Sedan break-through in the Battle of France. By eight o'clock elements committed included the 1st Battalion of the 7th Panzer Regiment (50 tanks) ; the 1st Battalion, 69th Panzer Grenadiers; the 2nd Battalion, 86th Panzer Grenadiers, and a battalion of the 90th Artillery Regiment. Shellfire registered on the 16th Infantry switch position in the pass at Hill 336, while the German infantry crawled forward from wadi to get within assaulting distance of the pass' defenders. Meanwhile the remaining 155's of the 5th Field Artillery Battalion were emplaced on line with the 3rd Battalion, 16th Infantry, and blasted round after round from rapidly dwindling ammunition stocks into the German ranks; the 2nd Battalion of the 16th Infantry detrucked at the fork of the Gumtree-Gafsa road under fire, and slogged into position on either side of the 3rd Battalion line. By mid-morning the German attack had stalled and as the oppressive mid-day heat beat down upon the attackers and defenders alike. Reserves from II Corps began arriving, including the 899th Tank Destroyer Battalion of full-tracked 3-inch guns, and the 17th Field Artillery, to reinforce the hard-hit 5th and 32nd Field Artillery Battalions. News that additional American tanks were on the way cheered the fighting men of the First Division.

In the early afternoon Company E of the 2nd Battalion, 16th Infantry, made a limited counter-attack southward from the vicinity of Hill 483, eliminating some of the troublesome German patrols who were searching out the hilly northern flank of the Hill 336 position. The former positions of the 32nd Field Artillery were retaken before German patrols could infiltrate and destroy the remaining equipment, and contact with the 3rd Battalion, 18th Infantry, which had been isolated from the Division by the morning counter-attack was made in the vicinity of the wadi west of Hill 482. A few German tanks, attempting to outflank the switch position from the south were bogged down in the soft mud of Chott (Salt Lake) El Guettar, a provident natural obstacle on the right flank of the Division Command Post.

In the late afternoon the Germans made another violent attack on the pass with reformed infantry supported by tanks, but the now well-knit defense force within the pass smashed the attack with mortar, machinegun and artillery fire.

On March 24th, the 2nd Battalion, 16th Infantry, relieved the 3rd Battalion, 18th Infantry, and were heavily shelled in the wadi west of Hill 482. The 1st and 2nd Battalions, 18th Infantry, on Djebel Berda, were attacked by the fresh 10th Motorcycle Battalion which had been the German battle group's reserve. Tired and badly cut up by the past two days' heavy fighting, these American Battalions fell back slowly on the heights of Berda. On March 25th the two weary formations were withdrawn upon Corps order and, together with the already relieved 3rd Battalion, 18th Infantry, regrouped at El Guettar. Meanwhile, the 26th Infantry had attacked the northern rim of the Djebel Moheltat, and from point 536 were beginning a tortuous battle through rocky and barren hills toward Hill 482 which was the key to the battlefield.

From this point on the battle resolved into a grueling grind in which the terrain was a deadlier foe than the enemy. The II Corps committed the 39th and 47th Infantry regiments and much artillery of the Ninth Infantry Division into the battle to regain Djebel Berda. A tank force of the First Armored Division, under Colonel Chauncey Benson, along with the 2nd Battalion, 6th Armored Infantry, were thrown into the fight which moved sluggishly but always forward, day by day.

The Germans displayed the great defensive skill, later to be so thoroughly validated in Sicily and Italy. Just what forces remained for the stout German defense was not clearly known. It was thought that elements of the 10th Panzer Division and the Italian Centauro Division remained in well-organized defensive positions. Skilled parachute reinforcements of the Ramcke Brigade subsequently were identified, along with Panzer Grenadier Regiment "AFRIKA." A battle group of the 21st Panzer Division defended well-laid minefields and a sharpshooting anti-tank screen of 88's bottled up the Benson Force in the center of the valley.

The zone of the First Division was now the rugged hills north of the Gabes Road, and, in conjunction with the 26th Infantry, the 16th Infantry attacked the horseshoe shaped Djebel Moheltat on the 28th of March, and were hurled back from wired-in, well-defended positions. On March 29th, the 26th Infantry advanced to within assaulting distance of Hill 482, and took the position on March 30th after a great effort and with considerable losses among the rifle companies. The 16th Infantry, operating outside of the horseshoe rim on the southern flank, advanced eastward, crevasse by crevasse, while its supply line was constantly menaced and frequently infiltrated by German patrols. The 18th Infantry meanwhile, after a short rest, had been assigned the task of advancing along the Gumtree Road. They had taken Djebel Hamadi (567) on March 27th, and then had moved south to cover the flank of the 26th Infantry by attacking the difficult position of Hill 574.

Orientation in this wild and mysterious country was a major problem. Units found great difficulty in accurately reporting their positions since maps were re-photographed French sheets surveyed in 1903, and of 1:100,000 scale. The terrain was cup up into ragged, rocky promontories, separated by deep wadies, all of which looked alike. To get a decent position coordinate, it was necessary to resect azimuths on the few truly identifiable features. This naturally required the compass-shooter to climb to the highest point of the position, a task made doubly hazardous by the discouraging attention and accuracy of the German snipers supported by 88's.

While the First Division was embroiled in the troublesome horseshoe, the Ninth Infantry Division was experiencing little success in capturing Djebel Kreroua. However, on April 6th, all infantry had reached their objectives against decreasing German resistance, and it became apparent that the Germans had pulled back to save their strength for the next party. With Montgomery battering through the Mareth and Akarit Line, the German defensive position at El Guettar was hopeless, and by the morning of April 7th, no Germans remained to be contacted. The tanks of the Benson Force moved through the gap at Djebel Kerousa, the 18th Infantry marched unmolested east to El Ayacha and beyond, and the 3rd Battalion of the 16th Infantry crossed to Gabes highway east of Djebel Krerousa, and met the equally weary doughfeet of the 47th Infantry Regiment to exchange felicitations mingled with condolences.

To many of the First Division who fought at El Guettar, it seemed doubtful that any great victory had been won. Some 1,800 prisoners had been captured, but only a disappointing 7% were Germans. It was believed that casualties inflicted upon the enemy were generally lower than those suffered by the American troops. By keeping firm pressure on the western German flank, however, the Eighth Army at Mareth was assisted by having reserves drawn off. Furthermore, in 17 days of constant fighting of the roughest sort, the First Division had proven itself. The Division was now an offensive team of proven ability and spirit and it had added a big scalp to its belt, the 10th Panzer Division, which received its death blow at El Guettar.

The second week of April, 1943, found the battlefield of El Guettar deserted, and while Montgomery's Eighth Army pursued the enemy northward along the coastal plain toward Enfidaville, the First Division briefly rested. Some units, when they were mildly exasperated, were ordered to clean up the battlefield. Amidst the colorful blanket of fragile desert flowers, troops on police detail wandered warily through a conglomerate litter, always watchful for the menacing 3-pronged sign of the detestable anti-personnel mine, known as the "S" or "Bouncing Baby." Piles of spent shell casings, burned-out tanks, the pitiful small piles of personal treasures abandoned by the wounded, and an occasional unburied corpse, attested to the fury of the past action. Already the opportunistic natives, ghoulish through poverty, rag-picked through the wadies and rocks, and occasionally one blew up on a live mine.

Finally the convoys threaded away from Gafsa toward the now familiar bivouac area in the hills north of Morsott. Native children thrust out anxious palms for the henceforth forever-lost hard candies and biscuits. The troops grinned at the sight of an old latrine trench festooned with flowers, which sentimental natives, confusing the wooden date-marker for a burial cross, tended with reverence.

Following a few days of rest and refitting the Division was again alerted. When II Corps effected the miraculous logistical switch to the north flank of the British First Army, moving some 150 miles through the British communication lines, the First Division was in the van in its usual prominent position. By April 16th leading elements of the Division took up positions northeast of Beja, in a new empty terrain of lushy green wheat fields and rolling hills, contrasting violently to the burned desert fringe of El Guettar with its sand and stark, tortured mountains. This new area was an old battlefield over which the British and Germans had fought vigorously during the winter months. Furthermore, lack of trees and ground cover made it the toughest of areas from a defensive point of view. The full II Corps sector resembled a right triangle with its point or apex resting upon Mateur. The hypotenuse bordered the Tine Valley, running generally northeast, and represented the Division's axis of advance for the projected attack.

The Axis armies were now hemmed into a quarter-circle inclosing Mateur, Bizerte, Tunis and Cape Bon Peninsula. Their defensive positions were uniformly strong. The principal worry of Von Arnim's Group "Afrika" was the broad Medjerda river valley, a natural corridor into Tunis. Stretching southeast from the Mediterranean were the American II Corps with the First Infantry Division on the right flank, the British First Army to the south fringe of the Goubellat Plain, the French XIX Corps in the mountains opposing Pont du Fahs and Djebel Zaghouan, and the famed desert Eighth Army, now getting a bitter taste of mountain warfare, from thence to the east coast, and again the Mediterranean.

The strategic plan required a coordinated series of attacks by all Allied forces, initiated on a counterclockwise schedule by the II Corps. It was anticipated that the main effort would ultimately be developed by the Eighth Army, or the British First Army. Neither the Americans nor the French were considered capable of major accomplishments, due to the mountainous terrain of their respective sectors.

The First Division jumped off the night of 22-23 April from a line opposing the three enemy strongpoints on Hills 575, 407 and 306, all located south of the Sidi Nsir-Tebourba road. On the left flank, the 34th Infantry Division was assigned the task of turning the enemy flank upon Djebel Grembil (Hill 609) and initially exploiting toward the Oued Djoumine Valley. On the southern flank, the 6th Armored Infantry was assigned key hills south of the Oued Tine to cover the right flank of the First Division.

The German force facing the Division consisted of elements

of the 334th Infantry Division, the crack Barenthin Engineer Regiment of the Luftwaffe, the 47th (separate) Infantry Regiment, the anti-tank battalion of the 10th Panzer Division, and assorted marsch battalions, tank and assault gun units.

The enemy facing the 26th Infantry Regimental Combat Team was advantageously established, especially on Kef el Goraa (Hill 575). The approaches to this strongpoint was through smooth and round-topped hills which offered little concealment except for occasional patches of short wheat. The enemy positions were strongly prepared and well camouflaged. Rocky hideouts afforded excellent protection against the air bursts of our artillery. During the attack on Hill 575, infantry and detachments of the 1st Engineers cleared 1,800 mines from the area.

The attack of the 26th Infantry jumped off before dawn on April 23rd behind a concentration fired by the 33rd Field Artillery Battalion and part of the II Corps Artillery. The 1st Battalion, 26th Infantry captured Hill 565 at 3:55 A.M. against light opposition. When the advance continued across the valley, heavy enemy fire caused many casualties, and the attack stalled 300 yards short of the main objective. Meanwhile, the 2nd Battalion, 26th Infantry, in support of the 1st Battalion, moved up to Hill 565, and its forward elements reached a point 1,000 yards south of Hill 575 in a flanking movement. Enemy troops on the forward slopes of the hill forced them back with heavy fire. Having failed to capture their objective, the two battalions withdrew to Hill 565.

On April 24th, First Division artillery intermittently shelled enemy positions on Hill 575. The 3rd Battalion of the 26th Infantry, having been relieved on the left by units of the 34th Division, moved up to support a renewed attack planned for April 25th. By this time the 16th Infantry had outflanked Hill 575, by capturing three important hills to the southeast. According to a prisoner-of-war report, the enemy pulled out of Hill 575 at 2:00 A.M., the hour when our attack jumped off, leaving only a rear guard. The 2nd Battalion occupied the hill at 3:50 A.M. and a few hours later the 1st Battalion had possession of Hill 533 to the north. The 3rd Battalion, 26th Infantry, advanced northeast of Hill 575 and continued along the ridge toward Djebel Touta (Hill 444) which was occupied in the afternoon. As the First Division moved forward, the 2nd Battalion of the 168th Infantry (34th Division) moved southeast from Hill 344 and took over Hills 533 and 575.

Early on April 23rd, while the 26th Infantry was making the initial attack on Hill 575, the 16th Infantry advanced into the hills to the southeast and by the end of the morning had taken Hills 415 and 374. The enemy fought stubbornly, subjecting our troops to mortar and artillery fire from the slopes of Hill 407. Hill 400 saw the hardest fighting and changed hands three times before it was finally taken, shortly before noon. On the next day, with Hill 400 in its possession, the 16th Infantry was able to capture three more heights: Hills 491 and 469 to the north, and 394 midway between 400 and 407. During the night of April 24-25, the Germans withdrew on the whole Division front. The 16th Infantry had played an important part in forcing this retirement. In the follow-up of the enemy movement, the 16th Infantry occupied Hill 342 as Division Reserve.

To clean out enemy positions on the Division's right, the 2nd Battalion of the 18th Infantry, with the 1st Battalion, 13th Armored Infantry (attached) advanced on April 23rd against Hill 350 on the west side of the Tine Valley. The early stages of the attack were successful, but counter-attacks by elements of the 10th Panzer Division from Hill 407 pushed the 2nd Battalion of the 18th Infantry off the high ground by 7:30 A.M. To protect the flank toward Hill 407, the 2nd Battalion moved with tank support through minefields around the north side of Hill 350 to attack Hill 306. After five hours of stiff fighting, marked by numerous counter-attacks, the 18th Infantry had captured both Hill 350 and Hill 306. In spite of heavy casualties, particularly in Company E, 18th Infantry, it went on to strike at Hill 407, a mile to the northwest.

The main attack on Hill 407 jumped off early the next morning, April 24th, against initial stubborn resistance of heavy fire of all weapons. Nevertheless, the hill fortress was in our hands by 4:00 A.M. There was much evidence that its power to resist had been weakened by poundings from our artillery, and especially by a heavy concentration laid down for an hour before the attack.

Threatened with the loss of all commanding ground in this area, the enemy continued to keep Hill 407 under heavy fire and counter-attacked Hill 306 about 9:00 A.M. Despite success at Hill 306, there were signs that the enemy was preparing to pull out to the east, and by the morning of April 25th a German withdrawal was under way. The 18th Infantry was thus enabled to move several miles forward. By 2:00 P.M., on April 25th, leading elements reached the western end of the long Djebel Sidi Meftah ridge (point 347), occupying Hill 340 on the way. Part of the heights at the entrance to the main Tine Valley had been conquered.

By April 26th, the First Division had attained its initial objectives and controlled all the high ground south of a line from Hill 575 to Hill 347 (Djebel Sidi Meftah). However, the Division now had a long flank on the left, exposed to enemy counter-attack from strong positions on high ground. Corps Headquarters saw that any further progress eastward would increase the danger to this flank.

The next move, therefore, were coordinated blows by the 34th and First Divisions. The 34th Division was to attack into the hills east and west of Sidi Nsir, with Hill 609 (Djebel Tahent) as a key objective. Supported on its flank by this attack, the First Division was to carry on its offensive eastward and complete the opening of the Tine Valley.

The ground facing the 34th Division was as hard to fight through as the area just won by the First Division. The German right flank was anchored on Djebel el Gara, west of Sidi Nsir and dominating the highway and railroad from Beja to Mateur. To the east, the enemy held Hills 435, 490 and 609. From these heights, as a result of the retirement forced by the First Division, the enemy line now ran slightly south of east to the eastern end of Djebel Sidi Meftah.

The First Division, with the 34th Division swinging into action on its left flank, resumed its attack to the northeast on April 27th. Progress in this direction would outflank Hill 609 and would still further clear the way for advance down the Tine Valley. Djebel el Anz and Djebel Badjar were the immediate objectives of this drive;

beyond them the Germans would have little commanding ground for continued defense of the approaches to Mateur and the Chouigui hills..

On the First Division's left, and under fire from the enemy on Hill 609, the 2nd and 3rd Battalions of the 16th Infantry advanced on Hill 531. This position, supporting Hill 609 and about a half-mile south, was partially occupied on April 28th, but the enemy still held the reverse slopes. On the next day the enemy counter-attacked against Hill 531, but Company I held the position.

Another dominating position was Hill 523, lying east of Hill 609. The 2nd Battalion, 16th Infantry, attacked this strongpoint on April 29th with artillery support, but made little headway. On April 30th the First Battalion, 16th Infantry, joined in the attack, and the hill fell to a bayonet charge before 3:00 A.M. The attack carried on north-east about a half-mile to take Hill 545. The enemy counterattacked furiously and recovered both positions, which were vital to his defense of Hill 609.

While the enemy counterattack was in progress, Company H of the 1st Armored Regiment was moving up from its bivouac near Beja to support the 16th Infantry. The enemy had succeeded in recovering both Hill 545 and Hill 523 before the tanks arrived. When the tank platoons of Company H moved into the valley before Hill 523, our infantry was pinned down by enemy machinegun and rifle fire. The 1st Platoon took up a defiladed position behind a steep cliff in the middle of the area while the 2nd Platoon attempted to move down the valley. Enemy 47-mm guns knocked out three tanks, including that of the company commander. The rest of the 2nd Platoon then joined the 1st Platoon in its defiladed position, and the tanks, once more moving down the valley, destroyed two 47-mm guns and a machinegun nest. The difficult terrain, however, prevented the tanks from advancing to their objective, and the infantry remained pinned down by rifle fire until the fall of Hill 609 made Hill 523 of no further importance to the enemy. The reconnaissance section of a tank destroyer battalion, attached to the 34th Division, established its observation post on Hill 523 prior to daylight on

May 1st. On the next morning our troops moved in, skirting the minefield left by the Germans at the base of the hill.

On the center of the First Division front, the 26th Infantry struck toward Djebel el Anz. The enemy began a withdrawal from points east of Djebel Touta late in the afternoon on April 27th. The 26th Infantry followed the withdrawal, and its patrols reached Djebel el Anz north of a track to Tebourda. On the next day, April 28th, a stiff contest developed for possession of Djebel el Anz and its surrounding heights. The 26th Infantry held part of the key hill before 7:00 A.M. and during the afternoon was compelled to fight off two counterattacks in which the enemy took heavy losses, especially from our devastating artillery fire. The 7th Company of the German 755th Regiment lost all but 30 or 40 of its men, according to a prisoner-of-war report. As night fell, the enemy was very active on Hill 286 northeast of Djebel el Anz. While our troops consolidated their positions during the next day, the enemy regrouped his forces for counterattack. Five times on April 30th the Germans tried to recapture Djebel el Anz, but every attempt was repulsed.

On the long ridge bordering the Tine Valley, the 18th Infantry encountered relatively less opposition and made the farthest advance to the east. On the morning of April 29th, the 18th Infantry occupied Djebel Sidi Meftah without opposition as far as point 281 and then felt out enemy positions on the north and south sides of Djebel Badjar. By May 2nd, heavy motor traffic indicated that the Germans were withdrawing to the north and east. The fall of Djebel el Anz and the enemy's failure to recapture it made his position on Djebel Badjar untenable.

From April 23rd to May 13th the First Division accomplished a 10-mile advance which gained for it the full control of the hills north of Tine Valley. On the other side of the "Mousetrap" units of the First Armored Division were matching this program.

At every point where II Corps attacked, the enemy had offered bitter and stubborn resistance, marked by frequent counterattacks to recover lost ground. Despite all their efforts, by May 1st the Germans were in a critical situation on the entire II Corps front.

The advance had dislodged the enemy from his best defensive positions in two areas. In the south, our main effort had fully opened the corridor to Mateur and down the Tine Valley. By his failure to retake Djebel el Anz and Hill 609, the enemy was left fighting on the edge of the high ground, with rolling country behind him to Mateur. In this country there was no such series of natural strong positions as the First Division had just conquered. Full use of our armor was now possible, and a successful American attack north from Djebel Badjar might easily become a breakthrough, cutting off German units still in the hills to the northwest.

The maneuvers of the Ninth Infantry Division had rendered the enemy's Jefna strongpoints untenable. The flanking columns of the Ninth Division had pushed so far northeast of Jefna that the Germans here also were hanging on to the edges of the last high ground protecting the Mateur plain.

To avoid disaster the enemy facing II Corps undertook a general retreat on the night of May 1-2, and again on May 3rd. Enemy forces in the southern sector withdrew eastward to positions located from Perryville south toward Chouigui and Eddekhila. Here, on a north-south belt of hills, the Axis forces might still hope to protect Tebourba and the Tunis plain. North of Garaet Achkel the Axis pulled back to the hills bordering that lake and prepared a last-ditch stand on the main road to Bizerte.

The enemy retreat was followed up at once by a powerful striking force. General Harmon, commanding the First Armored Division, ordered Combat Command B to move north from the Tine Valley to Mateur. At about 11:00 A.M., May 3rd, the 81st Reconnaissance Battalion entered Mateur quickly followed by other units.

The capture of Mateur meant that the main system of German defense in the north was broken. The pressure thus put on the enemy prevented him from effective concentration to meet the British drive in the Medjerda Valley. The II Corps had performed the impossible. They had broken through the German positions in what had been proven during the winter to be impregnable and impossible terrain.

South of the Mateur-Teburba road, the enemy had fallen back east of the Oued Tine to a defensive line in steep hills following the curve of the river. While the First Division advanced northeast from Djebel Badjar against the northern end of this line, the 34th Infantry Division was to drive to the east against Eddekhila and Chouigui.

The new German line in the southern zone east of the Tine ran from Kef en Noscura on the north to a cluster of strongpoints between Eddekhila and Chouigui, ten miles to the south. Rising steeply 600 to 1,000 feet above the plain, the hills gave the enemy very strong defensive positions protecting Tebourba. These might be turned, however, from the north along the Mateur-Djedeida road, and, if the attack of the British V Corps succeeded, the enemy on these hills would be cut off from retreat toward Tunis.

In preparation for an assault on the northern end of the German line, the First Division on May 5th occupied the high ground west of the Tine facing the hill mass of Djebel Douimiss, held by the Barenthin Regiment. The next day the 18th and 26th Infantry Regimental Combat Teams attacked across the Tine into these hills, supported by Company H of the First Armored Regiment. The armored unit was held up by minefields and the collapse of a bridge over a deep wadi. By nightfall the 18th Infantry had suffered numerous casualties. It was forced to withdraw west of the Tine during the night. This move left the 26th Infantry holding a salient on the right, and its withdrawal was necessary. The First Division was then ordered to maintain pressure against the enemy and to prevent any westward movement. Our troops held their lines west of the Tine on May 7th, and on the following day the Barenthin Regiment withdrew.

The conclusion of the Tunisian campaign, which resulted in the piecemeal surrender of all Axis forces by May 13th, found the First Division exhausted and considerably decimated. The 17-day campaign through the roughest terrain in northern Tunisia had been successful at a cost of 103 men killed, 1,245 wounded and 682 missing. Attrition in the rifle companies had been severe, with the remaining average strength of each amounting to little more than that of a reinforced platoon.

The amazing success of II Corps which had surprised both the Germans and British, had greatly enhanced the prestige of American arms among The Allies. Sharing the accolade were the men of the reliable RED ONE, who had re-dyed their shoulder patches deeply in the enemy's and their own blood. The tremendous skill of the First Division artillery, the doggedness of the infantry, the complete cooperation of Divisional Special Troops, as well as the uncanny ability of the troops to maneuver their transportation over incredible obstacles, all gave evidence that the First Division was still one of history's finest fighting formations.

As the troops entrained on dingy "40 and 8's," for the tedious return to Oran, the words of General Terry Allen were well-remembered: "We've been given a wet ball on a muddy field. Watch us run with it!"

◆   ◆   ◆

TUNISIA

As I Saw It

by

JACK THOMPSON

TUNISIA was mud and mines. Tunisia was a pattern of lengthening purple shadows and scorching hot sun, a land of torrential rain and dry heat, a land of choking dust and miring mud. Tunisia was Arabs with eggs and krauts with 88's. Tunisia was the dead; the dirty, faceless, grotesque dead, sprawled on the hot rocks and sand, among the brilliant yellow desert flowers, in the piney thicket or the stoney wadi. Tunisia was a heavy pack and cold chow. Tunisia was the flat, flat plain, the wrenching scream of a dive-bomber, the brief splatter of swift bullets, tracers in the night sky, the crunch of unfamiliar hobnails on unfamiliar sand. Tunisia was confusion. Tunisia was a testing ground of tactics, a "blooding" of the army. Tunisia was the sickly sweet odor of death, and the sardonic weary "glory" of victory. Tunisia was the amalgamation of men in battle, the curious welding of man to man in the arc of misery and achievement, in the unforgettable fact of shared experience. Tunisia was the first real test of America against the Axis, of weapon against weapon, of guts against guts with hand grenade, rifle, and knife. This land of the towering rocky djebel and its dark mysterious people was military pioneering for the army. It was defeat and it was victory.

Tunisia was all of this, and more, too. Tunisia was the "Red One." Inseparable, forever tied together in memory and history, Tunisia and the First U. S. Infantry Division.

I remember:

Sun slanted through broken clouds over the sodden landing field at Youks-les-Bains, Algeria, a one-time Rome bathhouse on the Tunisian border, as the dull hulls of C-47's winged in from the north. Tired GI's, who'd been on the go constantly since the landings at Oran, lurched out of the cargo doors, spilling out on either side of the old French gravel road. Company I, 3rd Battalion, 26th Infantry, had arrived, the first unit of the First Division to reach the border.

The doughfoot had come down on a hurry-up rush job from Algiers, 700 miles away, to reinforce the 2nd Battalion, 503rd (later 509th) Parachute Infantry which, on November 15th, a week before, had jumped to seize the airfield. With them, but over the twisting tortuous mountain road, came Capt. Gilbert Ellman, with a company of tank destroyers, of ancient out-moded vintage. And within a week Lieut. Col. John Bowen and the remainder of the 3rd Battalion were down there inside Tunisia, garrisoning Gafsa and Feriana, key road junctions.

In those early days the war was weird and new, as weird as the curious country. It was a "bits and pieces" war as the top brass tossed units in piecemeal to build up a line, screen off central Tunisia, and support the British First Army which was on the way, it hoped, for Tunis and Bizerte, far to the north. Tunisia was to have been a British chore alone, captured in orthodox fashion, after the

Algerian bases had been secured by the Americans. But Allied Force Headquarters thought it saw a chance to grab something for nothing, to win the race for Tunis by a bold gamble, and Lieut. Gen. Kenneth A. N. Anderson, commanding the British First Army, was sent eastward as fast as he could go. The British First Army was one in name only then, scarcely as much as one division, for the British build-up was still on the water or back in English ports. To bolster this force of three slim brigades, General Eisenhower snatched the 18th Infantry Regimental Combat Team off the beach, and by late November it was moving into the blood bath of "Long Stop" hill near Medjez-el-Bab. Up came the 5th Field Artillery Battalion which got mixed up with a combat command of the First Armored Division. Early rains drenched the country, making maneuver off the roads almost impossible in squashy quagmires, and there, in the mud, the tanks and guns bogged down, were trapped, and lost. That muddy night, east of Medjez, the armor lost 128 vehicles.

The idea, at Algiers, was Tunis by Christmas. With northern Tunisia in Allied hands, Field Marshall Erwin Rommel, German's shrewd "desert fox," would be sealed between the driving British First Army in Northern Tunisia and the Eighth Army in the western desert. Rommel would have little hope of ever extricating his famed Afrika Korps or its Italian allies. The Allied idea was good, but the German command, while surprised by the landings in North Africa, did not sit on its hands. Its reaction was sure and swift.

By plane and ship, from nearby Sicilian and Italian bases, the enemy poured men, guns, and tanks into the north, bolstering the small force there, which was largely Italian. General von Arnim took command. Before the weaker Anglo-American force could reach Tunis, the Germans were on the high ground with their 88's, and there they stayed, until the end of the campaign in May. With good air fields close behind their lines, they dominated the skies in Messerschmidts and Junkers, strafing at will the Allied columns and troop positions. A few British Spitfires sometimes did battle, but flying from bases far to the rear, their early efforts helped little. It was not until months later when our airfields moved far forward, that the enemy lost his air superiority to swarms of American bombers and fighters and squadrons of new Spitfires. Meanwhile, in the misery of the winter, the German bombers and fighters roamed our roads in daylight, or by night. The experience was a painful lesson in camouflage and concealment, and in road discipline for truck convoys.

It was all very new, very strange, and very confusing, in those early days. The men fighting in tiny units, scattered almost the length of Tunisia, felt forgotten, without a home: no regimental headquarters, no division headquarters, fighting together with unfamiliar units.

No sooner had Company I reached Gafsa than the doughs took off down the road to Gabes, with the paratroopers, behind the old tank destroyers. Doughty reconnaissance by courageous young Frenchmen of the Chasseurs D'Afrique, riding in beaten-up old motorcycles, or anti-diluvian armored cars, reported the approach of a column of light Italian tanks. Seventy miles north, General Welvert, of the French army, was screaming his heart out at Tebessa, the Algerian garrison town, inside the mountain passes. Welvert screamed for help. Another column of tanks was coming west through Sbeitla and Sidi-bou-Zid. His troops, native and French, with nothing but rifles and a few light machineguns and some useless anti-tank guns and a couple of batteries of 75's would be at the mercy of the tanks. The Americans must come at once, or at least split their force, and send him help. But the local American commander, then Lieut. Col. Edson D. Raff, of the paratroopers, refused, although technically he was under the French command. (He was also getting orders from AFHQ in Algiers. For months the whole command in Tunisia was a mixed-up mess of confusion among every headquarters, until after Kasserine, when order was restored — somewhat.) So the doughs, the troopers, and the TD's pushed out to El Guettar, where months later the Red One would make history. And there, on the approaches to that green oasis, the Americans checked the tank column, knocked out four to six tanks, and sent the Italians racing back to Gabes. Back in Gafsa, refueled for the long march, and using ancient French colonial buses, the forces moved north, and by noon the next day had engaged the second column of tanks, amid the yellow, crumbling Roman ruins outside Sbeitla, not only engaged the enemy, but knocked out a dozen more tanks, and sent the Italians, with their German officers, rushing pell mell back from Sbeitla, back through the pass at Faid to safety.

But the pass at Faid intrigued Raff and Bowen who now had his battalion together. Faid controlled the lower end of the mountain range, the Grand Dorsal. With Faid in our hands, we would have the high ground, and control the western sector of the plain to the east where some day Rommel might appear with his Afrika Korps. The strategic value of Faid seemed ovious to the men on the spot, and so it was captured, but not without a fight.

In the dark of the moon and the knife-like cold, Bowen's men and Ellman's TD's outflanked the pass, through an unguarded draw, and by daylight were on the eastern side. The TD's, shooting like crazy, moved out majestically (and incorrectly) across the open plain, and right up into the pass, while the 3rd Battalion, which had climbed a djebel or two started fighting down among the rocks, toward the pass from the topside, while the troopers attacked the western end of the pass.

The enemy had a makeshift force of odds and ends, but they had good positions, guns, and ammunition, and they weren't giving up — yet. Our TD's were driven back from the pass. German JU 88's swung over to bomb and strafe the Yanks. Our own P-38's appearing from the muddy field at Youks-les-Bains, came in to help, and bombed and strafed our own people, before concentrating on the Krauts. Bowen was getting ready for a final move down into the pass when the clincher was given by a couple of ancient French 75's which Welvert had managed to move up from the rear. Firing air bursts, which splattered hot steel into foxholes, the French guns changed the picture, and the Germans and Italians came tumbling out of their holes, behind white flags. Faid was in American hands. But because our force was small, Raff arranged for Welvert to garrison the pass with his native troops, while the American force withdrew to Feriana and Gafsa.

I remember:

The rains came, icy cold, slashing and cutting through sodden clothing, sending the dry wadies rushing over roads, tearing out bridges. And, in the south a piece of the Red One, a slim finger, almost alone, went on doing what it could. That was a time of swift night raids on enemy outposts, and daylight ducks for cover as Kraut fighters and bombers swept in. Maknassy and Sened station, two pin pricks on the roads to the eastern coastal plain, south of Faid. There, by night, small forces, such as Steve Morrissey's, crept in close and cut loose on sleeping Italians with mortar and machinegun, while our own outposts at El Guettar were attacked almost nightly by enemy raiders.

And in and out, among the rifle companies, buzzing over the roads toward Maknassy, and Sened, or sneaking out east of El Guettar, went a crazy Englishman, Capt. Thomas Roworth, of the Royal Engineers, who lived with the 3rd Battalion. Never happier than when he was planting a booby-trap, laying a minefield, or mining a bridge, Roworth brought courage and humor to his new friends.

Little by little, too, the Americans built up slowly in the south, against almost insoluble logistic problems. We ate British rations, for weeks, mushing our way through canned steak and kidney stew, prizing the Player's cigarettes, missing them when American cigarette-less "C" rations finally arrived, along with the ammo and gasoline and spare parts. Driblets of armor from the First Armored Division started appearing in January as the Americans cast their eyes longingly toward the seaport of Gabes, and the chance to cut off Rommel at the Mareth Line, a chance which went slipping by rapidly as the days drifted on through the winter. From Oran, finally, came II Corps, to coordinate American forces in the south. But its front was almost 200 miles long. Its commander, Maj. Gen. Lloyd R. Fredendall, too, was hampered by being unable to pull his units together into cohesion. As part of the British First Army, he took his orders from Anderson, and that dour Scotchman often instructed the American corps commander where to place units as small as companies and battalions.

More raids were made on Maknassy and Sened, combined doughboy and armored attacks, with the Germans, as usual, sitting up on the high ground and pooping artillery at the Yanks on the plain. January came, and with it American plans to push on out from the south, outflank Von Arnim in the north, cut Rommel in two near or north of Gabes, perhaps at Sousse or Sfax. II Corps encamped in tents in a ravine near Tebessa, began blasting deep rock caverns, should the Luftwaffe decide to take a crack at them, while the rest of the army snickered at this caution. Alec Stark moved the remainder of the 26th RCT, with the 33rd Field Artillery, down near Sbeitla. Combat Command "A," of the 2nd Armored took up positions around Sidi-Bou-Zid, west of the Faid pass, but the rest of the 1st Armored, in two combat commands, was held by Anderson in the north, with the British. In between the British, and the weak American positions, was General Koeltz' XIX French Corps, a heterogenous collection of poorly armed, but often courageous Algerians, Moroccoans, and Tunisians, and other "Ay-rabs." Just to complicate matters further, half the Americans were under French command. The situation had the makings of a first-class debacle.

I remember:

The Ousseltia Valley in January. German fighters sweeping over the muddy field, the flat plain, the few snow-white French houses, the Arab huts. German armor and panzer grenadiers coming through the northern end of the valley, sweeping aside the initial French resistance, churning on down into the valley, threatening other French forces on the Grand Dorsal, the eastern bulwark of the valley. Elements of seven French divisions (elements is the right word, for the divisions were nowhere near full strength) trying to fight tanks, and 88's, with old rifles, and a few ancient anti-tank guns, and knives. The curious dark-skinned Goums, creeping back silently from night patrol, with a few choice ears, sliced from the heads of the enemy, and highly prized around the local camp fire. CCB smashing back north up the valley, its half-tracks and tanks, running wild over foxholes of the enemy, forcing the Germans to retreat from the valley floor, while Stark, with two battalions, worked along the ridge line, cleaning of Krauts and Italians, until the French positions were restored. Another German push in the north, and Fechet's 16th Infantry, another Red One "fire brigade," coming up behind the hard-pressed British and French, to clean the Germans out of positions around Robaa.

The Germans were smacking at our weak points, keeping the entire II Corps front off balance, making the launching of II Corps' planned attack to the east impossible, and giving the British command a bad case of jitters. Back and forth, on the eastern side of the Grand Dorsal, air reconnaissance, foot patrols, agents, and prisoners reported considerable movement of German tanks and troops. Rommel was by this time back in strength on the eastern plains, his Afrika Korps being forced into a small area between the mountains and the coast, below Von Arnim's forces of the north. On his heels came Montgomery's Eighth Army, flushed with desert victory, but unable to keep contact with the skilled withdrawal of the "Desert Fox." Rommel needed more elbow room. He was also bold. A bold stroke might set the Allies back on their heels, might shatter their southern front, outflank the northern, and even force a withdrawal from Tunisia. The time was nearing for the stroke. Meanwhile, the Germans kept punching at our line, needling the weak spots, trying to hide their intentions.

Having punched at Pichon, Pont-du-Fahs, and other spots at the southern edge of the British line where it tied into the French, backed up by the Americans, the Germans took a crack at the Allies' south flank. At Faid. Early in February. Smashing into the pass with infantry, artillery, tanks, and a few 88's, the Germans snatched Faid from the French, but not until half the poorly equipped French troops were dead or wounded. Down on the plain, to the east of Faid, sat CCA of the First Armored. And it sat all day long, after the German capture of Faid, sat on its big fat, metal bottom, when, with the sun at its back, it could have counterattacked to snatch Faid. Anyone who had seen German fighting knew that it would be fatal to give the Krauts a night of grace, for in that night they would surely move up all their damned 88's. And that's just what happened.

To the great distress of Alec Stark, and part of his 26th RCT, this other Red One "fire brigade" was hurriedly rushed into position, with orders to attack in the morning, with the support of the tanks, and take Faid. By now the high command knew this was an important pass which should have been held like grim death. Only, of course, the Germans had moved in their 88's and beaucoup infantry, so that when the 26th started up the hill, the Germans were able to hold on, and slash the American lines. The attack was not successful, and the Germans retained Faid. Then came Kasserine.

I remember:

On the night of February 13th, in connection with a visit to II Corps headquarters, just after getting his fourth star (until then the Supreme Commander had been on a par with the British general, Anderson), Eisenhower asked to visit the front. A II Corps staff officer drove the general to Sidi-bou-Zid where he hung a few gongs on some of the soldiers, and then started back to Algiers. The next morning, St. Valentine's Day, Rommel came boiling out of Faid pass with a whip lash of tanks, guns, and men which set the Americans reeling back behind the mountain passes and the high ground around Tebessa, back into the bloody cauldron of Kasserine. Twelve hours after Eisenhower left Sidi-bou-Zid, the town was in German hands.

But the whole Kasserine fiasco was unnecessary.

For weeks Lieut. Col. B. A. Dickson, II Corps G-2, had been predicting the Germans would bust out of Faid. His boss, General Fredendall, begged General Anderson to let the American forces get together, to bring the Red One under division control and in one section of the line, or at least to bring the widely separated components of the First Armored together, so that II Corps would have a powerful mobile force, held centrally, and able to rush to the fire wherever it broke out. Fredendall was worried about Faid. But Anderson was more worried about Pichon. He was convinced the German attack would come there, where the Germans had come through before. Had the advice of II Corps prevailed, American armor, used as tank division should be used, could have smashed the German attack on the plains of Sbeitla and Sidi-bou-Zid. Instead, the Americans lost 54 tanks that first day (much of this, to be sure, due to inexperience and poorer tanks, for it was the first combat for CCA). A battalion of the 168th Infantry (34th Division), emplaced on Djebel Lesouda, was surrounded and captured, and the Germans were on the way to Sbeitla and Kasserine.

With Rommel at Sidi-bou-Zid, Gafsa, which had been sticking out like a sore thumb, became untenable, and the 3rd Battalion of the 26th was ordered to withdraw 50 miles to the hills protecting Tebessa. Back from Gafsa, gateway to the northern Sahara desert, the crude little French colonial center with its motley array of natives and its odorous brothel, came the 3rd Battalion, back past the French gendarmerie station at Feriana, past rows of Roman ruins and the two airfields at Thelepte which were being hurriedly evacuated by our fighters and fighter bombers, back into the hills. And on the last French truck, bouncing up and down on top of the ammunition, rode the scurvy belles of the brothel, rushing back to take up new positions in Tebessa (where they had a pitched battle with other girls from a rival house, a battle settled only by the intervention of the Corps' provost marshal and deputy chief of staff). The remainder of the 26th, withdrawing from Sbeitla, was ordered to take up positions in the mouth of the Kasserine valley which at that time was being protected only by part of the 19th Combat Engineer Regiment.

Kasserine, as far as the Red One is concerned, can really be sketched in very swiftly. When he finally realized the fat was in the fire, that the big supply base of Tebessa stood in danger of being captured, that the Germans very possibly could smash north through Thala and even on to Constantine, and turn or cut off his own British First Army, Anderson yielded to II Corps' pleading, and released CCB from the north, after the much weaker third combat command, CCC, had been wrecked trying to stem three German panzer divisions. CCB boiled down south, covered the withdrawal from Sbeitla, and was then ordered up into the Tebessa hills, to guard three southern passes. One battalion of the 26th, worn and weary, and the 26th Infantry Regimental headquarters, moved into Kasserine pass, on the east side. The engineers, on the west side, had no combat experience. And the Germans punched on through. Critics say the engineers were in poor defensive positions. Critics add that the American infantry and their supporting TD's also were in a poor position. At any rate, in the dark and later in daylight the Germans overran both positions, cleared the minefields, and rolled into Kasserine valley, while the battered Americans withdrew northward.

The British rushed tanks down from the north to support the Americans. Those tanks were Valentines and Crusaders, little match for German Mark IV's, and VI's (Tigers). Driven back to within two miles of Thala, northern exit of the valley, the British held, only after the arrival of the Ninth U. S. Infantry Division artillery, which by forced march of more than 750 miles from the Spanish Moroccoan border, arrived in the nick of time. CCB, moved hurriedly from its westerly position, was on the way to Thala, when it was turned around, and sent hurriedly down into the valley from Haidra, where it blocked the western side and the pass to Tebessa. Another block, threatening Sbiba, further east, was thrown by the 18th RCT, hastily deployed from Medjez. The remainder of the First Division moved in on Bou Chebka, in the Tebessa hills, with the 16th RCT coming down to flank CCB on the right near the main Tebessa pass.

Confusion and uncertainty. That was Kasserine. That and poor communications. Frequently without any contact with its "front line" Corps was jittery, and prepared to move north to Le Kouif. Most everyone else was jittery too, worn out, dog tired, under constant German pressure, unsure of units on the flank, uncertain of reserves, attacked by German planes. And still it rained, the rain sometimes turning into swiftly driven snow flurries.

The Germans made a last all-out effort in the valley, trying to burst into the pass for Tebessa on the 21st, only to be blocked by CCB and the 16th. This was close-in, desperate fighting, swaying back and forth on the hill's slopes and the plain, with artillery pieces being lost and recaptured time and again. It was Rommel's last effort, an effort made final by the arrival, after many pleas, of heavy American bombers (B-17's and B-24's) which joined P-40's, P-38's, and A-20's to smash German tanks and guns. British night bombers joined in as Rommel started back out of Kasserine, his columns jammed bumper to bumper in their hurry to escape being bottled in the valley. CCB and the 16th RCT, attached to it, were to have pressed close on the Germans, but something happened. Perhaps it was the usual foul-up in orders. At any rate they lost contact with the Germans who managed to pull back, and in a few days the Krauts were again in their old spots at Faid, Maknassy, Sened, and Gafsa.

Rommel's bold gamble was the last time the Germans were able to snatch the initiative. From then on the end was inevitable, although the fighting became even more severe. Only a few men moved in time to plug critical holes had prevented Rommel from seizing any of his major objectives. Now it was time for the Americans to regroup, reorganize, and go on to the offensive, which they did on March 17th, St. Patrick's Day, about one month after the Germans had smashed out of Faid on St. Valentine's Day.

I remember:

In the cool glades around Morsott and Bon Chebka, GI's rested, cleaned equipment, took on renewed vigor. For the first time the First Division was together as a team since it had landed at Oran, on November 8th. You could sense the difference immediately as you visited the regiments and checked "Danger Forward." Maj. Gen. Terry Allen and Brig. Gen. Teddy Roosevelt could smile again. After having their command ripped to pieces and fought like a revolutionary army, they once more had control over operations and the ability to use the units in interbalance. The top brass had also, at last, moved the entire 9th Infantry up to the front, and the 34th Division would soon see action. New Shermans were coming in to replace losses in the First Armored, and the future looked brighter.

But even with the future there was a sour note. The new operation for "Danger Forward" was the recapture of Gafsa. But, this was to be done only to help Montgomery's desert army, and the cocky Red One was not too happy about doing a chore like this as a sideline, but the plan was to make Gafsa a huge supply dump for the Eighth Army, now approaching Rommel, dug in along the old French "Mareth Line," on the southern border of Tunisia and Tripoli. Still there was cause for cheer. II Corps, long the orphan of the British First Army, at last was made an autonomous command, responsible only to the new field commander, Gen. Sir Harold Alexander, newly installed as Eisenhower's deputy. II Corps also had a new commander, Maj. Gen. George S. Patton, Jr., resplendent in shiny helmet, glittering stars, pearl-handled revolvers, freshly laundered cavalry breeches and polished boots, "Georgie," who once boasted, unseemingly, that the American infantry did not fight in foxholes, but on its feet. A cavalry-tanker, "Georgie" loved lots of dash.

On the night of the 16th, Division patrols moved down from the highland toward Gafsa over the No-Man's-Land, and in the morning, in a three-pronged assault, the Division invested Gafsa and captured it without any real opposition. Gafsa, being an untenable defensive position, its Italian defenders had wisely withdrawn to the east, in the hills flanking the oasis of El Guettar. With Gafsa secure, the Red One pressed on, capturing early bags of Italian PW's, before running into the natural defensive positions around El Guettar which were well manned and well gunned by Italians and Germans.

II Corps, so long bivouacked near Tebessa, then Le Kouif, and Feriana, moved down into Gafsa, as the First Division pushed hard against the unyielding hills. As the position developed, and it became clear that the Germans would hold grimly to prevent their flank from being smashed while Montgomery smashed at the Mareth Line, the Ninth U. S. Division moved in on the right of the First, and the First Armored Division (plus the 60th Infantry), operating in a valley to the left, began its efforts to storm through Sened again and gain the heights of the Maknassy pass. And it was there, at El Guettar, that "Danger Forward," fighting as a team, made its name synonymous with bitter fighting, expert maneuver, and victory.

Scrambling over the rocky djebels, inching along the dry stony wadies (dry only when the rains held off), living for days in foxholes hacked into the sides of seemingly petrified sand, and holding ground against fierce counterattacks. That was El Guettar, that and the flicker and glitter of German planes before they swooped down to dump their bombs. That and the 10th Panzer Division, reacting swiftly to the American annihilation of the original Italian force. On the 23rd of March the 10th Panzer, one of the German's finest armored divisions, swung its full weight against the Red One, backed by the whip lash of 88's cunningly emplaced in the dominating hills. Outmatched American TD's hung on, firing until they were knocked out. The massed fires of the Division and corps artillery ranged throughout the valley floor which seemed to swarm with enemy armor, as it came on, flanked by panzer grenadiers and other infantry.

The enemy attack carried into the American positions, stalled, and finally backed off, leaving the hulks of charred tanks smoking in the hot sun, in full sight of General Allen's command post in the green oasis. Not even the 10th Panzer could crack through the Division artillery, the punch brought up by a fleet of new TD's equipped with 3-inch guns, and by determined and now veteran doughfeet who crouched in their holes to take on the German infantry at close range.

That was the high water mark of the German attack by men ordered to hold off the "Amis" at any cost to prevent the sides of the piston from collapsing. Montgomery was hammering hard at the Mareth Line with a full army. II Corps pounded at the walls of the piston, and on Djebel Berda a battalion of Red One doughs hung on in the face of a roaring shouting attack by fanatical black uniformed panzer grenadiers, against whom the Americans finally used the bayonet, before escaping from an untenable position. Those were the nights, too, cloudless and clear, but sleepless because of the constant drone of German planes, the clusters of parachute flares, the crunch and thud and hard blast of bombs, the flutter of the deadly butterfly or anti-personnel bombs, the crack and splutter of anti-aircraft fire. Fighting by day. Worn and weary at night. And yet, little by the little, the Red One inched forward.

Anxious to out-do Montgomery, Patton champed at the bit, itching to shake his force free and drive the Germans into British laps. On the left, though, the armor and infantry could not penetrate the Maknassy pass where Germans had drilled almost impregnable gun pits for their 88's and longer range guns. Other fouled-up orders had prevented the Americans from going in earlier to attack before the Germans started drilling. And on the valley floor at El Guettar Patton tried to shake loose, like a cavalryman, with an armored task force under Col. Chauncey Benson, 1st Armored Chief of Staff. But as day passed into day, the II Corps chant of "Benson rides again," became hollow and humorless. On the sand hills outside El Guettar 88's pinned down the doughs, moving through what seemed an interminable series of arroyos and ridges, each as difficult, each as important, as the one just captured. Nightly supply lines to the rifle companies were cut by patrols coming out from the well-mined and well-wired German positions.

When the end came with a rush, victory seemed curiously flat, for the Germans had remained throughout masters of defensive strategy, a trait they were to repeat again and again in Sicily and Italy, and often in the campaigns of Northern Europe. The infantry reached their objectives on April 6th. On the 7th it was apparent the enemy had pulled out. At last, Task Force Benson had a chance to ride down the valley, and the push to the east went on, with contact soon established with reconnaissance from Monty's Eighth Army. All along the Grand Dorsal the enemy had broken off and was in full retreat north into the hills above Enfidaville. Flat though victory was, at least the Red One had this knowledge: their unremitting pressure and that of the other forces of II Corps had made Rommel's withdrawal difficult, and was greatly responsible for the successful Eighth Army rupture of the Mareth Line, by occupying the attention of forces Rommel otherwise could have committed against Montgomery.

I remember:

There was one more battle for the weary Red One, the final battle for Tunisia, and as usual, when II Corps, now under the command of a leader to become world famous in the final battle for Germany (one Omar Nelson Bradley) made its amazing 150-mile march north on April 16th, cutting across all the British supply lines, the First Division was in the van. The corps move put the Americans on the left flank of the British First Army, in mountainous positions the British had been unable to crack all winter. II Corps was to keep the Germans occupied in the north, and the Eighth Army would feint a major attack in the south, while the British First Army, in the center, with the French XIX Corps holding on the right, would deliver the main blow and burst through. That's the way the advance plan shaped up, final glory for the First Army alone. No one, except the Americans, thought the Yanks would amount to much. Only the plan went a bit haywire.

This time, for the last great push, the Allies advanced with the weight of air power, built up over long months, and now concentrated on the battlefield, instead of engaged in other missions. Bradley, faced with terrain as difficult as any around El Guettar, placed the Ninth Division near the coast, the 34th, which with little experience had put up a poor show at Fondouk (but later was to become a top drawer fighting machine) in the center, and the reliable workhorse of the war, the veteran First Division, on his right. They were to fight for the strategic heights, knock the enemy back, and make a hole through which the First Armored Division (then under Maj. Gen. Ernest Harmon) would plunge to turn the German line.

The Red One jumped off, and it started all over again, the old familiar pattern of the enemy on the heights looking down our throats from beautiful defensive holes in the rock which sheltered him from air bursts. With little cover, the doughs, backed up by the artillery, began working through patches of green wheat, against the numbered hills: 575, 407, 306, 565, 533, 444, 344, 415, 374, 400, 491, 469, 394, 350, 347, and 340. They read today like a comptometer's calculations, but from April 16th to April 26th, they were ten days of Hell. Attack and counterattack. Down and up the rocky slopes, always under heavy fire, seldom getting a gift, working with machinegun, rifle, and hand grenade, and the reliable "div arty."

With its initial objectives under control by the 26th, the First then turned to assist the 34th in just as rough an attack, the capture of the redoubtable Hill 609 (Djebel Tahent), key to the Corps front. Two supporting hills, Nos. 523 and 545, fell to the 16th RCT, but only after the division for the second time had fixed bayonets for a knife charge. And then, in a fierce counterattack, the Germans came back. They didn't stay long. Hill 609 dominated the terrain, and with its fall to the 34th, the other hills toppled too. The Germans were beginning to fall back in earnest now — April 27 — but the fighting was by no means ended, although by May 1st the German position was critical. All three infantry divisions and the armor were probing his last strongholds, before the Mateur plain and the approaches to Tunis. Falling back on the 1st and 2nd, to protect his dwindling defenses, the German line was penetrated on May 3rd by a sharp armored punch by CCB which carried into Mateur.

And that was the beginning of the end. What General Alexander, the British commander of all ground forces, had not believed possible had been accomplished. Bradley's II Corps — the 1st, 9th, and 34th Infantry, and the 1st Armored — had turned the German line in the north, through the worst possible country, turned it and broken it. The rest was inevitable. Unable to check the Americans, the German center buckled and the British First Army, straining at the leash, and preceded by a carpet of bombs, pushed on toward the glittering prize of Tunis. In those last days, the weary decimated Red One, had more stiff fighting against die-hard Germans, but the route was on. Ferryville and the great French naval bastion at Bizerte fell to Americans, just before the British entered Tunis. Caught between forces attacking from every point of the land front, and with his northern flank and center broken, the Germans began surrendering in droves. For miles and miles, farther than the eye could see, they came swinging in under white flags, often guarded only by one footsore G.I. They came by battalions and regiments, singing their battle songs, with full equipment, the cocky Afrika Korps, finally taken in defeat, in what up to that time had been the greatest defeat of Axis arms since the start of the war.

When the final prisoner bag was totaled, there were nearly 250,-000 prisoners. Thousands of others had tried to escape by sea and by air, but Allied fighters shot down scores of troop-carrying planes while PT boats swarmed all over what had once been an Axis lake, knocking off the small boats trying to reach Sicily and Italy.

The final surrender on May 13th, last of a series of capitulations, found the First Division still in position west of the Tine. Victorious troops shouted and caroused in the streets of Tunis and Bizerte. For the Red One, though, victory was a chance to rest. It had carried the brunt of the doughfoot fighting since November 8th, six months before. Committed piecemeal to battle by the policy of the top brass, fought only as a team at the end of the campaign, serving under British and French commanders as well as a variety of Americans, the doughty Red One had sparked the entire Tunisian campaign. Now in a hard won victory, it was tired and worn, its ranks riddled with casualties. It had earned a rest. It wanted a rest. But, unknown at the moment, the bitter challenge of Sicily, more mountains, and more

German soldiers, beckoned in the distance. There would be no rest for the Red One until the final victory, but in Tunisia it had again won its spurs as the crack American infantry division.

◆ ◆ ◆

CHAPTER III

SICILY

July 1943

The Situation

AS early as January 1943, the Combined Chiefs of Staff, in session on the outskirts of Casablanca with President Roosevelt and Prime Minister Churchill, had agreed Allied strategy for the Mediterranean Theater of War. Aiming, in Mr. Churchill's words, "At Axis-held Europe's soft underbelly along the Mediterranean," a decision was made to invade and conquer Sicily, as a necessary preliminary to the conquest of Italy.

The Island of Sicily, shaped like a jagged arrowhead, with its broken point to the west, forms a natural bridge between the tip of Tunisia and the Italian mainland. It's strategic position, lying athwart lines of communications between the western and eastern Mediterranean, has been an important factor, both in peace and in war, since ancient times. Even in this modern age of air power its control was of paramount importance to making Allied lines of communication more secure, and to the conquest of Italy. That is why, despite its small size, being roughly 140 miles long and 110 miles wide, and despite the heavy blow of the defeat in Africa, and serious reverses on the Russian front, some 10 Italian and 3 German Divisions were allotted initially to the defense of Sicily.

Planned to be the largest triphibious effort undertaken by the Allies, or in World History for that matter, the operation was to become known as "HUSKY".

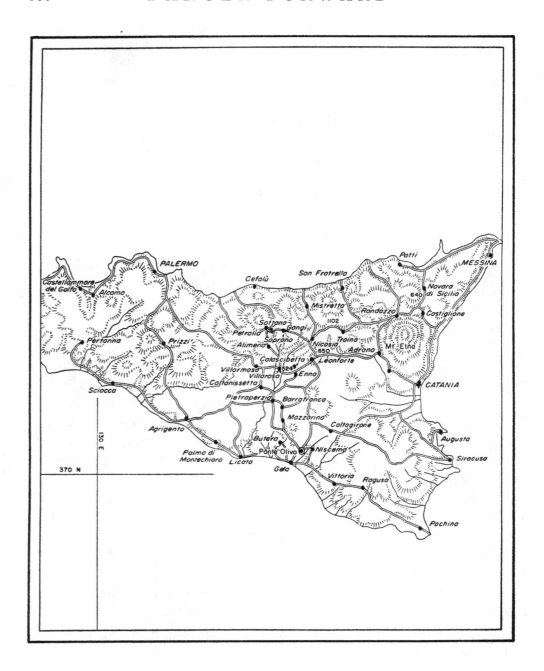

THE INVASION OF SICILY
July 10, 1943
The Record

THE dust of Tunisia had not settled, following the collapse
of Axis resistance in Africa, before the 1st Infantry Division,
worn from the heavy fighting in the Beja-Mateur area, was
assembled and routed westward by motor marches to the vicinity of
Oran where it closed on May 19, 1943. Bivouacs had scarcely been
completed when planning for operation "HUSKY" was initiated
concurrently with rehabilitation of personnel and materiel, and intensive training. Amphibious training, under the supervision of the
Amphibious Training School at Port aux Poules, was begun by
Regimental Combat Team 16, under the command of Colonel George
Taylor on May 26, near Arzeu; by Regimental Combat Team 26,
under the command of Colonel John Bowen, on May 28, near Mers
El Kebir; and Regimental Combat Team 18, under the command
of Colonel George Smith, shortly thereafter. All other divisional
and attached assault units, including Rangers under the command
of Lt. Colonel William O. Darby, were worked into the program
as early as possible.

As planning in Divisional Headquarters progressed, it became
evident that the scope and complexity of the operation were to be of
first magnitude. The 18th Allied Army Group, under the command
of General Sir Harold R. L. G. Alexander was to comprise the
landing force. It was composed, in the main, of the famous British
Eighth Army, under General Montgomery, and of the newly ac-
tivated U. S. Seventh Army under General George S. Patton, Jr.
Preceded by the Allied strategic and tactical air operations designed
to weaken Axis resistance and isolate the objective area, and by airborne drops, simultaneous assaults were to be made on the southern
beaches by the Seventh Army, and on the eastern beaches by the
Eighth Army, and a lodgement area secured which could be exploited
as rapidly as possible. All pre-invasion movements were to be coordinated with diversionary Allied threats against the Balkans and
Southern France, as well as against other parts of the Island outside

the objective area. The assault against the Gela-Vittora area was to be made by II U. S. Corps, under the command of General Omar Bradley, with the First Infantry Division (reinforced) on the left and the 45th Infantry Division (reinforced) on the right. Regimental Combat Team 18 was designated as floating reserve, under II Corps control.

Between June 8th and June 23, 1943, the entire Division was concentrated near Algiers, with the Division Command Post at Staouelli. Planning was continued, and a practice landing near Zeralda was made on June 24. Actual loading of landing craft was begun on June 26, and then, departed the next day for Tunis. The remainder of the Division (reinforced) began embarkation aboard transports on July 5, and sailed for a rendezvous outside Tunis on July 8.

By late afternoon, July 9, Malta had appeared and dropped astern, with Sicily only 90 miles away. The weather, generally calm until around noon, began to sharpen into heavy winds, not only making for a most unpleasant voyage but creating doubt in some minds as to practibility of landing operations. The wind seemed to slacken somewhat as the transport area off Gela was reached, and all preparations were completed about midnight for the landing assault echelons.

As the first groups were summoned to their boat stations, deck watchers could see fires along the Sicilian coast line. Bursts of tracers could be seen streaking into the blackness. Coastal searchlights flashed briefly and were doused. The heavy caliber shells from U. S. Naval vessels could be seen arching through the air and bursting on the beaches. The enemy coastal defenses in the vicinity of Gela had not been alerted until about midnight, when paratroops of the 82nd Airborne Division landed near Comiso, and throughout the Gela area, and caused enemy mobile groups to be sent out on a parachute hunt through the countryside.

Although the sea had moderated somewhat, the progress of landing craft was extremely hazardous; the first wave of the Ranger Force assaulted enemy defenses at Gela at 2:34 A.M. on July 10. The assault waves of Regimental Combat Teams 16 and 26 landed on their respective beaches about 2:45 A.M. All landings were successful and slight enemy opposition was met initially.

All units proceeded on their assigned missions, and the Division's Advance CP was in operation ashore shortly after dawn. Despite some harassment by enemy artillery and aircraft, men and materiel continued to flow onto the beaches in unending succession.

Coastal defense troops overrun by Regimental Combat Team 26 were mostly Italian, from various divisions and regiments including elements of the Asietta Division, the Aesta Division, Liverno Division, Automomous Coastal Defense Regiments and Bersaglieri. The principal initial beach resistance overcome by Regimental Combat Team 16 included pillboxes and machinegun detachments. Both units reorganized quickly and the advance continued.

The rapid movement of Division Troops across the beach, into the hill masses beyond the Gela-Comiso road, disrupted telephone communications between the enemy divisional headquarters at Caltagirone, and the troops in the Comiso-Ragusa area.

By 11:00 A.M., July 10, Lt. Colonel Darby of the Rangers had reported Gela taken, and by 1:30 P.M. the 1st and 2nd Battalions, 26th Infantry, had reached their initial objectives. By early evening, Regimental Combat Team 16 had reduced an enemy strongpoint at Pina Lupo, which had been defended by some twenty light tanks in addition to Infantry.

Although most landings of the Division went smoothly, in the earlier hours of the initial landings, elements of the 33rd Field Artillery Battalion ran into trouble. LST No. 313 carrying elements of the Battalion were dive-bombed by a single German plane which came out of the sun at 6:30 P.M., just after the craft had beached. A hit was made on the top deck, just above the white diamond painted on her side.

First, a two and one-half ton truck exploded; the entire craft became a raging inferno. Pieces of the ship and shells filled the air with singing death. Exploding small arms ammunition added to the din. Men were burned as they hung to the bow ramp which was down on the beach. Some men jumped to the pontoon dock section, not yet fixed to the beach, breaking arms or legs.

Some men jumped overboard, and only reached the beach when helped by a Captain from Division Headquarters. A Lieutenant, fully clothed, swam to some struggling men, but was carried away from the beach by a heavy undertow. A human lifeline was formed to bring exhausted survivors ashore.

Many of the personnel were taken off the LST by amphibious landing craft, which, directed by another Captain from Division Headquarters, eased up to the bow ramp. Some of the survivors were taken from the stern of the burning craft by another LST, whose skipper courageously ran his bow to the fantail of the doomed ship.

All the vehicles of Battery A, 33rd Field Artillery Battalion, and one section of Battery D, 105th Coast Artillery Battalion (Anti-aircraft) attached, were lost. Fortunately the howitzers had been brought ashore previously by amphibious craft.

During the whole of D-Day enemy tanks operating against divisional units were held at bay with bazookas, mortars, artillery, and naval gun fire. Fire support by the naval units was accurate and deadly, especially near the western beaches, and directed deep into enemy held territory for harassing effect, was extremely welcome to assault units.

Meanwhile, as II Corps floating reserve, the 18th Infantry Regimental Combat Team, commanded by Col. George A. Smith, Jr., had cruised back and forth off shore, awaiting the designation of a mission. While the Regimental Commander and Operations Officer were ashore looking for an assembly area, orders were issued for the 18th Infantry to land the night of July 10th on YELLOW and BLUE beaches. The first wave of LCI's hit the beach at 9:30 P.M., and all craft reached shore by 3:00 A.M., the morning of July 11th.

Considerable difficulty was encountered by the 18th Infantry in landing, because of surf conditions and the presence of an off-shore sand bar which could not be cleared by the landing craft. Much equipment was lost and one officer and two enlisted men were drowned. The 18th Infantry moved inland to an assembly area on the southern slope of a hill on the eastern side of Gela Plain, and was in position by 6:00 A.M. July 11th.

Although the 33rd Field Artillery Battalion had lost two guns in the rough water, their Battalion Commander, Lt. Col. Walter J. Bryde, had his Battalion in action by 6:00 P.M. that night. The

5th Field Artillery Battalion commanded by Lt. Col. Robert Tyson, and two batteries of the 7th Field Artillery Battalion, commanded by Lt. Col. George Gibbs, also were in action with the 33rd Battalion.

Confused fighting was in progress during the night of July 10-11. However, all units held their ground, pushed reconnaissance, and worked toward objectives.

The first enemy effort to throw the invaders back into the sea was launched on July 11, when having evaluated the situation and regrouped his forces, major enemy counterattacks developed. Spearheaded by German tanks of the Herman Goering Panzer Division, these attacks were heavy and sustained, and were repulsed only by one of the finest exhibitions of discipline and courage in the Division's history. Having moved ashore during the early afternoon of July 10, Division Headquarters found itself in the middle of the fight. Enemy tanks broke through between the 2nd and 3rd battalions of the 26th Infantry at 6:40 A.M., resulting in a telephone call to the Division Commander, Major General Terry Allen, from Brigadier General Theodore Roosevelt, Assistant Division Commander, who was at the 26th Infantry CP, and said:

"Terry—look! The situation is not very comfortable out here. The 3rd Battalion has been attacked by tanks and has been penetrated. The 2nd Battalion is in support, but that is not enough. No anti-tank protection. If we could get that company of medium tanks it sure would help. Is there any possibility of hurrying those medium tanks? If we are to take the (Ponte Olivo) airport we must have those medium tanks."

Every effort was being made to disembark the Cannon Companies of all Regimental Combat teams, and the remainder of the medium tanks of a Company of the 2nd Armored Division which had been unable to land previously. All available artillery, anti-tank, and naval weapons were brought to bear as quickly as possible. The Division Artillery Commander ordered all weapons into direct fire positions. By 9:10 A.M. German tanks were nearing the 2nd Battalion, 26th Infantry, and were taken under fire by elements of the 33rd Field Artillery Battalion and Regiment anti-tank weapons. Some 20 Mark IV tanks had attacked south down the Ponte Olivo-

Gela road, and swung eastward toward Division positions. Battery "B", 33rd Field Artillery Battalion, in direct fire positions in the area of the 1st Battalion, 18th Infantry, fired until two sections were entirely out of ammunition, when the battery was ordered to withdraw by sections. Three sections of the Battalion successfully withdrew, replenished their ammunition, and took up defiladed positions. One section, unable to withdraw because of direct enemy tank fire, disassembled breach blocks and withdrew only to retrieve their pieces an hour later. Out of an estimated battalion of enemy tanks, at least 50% had been disabled by early afternoon, of which 17 had been burned.

In the 16th Infantry zone, fighting was just as heavy. Only by herculean efforts was the Regimental Cannon Company disembarked and moved to positions from which it could give fire support. By mid-morning the Cannon Company of the 16th Infantry was in action on the Regiment's right flank. Under heavy attack, the Regimental Commander had ordered:

"Everybody stays put just where he is! . . . Under no circumstances will anyone be pulled back. Take cover from tanks! . . . Don't let anything else get through. The Cannon Company is on the way. . . . Everyone to hold present positions."

Lt. Col. Hugh Matthews, Regimental Executive Officer, observed thirty enemy tanks just off the road, about 1,200 yards northeast of the intersection of the Gela-Niscemi road. By 11:00 A.M., Lt. Col. Charles Denholm, commanding the 1st Battalion, 16th Infantry, was wounded seriously while personally manning an anti-tank gun, and was evacuated despite protest. Major Edmund Driscoll assumed command. The Regiment had only 3 anti-tank guns left out of 9; almost as many 37-mm guns were lost also. Colonel Taylor reported the situation as critical:

"We are being overrun by tanks. In Crawford's area (2nd Battalion) the enemy has 10 tanks in front of the Battalion, and ringed them with an additional thirty. We have no idea what is going on to the east of us at the moment. The 3rd Battalion is covering the main road."

Even the Division's Headquarters defense Platoon participated, in conjunction with an element of the 106th Coast Artillery Group and the 531st Engineer Shore Regiment in the repulse of an enemy infantry threat between the beach and a lake deep in the Division's right flank. Nor was enemy air idle. Losses of equipment along the beach continued; Transport K-40, carrying about one-third of the 18th Infantry transportation, was destroyed by bombing off shore near Gela. Several low flying enemy fighter bombers were shot down by anti-aircraft fire over the Division CP, the protection for which was provided many units.

At the height of the action, when the situation was most confused, with all elements of the Division, and attachments, holding their positions by tooth and toenail, the Division Commander directed the resumption of the attack at midnight. In retrospect, it would appear that the psychological effect of this order was of great magnitude, both on our own troops and the enemy for it later became evident that the enemy's morning action had been a piecemeal rather than a coordinated attack. In a vain effort to catch the invaders at their weakest, before the consolidation of the beachhead and the build up of personnel and supplies could be effected, the enemy had gambled and lost. Utilizing their superior mobility to move them to the beachhead area, the enemy had employed his tanks. without waiting for its accompanying infantry. When the tank attack was repulsed, even though at heavy cost to the Division, the results were disastrous for the enemy. His tank losses were so great that when the supporting infantry had arrived on the battlefield later in the afternoon, an insufficient number of tanks remained to enable the enemy to make the most effective use of his forces. On the other hand, as embattled as the Division was, the receipt of the Division order for the resumption of the offensive at midnight concentrated all efforts toward that end.

Nevertheless, enemy infantry reinforcements continued to arrive in assembly areas all along the Division front throughout the afternoon of July 11. All known and suspected enemy assembly areas were taken under fire by Battalion and Regimental heavy weapons, by Division artillery, and by naval craft whose heavy caliber shells were especially disconcerting to the enemy.

The 1st Battalion, 18th Infantry, was alerted at 7:30 P.M. to move eastward some 5 miles generally along the coastal road to take up positions protecting the east flank of the Division and Regimental Combat Team 16. The 2nd Battalion, 18th Infantry, with a 75-mm platoon of the Regimental Cannon Company in support was attached to Regimental Combat Team 26 and assigned the mission of seizing the high ground controlling the Ponte Olivo Airport, and securing the Field. At dark this Battalion reported: "Twenty truck loads of enemy Infantry on the left flank, detrucking in vicinity of morning tank attack. Artillery and mortars firing on them. Four or five German tanks in position about 1,000 yards ahead of our front line. Cannon Company has arrived; also a fresh load of mortar ammunition. Tanks to assist us would be wonderful."

Meanwhile, enemy infantry was detrucking along the front of the 1st and 2nd Battalions of the 16th Infantry. Mortars from a platoon of the 83rd Chemical Weapons Battalion, attached to the 2nd Battalion, 16th Infantry, were especially effective in firing on enemy infantry assembly positions, and these fires were reinforced by naval gun fire, as well as Division artillery.

Despite enemy reinforcements, the Division picked itself up by its boot straps shortly after midnight, and, in accordance with Divisional orders, surged forward all along the line. The 1st Battalion, 18th Infantry arrived in position on the Division's right flank in time to frustrate a minor enemy tank and infantry attack. At 3:55 A.M. on July 12, the 1st Battalion, 26th Infantry and the 16th Infantry were moving, albeit against strong opposition. In seizing it's objective, the 2nd Battalion, 18th Infantry, captured many prisoners and much materiel. Later, a sharp enemy tank and infantry counterattack gave the 1st Battalion, 16th Infantry some difficulty and necessitated a slight withdrawal. The fire of the Cannon and Anti-tank Companies, of Sherman tanks of a detachment of the 2nd Armored Division, and of Division Artillery, was so effective against a number of enemy tanks moving into the area in the vicinity of the road junction in the center of the front of Regimental Combat Team 16, that the enemy tanks were caused to disperse, leaving three "Tigers" and two Mark IV's ablaze, and at least one additional Mark IV disabled.

Before noon, July 12, Ponte-Olivo Airport had been seized and an enemy counterattack repulsed. Booby trapped 500 pound bombs found there were deloused by personnel of the ubiquitous 1st Engineer Battalion, under the command of Major William Gara. On the Division's left flank, contact with the 3rd Infantry Division had been established by the Ranger Forces. Many paratroopers, who had found their way back to units of the Division, and had fought with them throughout the action, were returned to the 82nd Airborne Division which was reassembling. And, most importantly, in spite of all enemy efforts, personnel, materiel, and supplies continued to pour in over the beaches.

No narrative of the Division's action during these days of bitter fighting could be complete without an expression of the Division's gratitude to the units which were attached to it for these operations, and to the paratroopers of all ranks of the 82nd Airborne Division. Although scattered in their drops prior to H-Hour, and in some cases as far as 35 miles from drop zones, Airborne units, in however small packets, reorganized themselves and took whatever offensive action appeared practicable on the spot. Even small detachments, and in some cases individuals, ambushed enemy troop movements, disrupted land line communications, and caused alarms without number, all deep within enemy lines. Not only was enemy control jeopardized thereby, but much wastage of enemy resources was caused. The accomplishment of the Division's mission was greatly facilitated. In working their way back to our lines, paratroopers requested permission to remain and fight with units of the Division. No soldier present during those critical hours will forget their example of aggressive spirit, and combat effectiveness. Similar tribute must also be paid to naval gun fire support and naval spotter aircraft, and to units of the U. S. and British Air Forces.

A captured enemy document, mute testimony of the effect on a first-class enemy unit of the action of the Division and associated units, read as follows: "Panzer Division Herman Goering, Division Headquarters, July 12, 1943: I had the bitter experience to watch scenes during these last days which are not worthy of a German soldier, particularly not a soldier of Panzerdivision Herman Goering.

"Persons came running to the rear hysterically crying because they had heard the detonation of a shot fired somewhere in the landscape. Others, believing in false rumors, moved whole columns to the rear. In one instance, supplies were senselessly distributed to soldiers and civilians by a supply unit that had fallen victim to the rumor.

"I want to state in these instances that these acts were committed not only by the youngest soldiers, but also by NCO's and warrant officers. Panic, 'panzer fear' and the spreading of rumors are to be eliminated by the severest measures. Withdrawal without orders, and cowardice are to be punished on the spot, and, if necessary, by the use of weapons.

"I shall apply the severest measures of court's martial against such saboteurs of the fight for the freedom of our nation, and I shall not hesitate to give death sentence in serious cases. I expect that all officers will use their influence in order to suppress such an undignified attitude in the Panzerdivision Herman Goering. Signed: (CONRATH) Commanding General, Herman Goering Division."

The interrogation of many prisoners also confirmed the hypothesis that the Division's midnight attack during the night July 11-12, ordered at a time when its situation could scarcely have been more parlous, had caught the enemy in preparation of his own attack and spoiled it in consequence. However bitter the fighting was thereafter, the issue was never in doubt after July 12, D + 2. The Division's beachhead was secured. It remained to expand that beachhead into a lodgement area, to rupture enemy efforts to contain the lodgement area, and to exploit such successive action to the maximum possible degree.

The 1st and 4th Rangers, the 83rd Chemical Weapons Battalion and two Companies of the 41st Armored Infantry were detached from the Division during the morning of July 13. The Rangers and Chemical Weapons Battalion joined the 2nd Armored Division. About noon Regimental Combat Team 18, having been released from its II Corps mission, was ordered to push north of the Ponte-Olivo Airfield and seize the commanding ground: Hill 180-Hill 260. This movement by motor and on foot was accomplished, and Mt. Ursitto was seized against opposition from enemy rear guards heavily supported by artillery.

Meanwhile, Regimental Combat Team 26 moved to secure commanding ground north of the Ponte-Olivo Airport, with Mt. Gibilscemi as the Combat Team's objective.

Regimental Combat Team 16, reorganized and pushed forward despite its heavy losses, which included Lt. Col. Joseph B. Crawford of the 2nd Battalion, who was seriously wounded on July 12. Company "G" of this Battalion moved into Niscemi before dark.

By 6:00 P.M., Headquarters, 105th Coast Artillery Battalion, joined Division Artillery Headquarters, and Battery "A" joined the 5th Field Artillery Battalion. All naval gunfire support parties were released to the Navy, and Division Artillery units displaced forward. Enemy aircraft continued to harass the Division both in forward areas and along the beach. Delayed action bombs, dropped in the area of the 7th Field Artillery Battalion, continued to explode for the next 48 hours.

Late the night of July 13, Colonel Bowen's orders to the Battalion Commanders of the 26th Infantry were generally as follows:

"Tomorrow we continue to advance. The Regiment will leap frog battalions forward, keeping one battalion in position at all times to cover the battalion on the move, and to protect against any threat that may develop. Following Lieutenant Falconieri's patrol, which has already moved out, Company E will move up to Pupa Hill. At 0600 in the morning, the 2nd Battalion will move out and join Company E, followed by the 1st and 3rd Battalions, on order. The 33rd Field Artillery Battalion will go into position to give fire support as indicated by the development of the situation. Division Headquarters orders us to go as far as we possibly can. Act aggressively—push!!"

This advance resulted in the seizure of Mt. Figare, Mt. Canolotti, and Mt. Gibilscemi, against scattered resistance, and thus made it possible for Allied Air Forces to occupy and begin operations from Ponte-Olivo Airport. The attack was continued with the 2nd Battalion, 26th Infantry, entering Mazzarino at 9:05 A.M., July 14.

Flanking the enemy's main positions in its zone of action, Regimental Combat Team 18, during the morning of 14 July, reconnoitered with its I and R Platoon north of the 2nd Battalion's objective and found Mt. Delle, Zolfora, and S. Cono cleared. Company F, at 1:00 P.M., contacted the enemy on Mt. La Serra; and the remainder of the 2nd Battalion moved forward to develop the situation. Passing through the 2nd Battalion, the 1st Battalion, 18th Infantry, attacked and occupied La Serra, after a stiff fight, causing the enemy to withdraw all along the line. Many prisoners and about 50 vehicles were captured in this action.

Regimental Combat Team 16 continued its advance along the road running north from Niscemi, overcoming many enemy delaying actions in the process. Several tanks were fired at, of which at least one was destroyed by the 7th Field Artillery Battalion.

That night, the Rangers assaulted the mountain strong point of Butera, on the Division's left flank, in one of the most brilliant actions of the war. Considered absolutely impregnable by the Italians, because of its extremely difficult approaches and its heavily organized defenses, the Rangers worked their way by stealth into the center of the defenses before they were discovered. Then, assaulting the garrison in hand to hand combat, they panicked the defenders, captured many prisoners, and forced the remainder to flee toward Mazzarino. Although a delaying position had been organized by the enemy north of Mazzarino, its garrison was also panicked by the arrival of the remnants of the Butera garrison, and immediately withdrew to Piazza-Armerina. Not knowing that Mazzarino had been seized by the Americans, several German Officers and men from Barrafranca, where a defensive position was being prepared, came into town and were captured.

On July 15, orders were passed to all units that First Infantry Division personnel could write home "from some place in Sicily", and could mention the fact that the Division had landed in Sicily on July 10, 1943.

All units continued to advance, with the 16th Infantry working a patrol into Caltagirone, which was repulsed, however, and withdrew after running into a German Mark VI tank which pursued it with fire. Enroute back to its Regiment, the patrol sneaked up on two Italians with demolition equipment stationed at a bridge, captured them, and withdrew the charges. Later they captured 11 prisoners from an enemy outpost position and brought them back to the Division lines.

During this time, the 1st Engineer Battalion had worked like beavers, maintaining beach exit roads, removing road blocks, repairing the demolished pier at Gela, clearing Ponte-Olivo Airport and installing 3 taxi strips, removing mine fields, providing forward water points, and constructing bridges.

On July 16, II Corps attached a Battalion of medium howitzers and a Battery of "Long Toms" to the Division; the 155-mm gun Battery was from the famous 36th Field Artillery Regiment, which had supported the Division in so many critical actions during the campaigns of Africa. As always, this support was most welcome, for on this date the Division butted its spearheads against Barrafranca, where a well organized defensive position, garrisoned by German troops, was heavily supported by artillery and tanks. Fortunately, the 70th Light Tank Battalion, under the command of Lt. Col. John Welborn, had become operational and was with the Division in time for this action.

The mission of assaulting Barrafranca was assigned to Regimental Combat Team 26. With the 3rd Battalion, commanded by Lt. Col. John Corley, some 700 yards south of the town, and the 2nd Battalion, commanded by Lt. Col. Derrill Daniel, almost abreast of it, the Regiment's plan was to swing the 1st Battalion, commanded by Lt. Col. Walter Grant, in an enveloping movement to seize the critical high ground west of the town in a coordinated assault.

Shortly after the attack jumped off, the enemy's reaction was heavy and quick. For the first time in the Division's combat experience it was fired on by a series of extremely heavy concentrations from "nebelwerfers". These large caliber rockets, of 150-mm and 210-mm caliber, in an estimated strength of one Battalion, had been emplaced behind the town, along with normal artillery support. Falling in the midst of the battalions, and on the Regimental Headquarters as well, these fires stopped our attack momentarily, until effective counter battery fires could be developed. Although the location of the enemy's rocket batteries was determined, Divisional 105-mm battalions attempting to adjust, with the Divisional Reconnaissance Troop observing, found the range too great; therefore the 5th Field Artillery, with its 155-mm M-1 howitzers and a unit of "Long Toms", were adjusted and began to fire.

About this time the enemy chose to counterattack with tanks, and about one Company of Mark IV German tanks were observed moving in the direction of the 3rd Battalion, 26th Infantry, having moved out of Barrafranca to the south along very well defiladed routes. Light tanks of the 70th Tank Battalion, which had taken some losses also from the "nebelwerfer" fire, were successful in ambushing an element of German tanks, knocked out several with their much lighter caliber armament, but were forced back. The 33rd Field Artillery Battalion, in direct support, also engaged the enemy, but observers had much difficulty in determining which tanks were friendly and which were enemy. Reeling from this blow, the 3rd Battalion, 26th Infantry, moved west and reorganized on the high ground to the left of the road running south out to Barrafranca. Shortly thereafter, while a Company of medium tanks from the 2nd Armored Division was being rushed to the support of Regimental Combat Team 26, the 3rd Battalion reported: "Enemy tanks now moving slow. Our artillery hitting close to them. Keep it up."

By midday this enemy counterattack had been stopped with heavy losses. In four coordinate actions, the Combat Team had destroyed 10 German tanks, while the medium artillery had destroyed 5; the remaining tanks withdrew into the town. By nightfall, units had worked their separate ways into and secured the town, sending patrols further forward to attempt to maintain contact with the withdrawing enemy.

During this day, July 16, Regimental Combat Team 18 had been concentrated in the vicinity of Mazzarino, with the 3rd Battalion north of the river. The 3rd Battalion of the 16th Infantry, which had been moved to a position protecting the left flank of the 26th Infantry during the afternoon, joined its Regiment at nightfall and later led it through Barrafranca enroute to Pietraperzia. During the early evening a task grouping was formed by Division Headquarters, based on the 70th Tank Battalion, and consisting of that unit, the 1st Reconnaissance Troop, and a composite element of the 1st Engineer Battalion. At dawn, July 17, this small Task Force, self-dubbed the "Rough Riders" because operating under the command of Brig. General Roosevelt, passed through the outpost line and drove north to secure a critical road-junction about five miles out of Barrafranca, from which it reconnoitered to the north, east and west.

During the morning the 3rd Battalion of the 16th Infantry, followed closely by the Regiment, pushed forward and occupied the high ground to the northeast of Pietraperzia, capturing about one company of Italian infantry and several Germans in the process. Regimental Combat Team 26 also moved forward, and occupied positions to the east of the town. It was evident the enemy, in attempting to save as much of his force as possible, was withdrawing to stronger positions south of Enna and Caltanisetta, blowing all bridges as he went. This enemy force was identified as coming mainly from the German 15th Panzer Division, reinforced by the 71st Nebelwerfer Battalion, and some of the 382nd Infantry Regiment.

About noon, Regimental Combat Team 26 was in contact with leading elements of the 45th Infantry Division, which had moved across the Division's rear to begin operations on the west flank. During the evening, the 18th Infantry was moved forward to assembly positions in the Barrafranca area. That night the 16th Infantry moved up to the Salso River, crossed it, and seized the high ground on the north bank, establishing a bridgehead.

Early the next morning, July 18, the 70th Tank Battalion, reinforced, under Division control, passed through the 2nd Battalion of the 16th Infantry, and pushed through to a heavily defended stream crossing in the direction of Enna; the ancient bridge, over a deep gorge, had of course been demolished by the Germans. It was evident that there would be a fight for Enna, the Island Capital and the GHQ for the Island's defense; originally it was in the zone of action of the 1st Canadian Division, operating to the east of the 1st U. S. Infantry Division, with the gap between them covered and contact maintained by the 1st Reconnaissance Troop commanded by Major Frank Adams.

Many stiff fire-fights between the tanks and the Germans occurred while a by-pass was being reconnoitered around this blown bridge, and while a detachment of the 1st Engineers were engaged in preparing a crossing for tanks and other vehicles. It was here that Lt. Col. Richard O'Connor, originally an observer from V U. S. Corps in Ireland who was Acting Executive of Regimental Combat Team 16, was killed while leading a reconnaissance patrol. A crossing was effected, however, late in the afternoon and a bridgehead established against extremely heavy opposition from German anti-tank guns and infantry; our tank losses were some three medium and five light tanks, while the Germans suffered severe infantry casualties and lost several anti-tank guns.

On July 19, Regimental Combat Team 18 moved by shuttling through Caltanisetta toward Villarmoso, about two miles west of which the 1st Battalion, gained contact and began to develop the situation. Having found the enemy Regiment ordered the 1st and 3rd Battalions to attack and seize the high ground north and south of the town. Although the 1st Battalion attack made good progress, the 3rd Battalion ran into strong resistance, as a result of which a general attack by the entire Combat Team was ordered with the objective the commanding terrain south of Villapriolo. Meanwhile, the same trucks which had moved the 18th Infantry returned for the 26th Infantry which was ordered to move two battalions forward to the road junction at Villarmosa, thence to be prepared to seize the town. Nevertheless, the attack of the 18th Infantry forced the enemy to withdraw to the north, making a direct assault on Villarmosa unnecessary. While the 70th Tank Battalion was licking its wounds and repairing battle damage, active patrolling was initiated in conjunction with the 16th Infantry, and strong enemy resistance developed to the north and east of the positions held. However a patrol from the 1st Reconnaissance Troop, advancing from the south rather than the west, did reach the important road junction south of Enna before it was driven off by enemy artillery fire.

At this time, II Corps ordered the 1st Division to size Enna, in compliance with which the 16th Infantry moved the 1st and 3rd Battalions east, and by cross-country movements occupied the high ground to the southeast of the town, and patrolled to its very outskirts during the night.

Early on the morning of July 20th, the 70th Tank Battalion, reinforced, drove on Enna via the main road, closely followed by the 16th Infantry, and against only scattered and ineffective artillery fire reached Enna before noon. The 3rd Battalion of the 16th Infantry, under its new commander, Lt. Col. Charles Horner, Lt. Col. Hugh Matthews having been relieved to return to duty as Regimental Executive, was accorded the honor of entering and mopping up the town, while it was being outposted by the Armored Task Force. As expected, many prisoners and much booty was captured.

As soon as the position was consolidated, the armor moved west toward Villarosa, where it joined divisional units about nightfall after having met little opposition except from enemy aircraft. The 2nd Battalion, 16th Infantry continued toward Calascibetta, which it seized despite some delaying action by two strong enemy machine-gun detachments.

At this time, the 91st Reconnaissance Squadron, formerly organic with the 1st U. S. Cavalry Division, became fully operational. Having seen its first combat in the Beja-Sejanane area during the latter part of the Tunisian Campaign, this unit was experienced, fresh, and "raring" to go. Its first mission was to cover the wide gap between Regimental Combat Team 16 and the remainder of the Division. This it did, most effectively; in fact, by infiltrating tanks and armored cars over what the Germans had considered an impassable mountain barrier, it developed a threat against the German south flank which caused a diversion of troops and greatly assisted the First Infantry Division in its drive northward to Petralia. Such flank guard missions, always posing the threat of an envelopment of the German south flank, were continued by the Squadron through the battle at Troina; it also covered the gap between U. S. Seventh and British Eighth Army, and maintained contact with the latter's 1st Canadian Division.

At 5:24 A.M., July 21st, the 2nd Battalion, 26th Infantry, was in the outskirts of the town of Alimena, receiving small arms and mortar fire; the 3rd Battalion was echeloned right rear with the 1st Battalion (motorized) behind it.

The Regiment requested air cover over the road between Villapriolo and Alimena until noon, because the poor road and demolished bridges were causing traffic tie-ups, presenting good targets for enemy planes.

By 8:30 A.M., the 26th Infantry had fought about five hours for Alimena and captured three hundred Italians. The 2nd Battalion, 26th Infantry, seized Hill 592; the 3rd Battalion took Hill 557. Patrols sent into the town received considerable sniper fire.

Although the 1st Reconnaissance Troop and tanks moved in to clean out enemy fire, this fire continued all day, even after Company F had occupied the town. Enemy artillery was especially active. Company B occupied the hill to the west of Alimena; Company G the hill to the east. The 1st Battalion moved up to the southern edge of Alimena.

The 70th Tank Battalion moved through and outposted the town, then continued east until stopped by a blown bridge.

The Italian garrison at Alimena had been covering the reorganization of Panzer Grenadier Regiment II of the enemy near Bompietro. The Lieutenant Colonel commanding the 31st (enemy) Infantry Regiment had been captured with this garrison.

The 5th Field Artillery Battalion, on moving forward to positions 3,000 yards southeast of Alimena, stated: "After marching under the worst road conditions the battalion has seen to date, position area was reached at 12:30 A.M. and occupation was completed by 2:00 A.M. Enemy mortars opened fire at 6:00 A.M."

At 1:00 A.M., July 22nd, the 1st Battalion, 26th Infantry, started for the high ground north of Alimena. Due to blown bridges, it was impracticable to use tanks for reconnaissance. The 1st Battalion cleared the hill and continued north with the 3rd Battalion moving up the road behind them. Approximately one kilometer east of Alimena both the 1st and 3rd Battalions, 26th Infantry, were pinned down by a heavy concentration of enemy artillery and mortar fire.

By noon the bridges were repaired so the tanks of the 70th Tank

Battalion could get through. Following a heavy barrage by the 33rd and 5th Field Artillery Battalions and the 17th Field Artillery Battalion, a coordinated infantry-tank attack was successful in the late afternoon. The drive was made for the high ground just south of Bompietro; tanks were in the lead, followed by the 1st Battalion, 26th Infantry. Next came the 3rd Battalion with its objective Hill 730. The 2nd Battalion, 26th Infantry, was in reserve. Tanks reached Bompietro at 6:45 P.M. and the 3rd Battalion took its objective at the same time; the enemy was cleared out of town by nightfall, and the town outposted.

According to the 33rd Field Artillery Battalion, "The enemy resisted stubbornly, and, for the second time in Sicily, showed artillery strength."

The 2nd Battalion, 16th Infantry, sent one platoon to furnish protection for Battery E, 36th Field Artillery Battalion, near Villarmosa. The remainder of the 16th Infantry was still in position covering Enna. At 8:00 P.M. the 16th Infantry (less Company F, which remained in Enna to guard ammunition dumps), moved on foot to Villapriolo.

The 2nd Battalion, 18th Infantry, left its Villaprido assembly area at 8:20 P.M. en route to Bompietro to pass through the 26th Infantry which had secured the heights overlooking the town at 9:15 P.M. Both the 1st and 2nd Battalions, 18th Infantry, moved by motor; the 3rd Battalion moved on foot.

By 4:40 A.M., 23 July, the 1st and 2nd Battalions, 18th Infantry, had detrucked at the road junction of Bompietro and moved forward. Both assault battalions seized Hill 1008 and, with the exception of two artillery rounds, were unopposed. A stiff fight developed for Hill 1056, which was nevertheless seized by the 1st Battalion. Patrols were pushed out to Petralia. A reconnaissance platoon of the 1st Reconnaissance Troop was sent to assist the 18th Infantry.

At 8:12 A.M., July 23rd, the 2nd Battalion, 18th Infantry, and two companies from the 1st Battalion, 18th Infantry, were in Petralia. The Regiment was ordered by the Division to establish a strongpoint at the road junction of the Petralia-Castelbuono road.

The 26th Infantry was ordered to move by shuttle to this road junction, leaving one battalion near Petralia to block from the west, and moving one battalion to Gangi to block from the east. One company of the 70th Tank Battalion and one platoon from Company A, 753rd Tank Battalion (medium) were attached to Combat Team 26.

The 1st Battalion, 18th Infantry, was moved to Mount di Corvo to protect the left flank of the Division; the 2nd Battalion moved to high ground east of Petralia to cover the road junction; the 3rd Battalion was sent to the high ground west of Petralia. The enemy was forced to retire to the north and east.

The Germans withdrew under cover of darkness from Bompietro to Sperlinga, with their 3rd Battalion, Panzer Grenadier Regiment III, covering the withdrawal. A strong position was organized five miles west of Gangi; the 2nd Battalion and the 3rd Battalion of the enemy were ordered to hold this position while the 1st Battalion and remnants of enemy Aosta Division occupied the high ground south and southwest of Nicosia and furnished a reserve.

The 18th Infantry was informed of a possible enemy attack from Nicosia, and that one troop of the 91st Reconnaissance Squadron (mechanized) was moving toward Nicosia, from the south.

Again the direction of the First Division's attack was changed, this time to the east.

A 16th Infantry Patrol to Villadoro was unable to find a suitable route for motor vehicles to that town. The 16th Infantry had also sent a platoon from the 1st Battalion as a combat patrol into the town. By mid-afternoon, July 23rd, the patrol was on the outskirts of the town, had captured nine Germans and was in a fire fight with other enemy troops in the town.

A company of light tanks of the 70th Tank Battalion was sent out on July 23rd to the 18th Infantry to be used as a reconnaissance party to reconnoiter the ground to Gangi. Heavy enemy artillery fire on the road east of Petralia prevented the reconnaissance party from moving forward at 3:15 P.M.

Enemy patrols were reported on the Division's left flank, but a 26th Infantry patrol and a 5th Field Artillery Battalion "Cub" plane found no enemy.

The 26th Infantry was ordered to move to the road junction east of Petralia and continue on foot to the high ground east of Gangi. This junction was captured and patrols proved Gangi unoccupied.

The 18th Infantry Reconnaissance Platoon (reinforced) with Engineers and an element of the 1st Reconnaissance Troop moved to the crossroads at Gangi, and the high ground east of the town.

A 16th Infantry patrol to Villadoro returned having contacted a platoon of the 91st Reconnaissance Squadron (mechanized) but found no enemy. The 91st Squadron also reported no practicable route for wheeled vehicles because of rough terrain.

The 26th Infantry was ordered to Gangi and moved by motors early July 24th, with objectives of taking Hills 1027 and 825, and thus straddle the road east of Gangi. The objective of the 1st Battalion was Hill 1027 and that of the 2nd Battalion, Hill 825. The 2nd Battalion cleared the road junction at Bompietro at 5:05 A.M., and was immediately followed by the 1st Battalion.

At mid-morning, July 24th, the 16th Infantry — under II Corps control — was alerted to move on one hour's notice. Plans were made for the movement, but the battalions remained in positions until dark that night, when the motor movement began to Gangi. With enemy artillery their only obstacle, the 2nd Battalion moved to its objective.

Goums — native French Moroccans — were attached to the Division again; this time with a strength of 280, and were to be committed in the tractless mountains on the north flank as soon as they could be brought up.

By 6:24 P.M., July 24th, the 26th Infantry was receiving machinegun, mortar and artillery fire — apparently German rear guard action; within 35 minutes the 26th Infantry was in the high ground east of Gangi.

The 16th Infantry, less one company, had been released to the First Division by II Corps. Since the trucks of the 47th Quartermaster Truck Company had to be returned to II Corps, the 16th Infantry was ordered to move to an assembly area near Gangi, using all available transportation.

Both the 1st and 2nd Battalions, 26th Infantry, pushed on to the east of Gangi, from Hills 825 and 1027. The 2nd Battalion advanced to and secured Hill 811 and sent patrols forward to Hill 824. The final objectives were to be Hills 937 and 825; the 1st Battalion was pushing north of the Gangi-Sperlinga road and the 2nd Battalion south of it.

The 26th Infantry was ordered to an assembly area southeast of Gangi at 3:20 A.M., July 25th; the 3rd Battalion reached the road junction southeast of the town by 7:30 A.M.

The 1st Engineers removed about one hundred new type German wooden anti-tank mines from this area; about thirty-five percent of these mines were "booby-trapped."

The final objective of the 1st Battalion, 26th Infantry, was Hill 825 — a big barren slab of rock. It was impracticable to occupy the hill since it was now commanded by the battalion positions on Hills 908 and 844. This fact was reported back to Division and again a similar report came back to the 2nd Battalion. But, after the 3rd Battalion had moved up behind the 2nd Battalion, Company G was sent on to the hill.

At daybreak, July 26th, the enemy launched a determined counterattack against Hill 937; Division forces could not hold the hill. By mid-morning, in the face of intense enemy mortar fire, our troops were forced also to withdraw down the west slope of Hill 825. The 26th Infantry was informed that four artillery battalions would support their counterattack. By this time the 3rd Battalion, 16th Infantry, and a part of the 2nd Battalion, had closed into the regimental assembly area near Gangi.

Having been ordered to assist the 45th Infantry Division on the north toward Castelbuono, the 18th Infantry sent out its reconnaissance platoon on the Geraci road. Contact was made with the 45th Infantry Division.

The 2nd Battalion, 26th Infantry, reformed, and following a heavy barrage by Division artillery on enemy infantry, mortars and artillery pieces, pushed back up Hill 937 and occupied it although the enemy remained on the eastern slope. The fire fight lasted all that day of July 26th. From an observation post in Gangi, enemy air-bursts could be seen smothering the top of Hill 937.

Coming up from the south the 3rd Battalion, 26th Infantry, seized Hills 962 and 982.

At 6:30 P.M. the 18th Infantry was ordered to move to an assembly area in the vicinity of Gangi, moving the 3rd Battalion by motor east from Petralia, while the other two battalions proceeded on foot. 16th Infantry for this movement.

Air forces and forward artillery observers reported one hundred enemy vehicles and some enemy tanks moving west from Nivodia. At 8:52 P.M. the 26th Infantry was ordered to send a reinforced company to Hill 1333 on the north of the Gangi-Sperlinga road. Meanwhile, the 1st Engineers sent a platoon to block a road from the north to the Petralia-Gangi road to prevent enemy infiltration. The platoon met patrols from the 39th Engineers, and returned to the battalion bivouac area as ordered. From its positions north of Gangi-Sperlinga road the 1st Battalion, 26th Infantry, sent out patrols to the north and northeast.

By 11:00 P.M., July 25th, the 18th Infantry's move to Gangi was completed. There were now six battalions of artillery supporting the attack plus Batteries E and F, 36th Field Artillery Regiment.

During the night the enemy pulled off of the eastern slopes of Hill 397 because he was pocketed between the 2nd and 3rd Battalions, 26th Infantry. Enemy interdiction fire hit the road north of Hill 937 every ten minutes—all night.

By 8:00 A.M., July 26th, the 1st Battalion, 26th Infantry, had sent out patrols to Hills 1122 and 1105 and reconnaissance in force to a line running from Hill 1122 southwest to Hill 912, thence southeast to Hill 821. The object was to send the battalion along this line, but plans went awry as they were pinned down by heavy artillery fire, mortars and machineguns.

The 5th Field Artillery Battalion dispersed a concentration of enemy vehicles at a range of 17,000 yards and searched the road behind.

By 10:15 A.M. the 91st Reconnaissance Squadron was south of Nicosia, and a reconnaissance platoon from the 16th Infantry had gone to Hill 1313.

The 1st Battalion, 26th Infantry, moved forward with its left flank on Hill 1122.

The Division plan was to have the 16th Infantry move east on the south Gangi-Nicosia road and capture Sperlinga; the 18th Infantry was to move north of the road and capture the high ground north of Sperlinga; and the 26th Infantry was to remain in present positions and assemble as Division Reserve, on Division orders. The attack began at 4:00 P.M., July 26th, with the 16th and 18th Infantry Regiments passing through the 26th Infantry.

The 16th Infantry Intelligence and Reconnaissance Platoon contacted the enemy on Hill 1333. After a three-hour skirmish, two enemy squads were driven down from the hill, which was then occupied by the 2nd Battalion (less Company F, which was still in Enna).

The 3rd Battalion, 26th Infantry, held positions taken the previous night and beat off three enemy counterattacks during the day. The 2nd Battalion also held its positions despite two enemy counterattacks.

By 6:00 P.M. the 18th Infantry was swinging wide to the north, in column of battalions—3rd, 1st and 2nd—along the high ground about one kilometer north of the Gangi-Nicosia road.

The 3rd Battalion, 16th Infantry, passed through the 26th Infantry and by 7:00 P.M. was approaching Hill 962, receiving fire from the north. A company of the 2nd Battalion was moving down to Hill 1192.

Prior to midnight, July 26th, the 3rd Battalion, 18th Infantry, was north of Hill 825 with the bulk of the Battalion on Hills 1115 and 1103. The 18th Infantry had not yet reached the enemy-held Hill 112.

Shortly after midnight, July 26-27, the 2nd Battalion, 16th Infantry, reached its second objective and the 3rd Battalion was on Hill 962, advancing to its second objective.

At 7:15 A.M., July 27th, the 4th Tabor of Goums passed the 1st Division Command Post just west of Gangi, en route to Hill 1558 to protect the north flank of the Division and interdict the north-south road leading from Nicosia to the coast, through Mistretta.

Meanwhile, the 3rd Battalion, 18th Infantry, placed Company I on Hill 1122 and the remainder of the battalion on Hill 1008. This battalion spent the day beating off enemy attacks. The 1st Battalion passed behind the 3rd Battalion and went for Hill 1558.

Although the 3rd Battalion, 16th Infantry, had captured thirty-two Germans and eight Italians, they were driven back to their original positions by extremely heavy enfilading fire from the north.

The Division requested immediate relief of Company F, 16th Infantry, which was still in Enna guarding ammunition dumps.

Given the mission of holding previous positions and containing the enemy by fire, while the 18th Infantry enveloped him from the north, and the 16th Infantry developed him from the south, the 26th Infantry held its ground despite repeated enemy counterattacks, especially against the 3rd Battalion on Hill 962. The Regiment was ordered to "clean out the enemy pocket on Hill 821 and consolidate the rest of its positions."

Company F, 16th Infantry, was released to the Division control at 3:00 P.M., July 27th.

By 3:30 P.M. the 1st Battalion, 18th Infantry, was at Hill 1558, and had full control of the north-south road out of Nicosia. "Long Toms" were firing effectively on this road.

At late afternoon the Goums were ordered to continue to their objective and coordinate with the 1st Battalion, 18th Infantry. An enemy counterattack against the 18th Infantry on Hill 1122 was beaten off.

The 70th Tank Battalion and the attached medium tanks, with about 28 light and 6 medium tanks serviceable at this time, due to battle losses, were alerted to "clean out the enemy pocket past Hill 962 on the main road." At this time the 18th Infantry had one company on Hill 1122 and two companies on Hill 1008, and one platoon on Hill 772, and one on Hill 741.

Forward elements of the Division were dive-bombed and strafed by enemy aircraft.

Division Headquarters notified all organizations that "Tanks of the Division will make a fast attack down the valley and then withdraw. The 18th Infantry will mop up the enemy pocket and then move to Hill 841, and attack towards Hills 784 and 782, at 5:00 A.M., July 28th. The 26th Infantry will clear resistance from Hill 962 and then move into an assembly area."

By 8:30 P.M. the medium tanks moved into position on the high ground and the light tanks were ready to deploy. The attack began and tanks dashed to a point on the road just south of Hill 962 before meeting any resistance. The 18th Infantry reported: "They sprayed for miles around for at least ten or fifteen minutes before receiving enemy fire." The tanks broke contact by 9:15 P.M. and were on their way back with the medium tanks covering the withdrawal.

After the tanks returned, the 18th Infantry sent patrols out to contact the enemy on Hill 821 and clear the hill by morning.

This tank attack caused confusion and disorganization among the enemy, and the loss of one 77-mm. gun and an unknown number of casualties. Division losses were three light tanks, and one man killed and five wounded; all losses were from incendiary bullets or thermite bombs.

Just before midnight Company F, 16th Infantry, reached the battalion assembly area and began detrucking.

According to the Division Intelligence Section: "Attack must have inflicted severe losses and shaken enemy morale since subsequent to the withdrawal of our tanks after dark, the position was mopped by Division infantry against only slight resistance. The fact that no enemy artillery was received by our tanks, either in the approach to the position or in the operation itself, probably indicates that the attack was unexpected and that enemy artillery was being displaced further to the rear at the time."

By 3:00 P.M., July 28th, the 1st Battalion, 16th Infantry, was moving forward; the 2nd Battalion was on Hill 1139 with a patrol to Hill 841; the Goums had consolidated Hill 1558, and the 3rd Battalion, 18th Infantry, was moving south to mop up the enemy pocket north of the road. Companies I and L, 18th Infantry, reached their objective which was the high ground east of Hill 821, just north of the main road, meeting slight resistance.

Supply to the 1st Battalion, 18th Infantry, on Hill 1558 was extremely difficult and was only maintained by carrying parties and mules.

At 6:25 A.M., July 28th, the 3rd Battalion, 16th Infantry, reached Hill 834 and was pushing east; the 1st Battalion was approaching Hill 834 with one company on the main road, and the 2nd Battalion was pushing east towards Hills 1139 and 651.

The 2nd Battalion, 18th Infantry, passed behind the 3rd Battalion to take Hill 841 and Hill 784; moves were made without enemy opposition.

Upon arrival at Hill 784, the 2nd Battalion, 18th Infantry, was ordered to take the high ground north of Nicosia, cutting the road. The 3rd Battalion was ordered to occupy Hill 951. Both battalions accomplished their missions despite enemy artillary fire.

By 8:30 A.M., July 28th, forward elements of Company L, 16th Infantry, had entered Sperlinga and found the town abandoned. Meanwhile, Company I pushed swiftly forward south of Sperlinga, and by 10:00 A.M. entered Nicosia.

Sniping was prevalent for about an hour with stiff resistance from enemy small arms fire coming from the high rocky ground in the north edge of the town. Just as ammunition was running out the defending enemy capitulated. Over seven hundred Italian prisoners were rounded up, together with a few German stragglers. The bulk of the remnants of the Italian Aosta Division deserted here. The German withdrawal was covered by the 1st Battalion, Panzer Grenadier Regiment III.

While the 2nd and 3rd Battalions, 16th Infantry, consolidated their gains, the 1st Battalion, preceded by the Intelligence and Reconnaissance Platoon, pushed northeast toward Cerami. For approximately two miles this platoon drew heavy machinegun fire from the high ground northeast of the road.

Before dark, July 28th, the 1st Battalion had moved into position and had knocked out several machinegun nests, capturing several Germans. However, heavy enemy machinegun fire prevented further progress.

At 7:30 P.M. the 18th Infantry was ordered to move the 1st Battalion to occupy Hill 1558, with one company on Hill 1509, the southeast extension of Hill 1508.

Goums were ordered to move to Hill 1082 just east of the road to organize and defend that hill. The 16th and 18th Infantry were ordered toward Hill 870; the 3rd Battalion had one company in Sperlinga. The 2nd Battalion, 18th Infantry was on Hill 917.

Both the 16th and 18th Infantry Regiments reported their battalions strafed early July 29th. The Goums were ordered to move at once to occupy and hold Hill 902.

By 8:35 A.M., July 29th, Hill 872 was cleared of the enemy and a company of the 16th Infantry was on Hill 823. Both the 16th and 18th Infantry were "progressing well" and the Division artillery was in position.

At midmorning, July 29th, the 26th Infantry was ordered to assemble close to and southwest of the front line. The leading elements of the 18th Infantry were on the 39th grid. The 1st Battalion, 18th Infantry, was on Hills 1558 and 1509; the 3rd Battalion, 18th Infantry was at Hill 951. A patrol to Mistretta returned after meeting opposition.

The 1st Battalion, 16th Infantry, was unable to progress rapidly because the enemy kept them pinned down by machinegun fire from favorable positions in caves. However, one by one the machineguns were liquidated. Late in the afternoon of July 29th the 2nd Battalion, 16th Infantry, commenced a flanking movement. Finally — just before dark—an assault by the 1st Battalion, 16th Infantry, resulted in the capture of the enemy machinegun positions. A large number of German prisoners were taken. Many enemy dead were found in captured positions.

After dark, July 29th, the 2nd Battalion, 16th Infantry, moved past the 1st Battalion on the right flank.

By 9:15 P.M. the 1st Battalion, 18th Infantry, was on Hill 1108. The battalion met only slight opposition and the Battalion Commander asked permission to enter Mistretta. This request was denied mainly to avoid possible mixup with the 45th Infantry Division, in the dark. About one hundred prisoners were taken. The 3rd Battalion, 18th Infantry, was ordered to attack and seize Hill 902; the 2nd Battalion, 18th Infantry, remained in position.

The 16th Infantry reached its objective and the enemy appeared to have been driven across the river south of the road. The Goums encountered a pocket of Germans and suffered some casualties. Elements of the 1st Reconnaissance Troop reached a point just south of Mistretta with no enemy contact. Artillery observers saw considerable vehicular traffic toward the east near Cerami.

Combat Team 39, 9th Infantry Division, (including the 39th Infantry, under the command of Col. "Paddy" Flint, and the 26th Field Artillery Battalion) was attached to the First Division effective midnight, July 29th. On the 29th of July the Germans withdrew to the high ground west of Cerami. During the night of July 29-30, despite a heavy Division artillery concentration on enemy positions west of the town, enemy elements withdrew to previously reconnoitered positions between Cerami and Troina.

At 2:30 A.M., July 30th, the 1st Battalion, 18th Infantry, was on its objective and the 3rd Battalion was moving east. The 2nd Battalion, 16th Infantry, was on Hill 913 and pushing toward Hill 816. By daylight, July 30th, the 3rd Battalion, 18th Infantry, was in the foothills of Hill 902 pushing toward the top of the hill.

The 16th Infantry sent patrols from Hills 809 and 816 to the river beyond the high ground in the vicinity of Cerami, to determine the state of the river banks and the condition of the bridges. The 2nd Battalion occupied high ground west of the Cerami River and south of the Cerami road.

On entering Mistretta by 8:45 A.M., July 30th, the 1st Battalion, 18th Infantry, found the town clear. A battalion of the 179th Infantry, 45th Infantry Division, passed through the 18th Infantry en route to the town.

The movements of artillery units forward were made on schedule despite complications caused by the movements of the 179th Combat Team over the same road from Gangi to Nicosia on their way north to Mistretta. Division artillery activity was limited to a few targets of opportunity and long-range counterbattery and interdiction fire.

The 1st Engineers swept the Nicosia-Cerami road for mines and reconnoitered blown-up bridges for bypasses west of Cerami.

By mid-morning, July 30th, 16th Infantry patrols reached the 40th Grid. The Regiment improved positions occupied during the night. The patrols made no enemy contact. The reconnaissance platoon came under heavy mortar fire and artillery fire while attempting to cross the Cerami River on the road to the town.

The 3rd Battalion, 18th Infantry, had slight opposition in taking Hill 902. The 18th Infantry was ordered to push patrols to the hills of Cerami. Meanwhile, the 91st Reconnaissance Squadron reconnoitered for a possible route for the 16th Infantry to Troina.

Patrols from the 3rd Battalion, 18th Infantry, were dispatched to Capizzi and found the town occupied, while patrols to Hill 1035 found this point unoccupied.

At 5:40 P.M. the Goums advanced to the vicinity of Capizzi. Coordinating with the 3rd Battalion, 18th Infantry, they drove the enemy from the town. At 7:00 P.M. Division Artillery reported to Division Headquarters that eleven battalions of field artillery were going to move forward that night.

Foot patrols from the 16th Infantry reached Hill 910 without incident; another patrol climbed the high ground toward Cerami. The enemy was observed dug in on the high ground southwest of the town of Cerami.

Early in the morning, July 31st, the 39th Infantry occupied the hill mass west of Cerami, and reorganized and pushed patrols to the east.

The 1st Battalion, 18th Infantry, having been in Corps reserve, was released by II Corps to the First Division at 7:55 A.M.

The 16th Infantry was ordered to assemble by battalions, keeping the 3rd Battalion in the vicinity of Nicosia, to feed, clothe and rest the men.

Having been alerted to pass through the 16th Infantry to attack Troina, the 26th Infantry was later informed that the Division might move the 26th Infantry to Cerami; it would take the 39th Infantry five or six hours to leave the town. The 26th Infantry sent reconnaissance to Cerami.

By mid-morning, July 30th, the 1st Battalion, 39th Infantry, was moving forward and the 2nd Battalion was on Hill 1127. The 4th Tabor of Goums reverted to Division control from attachment with the 39th Infantry Regiment. The Regiment was ordered to move on and seize Troina, where enemy resistance was building up.

Beginning at midnight, July 30th, seven artillery battalions fired nineteen concentrations of harassing fire until 3:00 A.M., July 31st. Beginning at 3:15 A.M., July 31st, nine battalions fired fifty-one concentrations until 5:00 A.M. Battalions firing were the 1st Battalion, 36th Field Artillery Regiment; 2nd Battalion, 17th Field Artillery Regiment, 1st Battalion, 178th Field Artillery Regiment, and the 5th, 7th, 32nd, 33rd, 84th and 60th Field Artillery Battalions. The 5th, 7th, 33rd and 26th Field Artillery Battalions displaced forward.

By late afternoon the 2nd Battalion, 39th Infantry, was on Hills 1127 and 1234 and the 1st Battalion was on Hills 1064, 844 and 1018.

The road junction in rear of the battalions of the 16th Infantry was dive-bombed twice during the day. Occasionally artillery shells landed in the regimental area. It became evident that the enemy was going to put up a stiff fight for Troina.

The Division plan of attack for August 1st was one battalion of the 39th Infantry to capture the high ground north of Troina; one battalion to capture the high ground west of the town; and one battalion to capture the high ground southeast of Troina. The attack was to begin at 5:00 A.M., August 1st. After the fall of Troina, the 26th Infantry was to pass through the 39th Infantry and attack toward Caesro.

By 7:08 A.M. the 91st Reconnaissance Squadron was one mile south of Gagliano, and was ordered to attack and seize it, thus protecting the Division's right flank.

The 39th Infantry encountered small arms and mortar fire just southeast of Hill 1209. The 18th Infantry was alerted to move into an assembly area late in the afternoon, as soon as the 26th Infantry cleared. The going was as rough as any the Division had encountered.

A tentative plan was made to have the 26th Infantry pass to the left of the 39th Infantry, capture Hill 872 and cut the road running northeast from Troina to Caesro; further, to have the 16th Infantry move to Hill 910 at 5:00 A.M., August 2nd, to launch an attack on Troina and the hill just east of the town in order to cut the road from Agira to Adrano; all available artillery was to support the attack.

On August 1st, the battalions of the 18th Infantry, taking a temporary "breather" in bivouac areas located a few miles northeast of Nicosia, were again "standing by." A report had been circulated that the 9th Infantry Division was to relieve the 1st Division.

At mid-morning, August 1st, the 39th Infantry reported that a counterattack against their 3rd Battalion on Hill 1209 was being repulsed by artillery fire; the 1st Battalion was nearing Hill 910 with one company on Hill 875 north of Hill 1034; the 2nd Battalion was on the south slope of Hill 1209. The 39th Infantry planned to attack with its 2nd and 3rd Battalions.

Having been informed that the 1st Division planned to attack during the night, II Corps suggested that if the 39th Infantry was capable of taking Troina, the 16th and 26th Infantry Regiments of the 1st Division would remain in place, since the remainder of the 9th Infantry Division would not be available for combat until August 5th or 6th.

Since the 39th Infantry was continuing the attack, with the mission of capturing Troina, the order committing the 16th Infantry and the 26th Infantry to the attack on Troina was revoked. The 16th Infantry was ordered to remain where it was; the 26th Infantry was ordered to extend the left flank of the 39th Infantry with two battalions. The 26th Infantry was further informed that the Goums would be on their left.

The Goums were ordered to continue the movement to Mount Basillo to gain contact with the 26th Infantry there. After contact was made the Goums were to be attached to the 26th Infantry.

By late afternoon the 91st Reconnaissance Squadron had entered Gagliano, after a stiff fight.

B-25's and A-36's were reported en route to bomb Troina, but both medium and fighter bombers flew over the town without dropping any bombs. Messerschmidt 109's and FW-190's bombed our installations in the vicinity of Nicosia.

By 8:30 P.M., August 1st, the 39th Infantry was still three kilometers from Troina. Just before midnight the 39th Infantry reported that their 1st Battalion on Hill 1034 had just received a serious counterattack at dark. Division Headquarters told the 39th Infantry that Division Artillery would concentrate the fire of two battalions between Grids 50 and 51. The Goums were unable to advance because of heavy enemy artillery fire.

Later the 39th Infantry reported "things under control," and that they were reorganizing Companies A, B, and C. Companies A and C had suffered heavy casualties.

The 16th Infantry was alerted to move one battalion to Hill 910 some time during the night to aid the 1st Battalion, 39th Infantry, which was just south of the road.

The 26th Infantry planned to move as ordered at 5:00 A.M., August 2nd, with the 2nd Battalion leading, followed by the 1st Battalion. The 3rd Battalion was to be held in reserve. The objective was the capture of Hill 872 northeast of Troina, and the cutting of the road running northeast from Troina to Caesro. The 26th Infantry was told that five artillery battalions could fire beyond their objective, one of which could fire to Grid 57, and the other four batteries to Grid 62.

By midnight, August 2nd, the battalions of the 39th Infantry were withdrawing to higher ground.

Thus began the toughest and most significant battle of the Sicilian Campaign. At least one German Battle Group, reinforced, had dug itself in for a "do or die" stand on excellent defensive terrain. The enemy occupied the high ground north, west and south of Troina, utilizing the town itself as an observation post and an artery of supply and communication. It was exceedingly important for the Germans to hold Troina as long as possible, and thus protect their withdrawal over the Straits at Messina.

Highway 120 was the east-west road through Troina. North of the highway, the enemy 1st Battalion, Panzer Grenadier Regiment III of the 15th Panzer Division, had dug in on the ridge to Mount

Basillo. On the Division's right on Mount Acuto the 2nd Battalion, Panzer Grenadier Regiment III of the 15th Panzer Division, was in position. Still further to the north on Mount Pelato, enemy elements believed to be a battalion of the 382nd (enemy) Infantry Regiment, were in position. The 3rd Battalion of the Panzer Grenadier Regiment III of the 15th Panzer Division, was in reserve.

South of the highway Panzer Grenadier Regiment I, 15th Panzer Division, was dug in on the ridge just west of the Gagliano-Troina road.

At 2:00 A.M., August 2nd, the mission of the 16th Infantry was changed and the regiment was ordered to remain in position on one hour alert.

The attack was launched at 5:00 A.M., August 2, 1943, with the 2nd Battalion, 26th Infantry, advancing to Hill 1035, Mount Basillo. The 2nd Battalion was pinned down north of Highway 120, about half way between Cerami and Troina, by intense enemy artillery and mortar fire. Subsequent attempts by the enemy to cut off the battalion by a flanking movement on the right of the road were repulsed. The 1st Battalion, 26th Infantry, advanced one mile from its rear position. The 3rd Battalion, 26th Infantry, was in reserve ready to move into position southeast or southwest of Troina.

The Germans were firing from Hills 1032, 1034 and 936, according to reports from the 39th Infantry.

At mid-morning, August 2nd, II Corps notified the First Division that the 9th Infantry Division was on the road and leading elements would arrive in the rear by early afternoon.

Meanwhile, the 91st Reconnaissance Squadron reported that the road north of Gagliano was heavily mined, delaying its progress to the north.

The 2nd Battalion, 26th Infantry, was just beyond Grid 50 north of and generally on the line with Hill 1234; the 1st Battalion was still in an assembly area south of Hill 1234. The 3rd Battalion was near Cerami.

The 16th Infantry was notified that former plans involving the entire regiment would be executed at 3:00 A.M., August 3rd. The regiment would send forward the necessary reconnaissance.

At mid-afternoon Field Order No. 20, dated August 2, 1943, was issued by the 1st Division. The mission of the Division was to attack at 3:00 A.M., August 3rd, to capture Troina, cutting the road leading from Troina to Agira, and from Troina to Adrano, and to develop the situation in the direction of Caesro and Adrano.

By 7:55 P.M. the 18th Infantry had taken Hill 910 south of Highway 120.

To facilitate coordination between the 26th Infantry and the Goums, these units were notified that the password between the First Division and the 4th Tabor of Goums for the night of August 2-3 would be "Countersign Bon-Bon; and Parol Chocolat."

By 11:20 P.M. the 39th Infantry had patrols moving toward Hill 1029. The 91st Reconnaissance Squadron was ordered to gain and maintain contact with the 16th Infantry. The 16th Infantry was thus informed.

The temporary relief of the 16th Infantry on August 1st was ended on August 2nd by a 1st Division order which sent the 2nd Battalion of the 16th Infantry (supported by the 62nd Armored Field Artillery Battalion) by motor to Gagliano with the mission of securing two small hills south of Troina. The remainder of the 16th Infantry was ordered to move behind the town of Cerami in Division Reserve. All moves were carried out without incident.

In a telephone conversation with the II Corps Commander, early in the day, Gen. Terry Allen said: "The 39th Infantry is having temporary trouble. The 1st Division is planning another Nicosia and we will do it ourselves. The 26th and the 16th Infantry will both make runs and pull the guards back. Appointment to have an early breakfast." (Meaning early morning attack.)

The II Corps Commander replied: "Apparently there is a lot in there."

Replied Gen. Terry Allen: "It's been built up; they need the main road. This will mean we can turn over to the 9th Division a tight zone. If it's all right with you, we can do this."

"O. K.," replied Gen. Omar Bradley, II Corps Commander.

While the Battalion Commander, the Operations Officer, and

Company Commanders, Ranger Platoon and Intelligence Section had gone ahead with the reconnaissance officers of the 62nd Armored Artillery, the Battalion Executive Officer had brought the 2nd Battalion, 18th Infantry, forward on trucks to an assembly area on the south side of Gagliano. The objective was Mount Bianco.

By 6:48 A.M. the 3rd Battalion, 26th Infantry, was on its objective — Mount Basillo. The Battalion Commander, Lieut. Col. Corley, verified his position by two rounds of smoke.

Two companies of the 3rd Battalion, 16th Infantry, were on the immediate objective — Hill 1025. However, they were not too well situated because a platoon of enemy mortars and another of enemy machineguns occupied positions between the two companies.

Meanwhile, the 2nd Battalion, 18th Infantry, went into position without running into any enemy troops. However, early in the morning of August 3rd, enemy patrols could be seen working up to the high ground on the right flank. In a fire fight, the Battalion captured one of the patrols.

At mid-morning, in an answer to a query from Division Headquarters, the Battalion Commander of the 2nd Battalion, 16th Infantry, reported: "Some of Company E were captured. Companies E and F are northwest of Hill 916. We had quite a few casualties; estimation: ten killed, thirty wounded. We are on top of hill with Germans."

The 1st Battalion, 16th Infantry, was ordered to move forward along the road leading northeast of Troina to Hill 851.

The 16th Infantry and the 2nd Battalion, 18th Infantry Regiment, were ordered to continue the attack to the northeast and capture the hill just southeast of Troina; the battalion was to coordinate with the regiment. A while later the battalion was told that the 1st Battalion, 16th Infantry, would attack the hill just south of the town in conjunction with their attack.

At this point the Division Operations Officer, Lieut. Col. Frederick W. Gibb, telephoned the Operations Officer, 16th Infantry: "What is your communication with Sternberg?" (Commanding Officer of the 2nd Battalion, 18th Infantry.) The reply was:

"Have him on Hill 193. Am sending him message: Gibb: "Continue the attack coordinated with the 16th Infantry. Arrange his movement so it will coincide with that of your 1st Battalion. I don't want him to start up there alone. Will send your coordinates to them. There must be a close liaison.""

Having attacked Mount Acuto, Hill 1333, earlier in the morning, and having been driven off by artillery, and about one hundred German troops, the Goums were in the river bed west of Hill 1333.

By 12:35 P.M. two companies of the 3rd Battalion, 26th Infantry were on Mount Basillo; the 1st Battalion was in position north of Troina. Seven field artillery battalions fired concentrations on Hill 1200, north of Highway 120.

By late afternoon, the 26th Infantry reported they had: "Contacted Corley (3rd Battalion); he is taking punishment from the northeast." The report continued: "White (2nd Battalion) in position and supporting by fire. Grant (1st Battalion) having a tough time."

The 16th Infantry was informed that their 1st Battalion was attached to the 18th Infantry for coordination.

Since the attack of the Division on August 3rd failed to dislodge the stubborn enemy from his positions around Troina, the remainder of the 18th Infantry (with the 32nd Field Artillery Battalion in direct support, and the 77th Field Artillery reinforcing the fires of the 32nd) was sent to the south to Gagliano to assist the motorized battalion in that sector and increase the pressure from the south of Troina.

The time for the coordinated attack of the Division was 3:00 A.M., August 4th. The Goums were ordered to take Mount Acuto. According to the Goums, enemy infantry, supported by mortars and artillery, was in force on their objective.

At 11:15 P.M., August 3rd, the 26th Infantry sent the following message to their 1st Battalion: "Close on Corley (3rd Battalion) by fastest route starting immediately. Corley in same location."

An idea of the severity of the attack on the 2nd Battalion, 16th Infantry, is given by this report by their Battalion Commander,

Lieutenant Colonel Matthews, to the Regiment. NOTE: (The Regiment had directed the battalion to check on Wozenski.) Replied Colonel Matthews: "I called him back toward me. The enemy (over two hundred) counterattacked. He was running out of ammunition. We got jeeps up to the bridge. He had a platoon and a half left. We can't get artillery in there. We had this thing stopped once but then the enemy came back as soon as the artillery stopped."

Meanwhile the 3rd Battalion, 16th Infantry, had reported: "Something is burning out front. We are running low on ammunition."

A prisoner told the 26th Infantry that the Germans had orders to hold at all costs and to fall back later to a line thirty-nine kilometers to the east.

As the 3rd Battalion, 16th Infantry, went forward on Hill 1034, the 2nd Battalion was to occupy positions previously occupied by the 3rd Battalion.

At 1:00 A.M., August 4th, the 3rd Battalion, 16th Infantry, attacked and advanced five hundred yards and contacted the enemy. The 39th Infantry reported that they had been counterattacked twice the previous night.

The 2nd Battalion, 18th Infantry, advanced to the high ground overlooking P Bianco. All weapons were hand-carried because it was impossible to find a route for vehicles in the darkness. The high ground was occupied at 4:00 A.M. without any enemy opposition.

When daylight arrived, August 4th, the 2nd Battalion, 18th Infantry, was surprised to discover that the battalion objective was a small hill hardly big enough for a platoon and dominated by all the high ground to the south and east. However the ground now occupied by the 2nd Battalion dominated not only P Bianco but the whole left flank of the enemy around Troina.

The enemy soon realized the importance of the high ground as it gave him the advantage of observation, and the 2nd Battalion became continually harassed by enemy combat patrols from Mount Pelligrino. The enemy action made it impossible at that time for the 2nd Battalion to continue the attack on Troina as ordered by the Division.

Meanwhile, on the Division's left flank the 3rd Battalion, 26th Infantry, stayed in positions and improved them as much as possible. The 1st Battalion seized Rocca di Mannia (Hills 1131, 1113 and 1126), driving the enemy from these positions with the assistance of a heavy artillery barrage. The 2nd Battalion advanced to a position on the right of the 3rd Battalion.

Since the Goums had failed to take Mount Acuto the day before, and had fallen back, the 1st Battalion, 26th Infantry (just south of Mount Acuto), was in position to protect the left flank of the Division.

Because of the difficulty experienced by all troops at locating their forward lines on the map, the 2nd Battalion, 18th Infantry, was refused permission to fire on targets hindering the advance of adjacent units, thus prohibiting the battalion from taking full advantage of its excellent observation.

The artillery support for this action was the 7th Field Artillery Battalion (reinforced by the 1st Battalion, 178th Field Artillery), in direct support of the 16th Infantry; the 32nd Field Artillery Battalion (reinforced by the 1st Battalion, 77th Field Artillery), in direct support of the 18th Infantry; the 33rd Field Artillery Battalion (reinforced by the 5th Field Artillery), in direct support of the 26th Infantry, and the 26th Field Artillery Battalion (reinforced by the 34th Field Artillery), in direct support of the 39th Infantry.

Artillery units were active on August 3rd and 4th over the entire front on observed targets of all kinds including a great deal of counterbattery. Five-volley concentrations were fired on August 3rd on an enemy strongpoint northwest of Troina, by the 5th, 32nd, 33rd, 26th, and 34th Field Artillery Battalions, and by the 1st Battalion, 77th Field Artillery.

On August 4th the remainder of the 65th Field Artillery Battalion gave additional reinforcement to the 4th Tabor of Goums. The 62nd Field Artillery Battalion gave additional reinforcement to the fires of the 32nd Field Artillery Battalion.

Major targets destroyed by the 1st Division Artillery were mortars, ammunition dumps, and vehicles (by the 33rd Field Artillery), as well as a troop concentration; an ammunition dump on Mount Acuto, by the 65th Armored Field Artillery Battalion; counter-battery by the 62nd Armored Artillery Battalion, setting fire to ammunition dumps; rocket gun by the 32nd Field Artillery, and counterbattery by the 1st Battalion, 77th Field Artillery Regiment.

The attack by the 18th Infantry with the 1st Battalion, 16th Infantry (attached), was held up by the enemy; the terrain greatly favored the Germans. Because of terrain conditions, the Division had to supply the troops by mules. Confusing ground features made it extremely difficult for the organizations to orient themselves. The 3rd Battalion was released to the Regiment from Division Reserve, and placed in an assembly area behind the Regimental Command Post.

Seventy-two A-36's bombed Troina at 5:00 P.M. and again at 5:15 P.M. Thirty-six planes made up each flight. Artillery concentrations were fired at 4:45 to 5:00 P.M.; again from 5:10 to 5:15 P.M., and from 5:25 to 5:30 P.M. with smoke being fired during the last period. The 26th Infantry reported: "The air and artillery bombardment was lovely; it was amazing to see the effect the air had on everyone."

By 6:25 P.M. the 26th Infantry moved forward and reported: "The enemy completely unnerved and the artillery fire is nil."

Moving along the ridge-line on the right of the 2nd Battalion, 18th Infantry, the 1st Battalion ran into enemy entrenched on the ridge in front of Mount Pelligrino. By maneuvering his companies, the battalion commander forced the enemy from the ridge. Eighty-one-mm mortars did an excellent job in denying the enemy the use of Mount Pelligrino as an observation post.

One platoon of Company G, 18th Infantry, seized the south half of the objective P. Bianco. Fierce hand-to-hand fighting preceded its initial attack, and at no time after the occupation of the hill were our troops and the enemy more than fifty yards apart. Both Division and enemy casualties were heavy.

On the 16th Infantry front, just before noon, August 4th, Company I was counterattacked on its right flank; machineguns, mortars and artillery were firing on one company. The 2nd Battalion asked for artillery fire. Later the 3rd Battalion stated that the fire was falling close to Company I and asked that the fire be raised five hundred yards.

A report came in from observation post: "Artillery blasting Hill 1034. Germans retreating from hill toward our lines. Our troops going toward retreating Germans."

As usual, the life of an artillery forward observer was "rugged." The following report was an example: "At the time Montague was hit, Ferra was close to him. His radio rolled down the hill; one of his radiomen was wounded; another is missing. What happened to him is not known. Probably pinned down and can't get back. Will try and get his radio as it is reported that it is still in good condition."

The 16th Infantry pushed two companies to Hill 1034. The 39th Infantry reported they were advancing. By 9:00 P.M. the 16th Infantry was moving forward after securing Hill 1034. Both the 16th and 26th Infantry Regiments were told shortly after 8:00 P.M. that our troops are too close in for a Division artillery "shoot" but each regiment should call for its own fire as needed.

The 2nd and 3rd Battalions, 26th Infantry, were on Mount Basillo with the 3rd Battalion on the north; the 1st Battalion was in a column of companies en route to a position behind the 3rd Battalion.

Mines, the inhuman device of World War II, were all over the areas. These mines were both anti-tank and anti-personnel; the latter chiefly the "Bouncing Betty." The 1st Engineers mine-detector teams were in constant demand.

Company F, 18th Infantry, and a company of the 16th Infantry were driven from a hill in front of Company F; the companies coordinated their attack to recapture the hill.

The 26th Infantry continued to draw heavy fire from the north and northeast. However, the regiment felt that it had control of the road.

The enemy still held the high ground north of Troina from Mount Acuto along the ridge east of Elia to the high ground, Rne Purrazzo. South of the town and Highway 120, the enemy held the high ground from Hill 1033 to Hill 816, thence southeast to Mount Gregorio and Mount Salici.

The enemy 1st Battalion, Panzer Grenadier Geriment III, 15th Panzer Division and the 1st Battalion, 15th Motorized Infantry, 29th Division, held strongpoints south and west of Troina.

Using one platoon, the 1st Battalion, 18th Infantry, worked through heavy machinegun and mortar fire to a point along the northern slope of the ridge just short of Mount Pelligrino. This was a hazardous operation since the enemy was still in possession of all the commanding terrain in the Division zone of advance.

This high ground was strongly defended by Panzer Grenadier Regiment I with barbed-wire and well-placed automatic weapons.

To counteract the enemy's advantage of commanding ground the 1st Battalion, 16th Infantry shelled his positions with mortar and artillery fire, intermittently during the day. Later a patrol worked up to Mount Pelligrino and found the crest unoccupied.

Meanwhile, by morning of August 5th, the 1st Battalion, 39th Infantry, was at Hill 1033, about 1,700 yards out of Troina.

The 2nd Battalion, 18th Infantry, consolidated its positions and secured the excellent observation point which looked into the enemy's flank, especially into his gun positions. After accurate artillery fire was placed in this area, reports showed there were at least fourteen guns and many prime movers abandoned or destroyed.

The prisoners taken by the Division were completely dazed by the great shock of the shelling and the bombardment. However, the enemy stubbornly stuck in their holes and later emerged to fight the advancing infantry elements of the 1st Division.

Troina was still in enemy hands; enemy units were fighting vigorously and Division troops had to repulse several local counter-attacks. Late the afternoon of August 5th, the Goums were detached from the Division and attached to the 9th Infantry Division.

Allied planes again bombed Troina, late in the day. This time there were eighteen planes, in two groups, one from the west, and one from the east.

Late that night, at 8:15 P.M., the 1st Battalion, 18th Infantry, reported to Regimental Headquarters that they had occupied Pelligrino but that they were not too secure; an enemy tank was firing on them. Strong patrols were sent to Salici.

Early on August 6th, the 3rd Battalion, 16th Infantry, reported that their patrols into Troina had run into machinegun and mortar fire from the ridge halfway into town. The battalion had one platoon on Hill 1034 with the full force going right up there to Hill 1025. There was still some resistance from machineguns and snipers on Hill 1034. "Trying to clean it out as fast as humanly possible" reported the battalion commander.

At 6:00 A.M., August 6th, the 1st Battalion, 16th Infantry, reported to Regimental Headquarters: "Out of water and supplies at 10:00 P.M. Receiving fire on hills at this time. After taking care of supplies had artillery on Hill from 10:00 A.M. to 1:00 P.M. Have received no fire from the enemy since 10:00 P.M. Moved up on hill at 2:00 A.M. without opposition."

The seriousness of the enemy's loss of the high ground to the 18th Infantry by now was apparent. The 1st Battalion moved on Mount Salici to find it unoccupied. The 2nd Battalion Ranger Platoon moved on to the high ground east of Troina, without opposition; the 2nd Battalion and the 3rd Battalion followed them on their objectives.

The 3rd Battalion reported: "An attempt was made to supply the 3rd Battalion, 26th Infantry, by air late yesterday but it was unsuccessful. All dropped behind the enemy lines."

Just before 8:00 A.M., August 6th, American planes began to bomb the 1st and 3rd Battalions, 16th Infantry. It was one of the penalties of close air support as the Division knew it in those days. Battalions had moved to their objectives fast before the air mission could be changed.

At 8:40 A.M., August 6th, Major Horner, commanding the 3rd Battalion, 16th Infantry, reported: "A patrol of seven men in town. Snipers in town. Enemy eleven kilometers the other side of Troina, northeast. The 2nd Battalion patrol in the south of the town. I am moving Companies L and I on it. The 39th Infantry and our own artillery not to fire on us." The Division was so informed, as were all units thereof.

By 9:50 A.M. the 3rd Battalion, 16th Infantry, reported the town clear of enemy. Later the 3rd Battalion asked for a battalion of engineers to clear the town, which had been heavily damaged.

C-47 planes successfully dropped supplies on Lieutenant Colonel Daniel's 2nd Battalion, 26th Infantry.

Meanwhile, Lieutenant Corley's 3rd Battalion, 26th Infantry, advanced to the southeast and succeeded in physically cutting the Troina-Caesro road. Patrols to Mount Acuto from Major Grant's 1st Battalion, 26th Infantry, found it unoccupied; the enemy had pulled out.

Before noon, August 6th, Colonel Matthews, commanding the 2nd Battalion, 16th Infantry, had one company on the high ground west of Troina. Major Driscoll's 1st Battalion was south and east of the town moving cross-country. The 3rd Battalion reported many injured civilians in Troina.

The 39th Infantry was ordered to assemble pending 1st Division orders for their relief; they were not to make any forward movement.

Just prior to noon, August 6th, 1st Division Air Support Party was informed that the Division had captured Troina and told to change all air missions to Caesro. By 2:45 P.M. the Gagliano-Troina road was cleared by the 1st Engineers.

On its objective at 4:15 P.M., Lieutenant Colonel Sternberg's 2nd Battalion, 18th Infantry, sent patrols to the east. Lieut. Col. Joseph Sissons's 3rd Battalion was passing through the 1st Battalion en route to a position east of the Adrano-Troina road. Lieut. Col. Robert York's 1st Battalion was still on Mount Pelligrino but was preparing to move forward behind the 2nd and 3rd Battalions.

At midnight, August 6th, Maj. Gen. Clarence R. Huebner assumed command of the 1st Infantry Division; Col. Willard G. Wyman became Assistant Division Commander. Brig. Gen. Clift Andrus continued to command the Division Artillery.

On August 7, 1943, the 1st Infantry Division was relieved by the 9th Infantry Division and became II Corps Reserve; many attached units were released.

During the battle for Troina, the 16th Infantry was counterattacked seven times; the 18th Infantry was counterattacked once;

the 26th Infantry was counterattacked thirteen times, and the 39th Infantry was counterattacked three times.

From August 7 to 12, 1943, the units of the 1st Division remained in bivouac area in the vicinity of Troina where rest, rehabilitation, and training were stressed.

The 5th Field Artillery Battalion was attached to the 13th Field Artillery Brigade from August 7 to August 13, 1943, at which time it returned to Division control.

At 7:05 A.M., August 13th, the 32nd Field Artillery Battalion was alerted to move to the vicinity of Randazzo and was there ordered to make a reconnaissance of that town. The plan was to have the 18th Infantry Regimental Combat Team—with the 5th Field Artillery Battalion and the 1st Engineers, and the 1st Reconnaissance Troop—make an advance east of Randazzo as soon as the town had been passed through by the 47th Infantry and attached units.

Field Order No. 30 issued by the 1st Infantry Division gave the 18th Infantry the mission of passing through the British 78th Division located four miles east of Randazzo, proceeding northeast, maintaining contact with the British on the right, and the 9th and 3rd Infantry Divisions (U. S.) on the left, and contacting the enemy.

The 1st Engineers cleared mines, for a turn-around for vehicles of the 18th Infantry, in the area at the junction of the Randazzo-Bronte roads.

At 8:45 P.M. the 1st Reconnaissance Troop passed the initial point at Cerami. At 10:00 P.M. the 18th Infantry passed the Paterno-Randazzo roads on the east edge of the town of Troina.

Foot elements of the 18th Infantry detrucked at the road junction of the Randazzo-Bronte roads west of Randazzo, and passed through the ruined town on foot.

With the 18th Infantry committed, the 91st Reconnaissance Squadron was again attached to the Division.

The move of the 18th Infantry was completed despite considerable confusion due to road conditions. Then began a slow march of the battalions in the order 3rd, 2nd and 1st, from Randazzo to Mojo, Rocca Bodia; and Company F to Novara di Sicilia. Unopposed but moving slowly because of numerous blown-out bridges, and extensive minefields of Teller, box and "S" mines, the 18th Infantry proceeded over the rugged terrain.

At 6:30 P.M., August 14, 1943, the 2nd Battalion, 18th Infantry reached the road junction of the Franka-Villa Novara roads where they bivouaced.

Early on August 15th the 1st and 2nd Battalions moved out without their transportation which could not follow the foot troops. They passed through the 3rd Battalion at 12:30 P.M.

By 4:30 P.M. the 2nd Battalion (less Company F) bivouaced two miles southwest of Novara. Company F proceeded into the town of Novara and occupied it without resistance, taking one hundred and fifty Italian prisoners, and a great deal of military equipment and stores, including 15,000 gallons of gasoline.

Company F sent an officer patrol to contact the Third Infantry Division. This was done at 8:00 P.M. at a point two miles north of the Coast road. The tactical employment of the Division ended at midnight, August 16, 1943.

The 1st Engineers reported that they had removed from the road, shoulders and bypasses to Novara, at least five hundred "S" mines and five hundred Teller mines.

The commanding officer, 32nd Field Artillery Battalion, stated that his battalion had lost more men because of mines, in this final phase of the campaign, than had been lost throughout the whole operation to conquer Sicily.

During the Sicilian Campaign the battle casualties of the First Division were as follows:

16th Infantry:

6 officers and 87 enlisted men *killed in action,*
1 officer died of wounds,
39 officers and 357 enlisted men *wounded in action,*
5 officers and 128 enlisted men *missing in action.*

18th Infantry:

3 officers and 50 enlisted men *killed in action,*
11 officers and 235 enlisted men *wounded in action,*
34 enlisted men *missing in action.*

26th Infantry:
  5 officers and 86 enlisted men *killed in action,*
  35 officers and 434 enlisted men *wounded in action,*
  6 officers and 164 enlisted men *missing in action.*
Total Casualties, First Infantry Division:
  Killed in action, 264.
  Died of wounds, 3.
  Wounded in action, 1,184.
  Missing in action, 337.

During the period July 10 to July 31, 1943, the 1st Engineers bypassed or repaired twenty-three bridges and nineteen craters, as well as clearing wrecked vehicles, rubble, road blocks, filling shell and bomb craters, and sweeping the entire route of the advance for mines. From August 1 to the end of the Sicilian Campaign an additional sixteen bridges and seven craters were bypassed or repaired.

In thirty-seven days of continuous fighting the 1st Division took eighteen towns and captured 5,935 prisoners.

The use of enemy mines became heavier during the final period of the Sicilian Campaign. In the defense and withdrawal from Troina, and Randazzo, the enemy succeeded cleverly in completely breaking contact by the well-planned use of mines and demolitions. The quantity of the mines, the manner in which they were installed, and the effectiveness of the demolitions, all point to long and careful preparations made long before the actual fighting had advanced to these areas.

As was expected by the 1st Engineers, mines were placed in many branch and dead-end roads. Where bridges were destroyed logical sites for bypasses were soon heavily sown with anti-tank and anti-personnel mines. Stream beds were invariably mined.

The problems of the 1st Engineers were increased when it was found that mine detectors were ineffective in the area six miles west of Randazzo to about six miles east of the town. Lava formations from nearby Mount Etna contained sufficient iron ore to prevent the accurate detection of mines.

Throughout the Sicilian Campaign the First Division Ordnance Light Maintenance Company repaired trucks, and wreckers; and crews were active in repairing 155-mm. and 105-mm. howitzers, rifles, machineguns, and removing knocked-out vehicles.

The Clearing Company, 1st Medical Battalion, had 2,030 admissions during July for wounds, injuries and disease, and 3,098 admissions during the month of August, 1943. Six of the battalion's ambulances were lost during the Sicilian Compaign; one was hit by a shell, two were lost when the K-40 was sunk by bombing, one was lost in a road accident, and two were lost when LST No. 313 was dive-bombed and destroyed on "D-Day."

Beginning July 13, 1943, the total mileage of all 1st Quartermaster Company vehicles averaged 5,300 miles per day.

The motto of the 1st Infantry Division still held true: "No mission too difficult. . . . No sacrifice too great. . . . DUTY FIRST."

◆　◆　◆

SICILY

As I Saw It

by

JACK BELDEN

Excerpted with permission from the author's "Still Time to Die," published by Harper & Brothers, copyright 1943 and 1944.

IT WAS the hour of twilight on July 9, 1943, and I stood with legs spread apart on the swaying deck of the *U.S.S. Barnett* and looked out across the Mediterranean. My eyes filled with dark mass of the frothing water, its sibilant surging swells, the soaring green waves flecked white at their summits. The sea ahead of me was an undulating, dappled path, where heavy transports, dripping and rolling, chased one another in a wavering battle column. On the rest of the sea, thousands of warships of the British and American navies, swaying in sinuous and menacing lines, ploughed deeply through the water and showed now their rising, pulsating bows and now the tops of their spray-clouded masts.

The air was boisterous with a leashed-in kind of wildness. All the noises of the sea and sky were humming as if they would break out at any moment into a violent, uncontrollable roar. The wind whistled through the superstructures with crazy laughter, the broken clouds scampered across the heavens in flight and the *U.S.S. Barnett* lurched, plunged, rolled and groaned across the sea which rose in green waves over the forecastle and splashed with a loud slapping sound on the upper deck where I stood.

As I groped unsteadily along the deck to the rail, a nameless sinking feeling welled within me and I looked with emotions of scared pity at the fleet of tiny landing craft which every now and then emerged shaking from the sea beside us and then disappeared from sight beneath a fresh mountain of angry water. Turning from the sea, I saw below me soldiers clinging to stanchions, holding onto ladders, and far off on the poop deck men were bending over rails with their faces toward the water. Even in the distance the faces seemed tense and greenish, and the bodies of the men beneath the uniforms appeared limp and sodden. Suddenly, below me on the deck I noticed a stir among the forlorn figures. Then beside me a voice yelled: "Jesus! There's a man overboard." Along with a group of army and navy officers and men on the top deck, I rushed for the port rail and examined the dark, angry waters for the sign of a human body.

We were heading around Malta on our way to assault the Italian island of Sicily, and our great invasion fleet, beset by storm and wind, had no time to pause and pick up this nameless atom that had so suddenly, so silently, so helplessly fallen into the Mediterranean.

Yet the men on the *Barnett* with hypnotic concentration examined the rough, torn face of the sea where that head had last been seen. Their eyes traveled backward slowly. The sea grew curiously, seemed to widen and lengthen tremendously till the enormous, unutterable vastness of it overwhelmed the spirit of the watchers and made their eyes grow faint with staring. Still the eyes continued on back, wave over wave, seeking in all that limitless desert

of water to find a tiny, nameless speck that a few moments before
had been a living, breathing soldier, perhaps a machine gunner or
a company cook or a veteran sergeant on whom a platoon commander
was leaning all his dependence for the coming battle.   And so the
men continued looking back, searching the waves for this unknown
atom, till at last their eyes reached the gray, bleak horizon, and
beyond that they could not go; for the horizon halted all, stopped
all and still it gave them no answer: What happened to the "crazy
little guy"? After staring fixedly at the horizon and once or twice
licking their lips, the men brought their eyes slowly back again across
the waves, but this time they were no longer searching for any mark,
sign or token, but were brooding at the immensity of the sea, perhaps
trying to fathom how this fleet — "the greatest amphibious force in
history" — could have once seemed so indestructible or so important,
or how they, tiny, unknown, molecules of that fleet, could any longer
trumpet their significance in the face of this — this ship-consuming,
body-drowning, spirit-engulfing, immense maw of water.

It was too much. It was too hard. We turned away with nausea,
hollowness, impotence.

Quietly now the crowd dispersed. The evening was growing
darker and almost everyone went below, the officers for a last-minute
conference, the soldiers to try to get some sleep that likely as not
would never come. Only the naval officers and men on watch
remained on the upper deck.

As the westering light faded, it seemed to me that the darkness
lent a sinister cloak to the sea. With the passing hours it appeared to
grow wilder. Under other circumstances, I might have found the
night thrilling and the sea strangely beautiful. But now to me, who
was thinking that we would have to launch boats on this sea toward
a hostile shore, the crashing of the Mediterranean and the howling
of the wind seemed appalling. It was bitter to think that after four
days of what the skipper of the *Barnett* had called a "Mediterranean
cruise," this sea should rise up out of nowhere and threaten with
destruction our landing boats if we should dare launch them toward
the shores of Sicily. It had all happened so suddenly, without warn-

ing, and when we were in the midst of the greatest calm, and almost without a care in the world.

For four idyllic days, the Mediterranean had exhibited all her fabled, summer-time charms, with the blue ocean carpet scarcely once wrinkled by an untoward wave. Across her serene and friendly waters, from Casablanca in the west and Alexandria in the east, from Tripoli in the south and Malta in the north, had sailed a combined British and American fleet of 3,000 ships, swarming with 150,000 men, nearly 1,000 tanks and many times that number of guns, rifles and vehicles, and all of these — ships, tanks, guns and men — had, without accident, without a single error, without an air raid or a submarine attack, met, coalesced and formed into one gigantic unit to attack the Italian island of Sicily. In the faultless unfolding of the plan and in the unrolling of one calm day after another, it had seemed as if some supernatural force were smiling on our venture.

Under these special circumstances the very perfection of the weather and of our plans alike had been conducive to an increase in the confidence of our spirits. The soldiers, informally stripped to their undershirts for comfort's sake, had gathered a platoon at a time on the sun-splattered top deck, and there, with the quiet air of students, they had examined the relief model of the town of Gela, which they were to assault, and none of them had betrayed the slightest nervous tension. Everyone had been in cheerful spirits, acting more like tourists going on an excursion to a foreign land than soldiers preparing to assault a hostile shore. Oh, there might have been private soul-searchings in the hold below between a soldier and his buddy, and there had been serious conversations such as those held by Brig. Gen. Theodore Roosevelt, Jr., and me in his cabin at night, when, with solemn faces, we had declared that the failure of our invasion would be a fatal blow from which the American people, desiring action against Japan and not Germany, might never recover. But this kind of talk had been only a kind of spitting on our luck to keep it clean, and none of us had been able clearly to conjure up a picture of defeat. In the calmness of the sea everyone undoubtedly had found a sedative for whatever turbulence lurked in his spirit. Briefly, we had been at peace.

But then at noon on this day of July 9, the very eve of our invasion, a fresh breeze had sprung out of the north, swung around to the west, sharpened into a blow and at last, toward the middle of the afternoon, had lashed the sea into a froth. The azure blue of the water had turned a deeper hue; the rhythmic, rippling swells had broken up into choppy, heavy waves, and the whole sea, mounting higher and higher, had at last assaulted our fleet, rocking the transports from side to side, crashing down with angry venom over our low-slung destroyers and all but swallowing the small tank-landing craft.

Because the sea, right up until the moment when we had turned toward Sicily, had been so calm, it seemed now, when it had turned rough, as if we had been lured into a trap. The appearance of that wind out of nowhere had made us feel as Odysseus must have felt, when 3,000 years before us, perhaps on this same spot, his sailors had loosed the winds of Aeolus and driven him from his sighted goal; that is, we felt the gods were against us, and we said the wind — this wind that had come from the north, had come from Rome itself, and we called it "Mussolini wind."

In spite of the colorings of cheer that had tinged the whole voyage up to now, the men were plunged into a deep gloom. As the sea grew higher and wilder, the men grew paler and more ill, sought the stillness of their bunks, where they lay miserably sighing to themselves, or came up on deck and vomited over the rail, and went down below and were sick again, too weary to stir.

Taking their mood from the state of their stomachs, they gradually became sick with anxiety and doubt. They despaired in the new and angry face of the sea. The old cheerfulness had gone out of them, and hour after hour they were enervated by the gloomy thought that they were no longer in control of their destiny. From the time this thought took root and began like a slow poison to pervade the ship, there had developed — as if the men desired to win back control over their fate — the counterthought that it would be foolhardy to go ahead with the plans for invasion.

Down between-decks fore and aft, where the motion of the ship was more violent, the common soldier had been too sick to give utterance to his thoughts, but his face clearly betrayed what he was thinking. Amidships on the saloon deck, where the ship maintained a comparative equilibrium, the officer, with more stable belly, however, had openly vented his feelings.

In that tone of hoarse irritation that a man uses when he is trying to convince not only his listener but himself, one officer had said to another: "It's goddam foolish, I tell you. What's the use of going ahead with the invasion when your boats aren't even going to reach shore?"

And a captain had said to me: "It's not fear. No, goddamit! It's not fear. There's just no sense in risking the whole invasion in this sea."

Later the commander of our transports, with a slow, subtle smile, had said: "Even if we can land them, the soldiers will be too sick to fight."

Anyone is afraid who suddenly meets the unexpected and the unknown at the very moment when he is going out on a dangerous mission, and in that way the soldiers aboard the *Barnett* had become afraid. And, like most of us, when things suddenly go sour, they blamed their new-found lack of enthusiasm wholly on something outside themselves. It was not seasickness or fear that made the invasion no longer feasible, but merely the blind confluence of misfortune. Nevertheless, the men soon began to realize that more than misfortune and a storm was required to postpone the invasion. Something told them that they were part of an already-begun drama and they had to play it through to the end.

The Sicily operation was so vast and complicated, dependent on the interaction of so many different forces, and was coordinated with so many geographic places and time elements that the invasion could not be called off at this late hour without throwing the British and American armies and navies into a chaos and confusion from which they might not be able to recover for months. So, though all of us voiced the desire that the invasion be postponed, yet within us we knew that it could not be delayed.

Within this emotional trap we all had struggled vainly, and no one had been able to see a way out. For a while we had clung to the hope (sponsored by the naval officers) that when the sun went down, the sea would grow calmer. But that had not happened. The sea, instead of growing quieter under the cover of night, had grown more boisterous. And, to cap it all, at the worst psychological moment, the sick and half-scared soldiers had seen that lost body tossing helplessly in the Mediterranean. That had been too much. A blind, hollow feeling of impotence had gripped us all.

But men can't live on hollowness alone for long. Those who wait on the threshold of battle must, because of the very futility of their waiting, clutch at straws of hope to tide them over the nerve-consuming period of predanger. So now, since there was no other source, the men wrested a last gleam of hope out of the very storm itself. If the sea was so rough, they now began to tell themselves, and if the wind were howling this way round Sicily, why then — if this were so — then no one on the island would expect us from the middle of the storm to launch an invasion on the beaches. And if this were so, we would swoop down on the enemy, take him by surprise and get our boats ashore before he had a chance to fire on us.

That was the way it was now. Many soldiers found cause for near exultation in the fact of the storm. They, and I, too, were buoyed up by the belief — not by any means a new one; for that was what we had always planned, only now the feeling was stronger — that now we stood a glorious chance of catching the enemy completely unaware, perhaps while he was still asleep in his bed.

So it was with this sense of bolstered confidence that in the middle of the night of July 9, 1943, I went below to my bunk to wait for the signal to launch our boats against unsuspecting Sicily.

"Go to your debarkation stations."

The voice on the loud-speaker rang with a harsh metallic note through the wardroom.

The men sat up and blinked their eyes, and for a moment all of them stared at each other with expressions that seemed to say: "This is it." Then a few of them broke out in foolish grins and rose slowly from their chairs.

"All right, let's go, gang! Let's go!" called the commanding officer in a brisk voice. He got up and strode down the wardroom, a tiny bundle of energy, and the others slowly followed after him, their heads bent toward the deck as if they were thinking.

It was pitch-dark in the passageways. In the inky blackness men stumbled against each other, but no one uttered a word. In silence we made our way toward the bulkhead door through which a little lightfrom the boat deck outside shone. As we passed through the door, a hand reached out and squeezed one of us briefly on the arm. "Good luck," said a voice. It was the chaplain.

The moon was still shining dimly on the deck, but though we could now see, we clung close to each other for fear of becoming separated. From every passageway men, shuffling in dreary, silent attitudes, were coming out to swell the tide of those going in on the assault waves. They made a depressing sight — a composite of dead and dull faces and drab bodies loaded down with military gear. As we turned the corner of a bulkhead, the man ahead of me halted hesitantly before a boat which was swinging violently back and forth, first toward the deck and then away from it. Several voices behind us shouted and tried to allay any feelings of doubt we had. As we hesitated, they shouted cheerfully: "Get in. What are you waiting for?"

These words, spoken to show us that we were at the right boat, did not produce the action desired. The man who was leading our group paused on hearing those words, raised his hands in a helpless gesture and called back to the others: "I can't get in." As he said this, the men back of us yelled as if they were going to throw a fit. The leading soldier, however, remained adamant and made no move to get in the boat.

From my vantage point, it was evident that he was quite right in refusing to do so. The boat was rocking to and fro on its davits, coming close against the ship's side at one moment and swinging far away at the next. The only way to enter the boat was to slide down a short knotted line and drop in. But to attempt to drop in that swinging boat would be suicidal. One slight slip would mean a plunge down into the water, which was slapping now with a loud and menacing sound against the ship's side below us. So both the soldier and I remained standing where we were, looking at the dark void between the swinging boat and the ship, making no attempt to get in.

The crowd behind us, growing impatient, again yelled imperatively at us. Goaded by the angry voices, the soldier by me said: "Goddamit, there's no one here. Where the hell's the navy?" At these words, the men behind us transferred their disapproval from us to the whole American navy.

"Dammit! Get some sailors!" one officer yelled.

"Jesus!" said another, "the way the navy's hiding, you'd think they was going to invade Sicily instead of us."

As yet the delay had not been serious, but in our overwrought state of mind it assumed exaggerated proportions, increasing our nervousness to a state of shaking, angry doubt.

"God!" said an officer who had come up beside us, "if we can't get our boats launched from the ship, what's it going to be like in the water when they start shooting at us?"

The soldier by my side laughed bitterly. "Snafu! That's us. Always snafued."

At last two or three sailors arrived, the boat was secured firmly, the soldiers slid one by one down the knotted ropes, and the boat descended past the ship's side into the choppy water.

As we drew away from the ship, our moment's irritability dropped away from us as quickly as it had come. There was an immediate sense of gladness at getting started and a heightened awareness. When we got away from the shelter of the fleet, this feeling, however, soon gave way to another. We became sick.

The rocking of the small landing craft was totally unlike anything we had experienced on the ship. It pitched, rolled, swayed, bucked, jerked from side to side, spanked up and down, undulated, careened and insanely danced on the throbbing, pulsing, hissing sea. The sea, itself flew at us, threw the bow in the air, then, as it came down, swashed over us in great roaring bucketfuls of water.

The ensign standing on the high stern of the boat ordered the sailor by the bow to close the half-open ramp. As he moved to do so, the helmsman in the stern yelled: "I can't see. . . ."

He did not finish his sentence. At that moment there was a loud hissing sound, then a dull squashing crash, and a wave of water cascaded through the ramp, throwing down those who were standing on the deck and overrunning the boat with water.

"Bail with your helmets!" called the ensign in a voice of extreme irritation.

Kneeling now in the puddle which sloshed up and down the length of the boat, the men scooped up the water with their helmets, staggered uncertainly to their feet, threw their load overboard and then went down on their knees again to repeat the process.

Meanwhile, the ensign kept the boat zigzagging over the water searching in the sea for the boats of our assault wave. From time to time he would shout out to another boat: "Are you the second wave?" When he would receive a negative answer, he would curse loudly, turn the boat in another direction and begin searching again.

For a long time we coursed back and forth over the water, picking up one boat here and another there. Then we went into a circle, going round and round in the shadow of our fleet till, certain that every boat was present, we broke out of the circle formation and headed in a line toward a blue light, which, shining to seaward, was bobbing up and down some distance ahead of us.

The uneven motion of the boat was now almost unbearable. Hemmed in between the high steel bulkheads of the boat, the men crouched like beasts, shivering from the cold spray, silent, but uneasy with imminent sickness. One by one they vomited, holding their heads away from their loosely clasped rifles, and moaned softly.

From that time on, our dash toward the unseen shore became a nightmare of sickness, pain and fear. The boat had gathered speed now and we were beginning to bound from one wave crest to the next with a distinct shock. There were no thwarts, no seats of any kind in the boat; only the deck itself to sit on and the steep, high hull of the boat to lean against. The motion of the boat threw us all against one another. My hand in bracing my rolling body had accidentally come to rest on the shoulder of a young boy. I looked down at him and saw that he was holding his head in both of his hands and quietly vomiting. "It's the motion that gets you," I said.

"That what?" the boy said.

"The motion. It's different from on the ship. You'll get used to it. You'll be all right."

"Oh, sure. The motion. You ain't kiddin'. I'll be all right." He bent his head down, a sudden spasm contracting his shoulders, and he spewed from the mouth. "Oh, sure, I'll be all right."

I stood up and took a quick look over the boat's side. Astern our great fleet fled, diminishing, sinking beneath the waves. The boat had begun to pitch and shudder now, swooping forward and down, jolting almost stationary for a moment, then lifting and swooping again; a shot of spray smashed aboard over the bows like a thrown bucket of water, and I knelt down again.

The boat pounded on. It rolled us against iron pipes, smashed us against coils of wire and jammed us on top of one another, compounding us with metal, water and vomit. There was nothing we could do but wait, herded helplessly between the high, blank walls of the boat, huddled together like blind men not knowing where we were going or what was around, behind or ahead of us, only looking at one another with anxious eyes. That not being able to tell what was ahead of us, to catch even one slight glimpse of the universe outside our tossing, rocking world, was almost unbearable, leaving us, as it did, prey to all manner of nighttime fancies. The unnatural and unwholesome motion of the boat, churning my stomach into an uproar, the bare and opaque walls of the hull, shutting out everything but the vault of the sky overhead, evoked in my mind a picture of the world outside that was fantastic and terrifying. Instead of feeling myself part of a group of American soldiers going ashore on a carefully planned invasion, I saw myself and the men as strange phantoms flung out across the maw of the sea, into the blackness of eternity, fast revolving away from any kind of world we ever knew. I felt as if we had been caught up in some mysterious rocket, and that we were being borne onward in this bouncing projectile of machinery toward a nether-world goal as incapable of taking command over our own destinies as a squirrel in a cage.

In a moment of hollow doubt I stood up, edging my eyes over the gunwale and looking out into the comparative world of light around us. The sea was sparkling with tossed spray. Ahead, and on either side of us, boats were dodging and twisting through the choppy waves, and from their sterns, waving from side to side with the motion of the boats, showers of gleaming water streamed out behind like the plumes of birds. What was causing the water to gleam was a wide streak of light. It sprang like the tail of a stationary comet from a ball of incandescent yellow that was shining on the edge of the blackness off to our left.

Suddenly, the light swung across the water, fastened on our boat and illuminated us like actors on a darkened stage. In the glare, I saw the green, pale faces of the soldiers and their bodies huddling close against the hull. Then the light shot past and over us.

"Why don't they shoot out that goddam searchlight?" growled a voice from the depths of the cavernous boat. "Jesus! We'll be drowned without knowing what hit us!"

"Steady there!" said the voice of an officer. "Take it easy."

Again I craned my neck upward, just getting the top of my helmet above the hull and looking out with fascinated eyes. The light had now swung onto a small group of boats which were thrashing wildly from side to side trying to escape off into the darkness. From somewhere ahead faint red flashes began to flicker like fireflies. Then red balls, describing a high arc like a tennis lob, arched over our heads and fell down toward the illuminated boats which could not seem to shake off the hunting glare of the searchlight. At this I drew in my breath and involuntarily I shouted: "They're shooting at the boats." Below me, from the soldiers crouching with their heads toward the bottom of the boat, floated up an echo: "Shooting at the boats — Jesus!"

Abruptly, our boat slowed down. Above me, and slightly to the right, hung a blue light, seemingly suspended in the air. Dimly I discerned the outlines of a naval patrol vessel. Out of the darkness above mysteriously came a metallic voice: "Straight ahead! Go straight ahead. You'll see a small light on your right. Land there. Look out for mines. Good luck."

It was all very eerie — rocking there on the sea and hearing a voice calling out of the black above us. But I had no time to think of this. Our engine gave a sudden full-throated roar as the ensign cut off the underwater exhaust. The boat leapt forward. The other boats behind us raced around to either side of us, and we sped forward like a charging football line. "Hurry!" I thought. "God! If we can only make it!" The sea cascaded through the ramp and a broadside of water catapulted down on us. The boat shuddered, bucked, then plunged onward in a confident show of power.

All my senses were now alerted to the straining point. A flush of thrill and excitement shot through me like flame. It was wonderful. It was exhilarating.

Smash! Pound! Roar! Rush! — toward the goal. Here we come! Whee! My mouth was open and I giggled with insane laughter.

The sailor by the bow tapped me on the shoulder. I peered around. The boy was pointing. Ahead — directly ahead — two strings of dotted red light were crossing each other. They came out from right and left, like two necklaces of strung red and black beads, and crossed each other in the air some distance before us.

"Machine guns!" the sailor shouted. "Theirs." The little fire-flies of light were growing very close now. "Going right through them!" the sailor shouted. He made a gesture with his hand across his throat. "Right through them."

Snap! I heard a sharp cracking sound. Snap! Snap! Snap! Jittering, I ducked down below the side of the boat. Then I half slid, half fell to the deck, huddling low with the rest of the soldiers. I was on fire inside, but outside I was cold. I could feel all my flesh jerking. It was not from excitement. No longer did I feel any thrill. The boat was pitching and rocking like a roller coaster. I knelt now and was sick. Gasping for breath I wiped the strings of sputum from my lips, drawing my sleeve across my chin. Dimly I saw the boy beside me on all fours with his mouth wide open and his head bent down. I tried to pull myself together and sidled over and held his head. My gesture was almost automatic. I told myself I had to be of some use. But I no longer cared about anything. The boat seemed to be spinning like a merry-go-round. Dazed, I wished that a shell would come along and end all this horror, wetness and misery. If we could only get out of this insanely rocketing prison. If the boat would only stop for just a moment.

Soon I was almost beyond feeling. All I knew was that we were enclosed in an infernal machine, shuddering through the darkness, toward the edge of the world, toward nowhere. I did not feel the boat slow down. I neither heard nor saw men get to their feet. At first, all I felt was a violent shudder. Then I heard the engine break out into a terrible throbbing roar. At last, there was a jerk and a bump and the boat came to a halt.

"Open ramp!" shouted the ensign at the stern.

Glancing fearfully toward the bow of the boat, I saw it swinging down, like a huge jaw opening. Halfway down it stopped, stuck. We could see nothing. Only a half-open hole.

The soldiers stared at the hole as if fascinated. Grappling at the side of the boat, they pulled themselves to their feet, and peered uncertainly out into the darkness through the ramp. For a brief moment they starred at each other, then bent their heads down, shuffling their feet. No one moved.

The ramp jerked down farther until it was level with the water. Still nothing could be seen. Still no one moved.

"Get off!" The commanding officer's voice was imperious.

No one moved.

"Jump off!" he hollered again. "You want to get killed here? Get on that beach!"

With these words he leapt out into the darkness. Another man with a coil of wire followed. The others hesitated as if waiting to see what happened to those who had jumped.

I felt I would go crazy if I stayed in the boat any longer. I advanced to the ramp. "Here it comes," I thought and jumped.

The water struck me like a shock. I kept going down. "It's over my head," I thought. My feet sank down and touched bottom. My chin was just at the water. I started to push forward. A sharp crackle burst the air near by. There was a whine and whizz overhead. Then a metallic, plunking sound as if something was striking the boat.

The water was growing shallower. I bent my knees, keeping only my helmet-covered head above the water. I felt as if I were wearing a shield. Finding I wasn't hit, I realized the machinegun fire was so far surprisingly light.

It was dark. The fires that had been visible from the ship could not be seen here. Ahead of me I made out a sandy beach, rising in a slight slope. Figures were crawling on hands and knees up the slope. Every few moments they halted and lay flat on their stomachs. By now the water was really shallow. I straightened up and dashed for the beach. Bullets snapped overhead. I threw myself flat on the sand. At last, I was on dry land.

I left our column and, passing through a narrow verminous alleyway, came out on a comparatively wide cobbled street. Jeeps, high-wheeled Sicilian wagons and knots of soldiers and small groups of ragged, tubercular-looking people were standing around the houses. Some of the people held goats tethered to leashes, while most of them just stood and stared. Over by one building, a small group of soldiers lay in a heap of straw that was piled on the sidewalk. Some of them were munching raw tomatoes and one or two were sleeping with their heads thrown back in an attitude of utter weariness. One soldier was going down the middle of the street with his rifle slung over his shoulder and a bottle of wine tipped to his lips. Elsewhere soldiers stood on street corners with their rifles held tightly, on the alert.

Everything was so different from what I expected, that in no part of the scene before me could I find what looked like a battleground. With all my staring I could not discover any evidence of a battle still being in progress. Yet I knew somewhere beyond the town, at least, there must be fighting.

I thought: "I must find out someone who can tell me what happened here," and seeing a building more imposing than the rest, inscribed boldly with the letters "DUCE!" which were now partially covered by an American flag, I entered.

I climbed a narrow wooden staircase and, turning at the top, I entered a low-ceilinged room, where, behind a desk, a red-faced American officer, with his nearly bald but still youthful head bared, sat tilted back in a chair looking up at three or four Italians who were gesticulating at him with some excitement. This was the commander of the Rangers who had directly assaulted and taken the town of Gela while we had been attacking it from the flank. At present, he had installed himself as mayor of Gela, and was trying to straighten out arguments that had already cropped up.

After the Italians had gone, and in answer to my persistent questioning, he wearily recounted how he had captured the town. From his story, I gathered that within seven hours of landing on the beach, he and his Rangers had smashed their way into Gela, knocked out two coastal batteries that were firing on our navy, stopped an Italian tank counterattack with rifles and grenades, wiped out enemy resistance, captured 400 prisoners and, before lunch, instructed the civil population of 32,000 on their future behavior.

It seemed like a pretty good morning's work to me and I asked him if it had been as easy as it sounded.

"Well, it was sort of rough for a while," he admitted. "About nine o'clock I thought we had resistance stamped out, so I sent the town crier through the streets to shout the news and tell the people that we were Americans that had come to help them. That brought the people out. . . ." — he paused and wiped his hand over his face — "and about then eight Eyetie tanks — there were real Fascists in those babies — came down from the hills and started zoomin' through the streets. They raised hell. . . ." — he laughed, as if remembering something. "We didn't have a damn thing ashore. I told everyone to get inside the buildings. But, hell, I didn't have to tell them. You should have seen them run. They climbed up on roofs and hung out the windows throwing down hand grenades and firing machineguns at the tanks. They might just as well have thrown cream puffs at them for all the effect it had. I saw one tank coming down a street and I chased around the block in my jeep, swung around a corner, ran up on a sidewalk and started shooting at him with my 30-caliber machinegun. I must have fired 300 rounds at him. It wasn't doing any good and the tank still kept coming on. I ran like hell then." He laughed again. "And I drove right down to the pier and found an anti-tank gun there and loaded it up on my jeep. I picked up an officer and we went after the tank. Every time we slammed a shell in that dismounted gun, she recoiled on the captain and knocked him ass over teakettle into the back seat. But we hit the tank and knocked it out. After that we got another tank cornered right in the middle of the street. We must have put it out of commission because it wouldn't move. But nobody would come out of it either. Everyone was firing rifles, machineguns and hand grenades at it, but that damn tank just sat there and no one came out. I said: 'Here, let me fix 'em,' and I fired an assault grenade at the tank, but that didn't budge 'em either. They were tough guys all right! Seeing they wanted to play rough, I thought I'd play rough too. So I took an incendiary grenade and walked up and slapped it on top of the tank. It began dripping down inside, and we saw a little smoke coming out of the tank; then the turret opened and they all poured out screaming like they were mad. After that we got another tank, and the rest ran away. It's been pretty quiet since then."

A sergeant, who entered during the speech, had waited in silence for his superior officer to finish speaking. But now he interrupted him in some impatience.

"Tanks are reported coming up the highway north of us," he said in a tone of affected nonchalance.

The commander did not seem surprised, as though he had expected this all the time.

"Well, they won't chase us around the streets like they did the last time," he said hurriedly and got up strapping on his pistol belt.

I went outside.

"Jesus! Look at that, will ya, Joe."

I turned at the sound of the soldier's voice and noted down at the corner of the street a slight commotion.

A little procession was coming along the cobbles, moving in the direction that led out of town. A cart, drawn by a small donkey, with its wheels askew, and wobbling from side to side, was coming down the road past us. In front of the donkey, several children ran back and forth, contorting their faces in grimaces of gamin horror. Three men, one of whom held the donkey's reins, walked just ahead of the cart, their swarthy, thin faces sweating profusely. In the cart, lying in a doubled-up crumpled position, was a half-naked peasant stained profusely with blood.

A lieutenant and I stood there watching, and an old and wrinkled man leaned out of an upper-story window, shook his fist at us and made several obscene gestures. As we went down the hill again toward the beach, we could still hear him shouting imprecations.

We wandered along the beach seeking my typewriter, which was to have been brought ashore on an amphibious jeep in one of the later waves. I did not know exactly where to find it and knew it would be a thankless search.

After a short walk, we noticed in the water, about twenty yards from shore, an abandoned jeep, over which the surf was running in babbling white waves. On a sudden instinct, I searched inside it and discovered my typewriter which was coverd with a thick goo-ey, white substance that clogged all the keys. It was hissing with a strange sound, as if some chemical reaction had been set up by the water. Feeling downhearted because I now could not write any story, I shoved the useless typewriter in my musette bag, and we ploughed on in search of the headquarters of the First Division.

Passing by the spot where we had landed the night before, I was amazed to see the great number of mines that the sappers had dug out of the beach. Either they had become wet, I thought, there in the sand and so had been rendered useless, or they had been set to explode only on contact with heavy vehicles. This latter was partially true; for, as we learned, several jeeps, including that of Brigadier-General Roosevelt — only, luckily, he wasn't in it — had been blown up when they landed after us. The sight of these mines roused in me a very conscious knowledge of how lucky we had been so far.

From one end to the other the beach provided an astounding spectacle. Tiny infantry landing craft were coming in all up and down the sea front, and other larger boats were edging toward the shore to swell the monstrous and ever-growing heap of beached war materiel. I looked with choked eyes at the endless, confused mass of men, of tiny jeeps, huge, high-sided ducks and more jeeps and heavily loaded trucks, stuck and straining in the thick sand or moving clumsily on the wire netting that the engineers had already laid down in some places as a road. Along the beach, on every side, from the water's edge to the shrubbery growing by the dunes, from every conceivable direction, there was the roar of motors, the sound of spinning wheels, the puttering of incoming craft, the buzzing of planes overhead, the shouts of drivers, the loud orders of traffic policemen, the curses of soldiers, mechanics, gun crewmen and officers. In the surf at the edge of the beach I saw abandoned trucks, overturned jeeps and smashed boats, and on the sands there were blown-up cars, a tank with its tread off, heaps of bedding rolls and baggage with soldiers sitting on them, waiting for transportation, mechanics struggling over broken-down vehicles, and supply troops gathering up broken-open boxes of rations. Where the wire-screen road had not been laid down, the crush of men, vehicles and guns became greater, and there sounded a ceaseless roar of shouts, curses and anguished straining machinery. Trucks, floundering to their hubcaps in the sand, futilely raced their engines as jeeps, jerking this way and that, tried to pull them out and soldiers put their backs against the trucks and heaved with muscle-tightened faces and deep grunts torn from their stomachs. Officers superintending beach traffic rode up and down in jeeps. Their irritable voices made only a slight impression on all the uproar, and their faces looked as if they despaired of ever getting any order out of the chaos. Despite it all, traffic still managed to keep moving and materiel kept flowing inland from the beach.

The sun was beginning to set now, and larger craft were steaming up to the very beach itself, opening their mouths at the water's edge and disgorging ducks, anti-tank guns and a few tanks. Two of these landing craft, loaded with anti-tank guns had just drawn up to the beach directly opposite where we were. The ramp had been let down and vehicles were beginning to move off. We were just passing by when our attention was seized by a mass of running figures. They were streaming away from the ocean with their faces turned up and backward in a look of fear, panic and expectation. At the same moment a tremendous clatter of guns ripped the air apart on every side. Genuinely alarmed by the fleeing figures and the sharp staccato of the guns, I did not pause to look around — for instinctively I knew that planes must be near — but turned and fled away from the water as fast as I could go.

Seized with the same momentary panic as everyone else, I was hastening across the sands when I heard the buzz-saw roar of a plane very close overhead. Instinctively, I looked up to see where it was. I caught one glimpse of a plane not 200 feet above me and at the same time a black cylindrical object dropping from it. Without hesitating I threw myself flat on the ground. In the same motion I jerked off my musette bag and put it over my neck. Then I heard a high, shrill whine in the air. Something shrieked by me, followed by a sharp, explosive crack and a crashing jar. The ground rose and struck me in the stomach and a splash of water slapped against me like slung shot.

Feeling that instant relief that anyone feels after a bomb has struck and he knows that he has not been hit, I squirmed in the sand and looked over my shoulder to the near-by water. There, directly behind me on the sea, from one of the large tank craft, a column of gray smoke could be seen climbing upward.

As I watched, the column spiraled out in clouds, and suddenly a billowing mass of black vapor burst over the deckhouse, hiding it from sight, and a dancing shower of orange sparks sprayed over the blue water. At this the men sprang from their shelters and rushed across the sands toward the stricken boat. I followed.

In a very few moments, shrieks, groans and shouted oaths rang across the beach, and beneath them sounded the sinister crackling of fire. The space on the beach around the struck ship began to fill up; soldiers came scurrying out of bushes, M.P.'s roared up on jeeps and in the meantime trucks loaded with ammunition rushed away in the opposite direction. Suddenly, from the depths of the ship came a series of rapid-fire explosions, a vast spray of sparks shot up in the air and lobbed down on the beach fifty yards away where ammunition was stored. The crowd drew back from the water, alarmed.

"Goddamit!" said an officer excitedly. "That'll blow up all the ammunition on this beach."

As if he had heard, and understanding the danger, the captain of the tank ship drew up his ramp and backed hastily away from the beach. The other boat followed, pouring a stream of water from a hose into her sister ship.

The crowd dispersed. Men went back to their duties. A staff officer of the First Division, who had remained behind staring as if hypnotized at the burning boat, shook his head sadly. "That's got our anti-tank guns aboard," he said. "It's going to be just too bad if they come at us with tanks tomorrow."

Only barely did I hear his words. I was caught up in some inner tumult at the magnificence of the scene before me. The whole panorama was one of the most purely spectacular I had seen in many years of war. As if all the army, navy and air ministers of the world had combined to produce it, the whole terrible, logical culminating menace of modern industry, the whole theatre of war — a very World's Fair of War — land, sea and air — lay here before me in all its gigantic, splendid, overwhelming meaninglessness. The hollow bowl of the sea formed by the descending twilight was filled with ships of every conceivable tonnage, size and purpose. The rim of the horizon ten miles out to sea was lined with transports — majestic assurance that our supply lines were still intact. And from the transports new hordes of tiny craft, like water bugs, were scooting toward the shore to add their own heaped-up loads and the chattering of their own roaring engines to the riot and the confusion already on the beach. Above this scene planes dove and rolled. Below them the flames from a burning oil tanker out at sea and the landing craft near at hand lifted up their scarlet hands, tingeing the gray ships and the olive vehicles and the drab uniforms and the dull sand and the green bushes with a ghostly quality. I was stifling with the harsh and menacing opulence of it, sick and fainting with the movement and the vast indigestibility of it all. The whole thing seemed utterly impossible.

"Wish I was a painter," said the lieutenant by my side. "Kinda gets ya, doesn't it?"

"Gets you, all right," I said, as we wearily went on to division headquarters. This was in a grove of lemon trees, beneath the brow of a hill about 400 yards from beach. As might be supposed, everything was a blur of confusion, with everyone stumbling over one another in the dark and lost soldiers searching hopelessly for their units. Two such men, we found under a tree, philosophically putting away the last of a box of K rations. They were parachutists and they had dropped down on Sicily out of the darkness the night before and become lost from their company, the fate of which neither of them yet knew. After many varied adventures, one of which included hiding for several hours in a tree, they had escaped back to our lines, bringing forty prisoners with them. One of the lost men, a sergeant, was so proud of his prisoners that he had made the lieutenant to whom he delivered them on the beach sign a receipt for them. This he now took out of his pocket and showed us with a pleased grin.

What impressed me more than anything else in the parchutists' story was the fact that though they were lost from their own unit and though they had been through a dozen dreadful adventures in the night and day, yet they hadn't abandoned their cheerfulness and were quite as ready to fight with the First Division as with their own Eighty-second Airborne Division. In short, they were able readily to adapt themselves to circumstances.

That was the way everyone was around camp that night. The bedding and the baggage had not come; nobody knew where anybody else or anything was, yet everyone moved about quite independently, taking care of himself.

Shouldering a blanket I went up on the side of the hill to sleep. The night was warm and clear. Out at sea there was the twinkle of our fleet's ack-ack guns. Closer at hand was the glow of the burning ship. Overhead the moon stood high in the sky, and the stars gleamed around it.

Gazing at the starlit sky, at the moon, at the flickering guns and the glow of the fire, I felt a thrill of sad joy. "How strange it all is! What can it all mean?" I thought. And suddenly, convulsively, when I thought of all the terror of the landing in the night, and all the weary blot and blur of the day, I knew how good it was to be alive.

CHAPTER IV

THE SITUATION
June 6, 1944

THE final approved plan for assault on the continent of Europe under the Command of General Dwight D. Eisenhower as Supreme Commander of the Allied Expeditionary Forces included substantial and direct effort by American Forces. This plan involved simultaneously daylight assault landings on a broad front by two separate American corps—V Corps and VII Corps—both under the operational command of General Montgomery, commanding the Twenty-first Army Group. Until sufficient American forces reached Europe to warrant the operation of an additional American Field Army, the First U. S. Army was to remain non-operational.

The VII Corps, with the 4th Infantry Division making the assault by sea and assisted by the 82nd Airborne Division and the 101st Airborne Division landing in the rear of the German coastal defenses, was to establish a beachhead in the neighborhood of Varreville near the southern portion of the east coast of the Cotentin Peninsula—"Utah Beach". The V Corps, with one combat team of the 29th Infantry Division on the right and one combat team of the 1st Infantry Division on the left, all under the command of the 1st Infantry Division, was to establish a beachhead on the northern coast of Calvados near St.-Laurent-Sur-Mer—"Omaha Beach."

The plan of assault on Omaha Beach was to land two regimental combat teams on a broad front, with two battalions of each regiment in the assault and one in support. In general, the right combat team— the 116th Regimental Combat Team of the 29th Infantry Division—

was to capture Vierville-sur-Mer and push through the defenses; the left combat team—the 16th Regimental Combat Team—was to push east along the defenses. Succeeding elements of the First Infantry Division were to drive inland and establish an initial beachhead to include vital high ground between the Aure River and the sea. Ranger units were to perform special missions.

The assault forces for Omaha Beach totaled about 30,000 personnel and about 3,000 vehicles, followed up on the same and next day by a further strength of about 25,000 personnel and about 4,000 vehicles.

The hour of the assault differed by some thirty minutes between Utah and Omaha beaches. This was due to the fact that the direction of flow of the incoming tide was up the English Channel and therefore high water (less three hours) occurred at Utah Beach some thirty minutes prior to the time it occurred on Omaha beach.

With the postponement of D-Day from June 5th to June 6th, due to adverse weather conditions, H-Hour for the assault was announced as "Utah Beach—6:25 A.M."; "Omaha Beach—6:45 A.M."

◆ ◆ ◆

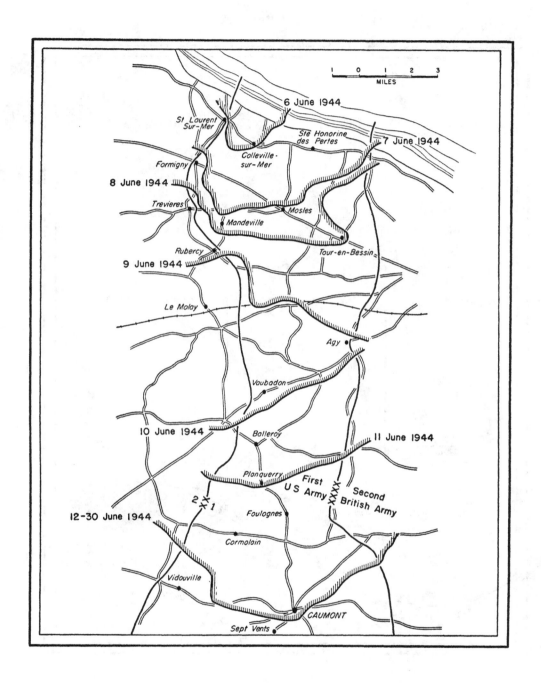

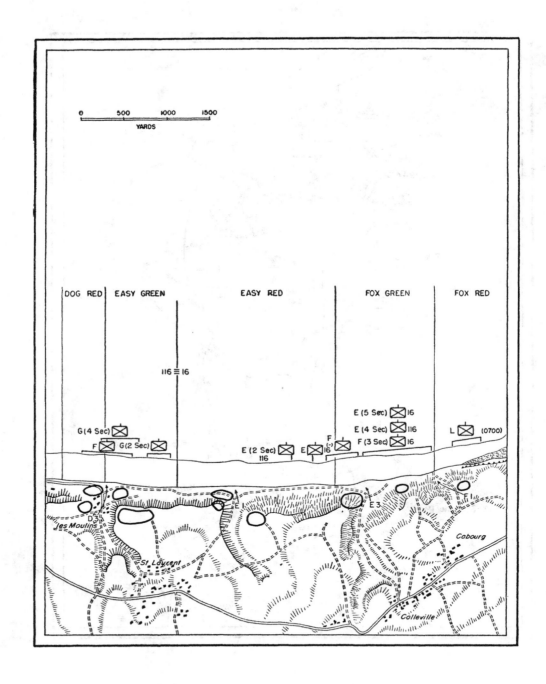

NORMANDY

The Record

June 6 to July 25, 1944

THE invasion of the continent of Europe, the supreme operation of World War II, found the First Division spearheading the attack at the most difficult point — Omaha Beach.

After the completion of the Sicilian Campaign the Division had
sailed for England where it arrived in November of 1943. In Dorset
County it settled to train and refit for the operation that lay ahead.
Major General Huebner and his staff immediately started work on
a series of invasion plans the last of which called for an invasion of
the Normandy coast by V Corps with the First Division carrying
the ball.

The mission of V Corps was to secure a beachhead in the area
between Port-en-Bessin and the Vire River from which our troops
would push southward toward Caumont and St. Lo, conforming with
the advance of the British Second Army. The corps would arrive at
the beachhead in four stages. The initial assault force (Force "O")
consisted of the First Division, reinforced to include two other infantry regiments with strong attachments of artillery, armor and engineers, as well as attachments of engineer and service units for movement to the beach. Chief components of the First Division, reinforced and numbering 34,142 men and 3,306 vehicles, were the 16th
and 18th Regimental Combat Teams, the 116th Regimental Combat
Team and the 115th Infantry attached from the 29th Infantry Division, and the Provisional Ranger Force made up of the 2nd and 5th
Battalions.

The follow-up force (Force "B") was scheduled to arrive off
the assault beach after noon on D-Day. It numbered 25,117 men and
4,429 vehicles and included the 29th Infantry Division, consisting
of the 175th Infantry and (attached from the First Division) the
26th Regimental Combat Team. Scheduled to arrive on D plus 1
and D plus 2, the preloaded build-up contingent had as main com-

ponents the Second Infantry Division and totaled some 17,500 men and 2,300 vehicles.

The loading plans of Force "O" and Force "B" were designed to fit an operation which would develop from an assault by one reinforced division into attack by two divisions abreast. Unity of command in the critical first stages would thus be assured. Maj. Gen. Clarence R. Huebner, commanding the First Division, would conduct the initial assault with a force that included units of the 29th Infantry Division, all under the initial field command of Brig. Gen. Willard G. Wyman, his assistant division commander.

Plans for the landings and movement inland were made so as to permit the early assignment of divisional zones to the First and 29th Divisions. These zones would go into effect on Corps orders, when Maj. Gen. Charles H. Gerhardt would assume command of the 29th Division with its normal components. In the meantime, in order to pave the way for this step, Brig. Gen. Norman D. Cota, former Chief of Staff of the First Division, then Assistant Divisional Commander of the 29th, was to land with the 116th Regimental Combat Team and assist General Wyman in handling the 29th Division units until they reverted to 29th Division control.

The First Division had been alerted on 23rd March to be ready for movement to marshaling areas on short notice. Actually, movement began on 7th May and was completed by 11th May for elements of the assault and follow-up forces. Once in the marshaling areas, troops were "sealed" in their assignments. During the last few days of May, they were moved from the marshaling points to the ports and "hards" for embarkation, their places being immediately taken by units designated to follow across the channel in build-up schedules. By 3rd June all troops of the First Division, reinforced, had been loaded, and some of them had been aboard several days. Portland, Weymouth and Poole were the embarkation areas. On the night of 27th May, a small enemy air attack on the Weymouth area caused loss of a few smaller craft. Aside from this raid, the loadings suffered no interference from enemy action and German air reconnaissance up to D-Day was on a routine scale.

General Eisenhower decided at 4:15 A.M., 5th June, to accept the risk involved in making the assault under the conditions of sea and sky expected for the next day. H-hour for Omaha Beach was set at 6:30 A.M. Low tide would occur at 5:25 A.M. and the first high water at 11:00 A.M. Sunrise was at 5:58 A.M. and sunset at 10.07 P.M.

The main convoy of Force "O" cleared Portland Harbor on the afternoon of 5th June; movement across 100 miles of channel to the assault areas was uneventful. The operation met no interference from action by enemy naval or air forces. Continuous air cover was provided for the shipping lane and for Allied assault beaches.

Weather conditions on D-Day were far from ideal for the assault operations. Visibility was ten miles, but there was a partial overcast to hamper bombing. The wind was still strong, coming from the northwest, and therefore producing its full effect on the coastal waters off the Omaha sector. A wind force of ten to eighteen knots caused waves averaging three to four feet high in the transport area, with occasional waves up to six feet. On the beach, breakers were three to four feet. This condition of the sea persisted until D plus 1 before the wind moderated. The effect of the sea on the landing plans was to be felt throughout D-Day.

The beach defenses consisted of minefields and beach obstacles. These included stakes, ramp obstacles, element "C," hedgehogs, tetrahedra and curved rails. The enemy was aided by the wreckage of landing craft which cluttered up the beach and hindered landing. By H plus 3 hours, the obstacles and wreckage had so littered the water's edge that unloading was seriously hindered. The beach itself was not wired, that is from the low water mark to the beginning of the turf. From the edge of the turf, however, to a point in the rear of the enemy installations on the high ground and bluffs, the area was well defended by double-apron wire, concertinas, and knife-rests. Numerous minefields had been laid and made more effective by the placing of minefield warning signs in both mined and unmined areas. Further to the rear, at a distance of 300 to 600 yards from the beach, concrete gun positions had been sunk into the sides of the hills. These contained 75-mm. and 50-mm. anti-tank guns and machineguns.

Beyond the first ridge, mortars had been emplaced; these were chiefly effective in the afternoon of D-Day.

The importance placed by the enemy on the beach defense is illustrated by a field order issued by Gen. Field Marshal Erwin Rommel, 22nd April, 1944: "We must succeed in the short time left until the large offensive starts, in bringing all defenses to such a standard that they will hold up against the strongest attack. Never in history was there a defense of such an extent with such an obstacle as the sea. *The enemy must be annihilated before he reaches our main battlefield.*"

A heavy naval and air bombardment preceded the assault of the beach by two battalions of the 16th Infantry and two battalions of the 116th Infantry. The bombardment knocked out several enemy installations but was not very effective against the concrete emplacements which were sited at an angle to cover the beach laterally. The unfavorable weather reduced the effectiveness of the support weapons. The assault waves of infantry as a result were to find themselves in a difficult situation. The fire was so intense and the fields of fire so laid out that it was virtually impossible to push beyond the beach until anti-tank weapons could be landed to penetrate the emplacements by frontal fire. Meanwhile, although the enemy had caused havoc among landing craft, he would not be able to prevent the landing of some follow-up troops.

The enemy position on the cliff overlooking the beach was finally pierced by the 2nd Battalion, 16th Infantry, at 10:00 A.M. The enemy troops on the high ground, however, continued to resist in place the troops which followed up this breaching, until killed or driven back by intense fire.

The keystone of the beach defense was the village of Coleville-sur-Mer, situated on the high ground to the east and to the rear of Exit E-1 (the Ruquet River Valley). It had to be taken to cut the beach area lateral communications.

The enemy had approximately one and one-half battalions manning the forward beach emplacements. These troops belonged to the 726th Infantry Regiment of the 716th Infantry Division. In addition, and unknown to Allied intelligence, the 352nd Infantry Division was by chance engaged in an anti-invasion training maneuver immediately behind the assault beach defenses. This gave the enemy a great advantage in the depth and in the initial strength of their position.

In the initial breakthrough, our troops were immediately engaged by that portion of the 352nd Division which was in the vicinity. The 914th and 916th Regiments with the 915th in reserve.

The 915th went into the line around Treviers when it became obvious that our advance was not being halted. To protect the right flank the enemy was to bring up elements of the 30th Mobile Brigade, including the 513th, 517th and 518th Mobile Battalions which were used to support the 352nd Division. These were not to arrive, however, until 7th and 8th June.

As the landing craft carrying the 16th Regimental Combat Team units came within a few miles off shore they passed men struggling in life preservers and on rafts. These men were personnel from foundered DD tanks, the first casualties of the rough seas. According to plan, Companies B and C of the 741st Tank Battalion were launched at H-50 minutes, 6,000 yards off shore, to lead in the first assault wave on the eastern beach sectors. In very short order the DD's began to suffer crippling damage in broken struts, torn canvas, and engine trouble from water flooding the engine compartment. Of the thirty-two tanks, two swam in and three others were beached from an LCT (landing craft tank) which could not launch its DD's because of a damaged ramp. In the 116th Infantry zone, the officers in charge of the tank-loaded LCT's had decided not to risk the conditions of the sea, and the thirty-two DD's of the 743rd Tank Battalion were carried in to the beach.

The assault troops experienced their worst disappointment of the day when they found the beach unscarred by air bombardment and soon realized that the air bombardment had had little effect on the beach defenses.

The Army-Navy Special Engineer Task Force had one of the most important and difficult missions of the landing. Their chances of clearing gaps through the obstacles in the first half-hour allotted to them were lessened by accidents on the approach to the beach. Delays in loading from LCT's and LCM's (landing craft mediums) and in finding their way to the beaches, resulted in half of the sixteen assault teams reaching shore ten minutes or more late. Only five teams hit their appointed sector, most of them being carried eastward, with the result that Dog Beach (the 116th's zone) received much less than the effort scheduled. As a further effect of mislandings, at least three teams came in where no infantry or tanks were present to give protective fire.

In net result, the demolition task force blew six complete gaps through all bands of obstacles, and three partial gaps. Of the six, only two were in the 116th's half of the beach, and four were on Easy Red, a fact which may have influenced later landing chances. Owing to the loss of equipment, only one of the gaps could be marked, and this diminished their value under high-water conditions. Their first effort made, the demolition teams joined the other assault forces on the shingle or sea wall and waited for the next low tide to resume their work. Casualties for the Special Engineer Task Force, including navy personnel, ran to forty-one percent for D-Day, most of them suffered in the first half-hour.

The infantry companies in the first wave came in by boat sections, six to a company, with a headquarters section due in the next wave (7:00 A.M.). Each LCVP (landing craft vehicles and personnel) carried an average of fifty-one men and an officer.

As expected, few of the LCVP's and LCA's (landing craft assault) carrying assault infantry were able to make dry landings. Most of them grounded on sandbars fifty to one hundred yards out, and in some cases the water was neck-deep. Under fire as they came in within a quarter-mile of the shore, the infantry met their worst experiences of the day and suffered their heaviest casualties just after touchdown. Small-arms fire, mortars, and artillery concentrated on the landing area, but the worst hazard was produced by converging fires from automatic weapons. Survivors from some craft reported hearing the fire beat on the ramps before they were lowered, and then seeing the hail of bullets whip the surf just in front of the lowered ramps. Some men dove under water or went over the sides to escape the beaten zone of the machineguns. Stiff, weakened from seasickness, and often heavily loaded, the debarking troops had little chance of moving fast in water that was knee-deep or higher, and their progress was made more difficult by uneven footing in the runnels crossing the tidal flat.

Many men were exhausted before they reached shore, where they faced two hundred yards or more of open sand before reaching cover at the sea wall or shingle bank. Most men who reached that cover made it by walking, and under increasing enemy fire. Troops who stopped to organize, rest, or take shelter behind obstacles or tanks merely prolonged their difficulties and suffered heavier losses.

In the first assault wave on the 116th Infantry's half of the Omaha Beach, Company E, which was supposed to land on Easy Green, veered a mile eastward from that sector. The three companies in the 116th's zone were in poor condition for carrying out their assault missions. By 7:00 A.M. Company A had been cut to pieces at the water's edge, Company F was disorganized by heavy losses, and one of the scattered sections of Company G, those in best shape, were preparing to move west along the beach to find their assigned sector.

To the east, in the 116th Infantry area, the picture differed only in detail. Easy Red Beach, over a mile long and fronting E-1 Draw, was assigned to the 2nd Battalion, with Companies E and F landing in the first wave. The bulk of both companies landed far to the east. The only infantry to come in on Easy Red in the first wave were two lost boat sections of Company E of the 116th Infantry, and one section each of Company E and F of the 116th Infantry.

Very different was the record of the landings on Fox Beach. Whereas four scattered sections of infantry came into Easy Red without many casualties, the bulk of four companies (three of them scheduled for more westerly beaches) landed on Fox against every possible handicap of mislandings, delays and enemy opposition.

Less than one section already accounted for (on Easy Red),

Company E of the 16th Infantry, touched down on the western part of Fox Green, the craft badly scattered over a front of nearly eight hundred yards. The final run-in was not costly, but crossing bands of automatic fire caught most of the craft as the ramps were lowered, and from there on losses were heavy. Most of them were incurred in the water and among men who stopped to drag the wounded ashore. So exhausted and shaken were the assault troops when they reached the sand, three hundred yards from the shingle bank, that most of them stopped there and crawled in just ahead of the tide. The greatest number of the company's 105 casualties on D-Day were suffered on the beach, in the first stage of assault.

Beginning at 7:00 A.M., the second group of assault waves touched down in a series of landings that lasted forty minutes, ending with the support battalions of the two regimental combat teams. The later waves did not come in under the conditions planned for their arrival. The tide, however, flowing into the obstacle belt by 7:00 A.M., was through it an hour later, rising eight feet in that period; but the obstacles were gapped at only a few places. The enemy fire which had decimated the first waves was not neutralized when the larger landings commenced. No advances had been made beyond the shingle, and neither the tanks nor the scattered pockets of infantry already ashore were able to give much covering fire. Consequently, much of the record of this period is a repetition of what happened earlier.

Casualties continued to be heavy on some sectors of the narrowing tidal flat though unit experiences differed widely and enemy fire, diverted or neutralized by the troops and tanks already along the embankment, was not often as concentrated as earlier in the assault. Mislandings continued to be a disrupting factor, not merely in scattering the infantry units but also in preventing engineers from carrying out special assignments and in separating headquarters elements from their units, thus hindering reorganization.

At 8:00 A.M., German observers on the bluff in sizing up the grim picture below them, might well have felt that the invasion was stopped at the edge of the water. Actually, at three or four places on the four-mile beach front, U. S. troops were already breaking through the shallow crust of enemy defenses.

The command group of the 16th Infantry landed in two sections; the first, coming in at 7:20 A.M., lost the executive officer and thirty-five men on the tidal flat. Col. George A. Taylor arrived in the second section at 8:15 A.M. and found plenty to do on the beach. Men were still hugging the embankment, disorganized, and suffering casualties from mortar and artillery fire. Colonel Taylor summed up the situation in terse phrases: "Two kinds of people are staying on this beach, the dead and those who are going to die — now let's get the hell out of here!" Small groups of men were collected without regard to units, put under charge of the nearest noncommissioned officer, and sent on through the wire and across the flat, while engineers worked hard to widen gaps in the wire and to mark lanes through the minefields.

The 18th Regimental Combat Team had been scheduled to land on Easy Red in column of battalions, beginning at 9:30 A.M. After passing the line of departure, the first wave ran into difficulties in maintaining formation and steering a straight course. There was much congestion of traffic toward shore, with craft of all descriptions maneuvering in every direction. The 2nd Battalion began landing just west of E-1 shortly after 10:00 A.M. As they neared shore, troops of the 18th Infantry had no impression that any progress had been made on the beach: The beach shingle was full of tractors, tanks, vehicles, bulldozers, and troops — the high ground was still held by the Germans who had all troops on the beach pinned down — the beach was still under heavy fire from enemy small arms, mortars, and artillery.

The underwater obstacles caused great difficulties, even though a narrow gap had been cleared near E-1; the Navy report for the transport group carrying the 18th Infantry lists twenty-two LCI(L)'s as lost on the beach, nearly all from being staved in by log ramps, or hitting mines. Nevertheless, personnel losses in the 18th Infantry were light.

On the right of E-1, the 2nd Battalion found an enemy pillbox still in action. Fire from a tank supported the infantry in a first attempt, but the attack was stalled until naval fire was laid on. A naval observer contacted a destroyer about 1,000 yards off shore and coordinated its action with the infantry assault. The affair was very nicely timed; the destroyer's guns, firing only a few yards over the crowded beach, got on the target at about the fourth round and the pillbox surrendered. Twenty Germans were taken prisoners. Thus, at about 11:30 A.M., the last enemy defenses in front of E-1 were reduced. Within half an hour, engineers of the 16th Infantry Combat Team were clearing mines in the draw, and the Engineer Special Brigade Group units were working bulldozers on the western slope to push through an exit. E-1 became the main funnel for movement off the beach.

While the main assault was proceeding on Omaha Beach, three companies (D, E and F) of the 2nd Ranger Battalion were engaged in an isolated action three miles to the west. Led by Lieut. Col. James E. Rudder, commander of the Provisional Ranger Force, about 200 men came in at Pointe de Hoe. Their primary mission was to seize that fortified position and neutralize its battery of six 155-mm. howitzers, which could put fire on the whole Omaha approaches, from the craft assembly area in to the beaches.

In less than five minutes from time of touchdown, the First Rangers, by one type of rope or another, were getting to the cliff top. Some, covered with mud from having fallen into deep crater-pools on the beach, had trouble in climbing. A few ropes had been cut by the enemy or had slipped from the anchorage. The first man up waited no longer than it took for three or four men to assemble, then moved out on prearranged missions toward the gun positions. They found themselves in a no-man's land of incredible destruction, all landmarks gone, and the ground so cratered that if men got fifteen feet apart they were immediately out of contact.

Only a few enemy were seen and these were quickly driven to cover in a network of ruined trenches connecting deep dugouts and emplacements. One after another, the small advance parties reached their appointed gun emplacements, only to find them empty. The gun positions, three of them casemated, were partly wrecked; the guns had been removed. Without hesitation, the Ranger parties started inland on their next mission: to reach the coastal highway, set up a defensive position cutting that main route between Vierville and Grandcamp, and await the arrival of the 116th Infantry from Omaha Beach.

The small force on the Pointe was soon in a state of approaching siege. Enemy snipers appeared in the fortified area, and despite several attempts, the Rangers could never clean out the mass of wrecked positions. Three or four Germans still held out on the tip of the Pointe in an undamaged concrete observation post. During the afternoon two enemy counterattacks coming from the direction of St. Pierre-du-Mont were stopped, the most dangerous one by accurate and rapid fire from the Ranger's only remaining mortar. The anti-aircraft position was still very much in action, and destroyer fire could not quite reach it. Communication with the advance party on the highway was intermittent, depending chiefly on patrols that occasionally had to fight their way through.

Back on the beach, with General Cota close behind the leading elements, the 116th Infantry had entered Vierville shortly before 11:00 A.M. Except for scattered fire from the outskirts when the advance was starting, no enemy resistance was encountered.

A platoon of Company B, 116th Infantry, went through Vierville out of contact with the rest and turned south toward the chateau. On the way, they encountered a German resistance nest, assaulted it, and took fourteen prisoners. A little beyond the chateau, the platoon was attacked by Germans who had just deployed from three trucks coming up from the south. The Company B unit, reduced to twenty-five men and lacking automatic weapons, withdrew to the chateau and stopped the enemy attack with well-aimed rifle fire. Here they were joined about noon by a platoon from Company A, 5th Rangers, which had just been coming toward the chateau across country. Neither party knew there were any other friendly forces near Vierville.

In the St. Laurent area, except for Company M, pinned on the beach flat near E-1 draw, most of the 3rd Battalion, 116th Infantry, had reached high ground by 10:00 A.M. and were starting to push south. As a result of enemy resistance in and near St. Laurent, they were to make only a half-mile progress during the rest of the day.

St. Laurent had also proved a stumbling block for the 115th Infantry, coming at it from the northeast. That regiment landed in front of E-1 draw far to the eastward of its planned landing beach just before noon. It took three to four hours to clear the beach, going up mostly to the east of the draw. Somewhat disorganized by intermingling with the 116th Regimental Combat Team, the battalions were routed by direction of General Wyman to reach assembly points a thousand yards inland, by way of St. Laurent. The 115th Infantry's transportation was not due in on D-Day, so the men were carrying as heavy loads as possible; the heavy weapons sections were particularly burdened with guns, mortars and extra ammunition to hand-carry.

Scattered harassing fire from snipers, mine fields and occasional machineguns also slowed down the movement. The 2nd Battalion reached St. Laurent, met opposition in the village, and spent the afternoon trying to clean out a small enemy force, estimated at not more than a company in strength. Once again the main difficulty for the inexperienced troops was to locate enemy fire positions in terrain affording so much cover. Toward dusk when the attack was finally well started, naval gunfire hit in the village, caused a number of casualties in the 2nd Battalion, and stopped the effort. The battalion was drawn south of St. Laurent for the night, where it joined the 1st Battalion. This unit reached a position near the Formigny road a few hundred yards south of St. Laurent, making slow progress against snipers and some mortar fire. The 3rd Battalion had not reached the St. Laurent-Colleville road by dark.

Elements of five battalions had spent the afternoon and evening of D-Day fighting through an area of about a square mile which contained only scattered pockets of enemy resistance. The effectiveness of the attacking forces had been reduced by a number of factors, including lack of communications, difficulties of control, and the absence of artillery and armored support.

Returning to the 16th Infantry zone of action we find that when Company G got past the bluff and started inland, about 9:00 A.M. they were bothered initially only by light sniping and occasional minefields. Company G made rapid progress for a thousand yards to the south and was advancing in its designated zone and according to plan.

The first objective was a German bivouac area a quarter-mile west of Colleville; from there the company would turn into Colleville. Company G approached the bivouac area about 9:30 A.M. and received heavy fire from automatic weapons and mortars on both flanks of its advance. A two-hour action followed, with house-to-house fighting before the enemy was driven out of the area.

Remnants of a Company F section and small elements of Company H and two sections of Company E, 116th Infantry, had followed Company G's route from the beach and joined up during the morning, giving a strength of about 150 men for the attack on Colleville, the keystone of the German defense.

Company G had felt itself isolated during this period, an impression which was characteristic of most of the inland fighting on D-Day. Actually, the advance from Easy Red had been followed up by a number of units which by noon were not far from Colleville. Between Colleville and Easy Red Beach, battalion, regimental and division command groups were working hard to organize the scattered assault and build up support. Contacts were irregular, however, the hedgerows cut off observation, and small enemy groups held on tenaciously in bypassed positions, from which they opened with harassing fire on the flanks of the advancing units and drew them into a mopping-up action that might consume two or three hours.

Other enemy groups, trying to get back from the bluff positions, added to the confusion by appearing in areas supposedly cleared up. In this fashion, small separate battles were developing throughout the day almost anywhere between E-1 and E-3 draws and south beyond the highway. Advance under these conditions was more or less blind, and coordinated action by the assault forces became almost impossible.

Lieut. Col. Herbert C. Hicks, Jr., commanding the 2nd Battalion of the 16th Infantry, had followed Company G toward Colleville and was endeavoring to get other units of his battalion toward that area. The only sizeable group he could find during the morning was made up of about fifty men of Company E, including Lieutenant Spalding's section from the E-1 strongpoint. This party reached the coastal highway about noon and pushed several hundred yards beyond to cover the right flank of Company G. Moving with a section of Company G, the group came under sniper fire from the rear and lost contact with friendly units. Later in the afternoon, deciding that they were in danger of being cut off, the Company E detachment withdrew toward Colleville.

Meantime, elements of the 1st Battalion were reaching the same general area. Companies B and C reached the highway by 1:00 P.M. near the bivouac area through which Company G had already fought. They spent several hours cleaning snipers out of the woods in the vicinity, and made about three hundred yards progress southward by dark. Company A, slowed in getting up the bluff, spent the morning and early afternoon reducing a machinegun nest in the woods at the edge of E-1 draw, halfway to the highway. It rejoined the battalion late in the day.

The 18th Infantry had landed in front of E-1 draw from 11:00 A.M. to 2:00 P.M. One after another, as the battalions started inland, Brig. Gen. Willard G. Wyman, Assistant Division Commander, turned them in accordance with previously arranged alternate plans from their original missions to take over those of the 16th Infantry. Enemy groups were still scattered along the route of advance.

A mile to the east of Colleville, the 3rd Battalion of the 16th Infantry had been fighting all day on its own, out of contact with the rest of the regiment. After taking the bluff strongpoint at F-1 draw, the intermingled units of the battalion were reorganized on the high ground behind the bluffs. The advance off the beach had been made by elements of six companies (including Company F of the 16th and Company E of the 116th), but the force that now moved inland numbered little over one hundred men. Patrols were sent ahead, but the three men sent to Cabourg ran into a German strong-point and were captured. Enemy groups were still to the rear near the bluffs and even attempted a counterattack in platoon strength. In the afternoon, the battalion moved into Grand-Hameau. With the enemy holding Cabourg in some strength, there could be no question of further advance. During the evening, other elements got off the beach, some seventeen tanks came up, and the 3rd Battalion occupied defensive positions blocking the coastal highway at le Grand-Hameau.

The 26th Infantry loaded in Force "B," arrived in the transport area at 1:00 P.M. and was ordered to land at 6:00 P.M. near E-3 exit, the 1st Battalion arriving first at a time when the situation on the left of the 16th Infantry was critical, was diverted by General Wyman from its original mission to the left flank of that regiment. The remainder of the regiment was ashore by 9:00 P.M. and received orders to put the 3rd Battalion in a defensive position on the road south from St. Laurent to Formigny, with the 2nd Battalion close behind it ready to attack through the 3rd Battalion in the morning. The battalions were moving to their objectives during the night.

General Huebner and the command group, First Division, landed on Easy Red at 7:00 P.M. and joined General Wyman at the Division Command Post located in the entrance of E-1 draw.

At the end of D-Day the assault on Omaha Beach had succeeded, but the going had been harder than expected. Penetrations made in the morning by relatively weak assault groups had lacked the force to carry far inland. Delay in reducing the strongpoints at the draws had slowed landings of reinforcements, artillery, and supplies. Stubborn enemy resistance, both at strongpoints and inland, had held the advance to a strip of ground hardly more than a mile and a half deep in the Colleville area, and considerably less than that west of St. Laurent. Barely large enough to be called a foothold, this strip was well inside the planned beachhead maintenance area. Behind the forward positions, cut-off enemy groups were still resisting. The whole landing area continued under enemy artillery fire from inland.

Infantry assault troops had been landed, despite all difficulties, on the scale intended; most of the elements of five regiments were ashore by dark. With respect to artillery, vehicles and supplies of all sorts, schedules were far behind. Little more than 100 tons had been put ashore instead of the 2,400 tons planned for D-Day.

The ammunition supply situation was critical and would have been even worse except for the fact that 90 of the 110 pre-loaded DUKWS (amphibious trucks) in Force "O" had made the shore successfully. Only the first steps had been taken to organize the beach for handling the expected volume of traffic, and it was obvious that further delay in unloadings would be inevitable.

First estimates of casualties were high, with an inflated percentage of "missing" as a result of the number of assault sections which were separated from their companies, sometimes for two or three days. On the basis of later, corrected returns, casualties for the First Division and its attached units were in the neighborhood of 3,000 killed, wounded and missing. The two assaulting regimental combat teams (16th and 116th) lost about 1,000 men each. The highest proportionate losses were taken by units which landed in the first few hours, including engineers, tank troops, and artillery.

Whether by swamping at sea or by action at the beach, materiel losses were considerable, including twenty-six artillery pieces and over fifty tanks. No satisfactory over-all figures are available for vehicles and supplies; one unit, the 4042nd Quartermaster Truck Company, got ashore only 13 out of 35 trucks (2½ ton), but this loss was much higher than the average. On the Navy side, a tentative estimate gave a total of about 50 landing craft and 10 larger vessels lost, with a much larger number of all types damaged.

In the early hours of D plus 1 Day, V Corps took command of the forces ashore, freeing General Huebner to devote his entire attention to the First Division. Mopping-up of the ground occupied on D-Day was a time-consuming process. All during the night, small enemy groups had been trying to escape from the area north of the Colleville-St. Laurent highway, filtering through the 16th Infantry's scattered units and starting sporadic fire fights.

In the early morning, as drivers of a battalion headquarters were getting ready to move toward a new motor park, they found and captured 30 Germans in the field next to their night position. Back at the beach, enemy snipers were so troublesome to the gunners of the 7th Field Artillery Battalion that they were forced to organize an attack on the bluff with artillery personnel.

These were typical of many small incidents that prolonged the confusion in rear areas. The major job was the pocket of resistance at Colleville, which was dealt with during the morning of June 7th, by the 2nd Battalion of the 16th Infantry. Company G was through the village by 1:00 A.M., and found enemy resistance weak. Some fifty-two Germans of the 726th Infantry gave up without a fight; the Company L patrol, captured at Cabourg the day before, had talked the enemy into a receptive mood for surrendering. Great damage to German forces in Colleville was inflicted by the 2nd Battalion of the 18th Infantry, posted south and southeast on the escape route from the village. During the night and morning, 160 Germans were captured and fifty killed in this area. The 1st and 2nd Battalions of the 16th Infantry spent all of the day mopping up, moving short distances south and southeast from Colleville behind the advancing 18th Infantry. At dark, they were still encountering scattered machine-gun and sniper fire.

The advance eastward toward Port-en-Bessin was accomplished without meeting enemy resistance in any strength. The 3rd Battalion of the 16th Infantry, supported by Company B of the 745th Tank Battalion, went straight down the coastal highway and occupied Huppain for the night. Supporting this advance, the 62nd Armored Field Artillery Battalion fired five missions, expending 685 rounds, and reported the destruction of an enemy battery of medium artillery. The 1st Battalion of the 26th Infantry went south to Russy (reached at 5:05 P.M.), and then east to a position about 1,000 yards from Mount Cauvin.

British Commando units were reported on the edge of Port-en-Bessin, and by evening a juncture between the First Division and the British 50th Division was in sight.

The attack of the 18th Infantry was slow in getting started but made good progress during the afternoon. The 1st Battalion met only small and isolated groups of enemy resistance and was effectively aided in dealing with these by the five tanks of the 741st Tank Battalion. The battalion crossed the Bayeux-Isigny highway shortly after noon and ambushed some cyclists from reconnaissance units of the 352nd (German) Division. The tanks reached the vicinity of Engranville at 2:00 P.M. and shelled the village. Enemy resistance lasted until evening, when G Company attacked and forced an enemy platoon across the river. The battalion then occupied a defensive position on high ground which dominated the approaches to the Aure River. The situation on its right flank was unsatisfactory as the enemy still held Formigny. The 3rd Battalion of the 26th Infantry, advancing down the St. Laurent road, had been stopped a half-mile short of Formigny by strong resistance from machinegun nests and made no progress for the rest of the day. This left the 18th Infantry at Engranville exposed to attack from its rear.

The 3rd Battalion of the 18th Infantry kept pace with the 1st Battalion, going through Surrain at 12:15 P.M. and reaching the Bayeux highway just north of the Aure River at 5:00 P.M. The river crossing was made without meeting effective resistance, and by midnight the battalion was in defensive positions southeast of Mandeville, on the flank of the important enemy base at Trevieres.

Still further east, a second crossing of the Aure River was effected by the 2nd Battalion of the 18th Infantry. Supported by a platoon of tanks from Company C, 745th Tank Battalion, this battalion left the Colleville area at 10:00 A.M. in two columns and reached the Aure River at 2:40 P.M. No resistance was met until Company G in the western column reached Houetteville, where enemy mortar and machinegun fire from across the river forced deployment. The second column, however, reaching the river south of Bellefontaine, rushed a platoon across the 300 yards of causeway and bridge before meeting enemy fire. Tanks went across to support the platoon, the rest of the company followed, and Company G side-slipped east to take the same route.

Driving the enemy out of their defensive positions, Companies F and G moved in promptly toward Mosles, leaving Company E to clean up by-passed pockets of resistance. Mosles, the objective, was entered at 5:00 P.M. Thirty enemy dead were found after the sharp action at the crossing, which cost the 2nd Battalion only a few men and one tank. A patrol sent down the Bayeux road reported enemy in Tour-en-Bessin.

By nightfall on June 7th, a part of D-Day objectives had been reached. Only in the Formigny-Trevieres area was the enemy in force sufficient to check the First Division's progress.

The situation at Formigny was clearing up during the early morning hours of June 8th. About midnight Company B of the 18th Infantry, helped by tanks of Company B, 745th Tank Battalion, attacked from the southeast and drove out a small enemy force, which lost ten killed and fifteen prisoners. North of the village, enemy machinegun positions continued to block the 3rd Battalion, 26th Infantry, until late in the morning. Initially the delay at Formigny was due to lack of contact between the two battalions attacking from different sides of the village. Coordination was regained by division controls.

On D plus two day main action in the First Division zone shifted to the left flank, where the 26th Infantry went after its D-Day objectives in the Tour-en-Bessin area. The movement had begun late on June 7th, when the 2nd Battalion of the 26th Infantry released at 5:45 P.M. from Division Reserve, was ordered to seize the high ground at the crossroads between Mosles and Tour-en-Bessin. The battalion moved southeast along the front of the 16th Infantry, crossed the Aure River at midnight a little west of Etreham, and reached its objective about 5:30 A.M.

Enemy artillery and infantry were reported in some strength at Tour-en-Bessin, and the 26th Infantry at 8:00 P.M. requested an air mission. Division notified the regiment that adequate fire support from artillery and naval guns would be available if the air mission failed. The air attack was made by fighter-bombers shortly before 9:00 A.M.; an armored patrol got into Tour-en-Bessin by 11:40 A.M., reporting the town: "empty and flat." The 2nd Battalion, reinforced by a company of the 635th Tank Destroyer Battalion, and Company

C of the 745th Tank Battalion, waited on the advance of the rest of the regiment before moving into the town.

The other two battalions of the 26th Infantry were slow in reaching the scene. The 1st Battalion, its objective the ground northeast of Tour-en-Bessin, pushed patrols through Etreham about noon, encountering only snipers; then, determined resistance from prepared positions stopped the battalion at the river crossing. The rest of the day was spent in efforts to get across, with artillery support made difficult by the presence of 2nd Battalion units not far to the southwest. By evening only one company of the 1st Battalion was across the Aure River. The 3rd Battalion was held up north to Formigny all morning, pending arrival of a battalion of the 115th Infantry which was countermarching from Louvieres to Formigny for the purpose of strengthening the sector north of Trevieres. Released to the 26th Infantry at 1:40 P.M., the 3rd Battalion started down the Bayeux highway toward its objective, Ste. Anne, just beyond Tour-en-Bessin. It reached the 2nd Battalion position at 6:00 P.M. and was ordered to jump off at 8:40 P.M. for attack straight through Tour-en-Bessin, supported by Company C of the 745th Tank Battalion. The force went through the town about midnight, the infantry moving in two files on either side of the road, with six tanks between the files at the head of the column. Directed by the battalion commander, the tanks sprayed sniper positions and suspected strongpoints. Light enemy resistance was brushed aside, and the column reached Ste. Anne about 1:30 A.M. in contact with enemy patrols retreating to the east.

The enemy-held corridor north of Tour-en-Bessin was now in great danger of being cut. At the end of June 7th, the Germans still held Port-en-Bessin and south of it the high ground along the Drome Valley.

The narrowing enemy pocket was held by remnants of the 1st Battalion, 726th (German) Infantry, reinforced on June 7-8 by some elements of the 517th Battalion, 30th Mobile Brigade, rushed up from reserve positions near Coutances and St. Lo. By evening of June 8th, there was a chance that much of this force might be trapped by an advance of the 26th Infantry. Very determined enemy resistance, however, held off the 26th Infantry at Etreham and stopped the British efforts to get past from Drome. A violent action at Ste. Anne, in the early hours of June 9th, kept the base of the corridor open.

The 3rd Battalion of the 26th Infantry had dug in hastily at Ste. Anne to meet an expected counterattack, with Company L just north of the village, Company I facing east, and Company K to the south. A light rain began to fall and visibility was bad. About 3:00 A.M. Company L's position was overrun by a strong German column including ammunition trucks, bicycles, and other vehicles, the presence of which suggested that the enemy was withdrawing from the north and had blundered into the American lines. What followed was a wild fire-fight, at close range, with both sides hampered by surprise and confusion. The 2nd Battalion held on in the village; tanks were of little use in the darkness, but effective aid was rendered by area fire from six battalions of artillery and naval guns, directed northeast and east of the village. Casualties in Company L were severe, due mainly to shells hitting two trucks loaded with men temporarily captured by the Germans. By 6:30 A.M. the 3rd Battalion had restored its positions, taking 125 prisoners who testified to the effectiveness of the artillery fire.

Although the enemy had lost heavily in men and vehicles in this action, the corridor stayed open, and Vaucelles, a mile east of Ste. Anne, was retaken from the British in the same period. During the night and early morning, the enemy managed to withdraw most of his force from the salient, at the cost of considerable losses and further disorganization. When the 1st Battalion of the 26th Infantry resumed its attack south of Etreham on the morning of June 9th, only light resistance was met from the remnants of enemy forces north of the highway.

With the 26th Infantry beyond Tour-en-Bessin, the First Division reached its D-Day objectives. This mission had been largely accomplished by two regiments, with all battalions committed and moving on a front so wide that intervals between battalions were as much as 3,000 yards. No enemy counterattack had developed, though it was known from interrupted messages that attack was ordered for June 8th.

Intelligence reports by June 9th warned of possible concentration of reinforcements, including armor, in Cerisy Forest. However, barring arrival of reinforcements, all evidence indicated that the Germans had now lost whatever chance they once had of passing to the offensive on the First Division front. They had continued their policy of the first day in offering dogged resistance at tactically important points, often from prepared positions. In hedgerow country, this had slowed down the First Division's progress, and the delay was increased by the willingness of small enemy groups and individuals to fight on in bypassed positions. Nevertheless, these tactics could not stop the advance, and they steadily wore down enemy strength. Most troops of the bypassed groups never got back; a major proportion were killed, and by June 9th, the First Division had taken over 600 prisoners. Enemy artillery, so effective on D-Day, was less and less in evidence thereafter.

After receiving warning orders, at 5:00 P.M., June 8th, the First Division units had a considerable task of preparation in order to continue the attack at noon next day. They were somewhat short of the assigned line of departure; Moulagny-Courtelay-Grivilly-Cussy. On the afternoon of June 8th, the 2nd Battalion, 18th Infantry, received orders to occupy high ground a mile southwest of Mosles, in what would be the assembly area for the 18th Infantry. The battalion met determined resistance near Moulagny and dug in for the night a little north of its objective. The other battalions of the 18th Infantry had to wait for relief by the Second Division. This took place on the morning of June 9th, delayed by the fact that the 3rd Battalion was engaged in a fire fight at the time of relief; furthermore, both 1st and 3rd Battalions then had to cover some distance to reach their assembly area. As for the 26th Infantry, D-Day objectives were just being reached on the morning of June 9th; the 3rd Battalion had been in a severe action with the enemy at Ste. Anne early that day, while the 1st Battalion was still slowed by enemy resistance north of Tour-en-Bessin during the morning. As a result, the jump-off on the First Division front was delayed one to two hours.

By Field Order No. 36, the First Division planned its renewed attack with two regiments abreast. The 18th Infantry, with Company C, 745th Tank Battalion, Battery A of the 62nd Armored Field Artillery Battalion, and Company B, 635th Tank Destroyer Battalion, attached, and the 32nd Field Artillery Battalion in direct support, was to advance on a front of about 4,000 yards, with Vaubadon and la Commune as objectives, on the Bayeux-St. Lo highway. The 26th Infantry with equivalent attachments and the 33rd Field Artillery Battalion in direct support, was aimed at Dodigny and Agy, on the same highway. Two battalions of the 16th Infantry, with the 7th Field Artillery Battalion in direct support, had the mission of clearing enemy resistance up to the army boundary from Port-en-Bessin to Vaucelles, maintaining contacts with the British on that flank, and organizing defensive positions in the Tour-en-Bessin area. The 2nd Battalion of the 16th Infantry was held in division reserve. Four battalions of artillery (three of them 155-mm. howitzers or guns) were in general support, two of them reinforcing the fires of the 32nd and 33rd Battalions. During the short night (twilight lasted until 11:00 P.M.). The enemy at first offered stubborn resistance from a number of organized positions, but these were widely separated, not held in strength, and given only weak artillery support. Once they were bypassed or overwhelmed, little further opposition was encountered. Enemy weakness was indicated by identification of the replacement battalion of the 915th (German) Regiment, the reserve battalion of the 916th, and the reconnaissance battalion of the 352nd (German) Division, as well as remnants of the 517th Mobile Battalion. Evidently, with no fresh troops at hand, the Germans were throwing in their last resources in a fashion that spelled disorganization.

Along the entire front advance was progressively slower from the left to the right flank. By the end of the afternoon, resistance began to fold in front of the 26th Infantry, attacking with the 2nd Battalion and the 3rd Battalion abreast. By 9:40 P.M. the 3rd Battalion had reached its objective, Agy; the 2nd Battalion got to Dodigny at 1:50 A.M. The 18th Infantry was held up by a strong point near the line of departure; this had to be by-passed and cleaned up by the reserve 2nd Battalion, which took prisoners and counted many enemy dead. By 9:00 P.M. the 1st and 3rd Battalions of the 18th Infantry were two miles behind the 26th Infantry units on their left, and Corps gave permission for the 16th Infantry to move from reserve to a position where it could guard the open flank and help the 18th Infantry if necessary. The 18th Infantry, however, made better progress as night fell, and kept on pressing against diminishing opposition. By daylight it was abreast of the 26th Infantry. Its objectives on the St. Lo-Bayeaux highway were reached at 10:00 A.M. and 4:00 P.M., June 10th. The 3rd Battalion, on the edge of Cerisy Forest, met signs of increased resistance near its objectives.

In an advance of six miles, losses had been slight. Enemy prisoners taken in this sector were open in their praise and particularly stressed the effectiveness of artillery support given the advance; fires had been concentrated on strongpoints, assembly areas, and road movements. The 7th, 32nd, and 33rd Field Artillery Battalions fired 22 missions on June 9th, for a total of 976 rounds. The batteries of the 62nd Armored Field Artillery Battalion (self-propelled 105-mm. howitzers) had been divided between the First Division regiments, to be used for direct fire in close support against enemy strongpoints. As a result of the character of the opposition, however, these batteries were not needed. The three artillery battalions used in general support still found observation a problem and delivered for the most part uncovered fires. Naval fire, using 6-inch guns of the cruisers, was again very helpful, one of the targets being a battery south of the 26th Infantry's objective. According to enemy prisoners, many field pieces of the 352nd (German) Division's artillery had been destroyed and all their gun positions had been abandoned. Enemy artillery action on the Corps front was limited to occasional fire by single guns.

On June 11th the First Division organized the ground won in its rapid advance. By this time the ground essential for security of the beachhead had been won. The advance had carried over twelve miles inland and had conquered the dominating terrain at Cerisy Forest. The principal objective in the next phase was the Caumont area.

A road junction of some importance, Caumont lies on a hill mass more than 750 feet above sea level, forward of the Cerist Forest and controlling the upper Drome Valley. Its capture would make the hold on the beachhead doubly secure; as a base for further offensive operations into the hilly country to the south, possession of Caumont would threaten the enemy's main lateral communications from Caen to the St. Lo-Vire-Avranches region.

By Field Order No. 37, issued at midnight June 11th, General Huebner directed the First Division's attack in essentially the same formation used before; the 18th and 26th Infantry Regimental Combat Teams abreast on fronts of about 3,000 yards, with the 16th Infantry in reserve, ready to assist the attacking regiments and to protect the flanks. The left flank was to be guarded by the 1st Reconnaissance Troop, and two troops of the 102nd Cavalry Squadron were to patrol in advance of the attacking units. Each regimental combat team included a tank battalion; the 18th and 26th Infantry Regiments had each a company of tank destroyers from the 635th Tank Destroyer Battalion. Six battalions of artillery were in direct or general support. Movement toward the line of departure (le Planqueray-la Butte) had begun during the evening of June 11th, but the 26th Infantry experienced road difficulties which caused a two-hour delay in the jump-off, scheduled for 6:00 A.M.

On the right, the 18th Infantry had a comparatively easy advance, led by the 1st and 2nd Battalions abreast. No prepared enemy defenses were encountered, and opposition was offered only by light mobile screening forces, operating in patrols supported by armored cars and an occasional tank. This operation was handled in well-organized fashion, pulling back on what appeared to be a prearranged schedule.

The 745th Tank Battalion, attached to the 18th Infantry, reported a minimum of contact with enemy during the day. By evening, the 18th Infantry had made a four-mile advance to the Caumont-St. Lo highway and was ordered to stop there and patrol, particularly on the right flank. Here, the 18th Infantry was two miles farther south than was Troop B of the 102nd Cavalry Squadron, and established a screen to protect this flank along the Drome River and made contact with the Second Infantry Division.

On the left, the 26th Infantry met much the same type of light relaying resistance, built around reconnaissance cars and a few tanks. By dusk the 2nd Battalion was on the edge of Caumont. Patrols probing into the village, found it held by the enemy. During the night the battalion endeavored to capture the village but was held off by determined resistance estimated at two companies, supported by five or six tanks of self-propelled guns. Company F penetrated into Caumont but was then forced back. With elements of the 743rd Tank Battalion leading, the infantry cleaned out the village by 9:00 A.M., in house-to-house fighting. The enemy lost several vehicles and an 88-mm gun in attempts to stop the tanks. Artillery observers, entering Caumont with the advance, reported that they had excellent observation into enemy positions for the first time since D-Day.

The 18th and 26th Infantry spent June 13th in organizing their positions for all-around defense and in patrolling forward and to the flanks of the salient created by their advance. By afternoon, strong enemy patrols were taking offensive action all along the First Division front, probing to find its positions and in some cases infiltrating well beyond the outposts. Patrol activity was so lively as to give the impression of counterattacks, and supporting artillery was called on much more frequently than during the previous day.

The 33rd Field Artillery Battalion, attached to the 26th Infantry, fired 895 rounds as against 39 on June 12th, most of it about 3:00 P.M. when a "counterattack" was signaled. Enemy artillery showed signs of revival, putting some accurate fire into Caumont. Although no real counterattack developed, it was clear that the enemy was sensitive to the advance into Caumont and that a new quality of resistance was beginning to show. Elements believed to be from the 3rd and 4th Companies of the 2nd Reconnaissance Battalion, 2nd Panzer Division, were identified. In fact, the bulk of that division was moving across the First Division front during the day, from west to east, and was being committed just east of Caumont in an action that was critical for the whole Allied front.

In summary, by June 9th the hard shell of resistance had been broken and the enemy was off balance. The only units resisting the advance were odds and ends of the 352nd Infantry Division, the 726th Regiment, and the 30th Mobile Brigade. Inner organization of these units was lacking, and elements were thrown into the line in platoons and in company strength. Enemy sniping had been active initially, and one sniper, after being killed, had turned out to be a woman in the uniform of a lieutenant colonel of anti-aircraft artillery. The small groups of Germans that became isolated in our rear areas had surrendered after their ammunition was exhausted. The use of enemy armor as a counterattacking force had been expected, but the few tanks that did appear were easily disposed of by infantry weapons.

On June 10th, the Reconnaissance Battalion of the 17th SS "Goetz von Berlichingen" Division had been engaged. The enemy forward position at that time ran from a point 1,000 yards south of Balleroy east to St. Paul de Vernay. The flow of prisoners that had been passing through the division cage was then gradually decreasing. On June 11th, prisoners captured numbered 1,036.

On June 12th, elements of the 3rd Parachute Division, which had moved from the Brest Peninsula, had been identified to the right front.

As a result of the first week's operation it became apparent that use of the 352nd Infantry (German) in the beach area to oppose the landing, had been a mistake. The breakthrough of the hard crust of defense left the enemy with no immediate reserve. He was forced to employ labor battalions, headquarters units, and all available personnel in the area. These forces were found to contain a number of foreign troops — Russians, Poles, Czechs and Belgians. Although the enemy fell back rapidly between June 8 and 13, he was able to hold units on the flanks, specifically the 2nd Division on the right of the First Division and the British forces on the left. On June 12th, after losing Caumont to the First Division, the enemy position threatened both of the Division's flanks.

Facing the First Division on June 14th in a half-circle were elements of the 5th Parachute Regiment, 3rd Parachute Division, the 304th Panzer Grenadier Regiment, and the 38th Panzer Engineer

Battalion of the 2nd Panzer Division. These troops proved to have good fighting qualities and comparatively high morale. The enemy began to dig in, constructing strongpoints, road blocks, wire entanglements, and sowing anti-personnel and anti-tank mines. Enemy artillery shelled Caumont almost continuously, and on June 15th the enemy launched a small counterattack. The 3rd Battalion of the 8th Parachute Battalion of the 8th Parachute Regiment of the 3rd Parachute Division, and the 38th Panzer Engineer Battalion of the 2nd Panzer Division attacked the 1st and 2nd Battalions of the 18th Infantry. First reports of the attack reached division headquarters at 9:00 P.M., but at 6:50 A.M., the next morning the 18th Infantry reported all was quiet again in its sector. The enemy lost heavily in this engagement without regaining any ground.

In anticipation of a continued push by the First Division in the Caumont area, the enemy undertook a partial withdrawal to the south on June 17th, but when it became evident that no further advance was taking place, he returned to his positions on a line about 1,000 meters south of the town. From June 17th on, it became increasingly difficult for patrols to penetrate the enemy lines, and there was evidence that the enemy was bringing up additional artillery.

On June 21st, the 2nd Battalion of the 2nd Panzer Grenadier Regiment, 2nd Panzer Division, moved into the sector west of Sept Vents, replacing the 38th Panzer Engineer Battalion which had suffered heavily in the counterattack of June 15th.

The period of relative inactivity between June 17th and June 30th, during which our air was often grounded by the weather, permitted the enemy to bring up badly needed reserves. These moved to the battle area using secondary roads and traveling by night. By June 26th, the enemy had two battalions of the 3rd Parachute Division and two battalions of the 2nd Panzer Division on the line with a battalion of the 74th Artillery Regiment of the 2nd Panzer Division in support. In reserve, the enemy was believed to have the 38th Panzer Engineer Battalion and elements of the 2nd Panzer Reconnaissance Battalion. The situation remained relatively unchanged on June 30th.

During the last week in June, the first use of psychological warfare was made on the Division front. Leaflets were distributed over the enemy positions by artillery fire pointing out the lack of enemy artillery and air support. Enemy propaganda leaflets found by our troops claimed a shortage of American doctors. The enemy also employed pornographic leaflets which proved more popular. Leaflets distributed over enemy positions by shell-fire, although lacking entertainment value, produced limited results, principally among the foreign elements of the 2nd Panzer and 3rd Parachute Divisions. Some deserters stated that their decision to come over to our lines was partially based on the circulars.

On July 14th, the First Division was relieved by the 5th Division in its position on the Caumont front. After a brief few days to re-equip and make plans the Division moved to the west to participate in the break-out from the Cherbourg Peninsula, the battle which is now incorrectly known as the "St. Lo Break-through."

◆ ◆

NORMANDY

As I Saw It.

By

DON WHITEHEAD

THE first soft layer of dusk had fallen over drab, war-weary London and veiled the patched windows of my Chelsea flat when the telephone rang. It was Ernie Pyle calling.

"Hey, Don," he said. "Come on over. I'm lonesome and want to share my jitters."

I left the flat and took one of London's funny little cabs through Hyde Park to the Dorchester Hotel where I found Ernie in his room finishing a column. He waved to a bottle on the table.

"Real Kentucky bourbon," he grinned. "I never saw the guy before in my life, but he wanted to give me the bottle and I wouldn't argue."

I helped Ernie re-type his column and then we sat and talked of invasion and the chances for success.

Nervous tension was mounting all over England and Ernie wasn't the only one troubled by the jitters. We all knew the invasion of Hitler's European fortress was drawing near but few of us knew the closely guarded secret of when. Nor did I want to know. The responsibility of knowing would have been too great.

The correspondents had been alerted to move out of London quickly, those of us going in with the assault troops. Our field equipment was packed. Now there was nothing to do but wait for the final call. The date was May 28, 1944.

Even then the little guy had a premonition that he would not live through the war. In unguarded moments his face was sad. He didn't like to be alone and he drew his friends around him as though they were a shield against some dark fear that was closing in on him.

I drew the blackout curtains and switched on the light.

"Who are you going with?" Ernie asked.

"I don't know," I said. "I hope it's the First Division. In my books the 1st is the greatest infantry division we've got."

Ernie nodded. "You can't go wrong with the 1st. I guess the 1st still is my favorite but I'm assigned to Bradley's headquarters. We'll be in about D plus 1."

Later we joined a group of correspondents at the Savoy and made a round of London night spots. Behind the blackout curtains there was music, laughter, glitter and a sort of reckless gaiety to ease the tension and the loneliness. Dawn was near when the party broke up.

It seemed I hardly had closed my eyes when the phone rang. I was ordered to report, with field equipment, to an address near Hyde Park. And when I arrived I found Ernie and friends from other campaigns lugging their gear into the office of Lieutenant Colonel Jack Redding, public relations officer. We sensed this call was the real thing and not another cover-up maneuver.

After lunch we were driven from London in jeeps which headed toward the southeast, traveling back roads where there was little traffic. We spent the night in a dreary temporary camp and next morning our little group separated to fan out to the various assault units in their assembly points.

Jack Thompson of the Chicago Tribune—an old friend from the North African, Sicily and Italy campaigns—and I were driven to an old English country house outside Portland. My heart leaped as I recognized our destination—*Danger Forward,* the headquarters of the 1st Infantry Division!

Major Owen B. Murphy of Lexington, Kentucky, said: "I've been throwing another extra sock in my bag each time I heard a rumor we were leaving. Now that you boys have shown up, I guess it's official."

It was good to see Colonel Stan Mason, the Division's chief of staff who had helped direct the 1st from the beaches of North Africa through Tunisia and Sicily. Stan Mason was one of the big reasons why the First Division was a great division.

And there was lanky Lieutenant Colonel Robert Evans, the capable G-2, and Major Paul Gale, big Lieutenant Maxie Zera from the Bronx with a heart as big as his voice, and many others who had made the long trip with the 1st.

We walked into the headquarters and Bob Evans introduced us to Major General Clarence R. Huebner—one of the finest soldiers and gentlemen I've ever known.

The general welcomed us warmly and with a sly humor.

"We're glad to have you with us," he said. "We'll do everything we can to help you get your stories. The people at home must know what we are doing. If you are wounded, we will put you in a hospital. If you are killed, we will bury you. So don't worry!"

I looked closely at this man whose division had been given the tremendous responsibility of leading the invasion assault. I saw a kindly face with a square jaw and direct blue eyes that twinkled with humor. I judged he was in his early fifties. He was physically fit and there was an air of confidence about him that I liked.

I found that Huebner had a great love for his 1st Division. He enlisted as a young man in the 18th Regiment and had come up the hard way through the ranks, distinguishing himself in the First World War. He knew the job of every man in his division as well or better than the men knew the jobs—because he had once held those jobs himself.

The general wanted his division to be the best in the entire Army. It wasn't entirely a matter of personal pride because Huebner knew that the toughest, straightest-shooting division won its objectives with the least loss of life. And if he was stern in his discipline, it was because battle casualties have a direct relation to discipline.

We made ourselves at home with the 1st, waiting for the call to go aboard ship. In the marshalling area, the equipment was being loaded and the troops were boarding the transports, LST's, LCI's and other invasion craft which jammed the harbor. Everywhere there was great activity.

Three of the busiest men in the marshalling area were Colonel George Taylor, commanding the 16th Regimental Combat Team; tall, quiet-spoken Brigadier General Willard G. Wyman, assistant divisional commander, and leathery Brigadier General Clift Andrus, division artillery officer (who later was to become the commanding general of the Fighting 1st).

I knew Taylor and Andrus well and seeing them reminded me of the Sicily invasion. Taylor's regiment had run into trouble when the Germans attacked the one-day-old beachhead with tanks. The 16th had fought tanks literally with everything but their bare fists and when it looked as though the tanks would smash the beachhead—Andrus' artillery turned the tide.

Clift Andrus was recognized as one of the finest artillerymen in World War II. And there on the beaches of Sicily he proved it. With only a few guns ashore, he got them into action almost at the water's edge and broke the counterattack. He had his artillerymen blasting at the tanks at close range over open sights in what was undoubtedly one of the great artillery battles of the war.

It was little wonder, traveling with men like these, that I felt secure when we went aboard the Coast Guard transport, Samuel Chase, on June 4. The Chase was the headquarters ship for Taylor's 16th Regimental Combat Team.

For 24 hours a storm swept the channel and kept the great invasion armada at anchor. But next day General Eisenhower made his decision and the fleet steamed under cover of darkness toward the beaches of Normandy.

There was a strange lack of excitement among the men aboard the Chase. In fact they seemed relieved the long wait was over, and that within the next few hours or days a decision would be reached in battle. Reality is so much easier to face than the subtle fear of the unknown and the waiting . . . waiting . . . waiting . . .

In the ship's hold, company commanders, platoon and section leaders studied a giant sponge rubber map of the Normandy coast. Every house, out-building, ridge, tree and hedgerow was faithfully reproduced on the model designed from photographs of the beaches where the 16th was to land. The men were memorizing every detail of the landscape which would help them in battle, figuring how best to reach their objectives while giving their men as much protection as possible from enemy fire.

They knew all that photographs and military intelligence could tell them about the terrain and the enemy defenses. But what they could not know was that, while they studied their maps and models, the enemy was moving a full division of infantry into the positions they were to attack!

This was a cruel, blind stroke of luck, this sudden shifting of the 352nd Division to the beach where the 1st was to land in the center of the Allied invasion drive. It placed the burden squarely on the Fighting 1st and no other assault force was to meet such a test of courage and stamina on the beaches of Normandy.

Up in the wardroom of the Chase, there was little to remind one of the tremendous drama being enacted. A poker game was in progress. A few watched the shifting luck of the cards. Others wrote letters or read books. If anyone mentioned what was ahead, it was with a wisecrack to mask his feelings.

Luck was running against a young captain in the poker game.

"Jim," he said, "give me another fifty pounds."

Jim shoved a wad of bank notes across the table.

"I'll pay you back . . ."

"Forget it! It's nothing but money!"

Later that night, Jack Thompson and I went to the cabin of Colonel Taylor and he unfolded the plan of invasion for us. Not until we were underway did we know our destination and how the Allies planned to smash into Europe.

The 16th Regimental Combat Team—supported by the 116th Regiment of the 29th Infantry Division—was spearheading the center of the invasion on the beach with the code name of "Omaha." The British was on our left and the American 4th Infantry Division was on our right.

Our initial assault force — known as "Force O" — numbered 34,000 men and 3300 vehicles. This was the spearhead, a reinforced unit stronger than two ordinary divisions, packing a terrific wallop. In addition to his own veteran 16th and 18th Regimental Combat Teams, Huebner was commanding the 116th Regimental Combat Team and the 115th Infantry, attached, from the 29th Division, a provisional Ranger force of two battalions, and attached units of artillery, armor, engineers and service units.

Following behind us was the 29th Division built up to a strength of 25,000 men and 4400 vehicles. And the assault forces had to be clear of the beach in the afternoon or else the follow-up waves would pour in on them.

As the Colonel explained the plan, I stared at the contour lines of the maps and saw the section of the beach where our assault boat would land north of the little town of Colleville-sur-mer was called "Easy Red." I wondered how easy it would be and how red the sands before another sundown. I wondered how many thousands of those battle-tough, homesick youths bobbing around us in assault craft would get beyond the beach known as Easy Red.

I remembered the interview in London with General Omar Nelson Bradley a few days before we left to join the invasion troops. The tall, grave Missourian was sure Fortress Europe could be invaded without the terrifying loss of life predicted by the gloom mongers.

"The invasion will be in 3 phases," he said. "The first phase will be to get a toe hold on Europe. And that will be the most critical of all. Then will come the second phase, the build-up. We must pour men and guns and supplies ashore as rapidly as possible. The final phase will be to break out of our beachhead and destroy the enemy's armies. . . ."

And I recalled sitting in a big drafty schoolroom in London and listening to Montgomery. He stood on a platform slim and straight with his hands behind his back, talking in his clipped, precise way like a headmaster lecturing a group of students.

"Rommel is a disrupter. Yes, he is a disrupter. He will commit himself on the beaches. He will try to knock us back into the sea. . . ."

Then Colonel Taylor's voice broke into my thoughts. "The first six hours will be the toughest," he said. "That is the period during which we will be the weakest. But we've got to open the door. Somebody has to lead the way—and if we fail . . . well . . . then the troops behind us will do the job. They'll just keep throwing stuff onto the beaches until something breaks. That is the plan."

Suddenly and for the first time, I began to realize the magnitude of invasion and its relentless force. Tomorrow we would hit the beaches and behind us would come wave after endless wave of troops, guns, tanks, and supplies to beat against the coast of Normandy in a mounting tide. It was as though man for centuries had lived, begotten offspring and labored toward this moment which would shape the world's history for all time to come.

General Bradley had chosen the veterans of the Red One to lead the way. He knew they had been tempered for the task on the sands of Africa and in the gray dust of Sicily. He knew they would not fail him.

This was the greatest tribute the commanding general of the American First Army could have paid to a combat division—placing it in the spearhead of invasion. For if the First Division failed then the center of the invasion front might well collapse and drag down the entire invasion in bloody chaos. It had to succeed, no matter how bitter the cost!

The ship came to life before dawn. Bells rang, chains clanked, booted feet clumped on steel decks and the ship's loudspeakers blared orders.

This was the day!

I struggled into my stiff, impregnated clothes which were a shield against gas attack, checked my gear and went up on deck as dawn began to wash away the darkness in the east.

We heard the roar of bombers overhead and saw the flash of explosions where the bombs burst on shore. Our air force was giving the enemy gun positions a pasting before the troops hit the beach.

And then my stomach tightened. The voice over the loudspeaker called the number of our boat. Silently our little group climbed over the ship's rail in the darkness and into an assault boat. The gray side of the Chase loomed above us and the boat was pitching in the rough channel. A cold wind whipped salt spray against our cheeks like pellets of ice. The water soaked our clothing and ran into our boots in icy rivulets.

All around us the LCVP's churned through the waves with their cargoes of seasick, miserable troops, disgorged from the ships spread as far as one could see in the misty graw dawn of 6 June. Amphibious ducks and tanks wallowed through the waves like strange monsters of the deep.

The tanks were one of the "secret weapons" for invasion to give the assault troops added firepower. They were buoyed up by huge inflated canvas doughnuts which encircled them. They were to go in shooting. But the storm which had swept the channel had made it a death trap. The tank crews drove toward the beach but few reached shore. Most of the tanks were swamped in the 6-foot waves and carried their crews to the bottom of the channel before the men had a chance to fight.

We circled near the Chase for a few minutes and then headed for the beach. The senior officer in our boat was tall, lean Brigadier General Wyman who had been with Stilwell in Burma. Wyman was to go ashore as quickly as possible, direct operations at close range, and organize Danger Forward, the advance command post, so that General Huebner could transfer his headquarters from ship to shore. Until the command post was organized, the nerve center of the First Division would remain aboard a ship in the channel.

The pitching of the boat made me sick. My teeth chattered from cold and, I suspect, a liberal dash of fright. My stomach heaved with every lurch of the boat and I knew there were thousands like me.

Major Paul Gale, who had been my companion on another landing in Sicily, grinned at me from under his helmet. I think Paul enjoyed the excitement and the sense of impending danger, but his wisecracks designed to cheer me couldn't stop the heaving of my stomach.

Soon we could see the beach—Easy Red Beach—a hellish inferno of battle. Shells exploded in the surf and sent up small geysers while bullets whipped up ugly little spouts of water. The thunder of our naval gunfire and the explosion of shells rolled over us now. Above the crashing shells and the sharp slap of the waves against our boat was the murderous hissing of flying shells.

General Wyman ordered our boat to pull alongside a patrol craft from where he could get a radio report of the initial landings and learn how things were going. A few minutes later he returned to the boat.

The situation ashore was bad. Everything was confused and behind schedule. Casualties were heavy. The engineers had not been able to clear all the gaps planned through the beach defenses. The invasion was stalled and somebody had to get in and help bring order out of the confusion.

"We're going in," the General said.

We left the patrol craft and moved in with the assault waves. Our coxswain found a gap through the barriers of barbed wire, logs, steel spokes and mines. The smoke of battle boiled around us, and we crouched in the boat and peered over the side at the carnage and destruction. Somehow we raced through the gap in the barriers on the crest of a wave. The LCVP grounded and we ran down the ramp and waded through the surf to throw ourselves on the beach with thousands of others hugging that precious little strip of sand and gravel.

From the water's edge the beach shelved upward for about 30 feet. Beyond this was a flat, open stretch rising gradually to a bluff less than 300 yards away. The sloping gravel shelf gave some protection from the machinegun and rifle fire pouring from the German positions on the bluff. But there was no protection from the mortars and shells which screamed in from nowhere. The beach was a shooting gallery and the men who came out of the sea were the targets.

Many officers were killed before they could reach shore. They died as shells smashed into their boats or as they waded toward the beach or as they stood on the few feet of French soil which they had helped to win. Boats landed far from their targets. Units were scrambled and left without leaders and without direction.

And so the men dug in on that narrow strip of beach washed by waves and blood. They piled up by the thousands, shoulder to shoulder. Machineguns were set up a few feet from the water. Tanks that reached shore leveled their guns on the bluff to answer the enemy's accurate fire. Mortar crews manned their weapons with the waves washing their boots. But nothing was moving off the beach. The invasion on Omaha Beach was a dead standstill! The battle was being fought at the water's edge!

I lay on the beach wanting to burrow into the gravel. And I thought: "This time we have failed! God, we have failed! Nothing has moved from this beach and soon, over that bluff, will come the Germans. They'll come swarming down on us . . ."

But as the minutes ticked by, no gray figures came off the bluffs. Our Navy was pouring a murderous fire into the enemy positions. From the beach too, disorganized as it was, there was a steady stream of small arms and machinegun fire. There was the heavy whack of the tank guns, too, and the thumping of mortars lobbing shells onto the bluff.

"We've got to get these men off the beach," Wyman said. "This is murder!"

Wyman studied the situation for a few minutes—and then with absolute disregard for his own life and safety, he stood up to expose himself to the enemy's fire. Calmly, he began moving lost units to their proper positions, organizing leadership for leaderless troops. He began to bring order out of confusion and to give direction to this vast collection of inert manpower waiting only to be told what to do, where to go.

Paul Gale was a lanky, dependable right arm to the General and slight Lieutenant Robert J. Riekse of Battle Creek, Michigan, was his aide and messenger through a steady rain of shells and bullets. Riekse went down with a severe hip wound before the day ended, but until he did, he was a stout helper.

Up and down that bloody strip of beach we went from group to group, from soldier to soldier. Under Wyman's direction, messengers began moving between unit commanders. They stepped over the dead and wounded, flung themselves flat as shells whistled in to splatter them with mud and gravel, and then jumped up to carry out their orders. And gradually the fog of battle began to lift a little.

On another section of our beach, Colonel Taylor was engaged in the same heroic task of organizing the troops pinned to the beach by enemy fire. With equal disregard for his own life, he moved along the water's edge organizing the men of his beloved 16th. There was no place to go but forward, and Taylor knew the sooner his men began moving the fewer casualties there would be.

There were many heroes on Omaha Beach that bloody day, but none of greater stature than Wyman and Taylor. They formed the core of the steadying influence that slowly began to weld the 1st Division's broken spearhead into a fighting force under the muzzles of enemy guns. It's one thing to organize an attack while safely behind the lines—and quite another to do the same job under the direct fire of the enemy.

I tried to keep pace with the General and with Major Gale and Lieutenant Riekse as they moved along the beach, but at times it was impossible because of utter exhaustion. There were times when I had to lie on the gravel beside the dead and wounded until strength came back to my legs. It was difficult to see how those men kept going as they did without rest.

I remember a wounded boy moaning in delirium: "Oh, merciful God! Please stop the hurt! Get me out of here! Get me out of here!"

Poor kid! It would be hours before anyone could listen to his plea and get him into a boat. Beside us men dug shallow trenches in the gravel with their bare hands. Blood ran from their raw fingertips. Bodies of the dead floated in the water and moved gently with each incoming wave, relaxed and peaceful; or stretched on the gravel in grotesque attitudes of frozen stillness. They had made their landing on another beachhead.

The wounded lay with eyes glazed by shock and pain and sometimes I helped them to crawl from the cold water which made them shake with chills. The medics worked over them staunching the flow of blood from wounds, easing pain with hypodermics, giving encouragement. The medics had no thought for themselves, or if they did gave no visible indication of it.

An LCVP ran onto a sand bar and the ramp lowered . . . a shell screamed into the craft and bodies hurtled into the water . . . men wading ashore with heavy equipment sank into the water without sound . . . jeeps ran down the ramps of boats and disappeared with their drivers . . . a youth came riding ashore on the rear of a half track . . . suddenly he gave a startled gasp and slowly toppled into the water, a round black hole between his open eyes . . . Medic Peter Kuffner of New York City darted into the water and dragged him ashore, but his battle was ended.

Time had no meaning. Minutes dragged like hours. All sequence to events was lost. Those hours on Easy Red Beach were one long, endless nightmare recorded in memory in sharp unrelated scenes.

In one of them while the shells were flying thickest and bullets buzzed like hornets, Private Vincent Dove of Washington, D. C., calmly climbed into the seat of a bulldozer and began dozing a roadway off the beach—the first road over which tanks and trucks and guns could move. He sat up there on his 'dozer with only a sweat-soaked shirt to protect him from a slug of steel. He had driven a bulldozer for 15 years before he entered the army. He wasn't going to let the Germans stop him now! And by some miracle he lived through the fire pouring from the bluff, his bulldozer snorting defiance.

Vincent Dove must have given courage to hundreds of men who saw him atop his bulldozer doing the job he was sent to do.

I joined Gale on one of his missions. As we walked crouching near the water he suddenly yelled: "Down!" I flopped to the ground.

A shell exploded showering us with mud and gravel. Gale came running over. "Are you hurt?" he said.

I spat out a mouthful of mud. "No. I didn't even hear it coming. Thanks."

"I didn't either," he laughed. "I just felt it."

I felt better, then. If anyone could laugh at a time like this, everything would be all right. Death was a constant companion on Easy Red Beach. I found that if you walked hand in hand with death long enough, then there was no fear. Fear was replaced with a sort of fatalism. You were either going to get it or you weren't.

A runner, Lieutenant John P. Foley of Trenton, N. J., came to the General's command post to report our troops had broken through the enemy defenses and were moving off the beach! The youth was worn with fatigue and he had been nicked by a bullet over one eye as he made his way through enemy fire. He brought the news we had been waiting to hear. News that the tide of battle finally had turned in favor of the Fighting First.

"You've done a fine job, Lieutenant," Wyman said. "You've shown great initiative." He gave Foley an affectionate pat on the shoulder.

Wyman and Taylor organized groups to wipe out troublesome strongpoints and diverted units from their original missions to support hard-pressed units. The attack of the 16th began to have cohesion and drive.

Slim, sardonic Captain Joe Dawson from Texas led his company —what was left of it—out across the mined flats and up the bluff held by the Germans. The mighty tide that seemed so puny and futile in the early hours of invasion hammered its way forward.

One of the strongpoints holding up the First Division advance was a blockhouse at the edge of a roadway leading from the beach to the high ground beyond. It controlled the exit marked on the maps as E-1. An 88 poking its snout from an embrasure in the thick concrete poured deadly fire onto the beach.

A destroyer moved to within 500 yards of the beach in a daring maneuver and began firing at the blockhouse. One shell exploded squarely in the gun opening and knocked out the position. The roadway from the beach was open!

We didn't know it then, but the Fighting First had whipped an entire enemy division in the battle on the beach! The Red One had whipped a strong enemy entrenched in prepared positions, and it had driven him back!

Rommel's beach defenders never recovered from this blow. His main defense force was shattered. He had no reserves near with which to counterattack before the follow-up forces poured ashore to support the assault drive.

German batteries on our right flank continued to hammer the beach but the small arms and mortar fire began to fade at midday and Wyman and his little party made their way across the flats to the blockhouse knocked out by the destroyer's fire. And the blockhouse became Danger Forward—the First Division's first command post on the soil of France.

This blockhouse today is a memorial to those who gave their lives on Omaha Beach. It is beautifully landscaped and neatly trimmed grass and shrubbery cover the scars of D-Day. It will be a shrine for always for the mothers and fathers of those who gave their lives on Omaha Beach.

When we entered the blockhouse it still reeked with cordite fumes and the thick concrete walls echoed the explosions on the beach. But it was a sanctuary and to us it represented the solid inescapable fact that the First had a toehold on Hitler's Europe.

Danger Forward quickly became the nerve center of the battle. General Huebner and his staff came ashore to direct the operations at close range. They brought with them a sense of security and the knowledge that the First was once more a united force.

As the battle moved across the bluff, Huebner moved his command post with it. It was difficult to tell whether Danger Forward was in or behind the front line. All night rifles and burp-guns crackled around headquarters. Guns blazed as small groups of Germans attempted to fight their way from behind the American lines. Snipers were flushed from within a few yards of the command post and no one knew from what direction a bullet might come.

Through the tangled, matted Normandy hedgerows the men of the First fought their way forward. They captured Colleville, cut the main coast road, repulsed enemy counterattacks, and drove on to capture the strategic town of Caumont, sitting on a hill which dominated the left flank of the entire American beachhead.

Once the First had a toehold on the soil of France, there never was any doubt of the Red One reaching an objective. General Huebner's command post had an almost professional atmosphere of calm assurance. The First Division from top to bottom believed it was the best infantry division in the United States Army—and conducted itself accordingly. Even the headquarters company was willing and ready at all times to pitch into a scrap—and more than once the cooks and clerks and headquarters troops picked up their guns and helped turn the tide in the First Division campaigns.

But in all its battles in Africa, Sicily, France, Belgium and Germany, there never was one quite like the battle of Omaha Beach. In that battle alone the Fighting First won a niche among the immortals of American history. Huebner's men smashed the main strength of the Germans and by so doing turned the key that unlocked the door to victory in Europe. Behind them came the floodtide that overwhelmed the Nazis in the west.

General Eisenhower was keenly conscious of the tremendous role played by the First Division in helping him win the first round of the battle for Europe and of the magnificent fight of the 16th Regiment in spearheading the invasion on Omaha Beach.

One day early in July he visited Danger Forward accompanied by General Bradley. He pinned awards for heroism on the chests of 25 First Division heroes that day, and this is the story I wrote:

1st Division Command Post, France, July 2—(AP)—Heroes of the Fighting First Division who led the American assault on France and lived to cross that hellish strip of beach where so many courageous men died stood in the shade of tall Normandy elms today and received their accolade from General Eisenhower.

For the occasion they had tried to clean the stains of battle from their clothing, but still their uniforms showed they were just back from the front lines.

No one cared about spit and polish with these men—least of all General Ike, who pinned Distinguished Service Crosses on the chests of 22 and gave Legion of Merit awards to two others.

These elite infantrymen had come through a test as great as any soldiers ever faced, and by their courage and leadership had opened the way for thousands of troops to follow.

They stood to attention on the lawn of an old gray chateau when jeeps carrying Generals Eisenhower, Bradley and Gerow halted before their ranks. General Ike jumped out of his jeep smiling. He wore a garrison cap, an air-force jacket belted at the waist, and his trousers were stuffed into paratroop boots.

He shook hands with Major General Clarence R. Huebner and then an officer began reading the names of the men receiving awards—

"Brigadier General Willard Wyman . . ."

On the thunderous morning of D-Day, this tall, square-jawed man moved up and down the beach with an absolute disregard for his own safety, getting troops organized and moving them inland to knock out enemy strongpoints.

Quietly he issued commands sending the doughboys against enemy strongpoints which were pouring murderous fire into our ranks, helpless on a shelf of gravel at the water's edge.

"Colonel George Taylor . . ."

This blue-eyed soldier had stood on the beach where thousands of his men were pinned down by enemy fire, and in a quiet drawl said, "Gentlemen, we're being killed here on the beach; let's move inland and be killed." And his men surged forward to break the German defenses and clear an exit from the beach which was a death-trap.

"Lieutenant Colonel Herbert Hicks of Spartanburg, S. C. . . ."

Troops under his command spearheaded the assault on Hitler's West Wall where a reinforced enemy division was waiting to meet them on the beaches behind concrete and steel fortifications. His gallantry and that of his men contributed greatly to the success of that bloody day.

"Major Charles E. Tetgmeyer, Hamilton, N. Y. . . ."

Under heavy fire, Tetgmeyer covered the length of the beach administering aid to the wounded. Time and again he went into the mine-strewn water and pulled wounded men behind the comparative safety of a shale barrier.

"Captain Joseph Dawson of Waco, Texas . . ."

Here was the man whose unit was the first to come off the beach and the citation said he was receiving the award for "extraordinary heroism." Deliberately he walked off the beach and moved across the minefields alone to draw enemy fire and give his men a chance to move in behind him.

"Captain Kimball R. Richmond of Windsor, Vermont . . ."

His assault boat grounded 400 yards from the beach, so Richmond and his men swam through a hail of artillery and machinegun fire. On the beach he organized his company and led it into the attack.

"Captain Thomas M. Marendino, Ventnor, N. J. . . ."

He led his men ashore and then, refusing to take cover from enemy fire, led a charge up a slope and overran a German strongpoint.

"Lieutenant Carl W. Giles, Gest, Kentucky . . ."

His landing craft was sunk by enemy fire, but he swam ashore. He saw 3 men hit by enemy bullets fall into the water. He went back and pulled them to safety. Most officers of his unit were casualties and he assumed command and carried out the mission.

And on down the list to Pfc. Peter Cavaliere, Bristol, R. I., who stood before the four-star general with a carbine slung across his shoulder. Cavaliere went forward to set up an observation post and, surrounded by Germans, shot 8 himself and clung to the post helping to fight off enemy attacks in the critical hours of invasion.

Others on whom Eisenhower pinned DSC's were: Captain Victor R. Briggs of New York City; Lieutenant John N. Spaulding, Owensboro, Kentucky; 1st Sergeant Lawrence J. Fitzsimmons, New York; Staff Sergeant Curtis Colwell, Vicco, Kentucky; Staff Sergeant Philip C. Clark, Alliance, Ohio; Staff Sergeant David N. Radford, Danville, Virginia; Tech Sergeant Raymond F. Strojny, Taunton, Massachusetts; Staff Sergeant James A. Wells, St. Mary, West Virginia; Staff Sergeant Kenneth F. Peterson, Passaic, New Jersey; Tech Sergeant Phillip Streczyk, New York City; Sergeant Richard J. Gallagher, New York City; T/4 Stanley P. Appleby, Clarksville, New York, and Sergeant John Griffin, Troup, Texas.

The Legion of Merit was awarded Colonel William E. Waters of Louisville, Kentucky, and Master Sergeant Chester A. Demich of Burlington, Vermont.

As Eisenhower moved down the double rank, he spoke a few words to each man, asking him his job and where he came from in the States. And after pinning the medals on their worn combat jackets he called the men together in an informal group.

"I am not going to make a speech," he said. "But this simple little ceremony gives me an opportunity to come over here and, through you, say 'thanks.'

"You are one of the finest regiments in our Army. I shall always consider the 16th my Praetorian Guard. I would not have started the invasion without you. . . ."

The First Division tipped the scales of invasion and lived up to the lyrics of their famed battle song: "The Fighting First will lead the way from hell to victory. . . ."

CHAPTER V

The Situation

ST. LO AND MORTAIN

26 July to 24 August, 1944

FIRST U. S. Army Field Order No. 3 of 1 August 1944 directed all units except V Corps to advance generally in a southeasterly direction; V Corps was to advance on Vire, seize the ground overlooking it from the north, and then hold its objective until pinched out by the advance of the Second British Army. The following day the VII Corps had advanced the 3rd Armored Division and the First Infantry Division on its right against light resistance to clear the Brecey bridgehead to a depth of between 4,000 and 8,000 yards. The next day VII Corps armored task forces had swept southeast and occupied Mortain.

On 4 August, the VII Corps, with the First, 4th, and 9th Infantry Divisions and the 3rd Armored Division continued to change its direction of advance to threaten the enemy left rear and tend to cut him away from Paris.

On 7 August, the enemy struck in strength at Mortain, occupied by the 30th Infantry Division. To the south the First Division crossed the Mayenne River and registered substantial progress to St. Fraimbault de Prieres.

The enemy attacks in the Mortain area had been made with more force than any previous effort in order to cut through our narrow bottle-neck between Mortain and the sea. Although repulsed with considerable loss to him in tanks and vehicles, there was every evidence that the enemy was concentrating additional armor east of Mortain and north through Sourdeval for a renewal of the attempt. Strong forces of fighter-bombers were directed against these concentrations, and a second attack did not materialize.

Between 10 August and 19 August, V Corps and VII Corps operated to tighten the lines around the hostile forces. The closing and final elimination of the Argentan-Falaise pocket on 19 August saw the virtual destruction of the Seventh German Army. The principal escapees were the remnants of the SS Panzer Divisions, for whom the infantry troops battled to keep the gap open. The carnage wrought during the final days as the artillery of two Allied Armies and the massed air forces pounded the ever-shrinking pocket, was perhaps the greatest of World War II. The roads and fields were littered with thousands of the enemy dead and wounded, wrecked and burning vehicles, smashed artillery pieces, carts laden with the loot of France overturned, and smoldering dead horses and cattle swelling in the summer's heat.

The last week of August 1944 carried the First Infantry Division across Northern France. Only scattered resistance was made by the enemy, proof of the destruction and defeat suffered by the Great German Army of the West.

The liberation continued in September from Soissons across the Aisne River and included Laon, in France, and Maubege, Bavai, Charleroi, Namur, Liege and Herve, in Belgium.

Again the First Infantry Division returned to the never-to-be-forgotten shell-pitted, grass-coated field of World War I—Soissons. Those of the First Division who had given their all in that long-forgotten-sometimes-remembered war of long ago, reached their ghostly hands for rusted rifles—then remembered, and in ghostly assemblage—stood at "attention" as they watched the old outfit carry on.

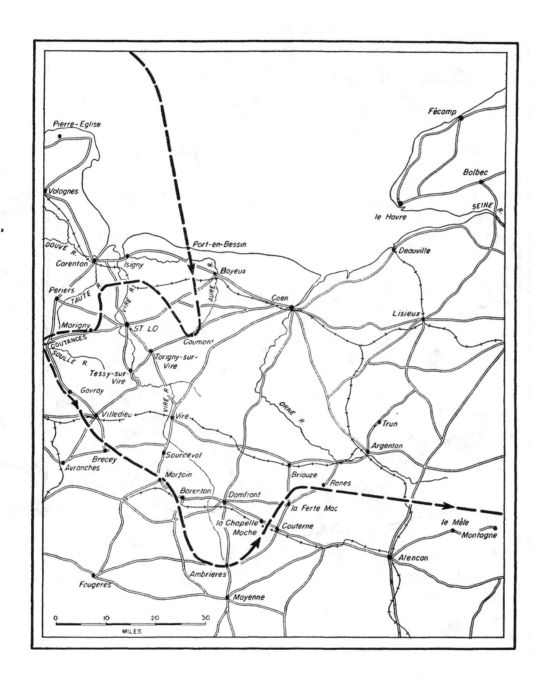

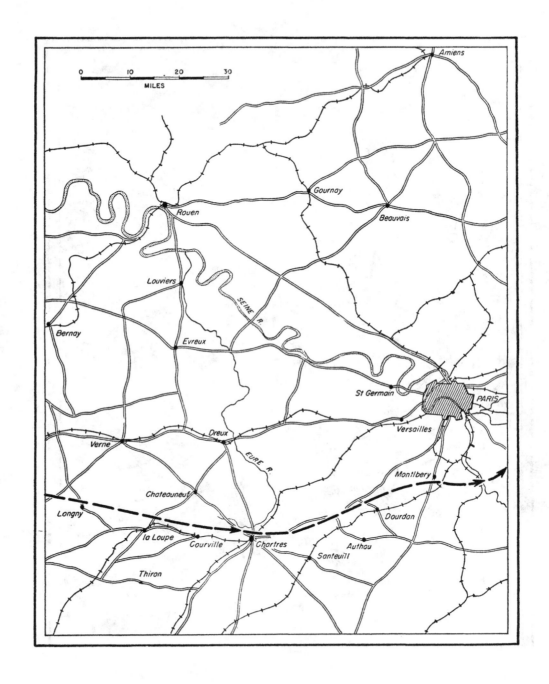

The Record

ST. LO AND MORTAIN
July 26 to August 24, 1944

TO HAVE a proper understanding of the operation of the First Division in its drive out of the Normandy beachhead and its rapid advance across France, it is necessary to review briefly the general situation, so often referred to in lower echelons as "the big picture." The important role played by the First Division in the action is enhanced and made more dramatic by a thorough understanding if the grand tactics impelling it onward as it drove far out into open territory where its accomplishments and its continued existence depended so largely on its own spirit and integrity.

The Normandy beachhead being secure, and with sufficient build-up being coiled within the beachhead, the man with the Red One on his shoulder, sweating it out in a foxhole, was beginning to think the war was going to be fought, perhaps for months, among the few particular hedgerows which he could see. Just incidentally, he knew that other outfits had battered their way into Cherbourg. The "Stars and Stripes" was publishing the glories of new divisions and even his own "Traveller" was mentioning these exploits. This did not particularly please Joe—*he* was supposed to be in the elite outfit. *His* First Division was supposed to be chasing the "Sal Boche" out of this newly-acquired fraternization territory, not these new outfits which were hogging his headlines. Of more serious concern to him at the moment was the fact that Jerry's positions in front of him had tightened considerably. There were no holes in the line, no fleeting expectation that the next day would see Jerry gone from his front. Joe had learned the hard way that a little relaxation of his offensive defense, his patrol control of "no man's land" meant additional punishment from German mortars and artillery.

The temporary stalemate of affairs was broken on 14 July when the First Division was relieved in the Caumont area by the 5th Division. CT 26 willingly turned over its hot corner to the 11th Infantry and started back to the division assembly area. CT 16 was relieved by the 2nd Infantry. Remaining Division units likewise turned over their French real estate to 5th Division elements. By moving back through the beachhead area in a swinging arc to the west, the First Division smoothly closed in its assigned bivouac area in and around the tiny little Norman village of Colombieres where units were to rest, recuperate and refit. Experienced men of the First Division placed little faith in the word "rest." They had learned from previous experiences that in warfare there is no rest. They knew that refitting was of the utmost importance and they also knew that the high command had a new plan cooking, one in which the First Division would again spearhead the attack. For hadn't Teddy Roosevelt told them many times that they were assault troops, known the world over as assault troops and hadn't General Huebner told them many times that the First Division would never sit on the sidelines when the high command had a big job to be done, a job requiring dash and competence, coordination, a job which must not fall behind schedule?

The man with the Red One on his shoulder was right. First Army now had its "Sunday punch" ready to throw. Operation "Cobra" was being put into effect. In general, this plan called for a breakthrough of German cordon defense surrounding the beachhead and an encirclement of that portion of the German forces caught in the area west of the breakthrough. Upon completion of this encirclement, a larger encirclement was to move eastward, again joining hands with the British thereby drawing the strings of the net tight around those German forces holding the defensive sector east of the breakthrough. Third Army under General Patton was to drive through the breach in the German lines, swing eastward through open country and encircle any escapees from the First Army's encirclement.

As soon as plan "Cobra" was given to the Division, the CG and his staff went feverishly to work. Maps of the new area showed town names that had previously been of concern only to G-2's. Roads into enemy-held territory took on an increasing importance. Hostile units deep behind their own lines were also up for operational consideration. Artillery fires had to be coordinated. Communications had to be planned for a very mobile situation. Rations, gasoline, ammunition must be ready and new problems were being encountered by our CIC as it planned to rapidly take over a community and as rapidly drop it to its own devices.

In its move from Caumont to the vicinity of Colombieres, the Division had operationally transferred from V to VII Corps. General Gerow had been most complimentary of the combat efficiency of the Division and had expressed regret in having to surrender it to General J. Lawton Collins of VII Corps. But to the man with the Red One on his shoulder that was nothing but normal for hadn't all other Corps commanders regretted losing this First Division? And hadn't Corps and Army commanders always wanted the First Division under their command?

The First Division was told to coil itself tightly behind the 9th, 4th and 30th Infantry Divisions, in that order, from west to east. The principal mission of the 30th Infantry was to secure the crossing of the Vire River, as far south as Tessy-sur-Vire, and to protect the left flank of the initial penetration. The 4th Division was given a narrow frontage in the center of the penetration and an initial objective at the south end of the penetration. These divisions were given specific instructions to clear all routes within their zones of action immediately upon seizing their initial objectives, in order to permit the First Division with 3rd Armored Division attachments and the 2nd and 3rd Divisions to swing General Hodges' "Sunday punch."

Just a word anent the support of the U. S. Air Forces. Their work had been nothing short of miraculous. The air over Northern France belonged to the U. S. Air Forces. Fighter bombers ranged the roads in rear of the German positions and allowed no daylight movement whatsoever. Bridges were bombed out, railroads made inoperative and the battle field isolated from its source of supply and replacement. Tactical mobility was a hazy memory in the mind of the German high command. Fleets of bombers moved deep into German territory. P-51s and P-47s roamed the skies raining death and destruction on anything that moved in Jerry's rear areas. Planes were available in ever increasing numbers, the weather promised to be fair, and an Air Corps strike of unprecedented magnitude was planned as the initial move in Operation "Cobra."

On July 19th, the First Division moved into assembly area and coiled just in back of the 9th Division. There it remained until the 25th of July. The weather had perversely become disadvantageous for the air strike so D-Day for Operation "Cobra" had been postponed until clearing skies permitted the execution of the planned saturation bombing mission. July 25th dawned clear and auspicious. Operational priority messages announcing this as D-Day received preferential handling as they sped over the communication systems to all echelons of command. H-Hour was set for 1100-B, and as this hour approached, the steady drone of planes overhead presaged the big event to come. Fighter bombers, 350 of them, streaked across and hit the narrow target strip along the Periers-St. Lo road. As they cleared the target area, the sky was filled with approximately 1500 heavy bombers. The roar of the motors alone was awe-inspiring. As they came over the target and bombs began to fall, the ground throughout the Division area trembled from the shock and concussion. Medium bombers took over and continued the destruction. Fighter bombers again came in and thickened the fires of the ground artillery which was pounding this same breakthrough area some 2500 yards deep and 6000 yards wide just in front of the 9th, 4th and 30th Divisions. At H-Hour, the "doughs" moved forward.

The heavy bombing mission, while morale breaking to the Germans, caused destruction surpassing the imagination. Anticipating the possible destruction of roads, planes carried bombs of 100 pounds and less, fragmentation, instantaneous fuze. Even so, roads were somewhat damaged. Large numbers of cattle caught in the area were killed. Enemy troops were either dead or shocked to the point of stupefaction. But true to Jerry's character, no shelling or no bombing ever succeeded in getting those few hearty souls with the Burp guns. Before the roar of the last planes subsided in the distance, that "B-r-r-r-r-r-r-p" could be heard in spots along what had previously been the German defensive position. How they managed this, no one will ever know but it seemed to be significant of the iron will and fanatical combative spirit of certain members of SS units. It served to caution the advancing "doughs" that death still lurked to their front and it must have served to strengthen the morale of any German soldiers within hearing. Futile and foolish resistance, yet by its sheer audacity it called forth a soldier's admiration for a brave man.

Liaison had been established between the 9th Division which was to make the initial hole in the defensive line and First Division which was to carry the ball on through. This liaison was close— about as close as one could hope to achieve. The two divisions had their command posts within a few hundred yards of each other and the First Division commander was actually in the CP of the 9th Division Commander where he could more effectively follow the action of that division. Before the ground ceased its trembling, messages began to pour into the 9th Division from its observation posts and forward units. Devastation of the bombed area was the only bit of information added to the routine report of the jump off, until—an urgent message arrived notifying the 9th Division Commander that two forward battalions had been caught in the near fringe of the bomb pattern and had been wiped out. It was unbelievable. Such misfortune simply could not be true. To the two experienced division commanders initial reports were expected to be unduly alarming but in this particular case, that sixth sense told them that the report was at least partially true. Lieutenant Colonel Clayman, a very brave man and an experienced battalion commander in combat, had given a most disconcerting report on his own battalion, one of the two in question. Disorganization in the two battalions unquestioningly existed. Closely following on the heels of this malchance was a report that somewhere up front General McNair had been hurt. Obviously, something had gone wrong. Action had to be taken.

The First Division coiled and ready to spring through the gap, was set in motion. Time was so very valuable. Every advantage had to be taken of the shock caused by the bombing. While the artillery fires maintained a saturation barrage on the front in the breakthrough area, the Division uncoiled southward. Men and armor surged forward. Light resistance, when met, was quickly brushed aside. Orders were to move fast and, down to the last man. The importance of speed was understood.

Before all units could clear the Bois du Hommet, forward elements of the 18th Infantry, passing through Combat Team 47, and driving southward, crossed the Periers-St. Lo road, at 7:00 A.M. July 26th, and raced onward toward Marigny. Enemy positions were bypassed by this lead battalion—the 1st Battalion.

The afternoon was wearing away. The 18th Infantry fought for and into the battered little village of Marigny, late that night and early July 27th. There a crossroads had to be taken and secured. The crossroads was taken, but "secured" at this early stage of the fight was a meaningless word. Jerry had occupied the nose of the hill just south of the crossroads and was interdicting it with every weapon at his command. Jerry understood the importance of that road net and assuredly he could not be bluffed off that defensive position. A battalion of the 18th was turned toward the hill but as darkness descended the Germans were still in their positions. Artillery was moving up and guns in position were pounding the Jerry position, but a square kilometer will absorb a lot of artillery fire without becoming untenable.

Combat Command "A" of the 3rd Armored Division hit Marigny, bypassed it to the right and rapidly fought its way through a disorganized enemy to its objective which was the high ground north of Coutances. There it laagered for the night. The armor had succeeded in its mission of arriving on the objective but it now found itself in the rather precarious position of being all alone in rear of a considerably larger force of Germans to the north.

By 2100 hours, in spite of darkness and confusion, it had become apparent that the German defenders were aware of an impending encirclement of their forces south of Periers and were showing evidence of becoming somewhat better organized as they fought desperately to re-establish their line at the point of penetration. The armor had succeeded in breaking through, as it was to do so often in subsequent engagements, only to find a bypassed enemy resistance holding up the supporting infantry elements.

Coincident with the fall of darkness, the German defenders on the nose just south of Marigny crossroads had quieted down with an apparent willingness to let well enough alone as long as they were not molested. Probing patrols, feeling their way along the outskirts of Marigny, discovered a narrow gap of some 300 yards in the German position to the northwest of the crossroads. An old trail shortcutting the crossroads was fortunately discovered in the gap. Division engineers attached to Combat Team 16 were sent in with bulldozers to make the trail passable. The original plan for CT-16 to closely follow on the heels of Combat Command "A" now appeared to be practicable of accomplishment. The engineers, working quietly in the darkness, drew little fire and expeditiously accomplished their mission. It was unbelievable that Jerry could ignore the obvious implication of this engineer work unless he was setting a trap. At best a 300 yard gap in any enemy line is a small hole through which to move a combat team. But speed was more essential now than ever. With the coming of daylight, the isolated combat command would probably be punished severely while a strengthened German position would make their support far more costly. The gamble of taking prompt action was great, but the certainty of failure if prompt action was not taken was clear in the mind of the First Division Commander, Major General Huebner.

The General's decision was prompt. Combat Team 16 must go through the gap at once. Preferably it would go through quietly with minimum or no disturbance of Jerry's position. To fully appreciate the risk of being taken, one must visualize the Division's right flank along which Combat Team 16 must move in order to reach the gap. The major encirclement of German forces was now on the Division's right flank. Although disorganized, they were still capable of placing considerable mortar and small arms fire on the road leading to Marigny. In effect, the move of CT-16 along this road would constitute a move parallel to the front of the encircled German forces. And on arrival at the gap CT-16, in column would have to pass close to the nose at the Marigny crossroads where the German position was unquestioningly strong. Small arms fire from the German position on the nose would enfilade the moving column which, because it was in column, would be in no position to fight back or protect itself.

In order to execute General Huebner's plan, the 2nd Battalion of the 18th Infantry which was confronting a German force on the nose was appraised of the plan and told to studiously refrain from drawing fire.

The 16th quietly and efficiently moved out. Tenseness was noticeable in every low spoken word. As the head of the column neared the gap, tenseness increased. Still there was no indication that Jerry would react. Gradually it became apparent as more and more of the CT slipped through the gap, that Jerry was not going to react—at least until daylight, and by that time the CT would be in hand, quite able to take care of itself. The first part of the mission was a complete success.

It is still a marvel to all concerned how Combat Team 16 managed to squeeze through this narrow gap during the night of 27 July. But it did, and with very few casualties. At daylight 28 July as CT-16 moved down the road to Coutances the picture became less optimistic. Jerry intended to contest every foot of the way and had mustered tanks and 88s to assist his defense. It looked like this was going to be a tough day.

The 16th Infantry had fought its way down to La Chapelle and on to the railroad through Cembernon. At 9:00 A.M. July 28th, the Regimental Commander, Colonel Gibb, reported heavy going. The gap at Marigny was being widened but the situation was still tense. The Germans cut off to the north were pressing hard to get out of the trap. Every minute lost in the drive on Coutances meant more Germans escaping from this trap. Fighting was severe and the going was slow. The Division Commander repeatedly called the regimental commander urging him onward and the CT responded magnificently. Supporting artillery fires were brought down extremely close to forward units. Armor was used to the maximum yet casualties were greater than at any time since 6 June. Road congestion to the rear only served to emphasize the urgency of rapid movement to the objective.

Mute reminders of the severity of combat along the route were evident as other elements of the Division raced along the road. German tanks lined the road with half charred crew members lying around or draped from the turrets. Here was seen an 88 taken to the upstairs floor of a farm house commanding a thousand meters or so of the roadway and here a German staff car with the occupants slouched dead in a sitting position just where they were riding. An American tank and a German tank were halted for the last time within a few yards of each other where one had surprised the other at a street corner; both having made the supreme sacrifice in a short and quick duel at 20 paces.

But the necessity for speed and still more speed, time and still more time, had not abated. A position on the high ground had to be held so the jaws of the vice could squeeze on the Germans remaining in the pocket. Having arrived on the objective, the men of the Division worked feverishly to establish defensive positions. Reconnaissance northward had to be pushed vigorously to meet other American troops attacking southward. The 4th Armored Division was fighting its way into the northern outskirts of Coutances while the First was driving in from the east. Mines and booby traps were encountered at every turn. German demolition experts had dropped trees across the city streets. Buildings were blasted and burned. With a roar, American armor from the north swept in, affected the juncture and swept on south to Granville. The Germans caught in the pocket were being cut into ever decreasing groupments and were slowly being gathered into POW cages. The breakthrough was successful, the initial job had been done. As the clock ticked away minutes and as General Patton's newly-committed Third Army spearheaded by the 4th Division raced southward to cut off the Brittany Peninsula, the First Division and the 3rd Armored Division changed direction in a sweeping move to cover the left flank of the Third Army.

Briefly bringing in the big picture, General Hodges' First Army with its VII Corps on the right was now to be on the inside of the encircling movement which was to swing east and north to an eventual juncture with the British. German forces caught inside this encirclement would be annihilated and the whole of Normandy released from the oppressive heel of the Boche.

Daylight hours the fighter bombers ranged overhead like angelic wasps. Rarely would an ME-109 or FW-190 slip through their protective cover to hit our racing columns. American armor moved deep into enemy territory blocking escape routes while infantry divisions pressed closely behind them to destroy enemy groups disorganized by these armored columns. Pockets of enemy cut off and trapped were pointed out to the fighter bombers who came in for the kill.

As the 3rd Armored Division and the First Infantry Division moved southeastward out of the Coutances area, they found the German forces contending their passage of the Sienne River in the vicinity of Gavray. Flanking elements of the 2nd Armored Division had raced by and through the area north of Gavray as the weight of the Division moved along the left flank of the Third Army. The breakthrough was thirty hours old now and the German high command was attempting to react. By day it could not. Our Air Force made enemy movement in daylight impossible. But at night the JU-88s droned ceaselessly overhead, apparently bombing at random in an assigned area.

On the night of 31 July, while the Division was taking advantage of darkness to exploit the daylight forcing of the crossing of the Sienne River at Gavray, enemy air activity concentrated on the Division area. The Division had moved into this area more or less on the heels of a flanking column of the 2nd Armored Division. That Division, with beautiful coordination with the Air Corps, had trapped retreating German columns on some of the sunken roads and had practically annihilated a German division. Wreckage of vehicles was so dense on roads it was necessary to call in bulldozers to push it out of the way to clear the road for one way traffic. Possibly, that stinging blow had evoked Jerry's retaliation. In any event, members of the Division will long remember the results of that retaliation.

JUs began droning overhead at approximately 23 hours. Large bombs were dropped on concentrations on the road which were revealed by flares. Antipersonnel bombs raked all cover. No unit of the Division went untouched. The Division command post in the vicinity of St. Denis le Gast received at least a fair share, disrupting communications, ripping to shreds all blackout tents and killing and wounding officers and men. The Air Support officer was killed in a foxhole and the General's aide was wounded. Communications were severed for approximately half an hour. Movement in the area was difficult due to a few remaining antipersonnel bombs which were exploding on a delayed action fuze. A nearby hospital had gone into bivouac for the night, remaining almost completely mobile. The Chief of Staff immediately sent a medical officer with a message to the Commanding Officer of the field hospital to set up his installations as quickly as possible to take care of the wounded. Fortunately, the night was not densely black. Starlight permitted a degree of visibility. Systematically the staff went about getting back to normal, reorganizing for operational efficiency, forgetting the raid which had ended as suddenly as it started and again becoming engrossed in the critical operation of throwing the Division across the Sienne River at Gavray.

At approximately 1025 B, 1 August, General Collins arrived at the CP, pointed his finger at the map and said, "There is your today's objective." His finger was on the town of Brecey and the high ground surrounding same; a continuation of the move straight south. Task Force X (of the 3rd Armored Division) under command of that gallant leader, Colonel Leander L. Doan, was spearheading the Division as an attached armored force. Colonel Doan was already on the road headed toward Brecey followed closely by the 2nd Battalion of the 18th Infantry. An efficient communication system functioned smoothly and with no loss of time this force was directed on its objective. By twelve noon both Task Force X and the 2nd Battalion 18th Infantry, were on the objective and buttoned up. This new mission had as its eventual objective the seizure of the high ground in the vicinity of Mortain and responsibility for the right flank of VII Corps.

Day and night the Division moved and fought. Speed coupled with mass action was paying dividends. Germans in the vicinity were demoralized or dead; debris and wreckage littered the roadside, with here and there a German corpse serving as a constant reminder that a lessening of pressure would permit scattered groups of demoralized

Jerries to assemble for concentrated action with an attendant increase in casualties. The net was obviously drawing tight again. The thin finger of armor and men probing into enemy territory was running into increasing opposition as Jerry began to guess the import of this move.

Mortain, a sizeable little city in Manche overlooks a pass in the mountain range leading from Avranches through Mortain to Domfront and, incidentally, is on a key road junction where the north-south road from Vire joins the east-west road from Avranches through Mortain and Domfront to Alencon. In this pocket northeast of Mortain—between Mortain and Caen, the Jerries were putting up a hard fight to hold the British on the right and prevent encirclement on their left by American forces. Falaise was at the eastern edge of this pocket although at the time there was hardly an expectation that the Division would swing in sufficient arc to find itself turned back northward toward Falaise and, incidentally, its Normandy beaches.

As the Division closed in on Mortain, the Jerries in the vicinity were getting a little bit tougher. Mortar fire on positions, on roads, and on probable command post locations showed a marked increase. From somewhere the Jerries had assembled some artillery and were using it annoyingly. Organized counterattacks on key ground seized by divisional elements gave warning that Jerry still had effective organization to our northeast.

In puzzling over the Germans capabilities, two very logical lines of thought were obvious. Jerry's effective resistance against the British in the vicinity of Caen indicated a sizeable force and an intention to hold that hinge. It was also obvious that a punishing blow could be delivered to the American forces by a German drive westward to the sea at Avranches thereby isolating that encircling force under General Patton and, more important to the wearer of the Red One, that portion of VII Corps which found itself at the time south of the line Avranches-Mortain.

For this operation the Division CP was established in a little valley northwest of Juvigny le Tertre. Just over the ridge to the left (north) German mortar shells were cracking on the hillside as if to give warning of the bitter fighting we were to have in that sector. CT-39 of the 9th Division, arriving in this vicinity, was attached to the Division at 1015 B on this, the fourth of August, for the express purpose of attacking northward to put pressure on this pocket of Germans. The situation was rapidly becoming tense. Fighting was getting back to a more severe and determined action. Divisional artillery was constantly throwing concentrations into possible German assembly areas to stave off a large scale counterattack. That night the Luftwaffe droned over the area throughout the hours of darkness. On the morning of the 5th of August CT-39 attacked north while the Division held its positions. Seconds and minutes were passing. The pressure of time increased the tension. Rapid movement had gotten into the blood of every man. This temporary stalemate should rightfully be only a matter of hours.

In anticipating a sudden move in continuation of the thrust eastward, the Division Commander alerted CT-16 and prepared it for a quick move southward. The Division command post was pulled out from behind the Division and reestablished out on right flank with no protection other than its own defense platoon. A critical road net could not be hampered by a command post move and its attendant slowing down of communications when word should come to break away from Mortain.

Almost coincident with this decision and command post move, orders were received to turn over the position in and around Mortain to the 30th Division and proceed with all speed to Mayenne. Units were ordered to make detailed preparations for a speedy and efficient relief. CT-16 was put on the road at once. Attached units of the 3rd Armored Division were alerted to move. As commanders and staff of the 30th Division came in to CPs they were quickly appraised of the situation, given guides, offered communication networks, and led to organized positions. As they went on to positions, hot spots were pointed out to them and recommendations from all commanders and staffs of the First Division indicated the advisability of taking seriously the possibility of a punishing counterattack in that vicinity. The gamble taken by the First Division was pointed out as a considered risk insofar as the location of its Division Command Post was concerned with due consideration given to the time element and the prospective move. It had been a constant regret among some members of the Division that these points were not sufficiently emphasized to possibly avert subsequent punishment administered the 30th Division by the counterattacks which developed before the 30th Division was completely set. The German 116th Panzer Division spearheaded this enemy drive toward Avranches and its failure to effect a breakthrough is not so much a blot on its escutcheon as it is a feather in the cap of the 30th Division. This 116th Panzer Division with its admirable commander, Major General Von Schwerin, was destined to cross swords with the First Division in subsequent actions, the General himself being in command of Aachen in the early stages of the fight for that city. The hectic combat career of Von Schwerin is an outstanding example of the unfair and callous treatment the German high command was capable of imposing on its senior officers who dared express a professional opinion which happened to be contrary to the naive hopes of their ostrich-like field marshals.

Speed again. The dust on the rural roads of northern France was settling on the tired faces of the wearers of the Red One. The late summer sun was bearing down pleasantly on rapidly moving columns as they wheeled through small French villages whose streets were lined with cheering civilians. Mayenne was just ahead and the Division was closing in on the city. Mortain was far behind and the sound of artillery and mortar fire was already hours in the past. Mayenne was reported very lightly held except for an uncertainty as to where one would encounter scattered German detachments, no serious action was contemplated. However Mayenne is on the western bank of the Mayenne River which flows generally north and south and just across this river at Aron an armored task force from the 5th Armored Division had bumped its head against a stone wall of opposition. CT-16 hit Mayenne, took it over and prepared to cross the river in force. A battalion of the 26th helped a combat command of the 3rd Armored Division outpost Gorron where everything remained quiet. Task Force X (3rd Armored Division) under Lieutenant Colonel Doan had already forced a crossing of the Varrene

River northwest of Mayenne in the vicinity of Amerieres Le Grand which permitted First Division troops to consolidate a bridgehead in this vicinity.

While in this location an artillery cub flying low over known enemy positions in the vicinity of Aron spotted a couple of Jerry trucks half camouflaged under trees along the roadside. Artillery was called in and hit the trucks in a matter of minutes, set them on fire and, to the alert eyes of the artillery observer, stirred up a hornet's nest of activity. To the astonishment of the cub observer, a long German column disclosed itself by seeking shelter from the artillery fire. Division artillery reported quickly to Division and with perfect coordination in a fashion that would please even the most disparaging critic of air-ground coordination, a squadron of dive bombers was called in and put on the target through the use of colored smoke shells in something less than ten minutes. This dive bombing smoked out some more of the enemy column so the leader of the squadron called in another squadron to continue the pommelling inasmuch as the first squadron's supply of bombs was exhausted.

Little further trouble developed east of Mayenne. A message from General Collins to General Huebner directed a conference between the two at Division Artillery's air strip on the afternoon of 9 August at which time the Division was ordered to change direction to the north moving via Couterne, Bagnoles, la Ferte-Mace.

The wheels started turning. Advanced units shot out their reconnaissance and the power followed closely behind. Supply was working nicely. Gasoline was on hand. Rations were ample. Action was not severe. Casualties were almost nil. Sweat was taking the place of blood and the undamaged countryside in its late summer greenness was little indicative of warfare. But the constant brushing by and bumping into isolated detachments of Jerries was sufficiently frequent to dispel any attitude of inattention to the possibility of sudden danger. As thick woods were hit, Jerries would be routed therefrom. Overhead at night the JU-88s still droned ceaselessly. G-2 reports from higher headquarters began to predict the size of the prospective bag of prisoners in the net that was rapidly being closed.

In these moves the individual found himself existing under bewildering conditions of physical comfort and discomfort as the case might be. One night he would find himself housed in an enormous chateau, the next in a foxhole under the stars. One day he would be in a severe fight. Perhaps that same day he would also roll through a peaceful French village at twenty-five miles per hour gazing into the smiling and cheering faces of the jubilant and friendly populace. An occasional bottle of wine generously given him by a Frenchman would help wash the dust from his parched throat and not infrequently, an apple tossed to him as he sped by would connect uncomfortably with his head. But Joe was happy; his morale was high and the world was a pleasant place to be. This rapid movement was a fine thing even though it did mean hours of uncomfortable riding and long hours of maintenance which left little time for sorely needed sleep.

Then Bingo. The Division swooped through Bagnoles De l'Orne, respite from both movement and combat, men of the Division began to see for the first time a hopeful civilian populace newly-emerged from the oppression and want they had known under the German occupation. The Division reached back and picked up its rear echelon and for the first time in days the whole Division was again assembled in something approximating a compact assembly area.

That in itself presaged a move. Since August 18 no fighting had taken place in the Division sector. The situation in and around Paris was receiving headline publicity. Although plans were in the offing for a long move to the east, there was still no definite date for commencement of the move. The Division had been away from the sound of guns for several days—seven days to be exact—for it was now late evening of the 23rd. Orders had just come in to commence the move eastward early on 24 August.

This move, one of the longest single moves made by the First Division, was a jump of approximately ninety-six miles. The route lay through Alencon and Mamers to Courville sur Eure. The First Division closed in the vicinity of Courville early on August 25th, without incident. During the early evening of August 24th, further orders had arrived which directed the First Division to push on eastward at first light in the vicinity of Etampes. The 3rd Armored Division was to cover this move. The mission of the Division was to establish a bridgehead east of and into la Ferte-Mace. Jerries were moving across the front from west to east. When they bumped into divisional units they attempted to bounce off to the eastward. Orders were to consolidate positions and hold on. Questionable juncture had been effected with the British forces fighting southward. The famous Falaise pocket was reportedly closed. All that had to be done now was to open the gates to the PW inclosure and pick up the remnants of the once famous German Fifteenth Army.

That the completeness of closure of this pocket was never quite effected is a matter of history, but to all intentional purposes the second big encircling movement had reached its climax and the high command signified "Mission accomplished." Interesting little incidents occurred along the front as the encircled Germans attempted to, individually and collectively, make their way eastward. Captured German vehicles manned by First Division personnel decoyed other German vehicles into the net and when astonished Jerries bumped and bounced off eastward they were gleefully permitted to bounce because Joe knew his old companion in arms on the right, the 9th Division, would soon have them in its PW cage.

As the bag of prisoners increased and the pressure lessened to zero, a few days of much needed rest was realized. Bagnoles as the name signifies, was a resort area and in the few days the Seine River in the vicinity of Corbeil and Melun comfortably housed elements of the First Division.

On the 25th, another uneventful move of some fifty-five miles ended with the Division closed in its assigned bivouac in the vicinity of Etampes as ordered. The next morning (26 August) the Corps Commander, General Collins, arrived at the Division CP, discussed the overall plan for further operations and issued the Corps order for the movement of the First Division across the Seine. Noteworthy at this time is the fact that General Collins, ever cognizant of the morale value of the Division's heritage, shifted the First Division to the left of VII Corps in a move destined to throw the First Division into Soissons where it had so gallantly fought in World War I.

No excerpt from the history of the First Division can be complete without mention being made of the spirit which motivated the famed organization. In World War I, it earned a reputation for dash, esprit and dependability. Concomitantly it developed a personality and a soul.

Throughout the intervening years of peace it retained a pride of heritage so that it entered World War II with a background of tradition, consumate pride and a more mature personality. In North Africa under fire, it again found its soul.

The soul of the First Division is its touch of immortality. Great men have led and guided the Division; little men have followed and executed. Both have given their hearts, their brains and their blood. And in so doing the Division has become bigger than any individual in it. No one man has made this Division. This does not mean that its great leaders failed to give it greatness. Just the contrary. But because of this all pervading soul, these men with a greater capacity gave more, or, if you will, absorbed and in turn reflected more of that inspiration which *is* the soul of the First Division.

◆　◆　◆

ST. LO AND MORTAIN

As I Saw Iit

By

A. J. LIEBLING

TWICE, with the First Division, I have been very nearly eaten by mosquitoes. The first time was in the oasis at El Guettar, where a soldier told me he had been awakened by a mosquito turning over his dog tags presumably to see if he had the mosquito's favorite type of blood. At El Guettar, survivors will remember, we were annoyed nights by butterfly bombs, which German planes used to drop along the highway and into the oasis, but the mosquitoes drew a greater volume of blood. A couple of men got hit by the bombs; everybody in the Division (including the visiting correspondent) got bitten hell out of. The gunk that was distributed to smear over the face and hands (D.D.T., like the Air Force, was invented too late to help in Africa) served only to encourage these Arabs with wings. Lieutenant Stevenson, General Roosevelt's aide, had a theory that if you left it off some mosquitoes would pass you up, like the epicures who don't like hot dogs without mustard. I should have thought that the atabrine the medics made us absorb daily would at least have served to make us taste bad, but Arab mosquitoes were no more finicky about their diet than Arabs.

In the last third of July, 1944, I left the First Army press camp at Vouilly, near Isigny, in Normandy, and moved my sleeping bag down to First Division, in some loathsome swamp back of a town generally referred to as St. John D-Day (St. Jean de Daye), which earlier in the month had been considered way out front. By now St. John and Hooey da Pooey (La Haye des Puits) had been organized and we were getting ready to go a lot further, fast. General Bradley had told the correspondents at a press conference what our side was going to try to do, and had outlined the task of the enlarged Seventh Corps (First, Ninth, Fourth and Thirtieth Divisions, Second and Third Armored). First was, of course, going to carry the ball, with some assistance from the armor. The other three infantry divisions were going to "open a hole" for these select organizations. When given a choice between going with somebody opening a hole or going with somebody walking through the hole, I always choose to accompany the latter. The polite way of saying it is that you get a better over-all picture that way. Also you live longer. However, things seldom work out as planned. I might have known that if First Division was pointed at a hole, the hole would turn out not to be there.

I arrived at Division after dark, but had no trouble finding it. I could recognize it by the mosquitoes. I could only assume that the El Guettar swarm had been following the Division ever since, getting fatter and sassier with continued good nourishment. Soldiers, who grow attached to animals, must have brought some along in barracks bags from Africa to Sicily, from Sicily to Dorset, the way they carry dogs, I told myself, and then transported some breeding stock across the Channel in LCIs. The only objection I could see to this theory was that the mosquitoes at St. John D-Day were too big to fit into a barracks bag. I decided that they must have grown considerably since June 6. After the first bite, which put a lump like a bowling ball on my left knee, I knew I was home again.

"Almighty God," I said politely to a nearby MP, "are they *shooting* these things at us, or are they self-propelled?"

"One touched down on the fighter strip near here today and they put 120 gallons of gas into him by mistake before he took off," the MP said. Everything about the Division was bigger and better, including the mosquitoes and the lies. The only improvement the Division hadn't acquired between El Guettar and the breakthrough was a fancy name. In Africa divisions had been too few and too busy to think up literary names for themselves, but in France, I had begun to notice, every new outfit coming in had a Chamber-of-Commerce title, like the Blood-and-Thunder Division, or the Hip-Hip-Hooray Division. I was glad that the First was still just the First. Also it was still beefing. Mostly, when a correspondent got into a division, soldiers would complain to him about how the Screaming Rockets Division, or the Escholtzia Division, or whatever it was, never got any notice in the newspapers. "To read the papers," they would say, "you would get the idea the First Division is fighting the whole goddam war!" In the mosquito swamp I met a soldier in the Signals Company who beefed because his division was getting too *much* credit. "Why do we get all these tough assignments?" he said,—"I'll tell you. Because we got too much publicity. We got even *Eisenhower* thinking we're supermen. Psychologically, it's bad for the other divisions. I think they ought to let them carry the ball once in a while. I would be content to just sit around until they get famous too."

So it was the First, all right. Camped in a swamp, eaten by mosquitoes, beefing like mad and preparing to play the star role in a big operation.

There are a couple more mosquito stories that I feel impelled to tell here. After all what men say is as much a part of their history as what they do—look at Patrick Henry. One soldier said, "I went to sleep in a barn last night, and when I woke up I was lying on my back out in the open, where a coupla mosquitos had drug me, and one of them had his foot on my chest and was saying to the other: 'Should we work on him here on take him out to the swamp?' The other one said, 'Aw, don't let's take him out to the swamp, or some of those BIG mosquitoes will get him.'" There was a tough little French lieutenant attached to G-2 who had served in the Foreign Legion in Indo-China. "Out there," he told Lieutenant Botsford and me, "we had double protection against mosquitoes. Every man had a big mosquito net, and under the mosquito net with him, a little woman. The woman would catch any mosquito that came through the net. At night the clapping of the women's hands, as they killed mosquitoes, sounded like applause at the opera." We agreed with him that it was a shame the War Department had not included both items in our equipment.

For this operation I had decided to travel with Divarty,—Divisional Artillery headquarters battery. This was a battery without guns—as I need not explain for the artillerymen, but a lot of the infantrymen didn't seem to know what it was then, and a lot of ex-infantrymen probably don't know yet. The headquarters battery merely had a switchboard, a set of maps, and a lot of telephone wires. Divarty was a small, traveling brain trust that moved quietly behind the front-line troops and called down fire on faraway Germans. Brigadier-General (later Major-General) Andrus, was Divisional Artillery Commander then, Col. (later Brigadier-General) Waters his executive officer, and there were Majors Boynton and Crocker, Lieutenant-Col. Pace, an uproarious Captain named Anderson and others I can't remember—my traveling family for a few days of the war. A correspondent gets himself a lot of different "families" during five years of war. He winds up remembering, generally with pleasure, twenty or thirty different little communities of which he has formed a part.

Divarty was under ordinary conditions an ideal place to follow the progress of a battle, or at least one division's part in it, because

Divarty controlled the Piper Cubs that served as the Division's eyes. The pilots and observers were not Air Forces men but artillery officers. They reported not only on targets and the effect of the Division's artillery fire but on all enemy troop and vehicle movements they observed. (Maybe this will be done next time by television, instead of Maytag Messerschmitt.) The information was routed through Divarty to Division, so it got to Divarty first. When ground observation was available Divarty had the best of that, too, for the artillery had its observers up in the line with advanced elements of the infantry. These observers had direct telephone lines to their battalions, and the battalions in turn to Divarty. Another reason I wanted to travel with Divarty was General Andrus, whom I had admired ever since I first knew him in Africa, where water was scarce and he had used left-over breakfast coffee to shave with. "Saves heating fuel too," he had once said. "It's warm." I figured that a man with such a direct approach to tactical and logistical problems was worth cultivating. And also the divisional artillery had shot through those Tenth Panzer Division tanks at El Guettar when the tanks were just about to overrun the oasis where I was. Such incidents are likely to give you a warm feeling about people.

Every night during the offensive Divarty would set up its command post in a farmhouse or barn within the Division area, black out the windows and chinks, and lay its wire to the battalions, which laid wires to their batteries. Then, after nightfall, when the Cubs came down, the officers would sit around a long row of tables—in an atmosphere that used to make me think of a newspaper copy desk during the slack hours—drinking strong coffee and playing cribbage while they waited for telephone calls. A call would come in, and Waters or Pace could hold a brief conversation, then remark, "Infantry patrols report some sort of Jerry movement at that road junction at 4124. Mediums can reach it." He would pick up the telephone again, make a call, and return to his cribbage game. Outside in the night the 155s would send a lot of high explosive screaming toward the dark crossroads.

I once asked the General what chance there was of hitting anything useful with that kind of fire, and he said, "About one in 50,000.

But if they have inexperienced truck drivers it will scare them and slow them up some." He always used to instruct Colonel Waters to pick a good big building for the command post, although everything bigger than a henroost was marked on the German maps, because, he said, he liked to be comfortable and he knew how hard it was to hit anything off a map anyway. He would admit the limitations of the artillerist's trade, although he is one of the best in the specialty. I used to get less nervous about incoming fire after talking to him. If you get hit it's an accident; which must be a great consolation. Observed fire, of course, is something different;—I'll never forget those tanks.

I watched the air bombardment that preceded the breakthrough from an upstairs window of the farmhouse Divarty was using then. The window faced south, toward the area, five miles away, that was to be bombed. There were three ridges, the first two topped with poplars, the third with pines, between the farmhouse and the target area. One stream of bombers came in to the left of the farmhouse, turned behind the third ridge, dropped its bombs, and came away to my right; another stream came in over my right, turned, and went off to the left. For two hours the air was filled with the hum of the motors, and the concussions of the bombs, even though they were falling five miles away, kept my shirtsleeves fluttering. Some of the soldiers, lying on the sloping ground under my window, rolled on the grass yelling happily, as though they were watching the home team pile up a big score. One guy yelled, "I'm glad my old man was born in Ireland!" "The more bombs we drop, the less fight there'll be left in them," another soldier said. Personally, since I had been in Paris when it was bombed in 1940, and in London in 1941 and 1943, to say nothing of a fighter field in Tunisia that Jerry used to bomb three times a day, I felt just fine about seeing Jerry get it in turn (as I supposed).

The only residents of the farm who seemed uncomfortable were a great, long-barrelled sow and her litter of six shoats, shaking their ears as if the concussions hurt them. At brief intervals they would lie down in a circle, all their snouts pointing toward center. Then they would get up again, perhaps because the earth quivering against their bellies frightened them. Puffs of black flak smoke dotted the sky under the first two waves of bombers; one plane came swirling down, on fire and trailing smoke, and crashed behind the second ridge of poplars. White parachutes flashed in the sun as the plane fell. A great cloud of slate-gray smoke rose from behind the trees where it had gone down. Soon after that the flak puffs disappeared; the German gunners either had been killed or, as one artillerist suggested, had simply run out of ammunition. The succeeding waves of planes did their bombing unopposed. There was to have been 350 medium bombers in the operation, followed by 1,800 heavy bombers and then 400 more mediums to clean up, and although I made no attempt to count them it didn't look as if the Air had short-changed us.

After the bombardment we waited all afternoon for the order to advance. We had heard that the divisional headquarters and the Fifth Field Artillery with its 155s were to be moved up by nightfall to positions beyond the Germans' morning line. That would mean of course that the real front line would be several miles further forward. As it happened, the breakthrough wasn't that abrupt. We didn't move until evening, and then only a couple of miles, to a spot that was still short of the morning jump-off point.

At nightfall neither the Division nor the Second and Third Armored had gone into action. The divisions up front had not moved forward perceptibly. Discouraging rumors were discussed in the Divarty mess that night. One was that Jerry had not been shaken by the bombardment, another that he had been annihilated, but that bomb craters had made all the roads impassable. I am afraid that we were pretty hard on the divisions in front of us. "Snafu," was a mild comment. What we didn't know, of course, was that we had been watching the bombardment of the Ninth and Thirteenth Divisions by the airplanes during the morning—that two battalions of the Ninth had been knocked out, and the Thirteenth had suffered 662 casualties. "The bombing of the 25th caused the Division as many casualties as the most severe day of combat," the history of the Thirtieth Division says. Naturally that had rather discouraged the boys who were supposed to make the hole. Lieutenant-General McNair, up front as an observer, had been killed. It was the second time I had been fairly near General McNair when he was hit. I had been a mile or so from him in Tunisia when he had been wounded. I guess my proximity just wasn't lucky for him.

Next morning at seven o'clock the 18th Combat Team kicked off. By nine o'clock we had word that the 18th had moved forward thousands of yards in the first hour, and all day long it kept moving forward, with what was reported as light opposition (if you were in the 18th you probably thought it was tough enough, but the few thousand yards between the dough and Divarty confer a great feeling of detachment. If you were there, or even if you were just reading about it in the newspapers, you know how the rest of that week went. One funny angle was my artillery fellow-travelers soon felt kind of frustrated. The infantry was moving so fast that the artillery was hardly ever called upon to shoot. Divarty felt a little like a fifth wheel. Here the mighty artillery of the First Division, which had saved it at El Guettar, blasted a way for it in Sicily, and smacked the el out of every djebel on the way to Mateur, was suddenly being pulled along in the dough's wake like a toy train pulled by a kid.

Whenever the Germans looked as though they might make a stand, according to G-2, some other American unit got behind them. By the fifth evening of our travels, Divarty found itself in a box. It was a gunner's nightmare; there was no place we *could* shoot without hitting some of our own people. Corps headquarters kept marking on the map things called "no fire" lines; they completely hemmed our guns in, and we weren't supposed to shoot across them. On that fifth night, the Division stretched out toward Coutances like a long finger. There were supposed to be Germans in front of us and on both flanks, but there was part of the Fourth Armored behind the Germans that the finger pointed at, and there were other American troops behind the Germans on our right, and the Third Armored somewhere out behind the Germans on our left. All the Germans in the area seemed to be trying to get out at once. Colonel Waters, a hustling, optimistic type, was so eager to get us well forward that he selected a CP for Divarty far up in the tip of the finger, in a spot where we felt for one night that we might be trampled to death by escaping battalions of the Master Race. The only American troops near us who had anything to fight with in case of a counter-attack (we didn't figure telephone tables and maps would prove very effective weapons) were the members of a Kansas tank destroyer outfit that I personally didn't have very much confidence in because the boys were always picking up motherless calves in their vehicles and carrying them around the countryside looking for bereaved cows who would adopt them. I figured they would be too soft-hearted to shoot anybody. One reason Waters had gotten so far forward was that General Andrus wanted to put some guns on Coutances, which was supposed to be full of Germans, before they could get out of there. But just about the time the wire crews laid the lines to the battalions he got a telephone call from Division—they had been informed by Corps that the Fourth Armored was in Coutances already, and poor old Pace, or maybe Boynton, went over and put another "No Fire" line on the map, which boxed us in 100 percent.

The artillery didn't get shot at much as it moved along in this offensive. It didn't seem like the same war as the one I remembered in Africa, when you couldn't move on a road without being strafed, and the Stukas used to divebomb the gun positions every time a battery started shooting. One night, I remember, the Germans brought off one of those Andrus 50,000 to 1 shots and landed a concentration on part of the 33rd F.A., causing a few casualties, but I think that was about all. Our Air Force may have flubbed up on that breakthrough preparation, but its general over-all job had been 99 percent effective. I only saw German planes once during the first five days of the offensive—about 15 rocket-firing Messerschmitts over the roads near Coutances. We were so spoiled by that time that we felt this was a hell of a note. The *Luftwaffe* had simply been hunted from the sky. As Colonel Mason phrased it: "Daylight hours the fighter-bombers (ours) ranged overhead like wasps." The burned-out German vehicles along almost every road were further testimony to the work the Air people had done before the ground forces had even reached the scene. General Andrus, not precisely an air enthusiast, even grumbled a little because he thought the planes had been *too* thorough. "If they had dropped one-hundred pound bombs instead of five-hundred-pounders," he once said, "they would have

killed just as many cows and they wouldn't have made such big holes
in the road." But I think he was a little touchy over not having
anything to shoot at.

The dead cows are one of my most vivid memories, not only of
the breakthrough, but of all the weeks of fighting in Normandy that
preceded it (most of them I had spent poking around hedgerows
with the 29th and 79th Divisions). They lay in the fields with their
legs pointing stiffly in the air, like wooden cows discarded from a
child's Noah's Ark, and their smell hung over the land as the dust
hung over the roads. During the hedgerow business a bovine stiff
was not always an unwelcome sight. Sometimes it offered defilade.
But after we once got moving they were just a horror. You need a
bulldozer to bury cows properly, and nobody had a bulldozer to
spare. The Mayor of St. Lo, who was in this country a year ago, told
me that the herds were back at full pre-war strength, and that is a
tribute to the lustiness of French cows, and bulls. At Divarty's fourth
command post there were more dead cows than usual, because, the
people on the farm told us, eighteen extra cows had arrived with the
Germans a couple of weeks before. There had been two sets of
Germans in the farm buildings—ten paratroopers who had showed
up driving eight cows, and forty S.S. men who had appeared driving
ten cows. The paratroopers, one of whom was a captain, had got
there first and taken up quarters in the farmhouse. The S.S. men,
arriving later, had billeted themselves in the outbuildings, but only
after a noisy argument, in which they had failed to get the paratroopers out of the house. The captain had too much rank for them.

The paratroopers had been fighting a long time and were fed
up, the people of the house said. A soldier who served as interpreter
had told the French family that the war was over, that Germany
was beaten. But the S.S. fellows, who had come from soft berths in
occupied countries, still talked tough. The S.S. soldiers had brought
a refugee family with them to milk the cows, the people at the farm
said. Every day the paratroopers drank the cream from their eight
cows and threw the milk away. They had seemed to be stuffng themselves in anticipation of a long period of post-war hunger. Both sets
of Germans had departed abruptly, but the S.S. had left one man

to guard the cows, presumably in case the American attack bogged
down before it reached the farmhouse. A shell had killed the cow-
tender. This Jerry had a letter on him asking his CO for permission
to go back to Essen, his home town, because he heard that his wife
had been killed in a bombing raid and he wanted to see what had
happened to his children. We figured he had not had time to send
the request through channels. Offensives disarrange so many plans!

The infantry operations during this first phase of the breakthrough were brilliant, I know, and some of the going was a lot
tougher than one would believe from the lightning rate of advance.
Only a great division can make tough going look easy. I was shocked
to read in Colonel Mason's excellent "Record," for example, that
on July 28 "Armor was used to the maximum yet casualties were
greater than on any day since June 6." But all a man can write about
is what he saw, and from the vantage point of Divarty the historic
breakthrough went, as the French say, *comme sur roulettes,*—"like
on rollers."

P. S. I left before all that excitement at Mortain.

CHAPTER VI

MONS AND AACHEN
August 25, 1944 to November 9, 1944

The Situation

TO RECOUNT the operation involving the breaching of the Siegfried Line, and the capture of Aachen, it is necessary to start in the vicinity of Mons, Belgium, where remnants of the First German Army attempted to escape from the pocket caused by the rapid advance of the First American Army, and the Second British Army.

On September 7, 1944, when the First Infantry Division swung from Mons, after five days of battle, and headed for Liege, five German Divisions—the 6th Parachute, 18th GAF, 47th Infantry, 275th Infantry and 348th Infantry—had been broken up and eliminated from the war.

More than 17,000 prisoners had been taken by the First Division alone, and an uncounted but proportionately high number of dead had been buried in the field. It was apparent that the captured Germans had been snared while hot on their way to the east, and the comparative safety of the Siegfried Line in the general direction of Aachen.

The disaster inflicted on the enemy in the Mons area broke up the German's strategical withdrawal and as a result VII Corps advanced rapidly to Liege, crossing the Meuse River and capturing the high ground in the vicinity of Henri-Chapelle, Belgium.

At this time a thorough study of the defenses of the Siegfried Line in the vicinity of Aachen was made, and it revealed two definite lines of fortifications, one which encircled Aachen, and the main defense line which lay between Aachen and greater Germany.

When the battered city of Aachen surrendered under the grinding pressure of a direct assault by the First Division on October 21, 1944, Germany lost more than a cultural city and an historic landmark. Aachen was also a coal-producing center and a key point in the Siegfried Line defenses. Aachen was a symbol of heroic resistance for the Germans as Stalingrad had been for the Russians. Aachen's defense was to have been a guarantee of the Reich's invulnerability.

The German people had been positively assured that Aachen could not be taken. Its defenders had been ordered by the Commander of the Seventh German Army to hold to the last man: "Your fight for the ancient imperial city is being followed with admiration and breathless expectancy. You are fighting for the honor of the Nationalistic German Army." But, unlike Stalingrad, Aachen crumbled and Nazi honor received a shattering blow.

When Aachen surrendered, however, it was apparent that the Germans did not intend to pull out of the Rhineland entirely. The fighting promised to be tougher and tougher; more German units were appearing daily in reorganized groups. This was a build-up to the Battle of the Hurtgen Forest—a forest nobody paid much attention to before, but which will never be forgotten, any more than the Argonne or Belleau Woods.

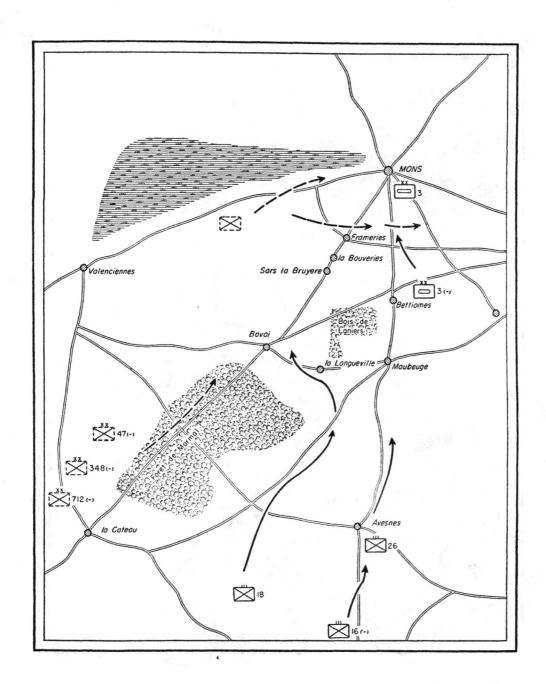

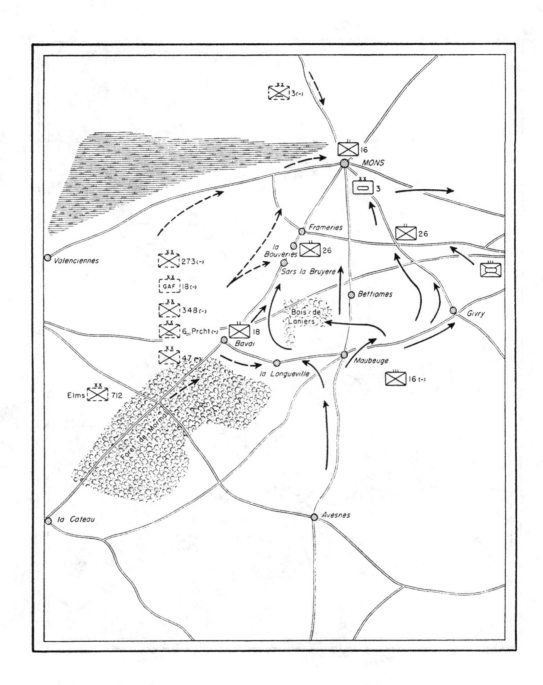

MONS AND AACHEN
August 25, 1944 to November 9, 1944

The Record

ON SEPTEMBER 11, 1944 elements of the 30th U. S. Infantry Division on the left of XIX Corps and to the north of the First Division, had established a bridgehead across the Meuse River. This left a wide gap between the left flank of the First Division and the right flank of the 30th Division. Since the First Division had been given the mission of protecting the left flank of VII Corps the 26th Infantry had echeloned to the left rear covering the gap.

A heavy reconnaissance screen across the First Division was being maintained by the enemy, and enemy artillery reappeared for the first time since the entry of the First Army into Belgium.

At this time, the First Division was ordered to send reconnaissance in force to the Siegfried Line and develop the enemy situation. The 18th Infantry on the left was ordered to send one Battalion (reinforced) forward to the Siegfried Line in conjunction with the 16th Infantry, which was also to send one reinforced Battalion forward on the right.

The attack jumped off at 8:00 A.M. September 12, 1944. The 18th Infantry ordered its 3rd Battalion forward, and the 16th Infantry ordered its 3rd Battalion forward. By noon September 12th both Regimental Commanders asked to be permitted to reinforce their leading Battalions with one additional Battalion. Enemy forces put up a stubborn fight although unequal resistance was experienced by the Regiments. The 18th Infantry met the most stubborn kind of resistance but the 16th Infantry moved rapidly and by nightfall, the 1st Battalion of the 16th had breached the initial Siegfried Line capturing many pillboxes. The 3rd Battalion, 18th Infantry had been unable to make any noticeable penetration by nightfall.

On the 13th of September both the 18th and 16th Infantry were ordered to continue the attack and capture all the high ground and its defenses south and southwest of Aachen. The 26th Infantry was ordered to prepare to relieve the two Battalions of the 16th in their own area, to permit the 16th Infantry to continue the attack to the northeast and seize the ground east of Aachen. In the 18th Infantry sector the 1st Battalion attacked to the right of the 3rd Battalion and rapidly took high ground west of Aachen-Liege road completely breaching the first initial Siegfried Line in that area.

The 26th Infantry moved forward and relieved the 1st Battalion, 16th Infantry, with the 3rd Battalion of the 26th. The 3rd Battalion of the 16th Infantry was still fighting in the Siegfried Line directly south of Aachen against very stubborn resistance and at the end of the day they were still heavily engaged cleaning out pillboxes, tanks, enemy self-propelled guns and infantry. It was quite apparent that the Germans had built defenses at Aachen along the southern outskirts of the city and since this was the first big city in Germany, the Germans anticipated that the Allied forces would immediately drive towards the city proper.

At this time it was decided not to put any troops in Aachen proper but bypass it on the east and drive directly towards the main Siegfried Line in a northeasterly direction, reach the line at that point and be prepared to exploit any success in that direction.

On the morning of September 14th, the 2nd Battalion, 26th Infantry passed through the Siegfried Line and cut off enemy forces that had been holding up the advance of the 3rd Battalion. By noon the 2nd Battalion had gotten behind the enemy and with the added pressure, the 3rd Battalion, 16th Infantry was able to break through and continue the advance to the northeast.

By nightfall both the 2nd and 3rd Battalions, 16th Infantry were just southwest of Brand. It was clear that the enemy was building up his forces as two new outfits, the 523rd (German) Infantry and the XIX GAF Battalion had been identified.

The 3rd Armored Division, attacking on the right, breached the Siegfried Line. By night of September 14th, an armored task force was reported just south of the Siegfried Line in the vicinity of Munsterbusch.

On September 14th, late at night, the 18th Infantry relieved the 26th Infantry. The 26th Infantry was ordered to attack northeast, secure the high ground southeast of Aachen and protect the left rear of the 16th Infantry. The 16th Infantry was ordered to cut the roads leading southeast of Aachen and then send reconnaissance in force to make contact with the Armored Task Force and reconnoiter the main defenses of the Siegfried Line.

On September 15th, the 16th Infantry cut the roads leading southeast out of Aachen, and continued the advance to the northeast. By noon the 1st Battalion of the 16th had contacted Task Force "Doan", 3rd Armored Division, with Company B, 16th Infantry. By noon of September 15th this force breached the Siegfried Line just west of Munsterbusch. By 9:25 P.M. the 16th Infantry occupied a position in the Siegfried Line.

On the morning of September 16th, 1944, VII Corps Commander ordered the 1st Division to assist the 3rd Armored Division in the capture of Stolberg and Munsterbusch. The 1st Battalion, 16th Infantry, in conjunction with Task Force "Doan" commenced the attack early that morning. By nightfall this force had made some progress toward Stolberg.

On the morning of September 17th, at 6:00 A.M. the enemy launched a counterattack on the 1st and 2nd Battalions, 16th Infantry. This attack was the first major enemy effort to drive off the First Division's threat to Aachen.

The counterattack of the enemy on September 17th was made by two Battalions of the enemy's 27th Regiment of their 12th Division. From prisoners it was learned that this organization had been withdrawn from the Russian front, reorganized and re-equipped in Germany and sent to Duren by train.

By 11:00 A.M. the counterattack had been beaten off and the 1st Battalion, 16th Infantry continued the attack towards Munsterbusch. By nightfall the 16th had made some progress against enemy resistance.

On September 18th the enemy attempted another unsuccessful counterattack, supported by artillery fire against Allied positions south of Verlautenheide. Meanwhile the advance of the 1st Division into Munsterbusch was heavily opposed by Battle Groups BOCKOFF (40 to 500 men) and SCHEMM, both composed of elements of the 9th Panzer Division. The defenses set up by these elements were well coordinated and stubborn. The terrain was well suited to delaying actions. Every house and at times every room in Munsterbusch was contested. Enemy artillery was more and more in evidence and our patrols were blocked off soon after they crossed our lines. In spite of the tenacity of the defense, however, prisoners and deserters picked up by the Division indicated that enemy morale was not too sound.

During the 19th and 20th of September all combat teams of the First Division improved their positions, with the 1st Battalion, 16th Infantry making local advances toward Stolberg. By late afternoon September 21, the 1st Battalion, 16th Infantry had seized their objectives in Munsterbusch.

On the morning of September 22nd, the 3rd Battalion, 18th Infantry which was on the left of the 18th Infantry sector, was attached to the 16th and relieved elements of the 83rd Armored Reconnaissance Battalion which had been holding the middle of the 16th Infantry sector. The 1st Battalion, 26th Infantry was released from the 3rd Armored Division and moved to the First Division sector. This Battalion had severe casualties and had to be refitted before being able to get into the lines again.

All during this period the 30th Infantry Division, part of the XIX Corps, worked up to the Siegfried Line in their sector, and were waiting for reinforcements before commencing the assault on the line itself.

Active patrolling had been instigated by the 26th Infantry Regiment towards the town of Aachen, to determine how strongly the town was held, and exactly in which direction it would be advisable to attack the town itself. Aachen was strongly fortified and garrisoned by elements of the 34th (German) Machinegun Fortress Battalion. It was determined that the best plan of attack would be to cut Aachen off from the rest of Germany.

On the morning of September 24th the enemy launched an attack against the 3rd Battalion, 18th Infantry which was then still attached to the 16th Infantry. The attack was beaten off, half of the attacking force (a special machinegun platoon) killed or captured, and another company was dispersed by First Division Artillery.

On September 28th and 29th the First Division consolidated their positions and maintained close contact with the enemy by active patrolling.

On September 29th the 1106th Engineer Combat Group moved in the positions occupied by the two battalions of the 18th Infantry south of Aachen, reinforcing the positions of the First Division before taking over the sector from the 18th Infantry.

At 12:30 A.M. October 3rd, the 27th (German) Division launched another attack against the First Division's front. This attack was sent in against the 2nd and 3rd Battalions of the 16th Infantry. The attack was supported by eight self-propelled assault guns, a self-propelled dynamite charge—"Goliath", and was preceded by an extremely violent artillery barrage during which time the enemy sent over more than 3500 rounds into the First Division sector. The "Goliath" was detonated harmlessly by a direct hit and artillery fire knocked out four of the enemy self-propelled guns.

Two companies of medium tanks from the 3rd Armored Division were alerted to assist the First Division in a counterattack role in conjunction with the First Battalion, 26th Infantry.

At 4:00 A.M. October 9th, the enemy launched another counterattack to prevent the First Division from consolidating on the high ground in the vicinity of Verlautenheide. Mortar fire and artillery fire drove the enemy out of Verlautenheide. At 10:30 A.M. the enemy launched another counterattack but they were again dispersed by artillery fire. Pressure on the 2nd Battalion, 18th Infantry continued throughout the day and not until 5:30 P.M. was the 18th Infantry able to resume the attack, with the 3rd Battalion pushing towards Haaren, and the 1st Battalion moving towards Crucifix Hill.

The 1st Battalion, 18th Infantry, continued the attack through the night and was successful in establishing road blocks on the Weiden-Aachen road and by early morning the 18th Infantry had two companies on Ravelsberg.

At 2:20 A.M. October 10th, a counterattack was launched against the 2nd Battalion, 18th Infantry in Verlautenheide which was repulsed by machinegun and artillery fire. By 3:00 A.M. one company of 1st Battalion, 18th Infantry was firmly entrenched on Crucifix Hill and had successfully repulsed a counterattack against their position at 6:00 A.M.

At 7:30 A.M. October 10th Company L of the 3rd Battalion, 18th Infantry launched an attack against Haaren and by 10:35 A.M. were on their objective in the northeastern part of Haaren mopping up. During October 8 to 10, 1944, 466 German prisoners were captured.

The general scheme for the reduction of Aachen was to give the Garrison Commander an ultimatum of twenty-four hours whereby if he did not surrender all troops and military installations within the town, immediate aerial and artillery bombardment would commence and the town would be reduced to rubble. It was estimated that Aachen was defended by approximately 5,000 troops—elements of the 246th Panzer Division, plus the original defenders or garrison troops.

At 10:00 A.M. October 10th, the ultimatum was delivered by the 26th Infantry.

On the morning of October 11th the 18th Infantry continued to mop up pillboxes within their zone of action and to reinforce and reorganize their defensive positions. By 11:00 A.M. no word had been received from the Garrison Commander of Aachen, although many white flags had been observed in and about the town, presumably put up by civilians. At 12:00 Noon the aerial and artillery bombardment of Aachen commenced and continued for the rest of the day.

At 5:35 P.M. October 11th, the Germans launched an attack with tanks and infantry against positions held by the 18th Infantry on Crucifix Hill. This attack was quickly repulsed.

On the morning of October 12th at 11:00 A.M., the 3rd Battalion 26th Infantry jumped off for the attack on Aachen proper with the 2nd Battalion driving west through the town and the 3rd Battalion west to capture the high ground on Observatory Hill and Lousberg. Steady progress was made during the day against stubborn resistance.

In the town of Aachen progress was slow and each house had to be thoroughly cleared of both enemy troops and civilians before passing on. Meanwhile it was apparent that a heavy enemy build-up was taking place northeast of the Verlautenheide ridge. VIII Corps reported that the 3rd Panzer Grenadier Division was moving north and could be expected in the First Division area.

The enemy launched a violent counterattack against Company G of the 16th Infantry, and against Company G of the 18th Infantry, and also against the entire left flank of the 16th Infantry position. The attack was supported by approximately eight tanks with the infantry elements coming from the 29th Panzer Grenadier Regiment. At 1:00 P.M. the enemy had overrun a portion of the 16th Infantry with tanks and infantry, but they were receiving heavy casualties from mass concentrations of mortar, artillery and machinegun fire. By 3:00 P.M. the enemy tanks were withdrawing and with the aid of mortars, artillery and infantry, the attack was repulsed by the First Division.

At 4:14 P.M. the penetration had been sealed off and the situation restored. The ferocity of this assault can be gauged by the fact that some 250 German dead lay in front of one company position.

At daylight October 13th, the 2nd and 3rd Battalions of the 26th Infantry had continued the attack on Aachen, and after the most difficult of all fighting, street fighting, had been able to form a juncture between the two battalions in the city. Progress was slow but steady.

At 2:40 A.M. October 16th, three companies of the 29th Panzer Regiment, in spite of terrific losses of the previous day, launched a coordinated attack of tanks and infantry on the left flank of the 16th Infantry. Again the attack was repulsed by machinegun, mortar and artillery fire, and by 11:00 A.M. all positions except one pillbox had been retaken. Prisoner of war totals rose proportionately and satisfactorily—400 were taken on October 13th and the bag continued to average 200 a day thereafter.

Late on October 16th a patrol from the 119th Infantry, 30th Infantry Division made contact with the 18th Infantry.

The 26th Infantry continued their attack on the town of Aachen and the 1106th Engineer Combat Group moved forward to gain contact with the left flank of the 2nd Battalion, 26th Infantry. Further progress was made in severe house-to-house fighting against fanatic enemy resistance.

At 7:30 A.M. October 19th the 18th Infantry was still fighting in Ravelsberg and by 10:30 A.M. positions were restored after inflicting heavy casualties on the enemy. At 2:30 P.M. the enemy launched a new attack in the same area, supported by tanks, and self-propelled guns. After two and one-half hours of heavy fighting the enemy was pushed back and the forward positions restored.

In the battle for Aachen there were not sufficient numbers of troops to hold the ground taken by the 26th Infantry so as to permit them to continue the advance. Since the First Division Reserve (1st Battalion 26th Infantry less one Company) was being used with the 16th and 18th Infantry Regiments in the many attacks they had received, it was decided to attach the 2nd Battalion of the 110th Infantry of the 28th Infantry Division to the First Division for a defensive role only. Their mission was to hold the ground captured by the 26th Infantry. In addition, Task Force "Hogan" comprised of one Battalion of Infantry and one Battalion of Tanks, was attached to the First Division for the purpose of attacking north of Aachen and seizing the northwestern portion of Lousberg.

By daylight October 10th, the 2nd Battalion, 110th Infantry had relieved elements of the 2nd Battalion, 26th Infantry on the left of the 26th, and the 2nd Battalion was in position to jump off on a coordinated attack on the center of Aachen, in conjunction with the attack of the 3rd Battalion, 26th Infantry and Task Force "Hogan", on Lousberg.

Task Force "Hogan" attacked at 7:30 A.M. and the 2nd and 3rd Battalions attacked at 8:00 A.M. By 8:35 A.M. the attack was progressing satisfactorily. However the medium tanks of Task Force "Hogan" had to be temporarily left behind due to soft ground. By dark some progress had been made.

The severity of the fighting on Lousberg indicated that the high ground was the area where the enemy was most ready to seriously dispute the First Division's encirclement of the city. Since the German High Command had believed that the main attack to reduce

Aachen would come from the south, all his main dispositions were in that sector of the city, and it was not until too late that the enemy realized the pressure from the east was backed up on the level of a full attack. Until the last the Germans expected another, more powerful assault from the south.

Lousberg however had been set up as a hinge in the defense of the city because it was learned that the adjutant to Colonel Wilck, the Commandant of the City, had convinced the Colonel that an experienced American Division would head straight for the commanding high ground. The Adjutant had dealings with the First Infantry Division in Africa.

At 7:30 A.M., October 20th, the 2nd and 3rd Battalions of the 26th Infantry, with Task Force "Hogan", continued the advance through the city of Aachen against strong resistance which included small arms, machineguns, antitank guns and mortars. At the end of the day Task Force "Hogan" and the 3rd Battalion, 26th Infantry were firmly on Lousberg while the 2nd Battalion, 26th Infantry had pushed completely through the center of the town and were nearing the western outskirts. The 2nd Battalion, 110th Infantry, had adjusted their lines throughout the day to come abreast of the left flank of the 2nd Battalion, 26th Infantry.

Activity on the 18th Infantry front was comparatively quiet throughout the day and contact was maintained with the 119th Infantry on the left.

At 7:30 A.M., October 21, 1944, the 26th Infantry, with the Task Force "Hogan" attached, continued the attack and at 12:05 P.M., Colonel Wilck, Commandant of the German forces in Aachen, surrendered to the 26th Infantry and made arrangements for the surrender of the remaining troops and installations in the city of Aachen. When he surrendered the city, Colonel Wilck had knowledge of the location and operations of only 500 of his men; more than 1,000 other troops were captured after the capitulation, however. They had just been cut off from the enemy command post and had become lost or had just quit and gone into hiding.

During the entire period for the Battle of Aachen, 5,637 prisoners had been taken by the First Infantry Division. The Division successfully held off many strong attacks by German armor and infantry, supported by the heaviest artillery concentrations that the First Division had ever experienced. At the same time, the First Division continued the attack against all resistance and assaulted and captured a fortified city.

It is believed that the success of the Battle for Aachen was due to the fact that the Germans, in the first place, had expected the First Division to attack the town prior to the attack on the main Siegfried Line itself; most of the defenses of Aachen were concentrated to the south and after fixing them with artillery, mortar and aerial bombardment, the enemy flank was turned from the east and north from a position which he had least expected the attack to come.

At the surrender of Aachen, Colonel Wilck the Commandant of the City admitted that "Germany is washed up. The 'V' weapons upon which the German propaganda leans so heavily can be no more than harassing weapons of no effect in the final outcome. Only America can save us, as I don't believe in miracles any longer," he said. The Colonel was asked if German resistance was at a low ebb, to which he replied: "Even if you surrender them in pockets the German soldier will fight to the end to carry out the Fuehrer's orders."

◆　　◆　　◆

MONS AND AACHEN

As I Saw It

By

MARK WATSON

UP TO THE crossing of the Seine, the western front campaign had broken neatly into 2 sections of equal length, if one goes by the calendar, but of quite different quality if one is counting either yardage gained or rains endured. The first 7 weeks were spent in battering a path from the beaches to St. Lo;

the next 7 in the series of leaps and drives which were to carry the American forces across the Seine, into and above and below Paris. Upon that lovely city the First Division's eyes had no chance to gaze. Others did the gazing. The Americans' drive to the northeast was continued without halt by VII Corps, the 4th Cavalry Group making a sweeping reconnaissance, followed closely by the three component divisions, the 1st on the left, the 3rd Armored in the center, the 9th Division on the right.

By this arrangement it was the First's privilege to be engaged for the next week in experiences as extraordinary as troops ever encountered—with wave after wave of retreating Germans, trying desperately to break out of the huge pocket into which they had been penned by the speed of the American advance. This new pocket, bigger than Argentan's, lay west and northwest of the course the First Division was following on the far side of the Seine. Out of it the frantic German divisions, vestiges of 3 armies, strove to scramble eastward to the temporary protection of the West Wall defenses by any road, and any means, and in any formation. The fugitives' efforts were to be no such skillful and well supported attacks as the First had been getting in Normandy, but a series of blind rushes (German communications and reconnaissance and forward intelligence were literally zero) made by vast masses of infantry without artillery support and almost without transport for their own wounded. German infantry had been encountered in Africa and Sicily and Normandy, but never Germans in any such desperate state as those whom the First experienced on the Soissons-Mons road.

Soissons was reached handily on 31 August. Our armor had ground its way down the highway where enemy resistance had been expected, and where it was certain a German supply column would try to push in. Here was the Villers-Cotteret forest (which the First had seen in 1918), which the Nazis had converted into one of the great storage areas for the western front fighting. It was still crammed with ammunition and equipment, so difficult was it for Von Rundstedt to find transport with which to move these goods to the troops who so badly needed them. It seemed a model storage arrangement, for the thick overhead foliage blocked aerial view not only of personnel and of the countless wooden shelters under which the waiting shells were stored, but of the narrow wood-roads which gave access to the entire grid-work. Allied bombing could have been done only blindly.

We pushed into the dark wood somewhat gingerly, wondering when we would run into enemy guards or, equally likely, retreating enemy troops replenishing their supplies from this copious hoard. A few must have been there, we discovered next day, but on this occasion there was no interference as we explored the dump and examined a few of the methodically arranged shelters. At each doorway, protected from the rain, was a checker's listing, the number of the shelter, the class of ammunition within, the amount on hand, the date of last inspection and verification. At each portal was a counter, exactly the right height for unloading from a truck, with a ramp leading downward to the shelter's storage-floor. Several of the huts which we saw that day we never saw again, for when we returned in the morning with a salvage crew we found there had been a night visitor who had blown up a row of the shelters before clearing out: where there had been orderly little wooden structures now was a row of holes in the earth, with shattered and blackened trees about.

There were other parts of the forest and the neighborhood which had an interest for men with long memories. In one of the dark lanes was found a lettered signboard at the foot of a hillock at whose top had been in July 1918 the observation point of General Mangin. The young men with me had never heard of Mangin, but I remembered well the name and face and brusque manner of that tough little Frenchman who in 1918 commanded the field army in which the First was included for the Soissons attack. I remembered that particular O. P., and also the cave within which lay our own corps headquarters. Some distance off I found again the escarpment on which I had stood for a time on that eventful July day 26 years earlier, and watched the American First and 2nd Divisions, flanking the 1st French Colonials, hammer their way through the German resistance and gain for Foch the great Soissons victory which was the turning point of World War I.

Beside the road lay another reminder, an international cemetery in which lay row after row of 1918 dead, most of the graves with German markers, a good many lettered in French, not a few in Arabic. Speaking of these reminders later in the day, I learned that General Huebner (wounded there in 1918) had been doing a little recollecting of his own. He suggested a short ride down another road. It was worthwhile, for there lay the dignified monument of this same First Division, bearing an inscription which I jotted down for later reference. It recorded the First's role in the Soissons victory of 1918, and the price of that performance in the 4 days' fight—2,213 dead, and 6,347 wounded. The World War I division was a larger unit than that of World War II, but 8,560 casualties were no handful then. The names in bronze were easily legible. So was the proud passage which was there quoted from General Pershing's tribute to his own First Division, and which should be re-quoted in every history of the eternal First for the inspiration of generations to come:

> The Commander-in-Chief has noted in this division a special pride in service and a high state of morale, never broken by hardship nor battle.

There was not much time for nostalgia so far as the 1944 crop of First Division veterans was concerned, for the reconnaissance reports warned of roaming Germans moving eastward. The cleaning-up of Soissons itself was easy and surprisingly profitable, for in the railway station itself were two fully made-up trains ready to move but with nowhere to go. The American Air Force's skillful bombing had shattered the outgoing railway tracks and done a particularly effective job on the tunnel north of the city, with a direct hit by heavy bomb at each entrance of the tunnel, timed so well as to catch a German train in the tunnel itself. The trains in the Soissons station were particularly interesting, for one of them was loaded with war materiel which the enemy would have been glad to get, and the other with food which *we* were glad to get: First Division messes for several days were enlivened by Westphalia hams and noodles, and tinned asparagus and some of the best canned cherries that ever dazzled a soldier who had seen nothing like that for months, and would not see anything like it again for still longer.

Northwest of the city, off the main route of the division, we came upon the almost unbelievable creation of Margival, the newly completed and never occupied headquarters for the German Commander in the west. It lay in a sheltered valley, where there had been no village, and hence where the Allied Air Forces would be unlikely to do any map-bombing on suspicion. It was such a triumph of camouflage that even from a moderate distance at the ground level one would fail to see it, and such a triumph of secrecy in building (by the Todt organization) that even the occupants of a nearby French village had never seen it and knew only vaguely that some kind of building had been going on with imported workmen. Yet beneath the forest of painted camouflage strips and netting lay broad concrete streets with spaced lamp-posts for night illumination. Beside the road lay the well-designed buildings, of reinforced concrete walls reaching far below ground-level, roofed with armor, comfortably and even luxuriously furnished for the great number of staff officers who were to have offices and quarters in this model headquarters. The council room designed for Von Rundstedt with its map-cases and huge table, perfectly lighted, almost made one wish that the war would halt around here long enough to permit its use by the Division. Fire-extinguishers were in their places, engravings on the neat walls (labels on the backs were invariably those of looted art-shops in Paris) comfortable work-chairs and easy-chairs in each officer's room and (model of German thoroughness) in each wardrobe a bootjack. About the edge of Margival were defense-post pillboxes but for precaution's sake no large anti-aircraft installations: those we later saw on the surrounding hills. It was all like a stage set, save for its decidedly permanent character, a truly perfect headquarters completed, by a jocular Fate, just too late to be of any use to its builders.

Out of Soissons we moved, along the road to Laon, following so close on the advance party that the highway itself was still almost empty, save at crossroads where elements had been dropped off to set up roadblocks to the west and keep an eye open for oncoming Germans. Yet so rapidly was the Division moving that when we retraced our route next day it was to find the right side of the highway clogged with advancing infantry. And it was coming none too soon, for the crossroads guards were sending out frequent reports of German patrols moving toward them and falling back after a brisk fire-fight to await the arrival of their own main columns.

There was a particularly lively fight engaged in by a battalion of our own infantry which had a battery of artillery attached for just this sort of business. North of Soissons it reached a crossroads from which our reconnaissance had been sending out signals to hurry forward. The battalion arrived almost simultaneously with a Kampfgruppe of approximately regimental strength coming in from the left. The Germans' light artillery had already moved into position so well concealed that our men could not locate it. Our artillery was accordingly handicapped, but only briefly. A light observation plane put into the air and soared defiantly through enemy flak until it spotted the concealed guns, and then gave firing data so quickly and reliably that in a matter of minutes the enemy fire had ended and the two infantry columns were engaged. The enemy still was too numerous for us, but he was not after fight so much as freedom, instructions having apparently been for the commander to get his men back to Germany with all possible speed. For whatever reason, a part of the enemy column continued the fight with out battalion, and the rest of it cleared the highway and made its way eastward in good order. We found consolation in the knowledge that there the fleeing Germans would run into the path of the 3rd Armored and, if that was passed, the arms of the warmly receptive 9th Division which was moving abreast of us some miles to the east.

That we kept running into enemy troops in march column, who were massed on the highway, instead of being well dispersed and covered, was our greatest surprise, for it seemed incredible that these German veterans would so expose themselves to attack. The explanation was, of course, that they were blind. The terrific pounding which the Air Forces had given them for days had destroyed the Germans' telephone and telegraph installations, with a few more being blown up by the French underground: the Luftwaffe was almost totally shattered: as a result the enemy had neither good information of what was going on nor any way of communicating what he himself knew. This same day, beyond Soissons, several small and terribly weary German columns were knocked off without difficulty because their commanders had never dreamed there were Americans in the vicinity until they ran into our roadblocks and a sweep of machinegun bullets from the roadside. They had no notion of whether they were blocked by a battalion or by a squad, the latter being the case very often. One of these columns was led by a dumfounded German major who explained that he had thought the road would be entirely clear for he had "only just received orders to march to Chateau-Thierry". At that moment Chateau-Thierry had been in American hands for 2 days.

To see whether this same sort of thing was common along our front (the V Corps lay to our left, and beyond that the XIX Corps, and still to its left the British and Canadians) we set out on a short exploratory trip, missed a warning landmark somehow, and eventually found ourselves in a series of hamlets near the Guise Forest, receiving from each group of villages a most tumultuous reception. It was all very flattering, to be sure, but not without its disturbing aspect, for what it chiefly meant, I surmised, was that we were the first Americans in. That proved to be the case, an ancient Frenchman adding that he had not seen an American since 1918. "Any Boches today?" I inquired. "Ah, yes, the brutes," said my informant, spitting contemptuously in the road. "There, and there, and there, and there." He pointed in all four directions. We moved in just one, put up for the night, and next day regained contact with the First as it moved across the Cambrai-Le Cateau-Charleville road and into the Mornal Forest.

From here past Maubeauge and into Mons (that same road over which the British Old Contemptibles had made their magnificent fighting retreat in 1914) was an almost continuous rat-race such as never before was met in my experience. The occasional encounters previously mentioned—with retreating Germans coming up from the left, running into roadblocks and into substantial American forces they had not dreamed of meeting—now became the rule at almost every cross-road. American battalion and company commanders welcomed these wanderers with bursts of fire which killed scores of Germans and induced hundreds, now leaderless, to surrender. Actions over, our well-pleased battalion commanders hastened to make their reports to regiment or division, only to receive the answer from an equally dazed headquarters that the same thing was going on forward and in the rear.

The east-bound tide of Germans ripe for disaster seemed endless. The main problem was not in defeating an already demoralized enemy, but in finding cageroom for the prisoners. The enemy dead were numerous, but they could be left to the villagers. The living prisoners had to be disarmed and guarded and transported back to prisoners' cages, and this was no small task for a division whose personnel was already outnumbered by its own prisoners. As August ended and September began, the road over which we had lately come was a most astonishing sight, with vast columns of bedraggled German prisoners trudging along in column, guarded only by a couple of American military police at the front of the column and a jeep load at the rear, with one or two machine guns or none at all.

Beside the road, sometimes standing in formation, sometimes allowed to rest wearily on the bank, were smaller groups waiting for transport or guards. When transport was available one saw American trucks jammed with standing German prisoners and not even one American guard save only the driver. There was still a typical road discipline. Repeatedly one saw columns of perhaps 500 prisoners, disarmed, dirty, weary, knowing themselves defeated and their country gone, respond instantly to a command, take up the march cadence and push on down the road to imprisonment but with heads up—even if they did look with uneasy forebodings at roadside fields where French or Belgian peasants were already digging long trenches for the burial of German dead, piled up like cordwood at the crossroads.

There was one highway where the spectacle sickened even men who had seen little save death and misery all these weeks. That was the place where a very long German double-column moving rapidly eastward and filling the entire wide highway had been spotted by an American fighter-bomber formation. The planes deferred their own mission long enough to sweep down and machinegun the helpless German unit from one end to the other. An instant later our own artillery, observing the planes' target, opened up with salvos which completed the destruction and left a much-reduced and miserable lot of prisoners to be gathered up. That was a road we had to use, over which accordingly bulldozers were driven to shove the dreadful debris off the highway. Young soldiers who had cheerfully said they never could see enough dead Germans changed their minds that day.

How could such complete disasters take place? These Germans were veteran troops, the very ones who had been making life both unhappy and uncertain for the Division for the past twelve weeks. They had proven themselves to be skilled and self-reliant soldiers. How could such men be slaughtered like sheep? How could they blunder ahead blindly into such obvious traps as were set for them at every crossroads? Probably discipline, which had made them such superb fighters, was working against them this time, for they were too weary, or too dismayed, or too much obsessed by the order to get east at any cost, or too confident that there were no Americans in their path, to exercise the individual alertness of which they previously had shown themselves capable. Perhaps the first blast of fire on the head of the column knocked off the leaders. For whatever reason, this sort of business went on hour after hour and mile after mile, until the Americans themselves were sick of slaughter. Our radio picked up the running oral report of an American aviator who had just spotted a retreating column of German transport—no trucks this time, for German gasoline was exhausted, but farm-wagons drawn by horses seized from the farmers. "The column is solid and a half mile long," we could hear him saying. "I don't see any flak guns and I will take it near the deck . . . Those are magnificent Belgian horses, and I hate to pot them too . . . Well, here goes." That meant another road blockade for our bulldozers to dispose of.

There were narrow escapes from unexpected collisions at dusk. The battalion with which we were moving toward Mons was looking for a place to bivouac and had its eye on a truly ideal spot just ahead of us, with water and a low wood-covered ridge leading back and to the side in a sort of V. As we got there we found that the preceding (the 3rd) battalion had worked on the same idea and was already installed with patrols placed, roadblock fixed, and machineguns set.

We moved on wearily through gathering dusk to another brook far ahead. We had hardly got there when we heard a lively fire-fight back at the V-wood. No help was asked of us and in time the firing ended. In the morning we found that a large and unusually combative enemy group had been on our very road, close behind us, possibly figuring that the very boldness of their design would protect them. They were wrong. The 3rd's commander had a fine grasp of bivouac security and, without knowing what the night would bring, had stationed his outposts skillfully, with machinegunners on both sides of the road in a V, as described, with his heavy weapons near the highway and pointing down it, and with his men bivouacked on the wooded ridge overlooking the road. When the furthest outpost detected the enemy approach, the warning was instantly picked up by a suddenly wakeful battalion. It was quite dark by this time, but the enemy's own rifle fire betrayed his whereabouts and from all the aroused Americans, on both sides of the V, with heavy weapons roaring straight into the enemy's front ranks, came a devastating attack. There were not many surrenders, and a great many casualties. The next day found the road littered with dead men and horses and upturned wagons. Through scattered stacks of clothing civilians from the neighboring countryside were already rummaging in search of the first booty the Germans had provided them. From broken field desks cascaded whole mountains of regimental and battalion and company paper which never would worry a quartermaster or adjutant again.

Further ahead there was another and much less bloody example of what can happen on a dark night. The armored column had shifted over to our road and it too was going into bivouac, each tank rolling through the gate into an open field, as directed by the M.P. with his electric torch. An extra tank rumbled up the road and was methodically waved into the field. It lurched across the ditch and followed the others toward the bivouac. But as it did, the M.P. started with surprise, turned his torch's beam on the big vehicle's insignia and hastily unslung his gun. "Kraut!" he yelled, and his companions leaped up beside him. A warning shot halted the tank, and out piled a German crew not much more surprised than the

Americans. The pilot had been quite plainly lost. He had heard
tanks moving, thought they were other Germans, and tagged along.
Our M.P. was able thereby to match the story of one of his comrades
who had been waving traffic past a crossroads by broad daylight that
afternoon, and was getting very tired of it. He suddenly beheld six
German infantrymen, hands above their heads, rising from the ditch,
where they must have been sound asleep. He grabbed his rifle, then
saw there was no harm in them, and slung it back over his shoulder.
"Can't bother with you," he said sternly. "Too busy. Get back in.
that ditch and stay there." When his relief came, he piled his own
private prisoners in the truck and sent them back to the cage.

At Mons came a change in plan. Instead of continuing to the
northeast, we would leave one regiment here for the mopping up and
move east by southeast toward Charleroi, then cross the Meuse at
Namur, and then push ahead toward Liege and Eupen and Aachen—
that famous old capital of Charlemagne near the junction of Germany, Holland and Belgium. (At one time the First had elements
in those three countries and in France too—probably a record for
divisions).

The new plan sounded easy. We had come very far and very
fast, and there were few of us who doubted that we would keep on
that same pace to the Rhine. How very wrong we were we learned
only by degrees. On September 2 (just before we pulled into Mons)
there was an army directive to division commanders, that they were
to conserve supplies, especially gasoline and ammunition. It meant
business, too, even in jeep-quantities, as we found when we prepared
to load up for a long tour of the new front. We made a shorter tour
instead, and as the Corps moved toward the Meuse and the crossings
of Namur and Huy and so into Liege, we became more fully aware
of the supplies tragedy which had overtaken the Allies, owing to the
almost incredible speed of their bound across France and Belgium,
getting further and further from the beaches and their source of
supplies, stretching thinner and thinner the line of communication.
With what seemed to transport officers like a runner's last gasp the
First Division crossed into the State Forest of Aachen, on 12 September. The First had reached Germany. A great goal was gained,

but our bounding days were over until February. And between now and February there were to be dark and bloody days for the First Division and for all our comrades on the Western Front.

Two days earlier the American entry to German soil had been heralded unmistakably by a battery of VII Corps artillery which had rolled up into Division area and taken position in an orchard beside the road. The guns were laid with noticeable elevation, obviously for something close to maximum range. The map-reading was easy: the target was German soil—the first to be reached by ground-based artillery. It was a little crossroads named Bildchen, just outside Aachen. It was receiving this dubious honor solely because of its bad geographical luck in being the nearest point in Germany and the only one in range of our guns. The gunners expressed curiosity over what the Bildcheners were saying, for, accustomed as the enemy by that time was to the descent of air-borne bombs, there would probably be something like despair over the arrival of artillery shells, for this could mean only that the American ground forces now were very close indeed. It was with interest, therefore, that Bildchen was visited a few days later when the Division kept the promise of the heralding cannon and moved down the road south of Aachen. There we passed the Bildchen crossroads. Scarred it was by the shells whose departure we had watched, but not nearly so much as our bloodthirsty hopes had encouraged.

Aachen we saw that first day only from the distant hills to the south. It was 13 September, and the guessing was lively about when the First would march into the ancient city. In our ignorance, and confidence that the First could do anything it wished, regardless of the halt in supplies, we surmised that capture would be easy in a week. If anybody had tried to say it would take more than a month he would have been howled down. But it was 16 October when finally the First, moving up from the southeast suburbs joined hands with the 30th, moving down from the northeast hills, and thus completed the ringing of the city. It was 21 October when the German garrison commander finally surrendered his 800 surviving troops.

The American high command was wiser than we, and knew that the city would not be readily given up. The original commander,

Schwerin, had recommended evacuation, which would have served the double purpose of protecting the ancient city from sure destruction, and conserving the garrison troops for more fruitful defense work further east. Schwerin's sound suggestion was rejected by Hitler, and he himself was recalled to Germany and oblivion, while his successor organized the local resistance.

The First, on instructions, passed to the south of Aachen and a little later the 30th Division passed to the north, attaining a part-envelopment which was due to make lamentably slow progress. There was plenty of other work to be done at the southeast, and the First set about doing it with a brusque drive into Rotgen, by way of the long-awaited Siegfried Line—or rather, as we were to discover, a spur of the real West Wall.

Surely there was nobody in the Division, by that time, who had not heard of the Siegfried Line, thought of it uneasily, and finally decided with soldier's fatalism that it could not be so much after all and certainly not enough to worry a Division which had battered its way across France and Belgium and now even a corner of Holland. The talk of "dragon's teeth" did not terrify the boys at all; this fairy-tale nomenclature, in fact, probably served to lessen the First's awe of the German creation.

However, there was no rollicking laughter among us that day when we moved up over a ridge near Rotgen and, starting down into the low valley on the other side, came suddenly upon our first sight of the Line. There it lay—five rows of gleaming concrete blocks of uneven shapes and heights, close enough to each other to block a tank and rugged enough to tilt a hurdling tank off its tracks and expose it to fire from the concealed batteries on the distant slope. Lengthwise the little valley the five rows reached, vanishing into a distant wood in one direction and over the horizon in the other. Short of them, at first escaping the eye, was a parallel ditch, some 15 feet deep and broad, and a very impressive tank obstacle itself—provided the attackers were seen in time and placed under fire from the concealed guns on the other slope. For the defenders there were at intervals sally-ports, in the form of narrow paths passing through the dragon's teeth and by a bridge over the moat. The whole path was mined, presumably. A final stretching of wire, and mines again, made an infantry attack something to undertake cautiously.

There was not much laughter among the Americans who looked down upon that spectacle and pondered what would have happened had a determined defense force carried out its proper mission at that point. Most fortunately for us it had done nothing of the sort. Our artillery had knocked out the pillboxes, concealed though they had been, and silenced the enemy guns, and then discouraged the enemy riflemen while our own infantry rushed the works. Thus protected, our engineers with great dispatch cleared the mine field, bulldozed a few tons of earth into one point of the great ditch and bridged the gap, blew out a fresh path through the dragon's teeth, and thus cleared the way for the American armor which rapidly spread out on the far side and went on with its normal business, closely followed by new waves of infantry and artillery. We were luckier than some of the other divisions, partly because the VII Corps had moved up so rapidly that the enemy did not have time to man all his West Wall defenses properly. Most of his defenders were dead west of Mons or in our cages. Even so, we had struck a soft spot and thought, in our relief, that we were through the whole Wall. We found otherwise very soon, and kept on finding out more for weeks to come, all of it extremely disagreeable.

Now this was a stunning experience to our replacements, who had not known the miseries of the beach-fighting back in June, nor the rugged days around Mortain. It was depressing for the veterans too, for the exhilirating success of the rapid jumps eastward after the St. Lo break-through, and the astonishing successes of a fortnight previously on the road to Mons had dimmed the painful memory of our losses in Normandy and led the old and young to the fond delusion that nothing now could stop the First—and (perhaps) lesser American divisions. The next few days on the line between Aachen and Stolberg slowly strangled that happy delusion. The Germans in their concealed defenses had wholly different ideas from the Germans we had blocked in their eastward flight back on the Maubeuge-Mons road. These new fellows had no idea of going east, and no idea of letting us go east either. They hammered back the First's attacks, and when opportunity offered they counterattacked with a fury that nothing but a death-stroke seemed to terminate. The talk had been of our meeting only German fortress-defenders made up of cripples and sick and aged: there apparently was some mistake in the estimate for we were running into extremely tough fellows who barred both our eastward path and also that sudden turn to the north by which we had hoped to finish the envelopment of Aachen. Our casualties rose, and among the new dead were many extremely valuable officers and non-coms who had gone unscathed through the bitter days which we mistakenly had thought were over.

It could have been a lot worse. That much we knew, and in it there was a crumb of comfort. Every German that had been killed before he could escape from the Argentan pocket, every German who had died in the frenzied rush west of Mons, every one of the huge bag of prisoners the First had made in those two great successes—all these were out of the way, and had they not been put out of the way they surely would now be facing the Americans in the West Wall, they and all their tanks and field guns which happily were out of business. That was all to the good, certainly. The record showed that the German First and Fifth and Seventh armies had been fearfully mauled by the American First Army all the way across France, and many of their component divisions had been obliterated. That was true, but nevertheless here was the German Seventh in quite un-ghostlike form once more squarely across our path. It now was composed of different divisions to be sure, and certainly no such divisions as we had destroyed utterly, but in this defensive warfare, in prepared positions, on German soil, with loyal civilians behind them, these new divisions were good enough to make a great deal of trouble for the stoutest-hearted invaders.

Our halcyon days were over indeed, for a time. Supplies of artillery were still short, just when we desperately needed artillery to batter through the Line. Our enforced slow-down had checked the troops in the flush of victory and, worse, had provided the beaten enemy with a breather. Perhaps worst of all, our vast superiority in the air, which had been mounting steadily, now had suddenly ceased to matter so greatly in the tactical fighting, for the weather had changed, and day after day was drenched with rain and fog so dense that not one of our numerous air squadrons could pierce it—a circumstance of which the enemy promptly took swift advantage. A fortnight ago it had seemed that all the advantage was with the Americans. Now, unmistakably most of it had shifted to the enemy, as suddenly as the Trojan heroes' battle advantage three milleniums ago had shifted with the whims of the Olympians, and apparently as irreconcilably.

It was not merely that our luck had run out. We were meeting opposition which would have been hard to best anywhere, and which we were well pleased had not been met at the point where the dragon's tooth line was breached. The First had taken a useful hill south of Stolberg, and the enemy wanted to get it back. The recovery mission was given to an SS battalion which ignored the up-hill handicap and, following an artillery pounding, started up the long treeless slope in sound skirmishers' fashion, a few individuals racing forward and then dropping while others leapfrogged them. Their trouble was that they had no cover, and when they came well up toward our positions they were met by a sweep of machinegun fire that left many of them kicking. The others came on undiscouraged, their own fire searching out the American machinegunners, but without full success. More of them fell. The others came on, and on, until the whole battalion was lost. A larger attack party from the same courageous and marvelously disciplined division made a second attempt, aided by heavier artillery and mortar support, but it too was beaten back, and the First held its ground. A wounded German who was hauled into our lines spoke with admiration of his captors. "We have been three years on the Russian front," he said, "and we have been beaten before. But it is the first time we have ever been stopped by small-arms fire."

We made attacks, too, which for the moment fared no better than had that German charge near Stolberg. The enemy's defensive positions were ingeniously placed and courageously held, and all over again the Americans discovered the perfection of a German defense in a retreat through the hills where guns could be left in concealment to cover every point of approach. Around Aachen, among other places, where Hitler had elected to make a stand, there was a plethora of ammunition in dumps. Little new materiel was coming forward, so well had the Allied Air blocked the routes, but the dumps which had been there for years were now at hand, and the attacking Americans suffered from it. Every foot of ground we gained that month was gained at sacrifice.

The First was not given to demonstration. Perhaps that is why the memory of one of its few ceremonies persists to this day. Fifty officers and men of the Division had been ordered late in September to General Huebner's headquarters, in a cottage which in normal times was occupied by the superintendent of the little mill in the ravine. The only agreeable thing about the cottage was that it stood on a small elevation, high enough to lift it from the mud into which the cold rains had converted the rest of the area. To it the fifty slogged through the mud that morning, and took their places on the slope, just as General Courtney Hodges, First Army commander, and Lt. General J. Lawton Collins of the VII Corps, motored up to the cottage, to be met by General Huebner. There was a short exchange of conversation, and then the three generals with a group of staff officers stepped up to the waiting fifty, now standing at attention in double rank. To each of the fifty went a battle decoration—sixteen of them Silver Stars, and two of them battle clasps marking a second winning of that trophy. To each went the respectful salute of the three generals, and with no more of a show than that the fifty then slogged through the mud back to their units to proceed with the day's fight. There was no flag, no brass band, no speechmaking, save the reading of the citations as each man received his award. My own notes of the event record that "the only field music was the whistling of the chill, damp wind sweeping over meadows which a few days ago were German soil." Of all these fifty only one was a field officer. The feats performed were all in the day's run for the First no doubt, but they were good. I recall one of the men was a staff sergeant who in gentler days ran a country grocery in Virginia; his particular exploit has escaped my memory but I recall that, also, he had never missed a day's action since he joined the division, and that included days when he was wounded. I recall another stalwart who some months before had been the only surviving non-com. of his section in a particularly hot fight; he took over the job of reorganizing what men he had left and starting a new attack; he did that five times, and took the position the section had been ordered to take. I hope those fifty pulled through the next four months of fighting, but I doubt it.

For the next ten days the First earned all the ground that it took, which was not much. The rain continued to fall, drenching all mankind and making the meadowland into a mudwallow, through which the tanks could not make their way with any effectiveness, any more than the airplanes could find their way through the opaque upper air. The losses around Hurtgen were mounting. So were those in our lines nearer Aachen. Supplies were still short and promises of betterment were few. Aachen itself was a misery. It could not be by-passed altogether for there was urgent need of its roadnet to help our supplies through. And so at last came the decision to pound a way through the narrow zone still separating First and 30th Divisions. On October 8 it was achieved, and two days later, when it was thought the Aachen commander's spirit would be broken by the completed encirclement which new German attacks failed to break, Army headquarters sent in an ultimatum: unless Aachen should surrender in two days it would be reduced by airplane and heavy artillery bombardment. The ultimatum was rejected and on schedule the bombardment began, while the weary infantrymen sat back and stared. From the observation posts on the hill south of the city it was a most extraordinary spectacle of demolition, twice repeated. From many windows were flung white sheets of civilian surrender but there was still no yielding by the garrison commander, and once more the infantry attacks began. On 16 October a deep gain was made in the southeast edge of the city and the next day the First pushed well into the center of the city. Yet not until 21 October did the garrison command surrender.

Aachen, shockingly battered, was ours, and the truth is that, for all its obstinate defense, it was not much save a symbol. We had taken a treasured city which Hitler had insisted be retained. But we still were four months from the Rhine, and before that river should be crossed, the First would have to keep a rendezvous in the Ardennes.

CHAPTER VII

HURTGEN FOREST

November 10, 1944

The Situation

FIRST U. S. Army—letter of instructions—October 26, 1944 stated:—"There has been an increasing evidence of an enemy build-up on the front of the VII Corps and the XIX Corps of the Ninth U. S. Army."

As of November 10, 1944 the order of battle of major combat units was as follows:—First Infantry Division; 3rd Armored Division, 4th Infantry Division, 104th Infantry Division, 47th Infantry Regimental Combat Team (attached to the First Division), Combat Command Regiment 5th Armored Division, and the 4th Cavalry Group.

The First Division was still a part of the main effort but now occupied a smaller sector to the south of the 104th Infantry Division.

On November 6, 1944 the 4th Infantry Division commenced to move to the north where it went into position in the Hurtgen Forest on the southern flank of the VII Corps.

The major effort of the VII Corps was to be made by the First Division which would pass through the front of the 47th Regimental Combat Team in the direction of Langerwehe, to seize the crossings of the Roer River north of Duren, assisted by the 3rd Armored Division on the left. The First Division objective was designated as the town of Gressenich and the Hamrich-Nothberg ridge.

Initially supported by the attack of the First and 104th Infantry

Divisions, the 3rd Armored Division was to attack when ordered by VII Corps in conjunction with the First Division, to seize the area Hastenrath-Werth-Kottenich.

The 4th Cavalry Group was directed to assemble in readiness (temporarily attached to the First Division) to be prepared to move to block initial crossings of the Inde River between Inde and Weisweiler.

The 4th Division on the right was to seize the crossing of the Roer River in the vicinity of Duren and to the south thereof, and to assist the later advance of the First Division to seize Colgone.

To support the attack of the First and Ninth U. S. Armies a comprehensive air support plan known as "Operation "Q" was evolved by the combined efforts of the ground and air staffs. Operation "Q" was the largest close support effort ever flown by the Allied Air Forces.

D-Day was to be between November 11 and 16, 1944. Bad flying weather was constant up to and including November 15th. On November 16th the day dawned overcast and cloudy. As the morning wore on the sky began to clear. At 11:00 A.M. there was a ceiling of unbroken clouds from 1,000 to 1,500 feet over the target area. At 11:45 A.M. the air attack commenced.

The First Division advanced some elements to the southeastern outskirts of Gressenich and commenced house-to-house fighting in that town, while others advanced to the edge of Hamich. Other First Division elements advanced north and northeast along the line of the Wehe and into the Grossewald east of Schevenhutte.

As the attack made progress in the First Division area, the 16th Infantry contained several counterattacks near Hamich. On the right the 26th Infantry resumed the attack and continued its progress through wire and mine defenses for a thousand yard advance northeast of Schevenhutte.

The Hurtgen Forest was as deadly as miserable, as unrewarding and as relentless a battle as the First Division ever engaged in. The woods were treacherous; the mud was thick and slimy. The roads were practically nonexistent and the weather became worse and worse.

It was slow going all along the line. The Tanks and the Tank

Destroyers were working hard but could make but little progress against the gluey mud of the area, and the supporting artillery, although it was really "putting out" could hardly hope to knock out all the enemy guns which were raising hell with the forward infantrymen.

That's the way it was in the Hurtgen Forest. Eventually it became a contest to see which side could outlast the other. The Germans had two divisions on hand and part of a third. Gradually the Germans were pushed back in the Gressenich Woods by the 26th Infantry in a bloody foot-by-foot tree-by-tree struggle. Through Histern the Germans were knocked out in a house-to-house struggle by the 18th Infantry. Casualties on both sides were heavy—each house, each hill, each hole in the ground was fought for, and gains were reckoned in yards—not the miles of the race through France and Belgium.

The lock was finally broken when Langerwehe was entered on November 27, 1944 and Hill 203 seized, and Frenserberg Castle had been cleaned out. On December 7, 1944 the sector was officially taken over by the 9th Infantry Division.

◆　◆　◆

HURTGEN FOREST
November 10 to December 8, 1944

The Record

THE Hurtgen Forest goes down in First Division History as one of the most unpredictable battles of World War II—for all time as far as that goes.

The most disheartening factor of all was the German mortar and artillery fire. The Germans had the best observation posts, and occupied the commanding ground. The Germans were everywhere, and in the thickness of the woods it was impossible to spot them, or divide them up so they could be developed or flanked. There was nothing to do but grind ahead from tree to tree, from hole to hole. Foxholes were not much protection; in the Hurtgen Forest every shell was a tree burst, and further, a foxhole was never portable.

The First Division expected a rest after the rough days on Verlautenhdide Ridge, and in the shattered streets of Aachen, but there was no rest. The First Division stayed in the line patrolling toward Quinx and the Wurseler Woods. On the other side of the line the Germans continued to build up in order to write off the loss of Aachen by stopping any further advances to the East.

On November 10, 1944, the Division moved out of contact with the enemy for the first time since the middle of July when preparations were being made for the breakthrough at St. Lo. This time the recess was for a total of six hours while the Battalions moved from their lines around Aachen to the Vicht and Mausbach area, to the south for the attack towards the Roer River.

A quick appraisal of the new ground showed that the First Division was up against a tough proposition again. The enemy had every advantage of the terrain, holding the open ground on the Gressenich-Hamich-Heistern-Langerwehe axis, and the thick woods on the east. The most important enemy position was Hill 232 which he used as an observation post as one officer musingly reflected: "This OP (observation post) was a 'natural'. From it the enemy could look down our throats in Gressenich, and observe the slightest twitch in Hamich."

The Germans had plenty of artillery to back up their position on Hill 232. It was estimated that about 200 pieces of artillery alone could be laid down by the enemy on any particular sector of the First Division front. The Germans were also dug in behind a cat's cradle of mines, concertina wire, and well coordinated final protection lines.

D-Day was set for November 16, 1944. At 11:00 A.M. it stopped raining for the first time in a week, and at 11:15 A.M. the Air Forces saturated the area with a preparation bombing.

At 12:45 P.M. the 16th Infantry moved out from Schevenhutte towards Hamich; the 47th Infantry Regiment of the 9th Division (attached to the First Division) moved out toward Gressenich, and the 26th Infantry started its slow and costly grind through the Gressenich Woods to the east.

It was slow going all along the line. The tanks and tank destroyers, though they were working hard, could make little progress against the gluey mud of the area, and the supporting artillery, although it was really "putting out" could hardly hope to knock out all the enemy guns which were pouring shells into the forward elements of the First Division.

Late in the afternoon the 16th Infantry had advanced with hand-carried weapons to the Hamich Line, but Gressenich was still holding out, blocking all the roads along the route of advance.

Hamich itself was a hold-off. Heavy enemy counterattacks from the village were turned off by the First Division, but German artillery likewise cooled any Division attempts to get into the town. On November 17th the 16th Infantry moved in and Hill 232 was neutralized by fifteen battalions of U. S. Artillery. Then the counterattacks started. The Germans threw tanks and self-propelled guns into action in an attempt to recover Hamich. German artillery also grew stronger than ever. The attacks went on night and day, and on several occasions the only way the Germans could be beaten off was by the First Division Infantry calling down artillery fire on their own positions in the town. Enemy tanks were knocked out by every means available—artillery and fighter bombers, and in one instance by a Doughboy in a second story window—with a Bazooka—sending a well-directed shot through the hatch of a German tank.

Allied Air was active in front of the First Division. At 11:15 A.M. November 17th, thirteen hundred heavy bombers from the 8th U. S. Air Force bombed in front of the First Division area. Ninth Air Force (U. S.) bombers repeated the attack at 2:25 P.M. At 3:00 P.M. one thousand heavy bombers from the Royal Air Force bombed in front of the Division line.

By 5:00 P.M. the First Battalion, 16th Infantry was consolidating its position; the 2nd Battalion, 26th Infantry had knocked out one pillbox and was mopping up enemy resistance in its area. The 1st Battalion, 47th Infantry was engaged in house-to-house fighting in the outskirts of Gressenich.

At 8:00 A.M. November 18th, the 3rd Battalion, 16th Infantry attacked Hamich. By 9:00 A.M. the 3rd Battalion had taken about one-third of the town of Hamich, but were receiving direct artillery fire from Hill 232. Five enemy tanks approached Hamich from the ridge outside the town, but First Division artillery knocked these tanks out before they entered the city.

Hill 232 was seized by the 2nd Battalion, 16th Infantry at 3:30 P.M. November 18th. The Germans counterattacked in the middle of the town of Hamich, concentrating their attack on the 1st and 3rd Battalions of the 16th Infantry. The 16th reported that ten enemy tanks and two hundred troops were in the center of Hamich at 9:50 P.M. By 11:30 P.M. the German counterattack had been repulsed, and two companies of the 16th Infantry were still in Hamich.

By the close of this rugged day, the First Division was consolidating its positions in captured territory, and prepared to attack the following day with the 26th Infantry.

At 12:30 A.M. November 20th, the 16th Infantry reported: "2nd and 3rd Battalions now in contact with the 18th Infantry. 1st Battalion, 47th Infantry and the 2nd Battalion, 18th Infantry in touch with the 18th Infantry." Further report said: "Attack will be delayed a half hour—reason: Company K moved on its objective in the dark and was disorganized by enemy tanks."

At 8:30 A.M. November 20th the attack was resumed. Artillery preparation was fired all along the First Division front. Four Infantry Regimental Combat Teams—the 16th, 18th, 26th and 47th (attached), backed up by the artillery fire of the 7th, 32nd, 33rd and 84th Field Artillery Battalions starting the ball rolling.

Fire-fights were engaged in several towns, Heistern and Hamich offering stubborn resistance. The town of Wenau was cleaned out by the 18th Infantry. One platoon of self-propelled 155-mm guns, recently attached to the 18th Infantry, rendered great service in Wenau. Progress was held up considerably by blown bridges, and culverts. Removing and marking minefields also slowed things down considerably.

With the most important line of resistance cracked at Hamich and Hill 232, the Germans withdrew slowly, contesting every village, built-up area, and terrain feature on the way. Enemy casualties were extremely heavy, and replacements came in the form of every available man in the area. Service troops from the rear areas, engineers, veterinarians and artillerymen were thrown in as infantry. Separate battalions and companies, such as guard companies from German Corps Headquarters appeared on the front lines.

The terrain most suited to the German defense, was on the easterly flank of the First Division, in the Gressenich and Wenau Woods. In spite of the heavy forest, soggy ground and slimy mud, the 26th Infantry pushed out to take Schloss Laufenburg, a castle strongly defended by the Germans. The Germans put up stubborn resistance, but were almost completely wiped out after one day's fighting.

During the night of November 20-21, the enemy brought up reinforcements. The Germans counterattacked but were beaten off early the morning of November 21st. The Commanding Officer of German forces in Heistern, a Colonel Kimbacher, was captured in an aid station, conspicuously marked with a Red Cross, from which the Colonel had been directing the counterattack.

On November 23rd, the three critical areas across the First Division front were in the vicinity of Hill 187, on the left, the high ground of the bend of the railroad between Nortberg and Langerwehe in the center, and several hills about one thousand yards out of the town of Langerwehe. The Germans resisted stubbornly at all of these points and their reduction was a slow and costly procedure.

Early the morning of November 4th, the 47th German Fusilier Company was almost totally destroyed by the 16th Infantry which passed around this company's left flank and attacked it from the rear.

The Castle of Schloss Laufenburg became the center of a hot fight between the 16th Infantry and the German 47th Volksgrenadier Division. The German Commander pulled his troops back into the cellar of the castle, and then called down artillery fire on his position to counter the attacks of the 16th Infantry. The 16th finally took Castle Schloss Laufenburg, but the Germans persisted and launched several counterattacks, all of which were costly in casualties—to the Germans only.

On November 24th, Schonthal was overrun by First Division troops, and the hill northeast of the town was cleared of enemy troops. Hill 203, however, continued to hold out and in the afternoon a powerful German counterattack, directed from Langerwehe, and covered by a heavy mortar and artillery barrage, hit the 18th Infantry, and the Germans retook the high ground north of Schonthal.

Bitter fighting took place on Hill 203. Both First Division troops and German troops were on this hill, and neither could drive the other off. The fighting rolled back and forth, until finally, on November 27th, the Division drove all enemy troops off the hill.

The Germans made another attempt to retake Hill 203, and Castle Schloss Laufenburg on November 23rd. German casualties were extremely heavy due to stubborn resistance of a practically new outfit of Germans—the 89th Infantry which simply refused to quit.

The reverse slopes of Hill 203 were well defended by a group of not more than 50 or 60 First Division troops, who, reinforced with excellently-sited automatic weapons, managed to hold control.

The Division continued the attack on November 24th, to seize the area Hucheln-Schilochen, crossing the Reichsautobahn and Inre River, relieving the 3rd Armored Division.

Fighting in the woods continued. Only the closest liaison between the infantry and artillery kept the First Division casualties down. Front lines became jammed close together, so difficult became the job of maintaining contact with units, due to the density of the forests.

On November 27th, the enemy position defending Langerwehe, and the open ground west of Duren, broke. During the night of November 26-27, the enemy brought up his first major unit from his hoarded reserves—the 3rd Parachute Division. Most of this outfit were young boys, 16 to 19 years of age, going into combat for their first time. The Germans tried to stage a super counterattack with the Parachutists, but failed and in the end, lost the Langerwehe-Jungersdorf position.

On the night of November 26th, the enemy situation was not

promising. Frenzerburg Castle, between the military highway and the railroad tracks, was still holding out, but it was dominated by the fire of troops of the 47th Infantry (attached to the First Division). Elements of the 16th Infantry were on high ground southeast of Gut Merberich, looking down on the buildings. A determined group of Germans was still contesting the 18th Infantry for the sole ownership of Hill 203.

The Germans concentrated on holding Frenzerburg Castle, and seemed to be reaching down deep into their bag of Reserves. The general plan appeared to be for the Germans to bring up a force of assault guns and take the Castle under fire. As the Germans started to move into assault position early the morning of November 27th, they were taken under fire by the 47th Infantry and decimated.

Meanwhile, the young Nazi Parachutists, full of high spirits and Nazi ideology, moved on to Gut Merberich. They had no more than reached the buildings when First Division Artillery registered square on the town, softening up for the attack by the 16th Infantry. The parachutists, who had never been under fire before, ran for the cellars, and were still there when the advance elements of the 16th forced the buildings. At least 75 prisoners were taken. To the north, the garrison of Frenzerburg Castle, unrelieved and not reinforced, was surrounded by the 47th Infantry.

To the east, another group of Parachutists (German) sent to relieve the battle group holding Hill 203, reached their positions just before the final assault of the 18th Infantry, timed to coincide with that of the 16th Infantry, pushed over the crest of the hill and overran the defenses. These German parachutists, like their comrades at the Gut, were overwhelmed by First Division preliminary artillery fire, and they surrendered in droves.

The 18th Infantry moved on to Langerwehe, cleaning out the woods to the east. By nightfall Langerwehe had been entered and was in the process of being cleared entirely of enemy elements.

At 3:00 P.M. the 3rd Battalion of German Parachutists, which was holding Jungersdorf, was pushed out by the 3rd Battalion, 26th Infantry after hard and heavy fighting.

To the south, other elements of the 26th Infantry, still working through the woods over a primitive and difficult road network, approached enemy positions in Merode. The First Division line was gradually being straightened out on a north-south axis, with all the villages on the line in First Division hands.

The position of the First Division was improved on November 28th when resistance in Stutgerloch was overcome. On the same day, the Frenzerburg Castle, which had been surrounded by the 47th Infantry, was taken, eliminating the last German pocket to the west of Langerwehe.

More than forty German dead were counted in Frenzerburg Castle, but the main body of defenders had escaped by a secret passage after refusing an ultimatum to surrender. The withdrawal was effected the night of November 27th, under cover of assault guns which moved up and shelled First Division positions.

On the Division right, the enemy positions at Merode were breached by the 2nd Battalion, 26th Infantry, which finally emerged from the woods and pushed two enemy companies into the town. Merode was unapproachable from the First Division side of town, by any heavy vehicles, or supporting weapons, while the Germans had an excellent supply net leading into Merode. The Germans made the most of this situation.

During the night of November 29th, the 2nd Battalion, German Parachute Regiment, which had withdrawn from Merode, counterattacked with powerful artillery support, and with assault guns.

The one track leading into Merode, from the First Division side of the lines, was taken by the Germans under intense artillery fire, and it was impossible to move up support weapons or reinforcements through the mud. A burned out tank lying directly across the road further impeded any relief.

The two companies of the 2nd Battalion, 26th Infantry, stood their ground, in Merode, but they were cut off from the rear, and attacked frontally by the Germans. They were hard pressed. Communication with these two companies did not exist and it was impossible to lay effective artillery fire from Division Artillery, on the Germans, this because of the lack of reported observation.

During the day of November 30th, the two Companies of the

26th Infantry continued to hold out in their part of Merode, but at twilight, November 30th, the Germans moved in and cut off the last hope of relief. Prisoners taken later reported that the remnants of Companies E and F, 2nd Battalion, 26th Infantry had been captured when their ammunition was gone, December 1, 1944.

On November 29th, a First Infantry Division order called attention to the fact that the First Division, in conjunction with the 104th Infantry Division, and the 4th Infantry Division, would continue the attack in its zone of action to secure crossings across the Roer River. The 104th Infantry Division was then Commanded by Major General Terry de la M. Allen, former Commanding General of the First Infantry Division, in its operations in Northern Africa and Sicily.

There is no doubt that enemy resistance to the First Division offensive of November 16th, 1944, was as tenacious and determined as any encountered in the Division's campaigns. By virtue of his stubborn resistance and reluctance to give up so much as a foot of defendable ground, the enemy was able to inflict a considerable number of casualties on First Division troops. In this he was aided by a terrain which was as unrelenting as the enemy himself. The deep woods through which the 26th Infantry forced its way, precluded the use of any support weapons except those which could be carried through the mud and underbrush, on a man's back. Enemy mortar and artillery fire, even heavier during this offensive than the concentrations laid on the Verlautenheide Ridge, in the Battle for Aachen, was increased in effectiveness by the high percentage of tree bursts obtained in the woods. Furthermore, the enemy was retreating over terrain which he knew intimately, and on which he had registered his artillery.

At the close of November, 1944, it was estimated that the German artillery was equal in number to that of the First Division, the first time such an advantage ratio had prevailed.

The morale of the enemy troops should have been shaky. It was not. Small groups, surrounded and cut off, refused to surrender. If the German command often sent suicidally small forces to perform what should have been battalion or even regimental missions, at least those forces fought until they were exterminated. Never before had

the First Division encountered an enemy regimental commander
personally directing local counterattacks, yet it happened during this
operation, when the Colonel commanding the 104th German Regiment, was captured fighting in an isolated and essentially hopeless
engagement.

The enemy's stubbornness, however, resulted in disastrous cas-
ualties. It is estimated that at least a battalion of infantry a day was
destroyed in the fighting around Hamich, Hill 232, Hill 187 and
Hill 203. Of the forty-one officers in the 104th German Regiment,
twenty-three were killed, wounded or captured by November 22nd.
Over 3,000 prisoners were taken and it can be said that the two
Divisions—the 47th Volksgrenadier and the 12th Infantry Division
(German) were destroyed.

On December 1, 1944, after two weeks of arduous fighting, the
Germans had succeeded in delaying the advance on the Roer River.
At Merode, the enemy had achieved a local success in holding the
town and eliminating two companies which had entered it. On the
other hand the Germans lost Hamich, Heistern and Langerwehe,
the framework of his defenses before Duren. In losing these towns,
however, the enemy suffered losses in personnel and materiel, and
in spite of his losses and his efforts, the line, on December 1st paralleled the course of the Roer River, and the natural defenses of the
terrain had been overrun.

This weakening tactical situation, however, in no way diluted
the enemy's determination to hold what he had. The Wenau-Merode
road was a very sensitive point; any effort on the part of the First
Division to move down the road was met by heavy and concentrated
fire, although the penetration of the 3rd Battalion, 26th Infantry
north of the road, met much lighter opposition.

The stutgerhof (large farmhouse) east of Langerwehe, was an
equally troublesome point. A platoon from Company I, 18th Infantry, which assaulted the house, was pinned down by intense artillery fire, and surrounded by enemy troops. After extremely bitter
fighting ten of the defenders were pulled out.

Enemy artillery, likewise, was at its high-water mark. It was
estimated that the enemy had available, besides the organic artillery

of the 3rd Parachute Division, the remnants of the 12th and 47th Volksgrenadier Division's Artillery, possibly that of the 3rd Panzer Grenadier Division, as well as normal corps and army artillery.

On December 1st, the 3rd Parachute Division (German) was opposing the First Division's advance. The survivors of the 47th Volksgrenadier Division, and of the 28th and 89th Regiments of the 12th (German) Division had been pulled out.

Luchem was the next enemy stronghold to be eliminated. It was reduced by a power play of infantry, tanks, tank-destroyers and artillery. On the morning of December 3rd, Luchem was held by elements of the 2nd Battalion, 8th (German) Regiment, and supported by a platoon of the 14th Company. The Germans considered themselves reasonably safe from any attack.

At 6:00 A.M. December 3rd, the 1st Battalion, 16th Infantry moved across the open ground between Langerwehe and Luchem and entered the western edge of Luchem.

There was no artillery preparation in the attack by the First Division on Luchem. The enemy was taken completely by surprise. As the infantry advanced, they liquidated the road-block shutting off the Langerwehe road. At daybreak, tanks and tank-destroyers were moved into the attack, and with their arrival, First Division artillery boxed in the area, to prevent the bringing up of reserves.

Although the Germans stubbornly defended the positions at the main crossroads, the town of Luchem was cleared in the afternoon. More than 150 prisoners were taken. The prisoners said that the sudden appearance of tanks had decided the question for them, further evidence that a few tanks may produce the German "hopeless situation" and consequent "honorable" surrender.

The German reaction to the seizure of Luchem, by the First Division, started with reconnaissance patrols, in the morning of December 4th. Shortly before dark, in the afternoon, movement was observed in the area northeast of Echtz, and First Division artillery, preparing for a concentration, had just registered on the area when the first elements of the attack left the enemy positions and advanced into Luchem. These elements were fairly in the middle of Luchem when First Division artillery caught them with fire from the four artillery battalions of the Division. Some of the enemy managed to struggle through to come to grips with the 16th Infantry but the back of the attack had been broken.

With the loss of Luchem, enemy activity went on the descendant. Artillery slackened off, and, although large-scale movements were observed, and attacked by Allied Aircraft, well behind the enemy lines, enemy activity in the forward areas was confined to minor reshuffling of troops and positions.

The enemy's attention swung to the north, where he mounted an attack, supported by ten tanks, against Lucherberg, previously captured by General Allen's 104th Division. The attack was unsuccessful, and did not spread to the First Division area. This decline of activity continued, interrupted by patrolling by both sides, until December 7th, when the Division was relieved by the 9th Infantry Division.

For the period December 9 to 16, 1944, the First Division was in bivouac areas in the vicinity of Henri Chapelle, Belgium, southwest of Aachen, Germany. All units, except the 16th Infantry, reinforced, began to rest, reorganize and re-equip. The 16th Infantry (reinforced) continued to be attached to the V Corps, in the Monschau area during most of this period.

◆   ◆   ◆

HURTGEN FOREST

As I Saw It

By

IVAN "CY" H. PETERMAN

SOUTHEAST of Aachen, where rocky ravines and the pillboxed slopes grow beards of bristling fir trees, lies the Hurtgen Forest.

Cold, gloomy and treacherous, it spreads its impenetrable mass, east to the impounded waters of the Roer, with the Plain of Cologne beyond, south to form alliance with the Schnee-Eifel. It is not one "staats forst" but several, consisting broadly of the Wenau wald, the Gressenicher, Merode, Hoch wald, Gemund, Rotgen, Munster and others—all segments of the Siegfried Line, and none of them benign.

Unlike Longfellow's murmuring pines and hemlocks, the Hurtgen is not primeval. It was hand planted in modern times at the order of the German General staff, and in that methodical process there was plenty of malice aforethought. Every natural advantage is screened; the thick spruce and balsams squat limbs to the ground, like football linemen challenging advance. The Hurtgen was not only shield and bastion, it provided a curtain for Von Rundstedt's Christmas offensive. And it thwarted every sortie aimed at the Roer River dams.

Today when winds blow down from the Eifel, across Hurtgen's conical spires toward wrecked Stolberg, smashed Duren, and twenty miles of ruined Rhineland lying between, the Forest may whisper of death and carnage, and the "green hell" it was in World War II.

Seven American infantry divisions and one armored combat team, tried to break the Hurtgen. All emerged, mauled, reduced, and low in spirits. Only two got all the way through: The First Infantry along the northern edge, and the 78th Infantry, which eventually seized the dams as the Roer campaign closed. Statistics reveal that for every yard gained, the Hurtgen claimed more lives than any other objective the Americans took in Europe.

The veteran 9th Infantry Division, ranging alongside the Big Red One as the Seventh Corps charged across Belgium, first ran into the murky Hurtgen. It was late September, above Elsenborn in what was called the Monschau forst, an assembly area throughout history, for German invasion of France. Here, an easy capture, was the large Wehrmacht camp, cleverly camouflaged in the woods. The 9th's artillery blasted the fir trees to kindling, but the Hurtgen resisted further advance.

The 28th Infantry tried next, up from Luxembourg to the vicinity of Rott and Zweifall, and thence into the labyrinth redolent of balsam. The Keystone doughs remained fourteen days; they drove over a matted mountain to capture Kommerscheidt and Schmidt, were expelled by an overwhelming panzer counterattack, came out minus one whole regiment, except for 350 men.

Next was the 4th Infantry's turn, and that seasoned outfit took possibly the worst losses of all, including its commanding general, "Tubby" Barton, whose health was ruined.

The Golden Arrow 8th followed, had no more luck than its predecessors, and the 5th Armored's CCR had a nibble. The 83rd in time had its chance, but the Hurtgen resisted them all.

When in March of 1945, six months later, soldiers of the 78th reached the dams, they passed the wreckage of six earlier efforts. Outside Kommerscheidt, beyond a wooded slope containing 2,500 German mines, they saw the 112th Regiment's dead, still by their vehicles in the snow, telephones and maps intact in the bunker CP, on top of which a Tiger tank had squatted, shooting the Yanks as they emerged. The 78th picked up thousands of mines, guarding every approach to the dams.

Such was the Hurtgen wald. Such its creeping barrage that erupted at each unwary step, marking its victim with a pillar of smoke toward which the defending enemy poured mortar and artillery fire.

Driving along the narrow, muddy roads—many a route was just a firebreak through the denseness—churning mud into the jeep until you literally had to kick it out or swamp the vehicle, the Hurtgen visitor in those days rode with the eerie feeling of being always observed. Although he could see no more than twenty yards into the thickness, the GI knew that hidden there, in ambush, in pillbox, bunker or slit trench, the Krauts were waiting. They specialized in tree bursts, splintering the tall firs, which dropped like javelins on troops below. Foxholes were roofed against this evil.

They had every road zeroed in. Every turn was a mortar target. Every crossroad an artillery objective. If the enemy were driven from one bunker, within a few minutes the new occupants would be shelled with direct hits. Germans in the next strongpoint had only to use the chart and pull the trigger. They could drop one in your lap as you wheeled down their "memory lane."

Small wonder then that when one American outfit withdrew, I wrote on November 16, 1944, the following description:

"When survivors retired from the Hurtgen today, they crouched in their vehicles, staring straight ahead. If there were heroics to recount, someone else had to talk. The men of this unit would not.

"Too many of their companions remained behind, too many were dead or missing. Too many grievously wounded and shattered in nerves and spirit. If they never saw Hurtgen Forest again it would suit them. If they never travelled its fragrant ravines, pitched another tent or hewed out a hut to ward off fragments and falling treetops, if they never saw a timbered slit trench, or smelled the tangy odor of burning cones and felt the springy needles underfoot, they wouldn't care. They had enough.

"They hated the Hurtgen Forest and all it defended. They hated its roads and ridges. They hated its cold and dampness. They hated its lurking death and the constant feeling of unknown danger. Yes, they hated the Hurtgen Forest where the stately Douglas firs with their epaulets of snow, ranged like frosted grenadiers, close-ordered on the hillsides—immutable, impenetrable, defiant. . . ."

It was muddy, mid-November when the Fighting First entered this formidable forest. It was a complicated assignment, that of taking the Gressenich-to-Langerwehe area, including a generous slice of the Hurtgen on the north, and the usual series of hills and towns along its edges.

The whole stretch was Siegfried defense, in depth. If there were no picturesque dragons-teeth tank blocks, there were minefields, booby-traps, shale slopes studded with automatic weapons, and mortars that seemed to be in league with the occult—so prompt were they to shower down if a doughfoot snapped a twig or rustled a branch as he moved among the trees. Moreover, the Germans knew this terrain like the back of their hands; if they used "pick-up" troops in certain spots, it was simply that anyone could defend them. We correspondents smiled at first when G-2 reported an outfit composed of veterinaries; the lads up front didn't think they were a joke. You didn't have to be overly clever to fan a field of fire from a West Wall position.

There had been a saturation air bombing prior to the first attack, which began November 16th. Clouds of U. S. 8th Air Force heavies, mediums, with dive bombers to finish any who remained above ground, shook the defenders, but did not shake them loose. The German-built bunkers were deeper and stronger than in the lines at St. Lo in Normandy, and there was no breach. Watching from the Stolberg Castle, which overlooked the First's area for attack, correspondents thought there couldn't be a live Kraut west of the Rhine. But there were.

They emerged when the raid ended, resumed positions, and any hope for a quick sweep with tanks was abandoned. General Huebner had moved from the rural menage west of Aachen and took up quarters at Vicht. The drive to Duren was cut out for infantry only.

From the outset, the Division realized this was no "vacation" after Aachen. If the 26th Regiment thought the approach to Aachen's barracks had been lively, if the Engineers prowling the hardwoods around those suburban hofs and nightspots above Charlemagne's old town, felt they'd lived through something, if the 16th and 18th battering Dawson's Ridge, Crucifix Hill, and the railway approach had been rugged, they quickly revised estimates in the Hurtgen.

Here as usual the Nazis had the high ground, the positions to command opposing movement, and ample artillery and automatic weapons to defend them. They also kept a quantity of tanks and SP guns handy in the woods, used them where needed.

During this campaign there was some scoffing at the type soldiers the Germans were using. At First Army briefings announcement that veterinaries were manning positions against the First Division, that new and beardless youth, or convalescents from hospitals were in the line, brought smiles. In retrospect, this seems rather wry humor. It must have been a grim joke to the Red One doughs. While such "pick-ups" could manage very well in certain Siegfried positions, the veterans of Tunisia, Sicily and the fight across France were meeting familiar faces.

Popping up like fresh dandelions despite repeated movings,

the 47th Volksgrenadier, the 12th Wehrmacht Infantry, and the 3rd and 5th Parachute Divisions had to be reduced again. The 3rd Para fought the First from Normandy through the Bulge. It was destined, by reason of Von Rundstedt's counteroffensive, to finish its days in front of the First, but miles west of the Hurtgen scenes. For at St. Vith in January, trying to dislodge the Yanks around Monschau, this prize Hitler outfit—possibly his very best—died in its tracks and almost to a man, as the First U. S, Infantry encircled and wiped it out beneath the snowy trees of the Wolfbusch.

During November there were many mad, inspired performances by the Germans. Remember, they were still enraged at the idea of Allied troops on their sacred soil. They were getting periodic pep talks, direct quotes from Der Fuehrer, to heave the invader over the border. Although Aachen, first large citadel of the Fatherland, had fallen, it stood at the very edge of Das Reich, and most of the frontier defenses still had to be reduced. The Siegfried Line was at least 20 miles deep in places, and at this strategic segment, the Hurtgen's dread hazards were not the least.

General Huebner picket the hamlet of Vich (or Vicht, depending on which map you used) for H.Q. If anything, it was drearier and muddier than the place he just left. The buildings weren't so good and there was no comparable schloss. G-2 was in a brick-stone house snuggled against a sidehill. I remember one day when a sizeable shell banged into the opposite hillside, just "a little over." You could hear the front rumbling beyond the ridge.

From Vich you took your choice on where you wished to see the war. If you liked hilly stuff, an exciting dash down an exposed road with 88-mm reception, you could try to see Hamich, the hard way. If you wanted both wooded and hilly terrain, the 47th Infantry, attached to the First Division for this operation, was not far off at Gressenich. But if you just didn't give a damn about life, and preferred being shot at from close range, a look at the 26th Regiment, up Hurtgen-way, was the place.

Members of the 16th might dispute this. They might argue if you wanted to shake hands with the Man with the Scythe, go visit Hill 232. It was enough to hear Captain Zera tell about it.

"You guys should see that hill," Maxie exclaimed. "Filled with dead. About 200 Krauts and something like 50 of our own men. We got a couple companies on it this afternoon, 2nd Battalion of the 16th went up there. The artillery worked it over plenty. Five thousand shells.

"Chewed up the trees with big stuff. The whole fifteen battalions of arty concentrated on that one little hill. Boy, you should see it!"

The capture of Hill 232 fell into half a dozen distinct acts. First, the artillery bombardment by the Americans. The Germans hastily got off the hill, or died there. Then, the 16th Infantry's 2nd Battalion charged up and dug in, placing automatic weapons. The Germans replied with their own artillery and mortars, laying down a scathing fire. But the Yanks held on, which fooled the enemy. When the counterattack began, the Nazis were annihilated almost to a man. The 16th kept the hill.

Another incident detailed at Division CP was one of those grisly things that occur just behind the firing line, but because they don't figure in the advance, are apt to be overlooked. A bunch of Krauts had surrendered, were herded into a stone barn. The Nazis, following fanatic custom that its OK to kill comrades who have quit, put down a mortar barrage, and one fat shell landed direct. There wasn't much need for PW trucks after the smoke cleared.

Later, when the QM detail arrived with the burial wagons, correspondents saw a pair of Negroes lugging the herrenvolk out, feet first. But a third darkie, unimpressed by the scene and light-hearted always, trooped behind the litter, strumming a salvaged guitar and loudly singing, "South of the Border."

Reflecting on the first ten days of this campaign, one is filled with admiration for the First Division's teaming of artillery with the infantry. By this super-effective fire, and the doughboys' quick follow-up, Herr Kraut certainly learned one thing: Once lost, a German position stayed lost. The overall net of German counter-attacks was worse than nothing. It was additional crippling loss.

Thus the effort to retake Hamich and Hill 232 in the early hours of November 19, an attack in force with considerable tanks and self-propelled guns, proved a dead loss. When some of the tanks got into the town, a favorite device—repeatedly used by the U. S. 104th Infantry which was driving parallel with the First through Eschweiler and Weisweiler—that of calling down their own artillery while the Yanks took cover in basements, shattered the dumbfounded Nazis. This was one ruse they never caught on to. Perhaps there weren't enough survivors to explain it when they escaped.

I am thinking in particular of the 116th Panzer Recon. Battalion, which was practically wiped out in Hamich during the above counterdrive. Those hardy fighters—among the better Wehrmacht armored units—had a taste of the Yank artillery trick in Schmidt, just prior to their performance in Hamich. There, pouncing upon the 28th Division's detachment which had entered the town only to discover superior German forces waiting, the 116th was shelled to a frazzle while in process of liquidating what they thought was an easy "bag." But it took a lot of pounding to convince a Kraut.

So things went as the first week's fighting chewed up valuable German forces and destroyed a well conceived defense. Hill 187 fell, Volkenrath with it. Wenau was taken by I Company, 18th Infantry. Schloss Laufenburg, verging the forest, fell to the 26th. The Germans rushed rear echelon outfits into line, for the Americans were approaching Duren and the Roer and might force Von Rundstedt's hand.

For there is now little doubt that the wily Field Marshall was saving his top drawer units for that big gamble in the Ardennes. Whether his grandiose scheme included a monumental "mousetrap play" is for military historians to decipher. But there was more than hydro-electric power involved in those Roer River dams.

Consisting of 11 connected dams, the largest called Schwammenauel and Urftalsperre, the Roer lakes covered 258 square miles with water, behind an earth and concrete wall whose core was 180 feet high. Both American and RAF bombers tried repeatedly but failed to crack the dams; when finally captured, only a few pockmarks indicated our bomb damage.

As everyone now knows, the seemingly senseless campaigns into the Hurtgen, entailing dreadful losses for practically no territorial gains, were part of the Allied strategy to get the Rhineland. Nobody knew what would happen if our forces crossed the Roer while German engineers held the control of those dams. A quick demolition, and millions of tons of water might surge upon our troops—if not to drown them, certainly to isolate them beyond supply, where German panzers could work them over.

Let us suppose, too, that Generals Eisenhower and Bradley had ordered the Ninth U. S. Army to lunge ahead against its mediocre opposition, crossing the lower Roer and moving toward the Rhine. With the dams still German-held, the First U. S. Army deeply involved in the Aachen-to-Duren operation, who would have swung around to halt Von Rundstedt's three panzer armies when they slammed across the Schnee-Eifel into the Bulge? Mired in the Roer's flood, caught without a mobile SHAEF reserve, the Allied cause would have been even more complicated than it became. These are factors but little considered when the chair-borne experts hold forth.

Suffice to say, the Americans did not cross the Roer until they were sure the dams no longer threatened. They did not get "sucked in" as the Nazis threw their celebrated Ardennes punch. Indeed, it was the reliable First Division which, with less than one day's respite from the Hurtgen, dashed from Aachen's rest area over the snowy summits of the Hoch Venn (highest area in Belgium) and blunted the Panzer's drive near Monschau.

All these things lay ahead, however, as the four regiments took turns chiseling through the Hurtgen in November. It fell mainly to the 26th doughboys to conquer the treeland, however. With the 18th, they sloughed through the sticky, rain-sodden woods, taking a village at the fringe, a castle here, a strongpoint there. If they got mortared in newly seized German dugouts, the men shrugged.

"It's safer at that, than trying to build new ones," they said.

I was one of the correspondents who made periodic jeep trips toward that front. Sometimes we got there, sometimes not. One mired vehicle in the slough-like firebreaks, and progress halted. If you became too noisy trying to turn around, friend Fritz would chuck a few at you, just for luck.

Thus things stood as the Division approached Heistern and Merode, two of the hottest spots it was destined to attack. Merode lay just out of the forest in the drabest of flatlands; the 26th was slicing toward it when Thanksgiving Day came around. A ferocious fight had settled Laufenburg Castle in the Americans' favor, but with the rest of the Division heavily engaged before Langerwehe, Hill 187 and particularly the castle outside the town, the 26th pushed gingerly downhill against the sharpest kind of resistance.

With Graham Miller, corresponding for the New York Daily News and a London paper, I arrived at Division headquarters about 1 P.M. It was unquestionably the dreariest Thanksgiving Day I've known. Rain pelted the countryside, the rivers overflowed with that yellow Rhineland flood, vehicles slid all over the roads, and even a few crazy Luftwaffers were scudding over the lines. It was a day to remain indoors, and with 30 miles from Spa already behind us, we were ready to rest, eat, and be briefed.

"Turkey dinner today," said Major Leonard Peters, the dapper Headquarters commandant. "Turkey for every dough in the outfit."

"Ha, that's a laugh. Now I'll tell one," said Miller.

"I mean it. We're delivering roast turk right up to the foxholes," Peters persisted. "Tell 'em Howard." Mess Officer Howard Wilcox dipped his mustachios in vigorous affirmative, allowing there would be turkey to last three days. "Those who are too busy shooting may get it tonight or tomorrow, but hot turkey sandwiches are being sent to the foxholes."

"I'll believe it when I see," the doubting Miller declared. "Somebody fill me in on the briefing. Who'll come along to the woods?" Full of Sergeant Carl Barone's specially prepared feast, I climbed in.

"The Hurtgen," said Graham, who had never been there before. I said nothing. We took off down the Zweifall road as Peters stood shaking his head. "Some guys don't know enough to stay out of the rain when they can," he announced.

Turning left, where the Engineers had widened a wood trail, the jeep in second gear climbed up a grade and into the forest. It was woods all around almost as soon as you left Vicht, but now the firs and hemlocks began in earnest. The road narrowed, the driver dropped into four-wheel drive. We passed some Engineers' tents at a crossing of firebreaks, but we didn't stop.

"Get your turkey dinners?" I yelled.

"Sure did. Get yours?" a GI responded. Graham made a note. He was wearing black leather fleece-lined boots for the first time. They had never been muddy, but this was the day.

Still climbing, we saw a soldier slithering down a slope. Blood had soaked his OD pants; he was using his M-1 for a crutch, the bayonet bent from thrusting into rocks and logs.

"How far to the dressing station?" he asked. It was about 200 yards. We didn't ask how he got it, and he didn't say more. We knew, however, that the front wasn't very far off.

Half a mile farther we saw a half-track parked. The driver signalled to be quiet, pointing into the brush. We got out, walking ahead of the jeep.

"Jerry just dropped one near me. Hears the tracks, I guess." We got back into the jeep but you couldn't hurry. The mud was coming over the footboards. Then we saw some medics working under the trees, and a GI walked behind two prisoners who kept their hands clasped on their caps.

"Where's Regiment CP?" Miller asked.

"Back of you. This is 2nd Battalion."

At this point a second jeep pulled into the clearing. It contained Corporal Bill Umbrell of Hummelstown, RD 1, Pennsylvania, and Sergeant Bill Tatom of Dos Cabazos, Arizona, with three large steamcans full of roast turkey and fixings.

"Where the hell did you come from?" a soldier asked.

"The Division mess. You guys hungry?"

Without delay they ushered Bill and his provisions behind a low dugout, carefully removing the can covers as messkits were opened. From the dugout entrance a voice warned: "Better get under cover. They've been mortaring this spot all morning." Graham and I ducked down the steps. The GI's continued with the food.

Lt. Colonel Darrell M. Daniel's headquarters was below ground, its best recommendation. Rain dripped through the heavily timbered roof, but you could move and settle into dry straw. A farm lantern provided light, the officers looked at us, amused.

"How do you like our accommodations?" Daniel asked.

"You fellows need a drink," said Miller, producing his rum flask. That helped. We explained about the Thanksgiving dinner, how it had just arrived.

"I still don't believe—yes, by God, I can smell turkey!" Captain Bernie Kotin, Chicago, started up the steps. Lieut. Elmer Killane of Cincinnati, Battalion S-2, was about to join him when something went "Crummpp" not very far away, and we settled back with Graham's flask. Miller, hesitating because he felt he 'jinxed' a couple of company commanders by visiting them near Aachen—both were killed—asked how far to the lines. Then, to try out his new boots, he went out to find the remaining company leader he knew.

That day the front line positions were about 200 yards from the battalion command post. Small arms fire rattled through the rain and mist, but the woods blanked out the sound of attacks down in the flatlands. After a while I went out, saw Orlando Schuyler, communications officer who had been with the First since North Africa. He said he'd trade the Hurtgen for a Tunisian djebel any day.

Medics were sending back some of the 26th casualties in that small area alone. Their own stretcher bearers all gone, they were making Kraut prisoners lug the last ones on their way to the rear. Tom Krucher, Moravia, N. Y., Ernest Marks, New York City, and Paul George, Beaver Falls, Pa., laid aside C-rations when they came up and saw the turkey. Jim Daniel, Bradford, Pa., Jacob Rosen, Philadelphia and Sergeant Al Yampaglia of Newark told how one of their crew had just been killed, trying to reach a wounded Yank. Lieutenant Eugene LaRocca, Hazelton, Pa., was in command of the medics.

From time to time a GI slogged up from his foxhole, bringing a German along. One of the Joe's, wearing no helmet and shambling through the underbrush as if herding the cows home in his native North Carolina, was puzzled when asked if he'd had his share of turkey. Nobody had told him it was a holiday.

"I've seen nothin' but these sour Krauts," he said. He had eight in tow. The Jerries tried for them with another mortar and we hurriedly returned to the dugout.

"You can get used to it up here," Captain Jim Libby, Burlington, Vt., said. "Just figure you can always be a little wetter than you are, a little colder, a little hungrier or more homesick. That keeps you going."

The colonel agreed.

"You must come up and see us some more. When you can spend more time," he grinned.

The officer didn't surmise, nor did I, but the next time we were to meet was in Nuremberg, exactly one year later. He was commanding a battalion on guard at the war crimes trial. It was again Thanksgiving, and I recognized him at once.

"We finally got out of that woods," he reminded. "Lost two whole companies at Merode, but we got the town. Sure I remember your visit—and how you guys looked when I asked you to be sure and come back, when you had more time."

But up at the 26th Infantry lines in the Hurtgen, the prospect of standing guard while Goering, Ribbentrop, Keitel and the rest heard their fate, never occurred. The object was to live until relieved. If you came out alive you had won.

It was nearly dark when we reached Division headquarters. We reported the turkey had arrived but E and F Companies had not received theirs. Wilcox swore when he heard.

"We have 60 more turkeys roasting. Those doughs will get some if I have to drive there myself tonight."

Correspondents Miller and Peterman were reasonably doubtful.

"You better take a guide, if you go," Graham cautioned. "That's the meanest bit of the war I've seen yet."

Anyone who fought the Hurtgen will agree.

As an offensive operation involving the full strength of the Division, First Infantry commanders are widely agreed that the Hamich-Heistern-Langerwehe reduction of West Wall defenses was the most difficult of the war. Losses were heavy, but with the attached 47th Infantry Regiment, the Division also had more men than in previous assignments. It did a conclusively successful job, too, against its most stubborn opposition and the worst possible terrain.

The drive continued from November 16th until December 4th when the 9th Infantry moved in and relieved. By then, however, the First Army front had bellied up to the Roer and was awaiting additional supply and regrouping before attempting to jump the river.

But who will forget events of those last two weeks in November? The fierce counterattacks by Germans, sometimes led in person by the officers who conceived it—the Boche was not yet convinced that he couldn't just barge in and retake what had been lost despite bitterest resistance—reached a crescendo in places like Hamich, Heistern, and Langerwehe, and on Hills 232, 187, 245, and 209, seldom, if ever seen in modern warfare. The German realized his Fatherland was being widely breached; even the lesser indoctrinated Krauts fought like madmen.

There was a battle long to echo in First Division recollection, around the Frenz Castle. That was just before the 18th Regiment cleared the way into Langerwehe, toward the end of the main drive. Huchelm, Schonthal had been outflanked and taken. Hill 203 had fallen. The 26th was bearing down on Jungersdorf from out of the woods, but the Krauts in Schloss Frenz still hung on. It was one of the last strongholds to fall and it wasn't much of a tourist objective when the First was finished with it. The place was full of "late" Hitlerites.

One of the last momentary victories for the enemy occurred at Merode. There, two companies of the 26th penetrating in a surprise attack, were countered viciously as their supply route was cut off, and after a night spent fighting a determined paratroop counterattack, were killed, wounded, or captured. The Germans had the advantage of complete artillery cover, tricked the Yanks into too rapid advance, then took the open road leading into Merode from the Hurtgen annex (called "Staats forst Merode") under fire, and the Division couldn't reinforce or rescue the two companies. That was the worst single loss of the whole campaign, but the 26th avenged it by ousting the Nazis from Merode on the 29th, reducing the little town to mere dust and rubble.

This temporary setback also had a profound effect on the 26th Regiment. It fought thereafter as if to avenge the men lost in that bad breakout from the forest; in the subsequent stand against the panzers near Monschau, the 26th Regiment, and in particular Lt. Colonel Daniels' battalion, fought as if inspired. At one stage they actually requested permission to "cut the whole Nazi invasion off at the base of the Bulge."

The Division's journal goes into details on these counterblows and the street fighting in Hamich, Heistern and Wenau, prior to the final achievement of objectives. But mere words do not convey the high-voltage effect of night prowling Panther tanks, a whole battalion of lost panzers crashing around under the leadership of a befuddled new lieutenant, the surprised but prompt reaction of frontline GI's with bazookas, and the almost phenomenal marksmanship of General Cliff Andrus' gunners in the artillery posts. Sometimes they broke up German tank sorties by the excellent device of direct hits. One or two of these, and the German column usually stopped. Time on target concentrations were stunning.

By the end of November the Division had bestrode the Inde River, a murky creek that wasn't much of a barrier except it marked the phase line. The 26th had finally fought out of the Hurtgen barrier, the 16th, 18th and 47th had all ground out their opposition. Corps and Army agreed the Fighting First had earned a good rest. It was so ordered, and General Huebner turned back to his old CP beyond Aachen. Before one day elapsed, the First was hastily ordered to help stop Von Rundstedt!

CHAPTER VIII

THE ARDENNES
December 17, 1944 to February 6, 1945

The Situation

ON DECEMBER 1, 1944 the concept of enemy capabilities was still as expressed by Intelligence agencies of the Allied Forces. The First (U.S.) Army presented the following evidence:

(a) Enemy capabilities.

(1) The enemy is capable of defense of the Reich west of the Rhine River, probably along the general line of the Ijssel-Maas-Roer Rivers and West Wall, and in the Third (U.S.) Army area Maginot Line-West Wall and the Rhine River.

(2) The enemy is capable of retiring to a defensive line behind the Rhine River.

(3) The enemy is capable of collapse or surrender.

(4) The enemy is capable of an air "blitz" to regain air supremacy in limited vital areas."

Since November 20, 1944, the Germans stubbornly contested every foot of ground in the zone of action in the First (U.S.) Army. The Germans defended with one Armored Division, one Parachute Division one Panzer Grenadier Division and eighteen Infantry Divisions.

On December 16, 1944, the Germans launched the greatest counteroffensive against Allied Forces since the Invasion of Normandy. The attack was initiated on the northern portion of the broad front held by the VIII Corps. It was supported by a heavy schedule of well-coordinated artillery fire commencing at 5:30 A.M. on front-line troops, artillery positions, and command post and communication areas.

After two and one half hours, long-range artillery concentrated on key rear positions at Rotgen, Eupen, Malmedy, Verviers and St. Vith, with the bulk of the firing in the southern half of V Corps sector, and all along the VIII Corps front. The area of the attack was a 60-mile front between the Eifel River and The Ardennes.

In conjunction with the attack, a special operation known as "GRIEF" was to be undertaken using American equipment, American weapons, American insignia and American uniforms. Thirty jeep loads of Germans were to make up operation "GRIEF."

On December 17th, the enemy resumed the attack. Many parachutists were dropped in the V Corps and VII Corps areas. These groups landed in small detachments and were seized before they could assemble.

The penetrations through the VIII Corps continued. At the same time in V Corps zone the Germans attacked vigorously toward Mutzenich, north of Monschau, but were thrust back. A counterattack by the 26th Infantry of the First Division was required to restore the position of Allied front lines at Butgenbach.

On December 18th, the Commanding General, First (U.S.) Army ordered the consolidation of the V Corps and VII Corps to meet a contemplated renewal of German counterattacks.

The German "Buzz Bomb" campaign reached its height during this operation.

An American correspondent wrote back home:—"Tradition, training and battle experience of crack American Divisions paid rich dividends in smashing the surprise German counteroffensive through the Ardennes in December, 1944. Unforgettable was the stand of the First Infantry Division which was in a rest area miles behind the front on the day the enemy attacks began, and by dawn the next day the Division was in the line holding the vital Monschau shoulder. This was the first place the German Panzers sought to break through toward Liege, and the rich American supply dumps dotting the rear areas."

It was a wonderful demonstration of the American civilian-soldier's courage, initiative and endurance—this grinding winter battle which, for hardship and suffering, made another "Valley Forge" of the forested, snow-covered Ardennes Forest.

Here are a few things which extreme cold and snow do to men and machines which make winter military offensives superlatively difficult:—

Wounded men flounder and are lost in piling snow, and may freeze before roving first aid men can find them.

Tanks are confined to main roads and are thus unable to move across open country thereby becoming better targets for ambushed enemy anti-tank guns.

It becomes progressively harder to move up supplies of food and ammunition over snow-blocked secondary roads, and some of it must be packed in.

Medicines freeze and front line "Medics" have to carry morphine syrettes under their armpits to keep them warm enough to use.

There are a thousand and one other problems that winter brings, but above all is a simple animal problem of how to keep from freezing to death.

And thus the coldest winter months were spent in the Ardennes from December 7, 1944 to February 6, 1945. Through the Ardennes Campaign the First Division, 2nd Division, 99th Division and 119th Infantry Regimental Combat Team made up the V Corps of the First American Army.

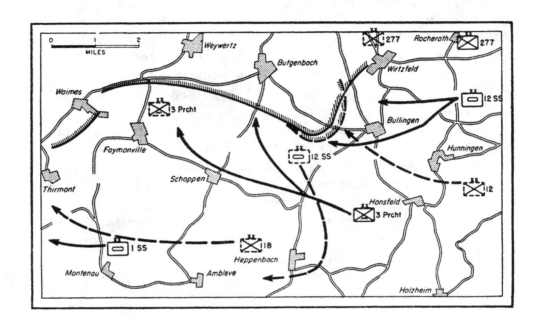

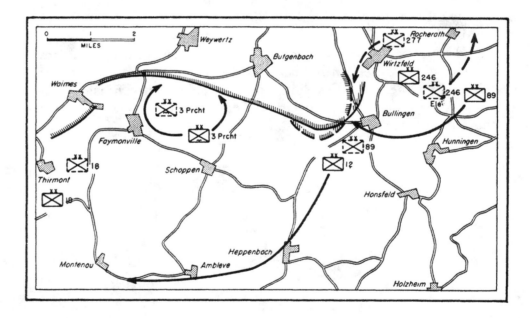

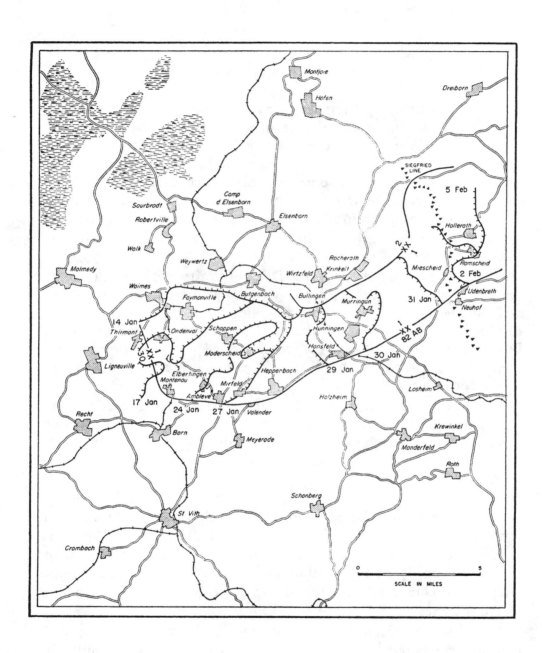

Montjoie
Hofen
Dreiborn
SIEGFRIED LINE
5 Feb
Hollerath
Camp d'Elsenborn
Sourbrodt
Robertville
Elsenborn
Rocherath
Miescheid
Ramscheid
2 Feb
Walk
Weywertz
Wirtzfeld
Krinkelt
Udenbreth
Neuhof
Malmedy
31 Jan
Waimes
Butgenbach
Bullingen
Murringan
Foymonville
14 Jan
Ondenval
Schoppen
Hunningen
Honsfeld
82 AB
Thirmont
Moderscheid
Ligneuville
Elbertingen
Hepperbach
29 Jan
30 Jan
17 Jan
Montenau
Mirfeld
Ambleve
Holzheim
Losheim
Recht
24 Jan
27 Jan
Valender
Born
Meyerode
Krewinkel
Manderfeld
Roth
Schonberg
St Vith
Crombach

0   5
SCALE IN MILES

T H E   A R D E N N E S
December 17, 1944 to February 6, 1945

The Record

WHEN the First Infantry Division was relieved after clearing the enemy from key positions west of the Roer River, a period of rest and refitting was anticipated. After six months of virtually unbroken combat, it was believed that a short period out of the line was in order, particularly as the heavy casualties of the recent fighting had reduced the strength of the Division, despite a continuous flow of replacements to sixty percent of its normal strength. Hitler's major counteroffensive in the Ardennes however, blasted these hopes.

Just as the last of the First Division units were pulling in to rest areas north of Eupen, the Division was alerted to move south and on December 7, 1944, the first units got under way. Given the key positions on the north shoulder of the "Bulge" the First Division took the full brunt of the repeated German assaults, and then started a series of night attacks which brought the Division to the Siegfried Line.

On December 16th, the Germans, implementing a capability which had existed since the start of the Allied drive to the Rhine River, launched a high-geared, meticulously-planned counterattack on the center of the American line, between Monschau and Echternach.

The enemy operation was designed as a monumental spoiling attack to cut off the Allied supply port at Antwerp, Belgium, and communications center of Brussels. One of the primary objectives of the German counterattack was the seizure of the enormous American supply dumps in the Liege, Verviers and Eupen areas. In fact the continued impetus of the drive hinged on the capture of the supplies.

The enemy's plan for the blow was carefully thought out, and carefully disguised. The Germans picked the terrain—an unlikely spot and therefore lightly held. The Germans waited for the weather and for the first week German operations were blanketed in baffling fog. The Germans built up enough supplies to catapult the initial momentum. They also gathered up all strategic reserves, including the 6th SS Panzer Army, and drove them through in a gamble that was far from unreasonable. Furthermore the Germans used every deception and surprise beyond the normal means at command and went all out in labeling this operation "GRIEF."

On December 17, 1944 the Command Post of the First Infantry Division was at Sourbrodt, Belgium. The Division was attached to the V Corps.

The 26th Infantry had two Battalions in the line to the south of and a little east of Butgenbach—a hill mass. The First Battalion was at Elsenborn. The 47th Infantry held Mutzenich. The 18th Infantry was east of Eupen with orders to back up the 47th Infantry. One Combat Team of the 30th Infantry Division was to move through the 16th Infantry to Malmedy.

The German plan was to drop 700 parachutists behind the American lines to seize the important road junctions between Eupen and Malmedy, and block the American troops which could be pulled in from the north where the main strength of the Allied Armies had been committed in the drive on the Rhine.

In conjunction with the parachutists, special troops in American uniforms, equipped with American transportation and Sherman tanks, would spearhead the German Panzers to spread confusion behind the American lines and disrupt the organization of resistance. It was planned to have these special troops race toward the American rear, shouting "The Germans are 500 yards back" to stall Sherman tanks at critical points in the American road net, and in general, carry on many other such divertissements.

Things went wrong, at least in the northern sector, from the start. On the night of December 16-17, nearly 700 parachutists were dropped in the general area of Malmedy-Eupen woods. They were (as established from prisoners) taken by the 18th Infantry and identified as a special unit led by a Colonel Von der Heydte and culled from various parachute Divisions on a "voluntary" basis.

Colonel Von der Heydte was a veteran of the Crete landings and a former holder of the $16,000 Carnegie Fellowship for the study of International Law in Vienna. In spite of this distinguished leadership, the plan went awry. None of the parachutists had been told of their mission, other than that further instructions would be given once they landed. The noncommissioned officers of the parachutists only knew that they were to hold certain road junctions—beyond that they knew nothing.

A crosswind and bad briefing of the Junker-52 pilots scattered the units and their weapons and equipment over an area far wider than planned. Much of the equipment was lost during the fall and broken. The radios were knocked out and reorganization was sketchy. With no secondary mission, these parachutists who managed to reassemble, hid out in the woods harassing isolated vehicles and taking a few prisoners. They were entirely unable to block the arrival of reinforcing troops.

On December 16th, with the First Infantry Division in a rest area, north of Eupen, it became apparent that the enemy was planning a breakthrough and the Division was accordingly alerted. By 3:00 A.M. December 17th, the 26th Infantry was sent down to Camp Elsenborn on the northern flank of the breakthrough to contain the enemy's drive and prevent it from spreading north. The First Division (less the 18th Infantry), and elements of the 18th Infantry, unmolested by Von der Heydt's parachutists, was in position twenty-four hours later. From that time to the end of the period, the enemy's frantic efforts to break through by the Bullingen-Butgenbach-Weismes route of approach, to the dumps of Spa and Verviers, were blocked off by the First Division.

The German attack in the north around Monschau and Bullingen was slow in starting. On December 17th the enemy attacked Monschau in some force, but was turned back by Division Artillery. Subsequent attacks, which did not seem to be pressed to the full extent of the German's potential, were likewise repulsed.

The first elements of the 26th Infantry only reached Camp

Elsenborn to the north at 7:00 A.M. December 17th. Consequently, something of a race developed between the 26th Infantry and the 12th SS (German) panzer Division for the occupation of Butgenbach, the next town on the projected northern route of the enemy. Before dark on December 17th the 2nd Battalion, 26th Infantry, had taken over the town of Butgenbach and were defending the high ground to the southwest against any thrust from Bullingen.

The 16th Infantry was on its way down from its bivouac area in the vicinity of Verviers to take up positions north of Weismes. The 18th Infantry remained just south of Eupen on an anti-parachute mission.

During December 18th the enemy continued attacks to reach the assigned road net from the east, putting heavy pressure on Krinkelt and Rocherath, and finally occupying these towns after the 2nd and 99th Infantry Divisions (U.S.) had been ordered to withdraw by the V Corps.

With every day the Germans delayed, their opportunity of breaking the line and getting control of the Elsenborn and Malmedy roads lessened. During the day of December 18th, the 18th Infantry was moving south to take up a position in the line after sweeping the woods south of Eupen for parachutists.

Members of Von der Heydt's ill-starred crew of parachutists kept showing up all over the sector. The Colonel himself, trying to beat his way back to the German lines, called for an ambulance in the vicinity of Monschau a few days later and asked to be evacuated. Although well aware of the failure of his mission, Von der Heydt asked an interpreter to notify him should the German radio announce that he—Von der Heydt—had been awarded the "Swords of the Knights Cross."

At 6:15 A.M. December 20th, the Germans attacked in greater strength but with no greater success. The 2nd Battalion, 26th Infantry reported contact with the enemy—a heavy force of tanks and about one battalion of infantry. At 8:15 A.M. the attack had been completely repulsed; eight tanks had been knocked out and were burning, and all First Division positions had been restored.

On December 21st another assault was launched. Into it the

enemy put everything they had at command, as well they had, too, for by this time a break through to the west to come to the rescue of the beleaguered First SS Panzer Division was imperative.

At 1:30 A.M. December 21st, the Germans opened up with machine-gun and tank fire on the 2nd Battalion, 26th Infantry positions southeast of Butgenbach. Artillery was brought down by the First Division and the attack was disposed of quickly. At 3:00 A.M. the Germans laid down an intense, concentrated artillery, nebelwerfer and mortar barrage. The battalions were blanketed and communications were reduced to radio and no contact at all was possible with the forward elements of the 2nd Battalion, 26th Infantry. When the inevitable follow-up thrust developed, the First Division Infantry was ready for it.

The Division Artillery fired nearly 10,000 rounds and succeeded in putting a serious crimp in the assembly of the enemy reserve, and following troops. In spite of this disruption of his rear elements, however, the enemy drove his attack hard and a slight penetration was made.

Five tanks which hit between Companies "E" and "F", 26th Infantry, got through Division lines, but the infantry elements held fast and cleaned out the German Infantry following the tanks. The enemy tanks which got through, although working on borrowed time, succeeded in pinning down the 2nd Battalion Command Post with direct fire at a range of 75 yards and overrunning Company "E" Command Post. Anti-tank guns near the 2nd Battalion Headquarters destroyed four of the enemy tanks. By 11:40 A.M. the full force of the enemy assault began to abate and the situation in the Company "E" and Company "F" area was restored. The brilliant defense by these two companies, under the most difficult conditions, is all the more remarkable when it is recalled that both companies had been virtually wiped out twenty days earlier in the Merode fighting.

The enemy again hit Company "F" with tanks, but the Division Artillery responded with alacrity and decision. The enemy did not come to grips with Company "F" in consequence.

Although the 25th Panzer Grenadier Regiment was pretty

well eliminated as a potential in the fighting of December 21st, the Germans continued to place highest priority on cracking First Division defenses to allow them to roll up the Butgenbach road. On December 22nd, the 26th Panzer Grenadier Regiment was committed to succeed where the 25th had failed. For a while this new outfit almost succeeded again with a heavy tank support. Tanks started north against the First Division positions shortly after noon, attacking from three points west of Dom Butgenach. Enemy infantry following these tanks managed to push the First Division lines back. At 9:40 A.M. an undetermined number of Panzer Grenadiers had forced through Division lines, splitting both Company "A" and Company "K" of the 26th Infantry.

Elements of the 18th Infantry were committed to hold further penetrations. Company "B", 26th Infantry advanced to restore the ground and Company "A" attacked due west to close the gap. Later, around 4:00 P.M. elements of the 18th Infantry moved in and helped in retaking the ground. One tank was still behind Division lines, after the fighting was over, but managed to escape after dark.

This second attack, which was equal in intensity to that of the 25th Panzer Regiment, the day before, was, in the end, equally disastrous to the Germans. In the two days fighting, it was estimated that the Germans lost more than 44 tanks—more than 44 to a certainty since that number was actually seen and counted. The 26th Infantry estimated that it had inflicted over 1,200 casualties on the Germans.

Movement in front of the First Division sector, on December 23rd was heavy but undetermined in purpose. Horse-drawn equipment was observed moving across the Division Sector, indicating the arrival of purely infantry units. Small attacks came in against the 16th and 26th Infantry Regiments, but they were obviously intended as holding efforts rather than serious attempts at penetration.

From December 23rd to the end of December, the Germans continued to bring Infantry elements to replace their Armor, and build up an artillery concentration with both field and anti-aircraft southeast of Bullingen. Movement on the limited road net in front of the First Division line continued heavy, and was taken under punishing artillery fire.

On December 26th prisoners and documents indicated that the 3rd Parachute Division (German), still held the western flank of the First Division position. To the east it was believed that the 12th (German) Division had moved into the line.

On December 28th both the 3rd Parachute and the 12th Division had been identified as being in front of the First Division. The failure of their last ambitious attack apparently convinced the Germans of the futility of trying to force their way through the First Division defenses. Enemy activity for the balance of December, 1944, consisted only of busy digging and moderate counter-patrolling. The Germans, however, continued to lay artillery fire on Division forward positions, and to extend their efforts to interdiction of roads in the rear areas.

The stand of the First Infantry Division southeast of Butgenbach put a spoke in the wheel of the German's plans. With the First Division jutting out in a salient, the overloading of the road network to supply the enemy being harassed by the effective, devastating fire of the First Division Artillery just about wrecked the over-worked vaunt of the Germans:—"Paris by Christmas."

The tactics of the 150th Panzer Brigade of the Germans—the power behind the operation "GRIEF", were never successful due to greatly increased security measures taken by the Division. Although no established penetrations of Germans (in American uniforms) took place in the First Division zone, an idea of the effectiveness of control can be readily seen in the case of a strange officer from higher headquarters, who got lost on his way to one of the Regimental Command Posts and ended up on a road leading through one of the Regimental Command Posts of the First (U.S.) Infantry Division. Within an hour of the first alarm this strange officer had been arrested four times and checked for identity.

"The road back" to the Germans—led to nowhere, and they gave evidence of fighting it out to the end. A number of American prisoners taken by the First Panzer Division southwest of Malmedy on December 17th, were disarmed and shot by their captors.

More than twenty-five civilians were murdered in Stavelot by the same outfit. On December 28th a 3-man German patrol entered the lines of the 16th Infantry with the indication it wanted to surrender. It was discovered however, that one of the Germans was carrying a machine-pistol behind his back. This patrol was eliminated.

German artillery during this period was consistently strong, although it reached the intensity of the Hamich Woods only on the few occasions before an attack. At the end of this period, considerable artillery build-up was still reported southeast of Bullingen.

During this entire period the German Air Force put in an appearance in greater strength than the First Division had encountered since the European Campaign started.

Meanwhile, the weather was steadily getting worse. During the first days of the German breakthrough, it was miserable enough —soupy fog and the old First Division brand of mud—composed of equal part of chocolate tapioca pudding and soft tar—but on Christmas Day the freeze started under clear, cloudless blue skies which gave the Allied Air Force its first crack at the endless German columns and the First Division Artillery its first chance to see what it was shooting at.

After December 30, 1944, the real bit of the weather set in. Snow piled up four and five feet deep. The temperature went below freezing and stayed there. It snowed for hours at a time, and a stiff cutting wind piled the snow into enormous drifts. This kind of weather continued endlessly.

Reports from Intelligence Section and from Operations Section also, showed plenty of activity on the part of the enemy for the week preceding Christmas Day of 1944. The Germans stubbornly insisted on attempting their planned breakthrough, using every conceivable form of deception. The advance, precautionary measures taken by First Division Security thwarted the fondest hopes of the Germans to reach American supply dumps.

German air appeared to engage in numerous dog-fights with American planes and consistently finished second best. Division anti-aircraft figured prominently in these daily forays and their box-score was mounting with hits.

On January 1, 1945, the Germans were on an operational see saw. The German plan of an unchecked drive to the Meuse River had been blocked in the west, and their planned drive through the First Division had failed, with serious losses.

On January 1, 1945 the mission of the First Infantry Division was to continue to defend the Butgenbach-Weyertz-Weimes Sector; maintain enemy contact by active patrols; harass the enemy; maintain contact with the 2nd Infantry Division on the left and the 30th Infantry Division on the right. The 26th Infantry was on the left of the Division Sector, southeast of Butgenbach; the 16th Infantry was on the right; the 18th Infantry occupied the center of the sector and Task Force "DAVISSON" continued to secure the dam in the vicinity of Walk and to maintain contact with the 30th Infantry on the right.

The First Division received orders—Headquarters, V Corps—January 2, 1945—outlining the attack of January 3, 1945. The First U. S. Army was to launch a coordinated attack. V Corps was to continue to hold defensive positions against any enemy attempt to penetrate from the south and east; to patrol on D-Day at H-Hour, supported by artillery and in such strength as would lead the Germans to believe a general attack was being launched. The First, 2nd, 9th and 99th Infantry Divisions (U.S.) were to send Combat Patrols to the front within the Division Sectors.

This attack went off as planned and the various phases of its planning went off on schedule. There was a noticeable withdrawal of German forces in several thinly-held spots, but still the resistance of the Germans was a stubborn and as pronounced as at the beginning of the drive. The weather continued extremely cold; snow was still piled up four and five feet deep. The sharp, cutting wind whipped the snow into drifts and it continued to snow.

It was into this weather that the First Division attacked on January 15, 1945. The Germans had come to the end of the line as far as their ambitious counterattack went; it was now the Allies turn. The Germans did not appear willing to give up any ground already won, and they continued to put up a stiff fight. Over and above the German's determination, however, were the difficulties of the terrain and weather; both presented conditions which were almost insurmountable.

The terrain comprised a series of high ridges and deep draws usually heavily wooded. These obstacles, difficult enough in themselves, were greatly increased in the bad weather. A deep snow running as high as five feet in drfits, covered the area. The ground was frozen, making it extremely difficult to dig sufficient cover.

The weather was so bad that during the battle, prisoners often expressed surprise that the First Division had been able to attack at all. The only advantage that the weather presented was that the First Division was often able to achieve surprise because the Germans did not believe that an attack was possible under the prevailing conditions.

The initial objectives of the attack of January 15, 1945, were Faymonville and Schoppen. The going was tough. Complete mine detection was next to impossible, and in at least one case a tank was knocked out by one of our own mines, buried so deep in the snow that it did not register on the detectors.

The Infantry found the going as difficult as wading through waist-high water. A man carrying his equipment could go no more than 300 yards without stopping for a rest.

Faymonville was taken after a hard and bloody fight, and Company "K", 16th Infantry got into a hornet's nest east of the town. The 18th Infantry was having tough going against well-emplaced German positions on the Klingelberg Hill to their front, but the attack pushed on.

On January 17th the First Battalion, 18th Infantry pulled out and swung around to the west to back up the 23rd Infantry of the 2nd Division (attached to the First Division for this attack).

The march, continued through the snow and across country, was one of the coldest on record, and one of the meanest, but the 23rd Infantry got through and into position with practically no rest— and on to the attack.

On January 17th, the first German resistance to the attack of the 18th Infantry hit Company "K". The First Battalion (German) 5th Parachute Regiment attacked, supported by two tanks. They were repulsed.

On January 19th four more German-held towns were taken in the worst weather of this campaign. Eibertingen, the first town, was defended by a force of about 130 replacements and stragglers from the Rohr Busch. Entrance to the town was blocked by a large number of wooden box-mines. Self-propelled guns and one tank were in the town which faced the 23rd Infantry. It was only after heavy artillery concentrations forced the Germans to fall back into the town that the Infantry was able to move forward and seize several houses on the northern edge of town.

The Germans counterattacked immediately and bitter hand-to-hand fighting resulted. By 2:00 P.M. the Germans began to pull out toward Deidenberg. One hundred prisoners were taken and more than thirty-five enemy dead were counted in the streets. The towns of Montenau and Iveldingen, also taken by the 23rd Infantry, put up less resistance and only 22 prisoners were taken from these two towns.

On January 22nd, with the line running roughly on the axis Deidenberg-Eibertingen-Schoppen, the First Division attack held up except for readjustment of the lines and mopping up of stubborn areas. The most stubborn area was the Butgenbacher Heck Area, where elements of the 89th (German) Volksgrenadier Division were deeply and skilfully dug in. The First Infantry Division troops succeeded in clearing about 800 yards of the northern edge of the woods in the face of extremely heavy small-arms and artillery fire, and the relentless weather and terrain.

On other sectors of the front the enemy took advantage of the breather to reorganize his shattered forces and feverishly erect defenses. This activity, with concomitment stubborn defensive action on the part of the enemy troops in the Butgenbacher Heck Area, continued to January 24th.

On January 24th, the German's Morscheck position, which he had captured in the early stages of the December action, was retaken. The Morscheck crossroads, possibly the best organized of the German's defensive positions, and probably where he least expected an attack, was held by the First Battalion (German) 1055th Regiment. This force was divided by the attack of the 18th and 26th Infantry Regiments, and both Regiments continued to push on, south and southwest, against stubborn but disorganized resistance.

On January 25th, the Germans were cleared from the ridge southwest of Moderscheid, and the towns of Amel and Mirfeld were taken.

During the next two days, January 26th and 27th, as the First Division attack halted, German activities were confined to further work on his defenses and counter-patrolling. On January 27th two of the First Division outposts were pushed back about one thousand yards by a stronger enemy force. One of the outposts were retaken however, by a heavy concentration of fire from Division Artillery.

On January 28th the First Division turned to the east again. The German "Bulge" appeared to be all washed up, and it was now the turn of the First Division to do the pushing. Murringen, Hunningen and Honsfeld, the last German-held towns in front of the First Division Sector, along the German border, fell on January 30th, and three days later the First Division was up against the Siegfried Line for the second time.

Defenses of the Siegfried Line, an unknown quantity until the positions were tested, proved to be as stubborn as the first cracking of the line at Aachen, around Verlautenheide.

While the 23rd Infantry was battling in the woods, the First Battalion, 18th Infantry cleaned out a massed force of Germans in an pocket south of the Amel River. The complete surprise of this attack resulted in the capture of three 88-MM guns, four 105-MM howitzers, a halftrack and an ammunition dump. These two actions on the western flank of the Division netted a total of 236 prisoners for this day. To the east, the 16th and 18th Infantry Regiments continued to work their way south under heavy artillery fire.

On January 28th the towns of Hepscheid, Heppenbach and Walender were cleared of the Germans, and the First Division, taking advantage of the enemy's disorganization, pushed rapidly up the Hepscheid-Honsfeld road to a high point about one thousand and fifty yards west of Honsfeld. Fighting in the streets of Honsfeld was over as soon as Division tanks appeared. However, one tank got stuck in the snow and the town was taken by the Infantry, solely.

The last enemy-held towns in front of the German Border—Murringen, Hunningen and Honsfeld, fell to the First Division on January 20th, after moderate fighting which netted 350 prisoners. The attrition which the enemy had been suffering since the start of the Division attack on January 15th, was noticeable in the defense of the last enemy-held towns on the German Border. Although the terrain was still excellent for a German defense, the Germans were unable to round up enough men to man their defenses.

Although the Germans had withdrawn considerable distance to the east, the continued heavy snow and rough going hampered the movements of the First Division. In spite of the weather and terrain hazards, however, the First Division continued to push to the east, and enemy screening forces were pushed back from the approaches to the high ground northwest of the Holzwarcke River, on January 31, 1945. The fighting during January of 1944 marked the grand deflation of the German's ambitious plan of December 15, 1944.

The effect of the Russian advances in the East, on the enemy's policy in the West cannot, of course, be assayed. It unquestioningly forced major changes in the plan of holding west of the Siegfried Line. Prisoners taken by the First Division, after the Russian Offensive got under way, indicated that the official German information still controlled the reports from the East, but that "grape-vine" rumors had given the prisoners a fairly accurate knowledge of events. The general attitude in the prisoners cage was:— "Why not let the Americans advance?" . . . "Our real enemies are the Russians."

One element which aided the Germans in their delaying defense (although it operated against him by increasing his losses), was the bitter weather. Terrain which could have been a minor problem, in supply and evacuation, during the summer, presented almost insoluble problems under a two-foot cover of snow.

The progress of the Infantryman through this obstacle was painfully slow. Points had to be changed every 75 to 100 yards. Machine gunners and mortarmen were barely able to move at all. Moreover, the temperature added its weight to the difficulties. Frostbite and freezing were common. Radio mouthpieces froze; signal wire froze and broke. Laying wires at all was extremely difficult and repairing a break almost impossible. A wire crew from the 16th Infantry worked six hours to locate a break in 1,000 yards of wire buried under four feet of snow.

Evacuation of wounded was equally serious when only a "Weasel" was able to cover the ground. Mines were very hard to locate, and in one case a valuable "Weasel" was destroyed traveling over a cleared road. The snow had packed down just enough by traffic to allow the weight of the vehicle to detonate a mine. Since most of the terrain covered by the First Division, in its advance, was open ground, there were no villages or houses to shelter the troops. Many of the Companies spent two or three successive days with no more shelter than they could dig for themselves in the frozen ground.

On February 1, 1945, the enemy's position gave him little cause for self-congratulation. The great counteroffensive which had looked so promising six weeks before, had been reduced from a salient to a "Bulge," to a desperate defense of what little ground remained to him in the west of the Siegfried Line. Moreover this defense, although desperate, was conducted by the Germans with an apprehensive eye over his shoulder.

While the Allies were threatening to push on to and possibly through the Siegfried Line in the west, the Russians were piling through the eastern defenses in Army Groups. The greatest threat to Germany of course was in the East.

On February 1, 1945, the 3rd Parachute Division and elements of the 89th and 277th Infantry Divisions (German), were opposing the advance of the First Division (U.S.). All the units were in straitened circumstances and had been pushed back toward the German start line of the December 16th offensive.

On February 2nd, elements of the First Division penetrated the Siegfried Line for the second time in the European Campaign. Defenses of the Siegfried Line, still remained stubborn. The attack by the First Division jumped off at 5:00 A.M., February 2, 1945. In the attack on Scheitert and Ramscheid, the Division units ran into two rows of dragon's teeth generously fortified with mines, both anti-personnel and anti-tank. At Scheitert the Germans put up hard resistance with machineguns and mortars, and the First Division was unable to enter Scheitert until shortly before dark. Supporting tanks and tank-destroyers of the First Division spelled success in entering Scheitert.

On February 3rd the Division attacked in the Hollerath "Knee" Sector. Again—on February 4th, the Division continued its 20th day of continuous attack in this sector. Hollerath, an important communications center, fell to the Division and the breach through the Siegfried Line, to the north of the Hollerath "Knee" was widened against stubborn German resistance.

The chief delays imposed on First Division troops were the miserable road conditions, enemy mines and the hostile terrain. By dark the high ground in the vicinity of Hollerath had been taken and consolidated. The final clearing of the remaining enemy pillboxes between Udenrath and Hellenthal was achieved on the 5th of February, 1945 when the First Division was relieved by the 99th Infantry Division. During the 21st consecutive day of attack, nearly 2,000 prisoners were taken; 28 anti-personnel pillboxes and 22 troop shelters were also taken.

The First Infantry Division Command Post opened at Aywaille, Belgium on February 6, 1945. The Division rear Command Post remained in Hunningen.

THE ARDENNES

THE BATTLE OF THE "BULGE"
December 17, 1944 to February 6, 1945

As I Saw It

By

IRIS CARPENTER

A NOTE on the bulletin board at Spa's Hotel Laaken read "Special briefing at 1300 hours tomorrow at First Division H.q."

The Laaken was our official press camp. It was characterized by cavernous corridors, the smell of cooking and latrines, but there is no doubt that the none too clean rooms, bereft of everything but army cots and duffle bags, would have seemed tolerable enough to those of us inured to combat conditions, but for the discovery of a small hotel across the Casino Square called the Portugal, where the floors still sported carpet (faded but still carpet), where the beds were soft, the meals black-markedly superb, and where Madame, with sons Robert and Charles, waited to make war easier for anyone who would pay the price for it. Thereafter, "The Portugal" housed most of the correspondents and became the press club.

Having noted the briefing for next day, we expected to find "Maxie" . . . Captain Maxie Zera, Public Relations Officer for First Division . . . waiting there to give us details. Sure enough he was. No sooner had we set foot outside the Laaken on our homeward way, than the bellow of his favorite song came booming across Casino Square to hit like an artillery barrage. "We'll take the hit out of Hitler, the muscle out of Lini, when the Yanks come rolling along."

"I'm having one of Robert's biggest steaks before I meet Maxie" announced Hal Boyle of A. P. firmly."

"Me too," agreed Jack "The Beard" Thompson. "I haven't eaten all day. I don't care *what* gives in the First. They can be making their biggest jump off yet, but I've got to eat before I get set for an evening of Maxie's singing."

They ate. But with Maxie accompanying. By the time we reached the Portugal he was in the dining room to welcome each of us with a roar of song, improvising words and music as was his custom.

Maxie was always the life of any party, but tonight the great organ of his voice poured from his stocky, powerfully built frame with gusto which was exceptional.

Song over, he greeted each of us with "Listen kid" . . . it was always "Listen kid", with that eager, sibilant punch they give to it up in the Bronx . . . "You comin' tomorra. You *gotta* come. It's the biggest thing yet!"

It was always the biggest thing yet for the biggest division ever with Maxie. But tonight it really *was* the biggest thing for them yet and the extra oomph in Maxie's party spirits was wholly justifiable. For after six months in the line, the First were going out for a rest!

"We got steak for lunch," Maxie informed us. "Then the Old Man's got sump'n to say. And I mean sump'n. It's a story! You know Maxie when he says it's a story!"

We did. So by noon every jeep in the press camp had whooshed its way through the drizzle and every correspondent in the camp had squelched through a muddy garden into the cottage "Forward from Stolberg" which was Headquarters.

Waiting for us, grizzle haired, quizzical eyed and smiling, was the "Old Man" . . . General Clarence Huebner, the man who had objected "God! I don't mind dying, but at least I'd like a say in how I send other men to die" when he received the orders which were to send his men spearheading into attack over the beaches of Normandy . . . not nearly enough of them in the first waves, the General thought, for the work they had to do.

That had been a hundred and eighty-two fighting days ago. And only five of them out of direct contact with the enemy.

Now, guns hurling shells at German troops on the other side of the Roer valley made the brown roses on the dreary papered wall back of the big map tremble a bit as the General turned to it. He ran his finger along the black crayoned line which marked the Division's line of advance . . . advance during which it had captured thirty-two thousand, three hundred and seven prisoners, fired seven and a half tons of metal at the enemy, cleared roads equal to the width of the Atlantic of mines, and laid communications of double that width.

"It started," the General told us, "with my reading Admiral Hall's order of the day. She's on. Let's go! I am not going to brief you on what has happened since. At a time like this when we can look back on such a six months work, it is fitting that a soldier should be here for that purpose. I have therefore brought here Sergeant Ehlers."

General Huebner dropped an arm around the shoulder of a boy we had all supposed until then to be waiting to hand notes or the briefing stick.

"Sergeant Ehlers is a platoon leader. He did things that it is unbelievable that any man could do and live. It is not merely the doing of such deeds. Magnificent as they are, that makes this great division, but that other men live up to the doing."

Quietly General Huebner informed us that the Congressional Medal of Honor had just been awarded to 22 year-old Sergeant Walter D. Ehlers, of L Company, 18th Infantry of the First Division, to top off a Silver Star and a Bronze Star with clusters. Then he outlined deeds which sounded like a one man war.

In Normandy the Sergeant had wiped out seven Germans in one hedgerow nest before leading his squad on to their objective. After this, he knocked out an entire gun crew, and the crew of another mortar which was pulverizing his men. Next day, finding his squad in trouble, he went to the extremity of his line and stood up to attract fire on himself while his men could withdraw. One bullet wounded him and knocked him down, but he got up, fired at and hit the attacker. Then he discovered that one of his gunners had been wounded. Ignoring his own wound, he carried the soldier to safety and then returned to his command over the field which by this time was so covered with fire that for any living thing to cross it and live seemed impossible. He refused to be sent to the rear with his wound and continued to lead his squad all across France to Stolberg, Germany, where it got into a street fight with some tanks. Enemy riflemen climbed on one of them, whereupon Sergeant Ehlers advanced to the middle of the street, and paying no more attention to the bullets whipping past him than if they had been rain on his hometown farm in Kansas, he stood there picking off the men on the tank as calmly as though they had been rabbits.

While this portrait of a hero was being etched, the hero himself rumpled one hand through his shock of lank black hair, and wiped the other back and forth over the corner stove, which hot as it was, burned less seemingly, than his embarrassment.

We had been given time for questions but it was soon evident that the kid from Kansas. . . . "He just helped Dad on the farm" . . . was far less nervous facing Germans than correspondents. To our request "Tell us a bit about the action in your own words" he gulped a couple of times, and finally stuttered awkwardly "Best idea you can get about it is by reading about it in the citation I reckon."

"Sure, let's do that," urged Maxie, "'n then you can all get around, a few at a time, 'n ask him anything you want."

General Huebner nodded, gave the Sergeant's shoulder a small encouraging thump, the rest of us a smile, and went into the next room while we got down to work.

Maxie seated himself on a stool beside Ehlers to make the ordeal easy as he could. "See here now, forget these folks. You just tell old Maxie what happened when you found that gunner was wounded after you'd stopped one yourself."

One member of our camp, however, had not the slightest intention of permitting Maxie to parry, soften, or change the wording of the one thing he wanted to know . . . "Do you hate Germans so you *like* killing them?"

Maxie blocked it a couple of times by asking something else.

The correspondent repeated it until the soldier finally looked up and directly at him. Then, speaking slowly, with the manner of one obviously thinking to the conclusion of a painful problem, he said "Sir. I don't hate anybody. And I don't like to kill anybody. But if somebody gets in my way when I have a job to do so I have to kill him so I can get on with it, why then I kill him and that's all there is to it."

No man ever said so simply how little and how much it takes to be a soldier.

It was because of such soldiering that the Division record was what it was before the men went back to their rest area near Verviers . . . went back for their first chance in six hellish months to live like human beings, went back to showers; to the benison of clean clothes; to the bliss of staying in houses for long enough to get not only dry but warm. . . .

Then, with what High Command described as "Complete tactical surprise," came the breakthrough.

It came on the 16th of December, after thirty jeeploads of German soldiers and a few tanks had already infiltrated through our lines. The soldiers spoke English (many of them with an American accent) and wore American uniforms complete to dog tags taken from our wounded and dead. The tanks captured were American, marked with our five pointed star. Their mission was to penetrate our forward positions, re-routing traffic so that reinforcements and supplies reached German lines instead of ours, cutting communications, sabotaging, and generally causing all the confusion possible. They did a swell job.

Before dawn, eight hundred paratroopers dropped behind our lines in the forest between Monchau and Eupen (which was V Corps Hq.) With dawn, fifteen divisions, comprising Von Runstedt's fifth and sixth armies, surged over the thickly wooded, tightly crumpled Ardennes hills on a sixty mile front.

The Germans, with four brilliant infantry and tank thrusts, breached the four weakest points on a long and much too lightly held front. In the first hours, the break that mattered most was the five mile gap sundering our 99th and 106th Divisions at Losheim, around the area which came to be known subsequently as "Hot

Corner." Through this gap the enemy avalanched tanks and men to drive a wedge between the First and Third Armies, and cut off, around St Vith, the poor 106th Division who were doing their best (after only five days in the line and on a twenty-six mile front,) to stop the cream of Germany's Panzer divisions.

At First Army Headquarters in Spa, only a few miles back, and right in the line of the enemy's main thrust, the only troops available for defense were the "Palace Guard."

The "Guard" had earned the nickname . . . with a derisive infliction . . . from combat troops who thought guarding Headquarters in nicely pressed uniforms was very far removed from the business of real soldiering. They consisted of twenty-five military police, a small number of armored cavalry troops and a few Belgians. All they had to fight with were six "ack-ack" guns, five half tracks, three assault guns and the weapons the men could carry. With them into action went engineers, cooks, clerks, drivers . . . even the censors from the press camp . . . to fight, to build road blocks, to mine bridges, to do anything that would delay for a little while those grey-green waves breaking through the wall of steel in which we had so complacently believed them encircled for final annihilation.

On the night of the 17th, First Army sent along an officer from their Headquarters at the Hotel Brittanique to the Press Camp to give us a special briefing. "There is nothing much to say," he told us "Except that the Germans have broken through at several points and that the situation is extremely fluid." How fluid we well knew, for several of us that day had been back of the German lines!

We filed the wretchedly inadequate picture which was all that censorship permitted, and went apprehensively into a night reberverating to a new sound . . . the curfew bell. Citizens were to remain in their homes. Spa was again in the front line.

First Army might try to keep the seriousness of the situation from the correspondents and the rest of the world but there was no fooling the Belgians. Every one in Spa knew to a kilometre how far away the Germans were. White and scared they hurried home . . . not wasting time on so much as a "Good night."

At the Portugal Robert was battening the place up to withstand a seige. "There will be no dinner," he informed us. "The cook has run away so the Germans don't get him."

Grimly, Jack Thompson advised us to "get ready to pull out and take darn good care to leave no papers and notebooks around" Hal Denny, late of the New York Times, grumbled that he thought he had done with retreating back in Africa. Lee Carson of I.N.S. hair in a red bow, and the rest of her lovely body swaddled as usual in much too big combat pants, boomed "Clear out all that junk in my room. *Goddamm* the Germans!"

Next morning, despite briefing which could detail nothing except that paratroops were thick in the woods around and German tank columns shearing ahead so fast nobody knew where to expect them next, some of us decided to risk trying to get to Malmedy, while the rest jeeped over to V Corps at Eupen.

Twice machineguns chattered among the pines which had for weeks been very back line area. Then we rounded a bend to find an armored car carrying men of the First Division.

"So much for our rest period" jibed the driver. "And to think that in another hour . . . just one more hour . . . I'd have been on my way to Paris. Now here we are huntin' Goddammed paratroopers."

The Division moved on the 17th to Camp Elsenborn on the Butgenbach ridge still miraculously in our hands despite the torrent of armor that rushed against the 2nd and the 99th Infantry Divisions on the previous day. With what remained of the 2nd and 99th, the First had now to contain the enemy and block the 6th Panzer Army's drive to Liege. . . . Liege, which contained in the greatest supply dumps ever assembled in Europe, pretty well everything necessary for the Allies final subjugation of Germany.

Germans already occupied the town of Bullingen, and were racing up from it along the ridgetop road towards Butgenbach, next town on the route of advance, as the First rolled down the ridge to be first in the town and deny it's road to the enemy as a supply route to their already successful breakthrough farther south.

In the opening hours of attack, the Division, though they did not know it at the time, delayed the head of the First Panzer Division (which had just sheared so devastatingly through the gap in our lines) by shooting up its tail. The delay also held up the onslaught of the 12th S.S. But not for long. A breakthrough at Butgenbach was a "must." On it depended the enemy's main chance of exploiting the tremendous advantage gained in his initial surprise.

First real appreciation of the importance which Von Runstedt attached to it came to E Company of the 26th Infantry on the morning of the 19th. Twenty truck loads of German infantry and what appeared to be dozens of tanks, came careening out of the dawn mist like ghosts, except as the boys said "There was nothing ghostly about them when they got close." The tanks came first, to roll right over our foxholes, dropping their long guns and firing down to blast men and holes together. Luck was with us in only one respect. The holes were good ones . . . deeply dug and re-inforced with pine trunks . . . and the ground was frozen hard enough for the tanks to roll over without breaking the holes in. So, if the tanks guns missed them, the men could crouch while the tanks passed, and then rise up out of their holes to shoot up the succeeding waves of infantry.

After an action lasting less than an hour on this first morning, E Company counted over a hundred enemy dead in front of their positions. It was that kind of fighting, and it went on and on in ever rising crescendo through four days and nights.

On the morning of the 20th tanks again came in with the dawn. They ran systematically up and down our foxholes, and then went on down the Butgenbach road right to the 2nd Battalion C. P. This C. P. was a farm which had been used as a hospital and abandoned in a hurry . . . such a hurry that the nurses had left some of their clothes behind. Such souvenirs of course possessed a G.I. appeal which was irresistible, and the Germans must have wondered mightly about the make-up of men who could fight and die as Americans fought and died during this period, with petticoats furled to their foxholes and brassieres decorating their combat jackets!

Commanding 2nd Bn. C.P. was Lt. Colonel Derrill M. Daniel

who looked out upon this particular morning to see three German tanks positioned within fifty yards of him.

In civilian life Daniel is an entimologist. Dispassionately as though he had been dissecting a bug, he rounded up the clerks and cooks, drivers and medics who comprised his staff; armed them, posted them, and told them "Hold Fast." They did though the tanks got close enough as one of the cooks said "To ram its bastard guns through the windows."

Communications to Division were out, so Daniel sent messengers to ask for "all the fire you can throw in the backyard." Division ordered it, and got back this message." "We've been firing all we've got like crazy now for three hours. What in hell goes on down there?" Hell was going on. With fire from our own artillery as well as from German tanks drenching them, the C.P. buildings looked a sorry sight.

A sergeant, whose name unhappily does not appear in the records and is no longer legible in my notes, decided that it was high time that something was done about the lead tank. He had never, until that morning, fought anything tougher than an index file; but he took a bazooka and a couple of drivers, made his way out of the farmhouse and around to the back of the tank and knocked it out. The other two tanks withdrew and Division received the laconic message "Attack repulsed. Send litters."

Out in front of the C.P., companies E. and F. were mopping up the enemy as unconcernedly as though they did not know that the tanks were milling around in their rear. Company Commander First Lt Charlie Ray, a blue eyed, rosy cheeked devil-may-care youngster who looked not a day over seventeen, and Company Commander Pierre Stepanion . . . dour as Ray was debonair, had no idea what the big picture was "and no Goddam time to worry about it either." Time and again the German tanks rolled through their positions. And time and again, though convinced that half the German army must be trying to bust through the little neck of woods it was their bad luck to have to defend, the companies held.

From "Shaef", "Ike" phoned General Bradley regarding the

vulnerability of the sector. "The German's cain't break through" Bradley chuckled "I've got the First Division there!"

But they did break through.

It happened on the fourth day of attack, when two of our platoons got a hammering that gave the enemy the objective for which he had fought so fanatically through almost a hundred hours . . . a gap in our line.

The gap was driven between "A" and "K" companies of the 26th just south of the town of Butgenbach. It was 800yds wide, and carried the vital road through Waimes to Malmedy. Through it the Germans could have poured men and tanks to change the whole combat story of the Battle of The Bulge. The fact that they did not do so was due primarily to fifty men . . . fifty men whose courage and resource kept the enemy ignorant of the fact that there was nothing between him and clear passage to the north for just long enough to prevent his taking advantage of the fact.

Our strength, after four days of heavy casualties, was such that we had nothing left to commit except one battalion of the 18th which was in reserve some miles to the rear.

Colonel Jeff Seitz commanding the 26th Regiment got assurance from Division Headquarters that the 18th Battalion would be trucked down as soon as possible, but the soonest possible meant a delay of hours in which the enemy could exploit his gain to catastrophic purpose. He gloomily studied his situation map on which companies from his three battalions were already scrambled together and extended to the utmost, then reached for the phone and called Lt. Colonel Rippert, commanding the First Battalion.

The gap had been cut on the left flank of Rippert's "A" company. At his command post in the town of Butgenbach he had just received news that a group of panzer grenadier riflemen had penetrated into the town itself, and had dispatched five tanks (all he had) to deal with them as Jeff's call came through:

"Jack, how is it down there?"

"Bad. Very bad," Jack told him, "We've got a gap 800 yds. wide and as far as we know Jerries lousing up the whole countryside. Last report has 'em in the town between our two C.P.'s."

(Jeff's regimental C.P. was in town about a half mile behind Jack's, "I've just sent out tanks to work on 'em."

"Well, keep at it. I'm having to pull your "B" Company back and send them around to attack down through the gap. Company "A" will have to fan out and attack too as best they can. Jerry wants that road. I've got a battalion of the 18th coming down but we've got to hold till they get here."

That conversation took place at 9:40 on the morning of the 22nd.

Company "A" was commanded by 1st Lt. Charles M. Robertson who "got it" in both his long legs only a few weeks later.

"Do the best you can Robbie," Colonel Rippert told him, "We can't let 'em get that road."

"I'll work back, then around and out from my left flank," Robbie said, "But I'll need some men to fill up on the right flank."

"God knows where they're coming from but we'll send what we can," he was promised.

They turned out to be ammunition carriers, wiremen . . . who obeyed Rippert's terse, "Drop whatever you're doing men and get going." . . . and they held the line while Robbie and his column set out.

Instead of fanning his men out to attack across the gap, Robbie marched them back to the rear and around it. They passed a C.P. who were so perturbed to see them that they immediately phoned Division, "Have just seen fifty men from "A" Company. Know "B" Company is pulling back. But this is "A".

"We'll check," Division assured them. But by the time they had it figured out Robbie's column had linked with "K" and was strung out across the gap wherever its fire power could hurt most. "B" Company, led by Lt. Maumus, fought their way in behind them to such purpose that the 18th, who did not arrive until late afternoon, were able to postpone their attack until next morning.

Thus, in those crucial first days, was the "Iron" shoulder anchored. And from this first point in our line that the Germans hit and could not break, began their defeat. From this point we built the line westward. . . .

There was little space in our dispatches to detail action or stress the significance of the part the First had played. So much else was hapenning so fast.

There was the stand of the 101st at Bastogne.

There was 7th Armored's purchase of time at St. Vith, as, in the middle of the salient, with the enemy practically surrounding them, they fought like demons for the six days which were enough for us to stop the breakthrough and hold it.

There were the atrocities being committed by the S.S.

There was the atmosphere of fear which permeated the country-side so it felt tangible enough to reach out and take hold of. Children no longer ran out to convoys to beg "cigarette pour papa." They clustered in doorways concerned only that American armor still flowed to instead of from the front.

We had said goodbye, with a German tank column only two miles away, to Madame and the Portugal. We retreated, with the rest of the so nearly captured First Army Hq. to Chaudfontaine near Liege (where we lost our Colonel and a correspondent when enemy planes strafed our camp). We retreated again, by which time we were more than three jeep hours behind the front and ex-pected to have to move back still farther.

The Bulge looked like a Christmas stocking with the toe snag-ged out of it. Monty had taken over to move in so many divisions that we began wondering if he intended to leave the troops room to fight.

His first suggestion upon assuming command had been to straighten the line between Malmedy and Monchau and give up the hot corner at Butgenbach. Had General Hodges agreed it would have been a very different Battle of the Bulge story for the First Division. Instead, the General pointed out that thousands of men and vehicles could not be moved back over the one swampy road south of Eupen without enormous losses and got the British commander's permission to leave well enough alone.

Patton finally beat back the German's effort to capture Bastogne. Hodges looked at the mere nine miles which was all that separated his firm north shoulder from the British at Dinant. He wondered whether to avail himself of Monty's authorization to pull back his right flank or gamble on the bold stroke of attacking to close the gap and link with the British.

The decision made, the commander on the spot . . . "Lightning" Joe Collins, reached for his phone and gave the order for attack which permitted the "Hell on wheels" (Second Armored) division, not only to link with the British, but pulverize the German 2nd Panzer division which they caught out of gas near Celles.

Second Armored were barely through dealing with them when Monty gave word to begin squeezing back the toe of the stocking.

The attack was to begin at dawn on the 3rd of January. Collins, spearheading with Harmon's 2nd and Rose's 3rd Armored divisions, was to follow the conservative course of driving back the toe to link with Patton's 3rd Army at Houffalise. The Americans had hoped to follow the strategy which General Bradley had advocated . . . of zipping across the base of the Bulge from the "Iron" shoulder to join Patton at St. Vith, and cut off the enemy pulling back over his only two usable roads.

To maintain surprise, units did not assemble until the last possible moment. However they assembled at all is something no one will ever know.

This country of razor backed ridges, canyoned, swift flowing streams and deep woods, is no terrain for armored attack at the best of times. On the morning of January 3rd it was blanketed in a mist that froze everything it touched. Snow was deep on roads, rutted with traffic, and topped with sheet ice over which tanks slithered and skidded helplessly as a beginner on skis. They slid into each other and off the roads, to chew up signal wires so that units found themselves on zero hour with no communications and half their vehicles out of action.

Air support was impossible because of the fog. "Things couldn't be worse," the men said. But they were when the sun came out . . . exquisite, icing the pine trees, throwing long blue shadows on the glinting slopes and showing our men up so they stood out against it all like a black eye on a preacher. The Jerries, wearing special white snowprufe uniforms picked them off the minute they moved. We painted our tanks white after the Germans showed us how, and wrapped our soldiers in sheets collected from Belgian civilians. But we didn't do it nearly soon enough.

During this attack the First played an unfamiliar role. It was their job to keep the enemy on their sector believing that the fight raging to the southwest was diversionary, and that he still had to contend with a main smash through from the northern shoulder. They mined themselves in and maintained patrols, never knowing when they were to attack or when the enemy would attack them.

It was a time which gnawed resistance to snapping point. The tension which never lifted, the freezing fog through which anything could emenate too late to do much about it, and the oppressive silence of the dank, dark forest, tautened nerves and had men so trigger sharp they fired at any noise or shape. To move from a foxhole was to run serious risk of being shot by a buddy. Twice in the morning reports morale was described as low. . . .

Then, almost a month after the Battle of the Bulge had started . . . the day before we linked with Patton to close the gap at Houffalise . . . the First got word that they were going in to attack again.

Von Runstedt, pulling his divisions back through the Seigfried Line, knew that his gamble had failed but he was selling every tree, every yard for every second of time it would buy . . . time that would give him the chance to organize his forces back of the River Roer.

The First were to drive south through Faymonville. They were to clear the road to Schoppen so that the 7th Armored could pass through for a triumphant re-occupation of St. Vith, from which the Germans had driven them a month previously.

On the map the objective looked reasonable enough. On the ground it meant fighting through a defile, crossing a river and storming hill after hill, with the enemy plastering mortar, H. E. and small arms fire to cut company after company to ribbons.

All three regiments began attacking on the 15th. "I" Company of the 18th was having the worst kind of trouble taking a hill which my rather weatherbeaten notes say was 587.

Numbers of the hills aren't important any more. They were then, of course. So important that the records are concerned only with hill numbers and map co-ordinances where action occurred. The men were expendable. Getting and holding the ground was all that mattered.

"I" Company got their hill, and were promptly pinned down by drenching mortar and withering machine gun fire from the front and both flanks. "They're digging in, poor bastards, as best they can," they told us at Battalion C.P. "But I ask you how in hell can a guy dig himself in when the grounds frozen so goddammed solid it takes a grenade to make a hole in it?"

"L" company had no chance to dig. The objective was a hill too . . . across a flat open space and pretty looking as a Xmas postcard to everybody but the poor guys who found crossing that open space mean't wading (for the snow was waist deep) through the main field of fire.

Past Faymonville, which had to be taken house by house in fighting nobody who lived through it wants to remember, the going got tougher still. The worst of all was where the defile narrowed and the men had to cross the stream to be stopped cold by stuff pouring in on them from the high ground on both sides.

Next day the bodies were still lying where they had fallen. More distressing than the number was the fact that so many were dead of wounds which would never have been fatal under ordinary conditions. One fair haired kid jutting out of the reddened snow had no more serious hurt than a fragment torn leg. He had frozen to death, as so many did, while waiting to be taken out.

Nothing on wheels would function in the deep snow. The only vehicles which would operate were weazels . . . sort of tank tracked jeeps . . . and there was only one of them to a battalion. Imagine trying to supply food, ammunition and the other combat needs of a battalion with one vehicle capable of carrying only 1200 lbs. The First had to do it all through those dreadful days.

It meant of course that a man had "Had it" if he stopped one. His life expectancy in that freezing cold was thirty minutes. And he knew that he could not be got out in thirty minutes.   If he was, his reaction was like the boy's in the battalion aid station at Faymonville who told me what the score was, but wouldn't give me his name, "To hell with my name Ma-am . . . use the space for Christ's sake to tell the folks back home what its like out here."

How could you tell them,   How could you convey with words cold which burned fingers as they touched metal, jammed automatic weapons and even condensed and froze breath on the diaphragms of the microphones so that our radios would not work.   What narrative form could paint the suffering of men who had no sleep for as long as three days and nights, no hot meal for days, no overcoats or blankets because they could not be brought up over the impossible roads?   How could you describe the feelings of men who day after day had to fight in conditions which only polar bears could find tolerable . . . conditions which could not be worse for fighting?   Did they grumble?   Of course they grumbled and blasphemed like hell.   But they fought like hell too.

Operational instructions had ordered the Ondenval Defile cleared for the 7th Armored to move through by January 18th. Clearing it cost the First so dear that they had to keep the 7th waiting.   Not until twenty-four hours after the deadline were they able to inform Hq. that they were set on all objectives and that the armor could get rolling.

By this time the division was battered to an extent that hurt to think about, Maxie was so down that for the first time on record he could not get up any enthusiasm for the fact that the censorship wraps were finally off and that we could now dateline copy "With the First Division".

The news clips which came back in the letters from home could give a little back to the boys for all they gave through every combat day.   Not much.   But at least they made them feel (no matter how cynically they might wisecrack) that there was something that the folks back home thought worth while to the hard, terrible and supremely self sacrificing business of soldiering.

Because of it, Maxie had his robust pride in his job, and played to the hilt his fabulous act of singing and posturing and never letting up for an instant on anything that would produce another inch of copy with a First Division dateline.

In these days of the fighting in the Ondenval Defile Maxie was as limp and dispirited as a thawed combat jacket might have looked if anybody had been able to find one in that area. He had no stomach for the tiniest boost to a story. His briefings came out in a flat, dejected monotone ending with "I'll phone press camp when you get back in case there's anything else."

There always was. And there was never space enough to tell it as it deserved to be told.

With the re-occupation of St. Vith, it was obvious to the world that Von Runstedt had lost the greatest battle in German history . . . the battle that lost not only the war, but the chance of keeping the shame and ignominy of defeat from happening on the sacred soil of the Reich.

From this point on, it was through the Seigfried Line to the Rhine. This is the dispatch with which I ended my story of The Battle of the Bulge:

With the 1st Infantry Division. January 28th, 1945.

"Leaving Von Runstedt's troops no time to do more than sweep the snow from their re-occupied pillboxes on the Seigfried Line, this division, with other troops not yet releasable (it was the 82nd Airborne Division) jumped off at four o'clock this morning on resumption of their drive to bend the Bulge back in the German direction now that they have ironed it out of the Belgian one. I said "Jumped off," but waded would be a more accurate description because it was just that.

There were three feet of snow over level ground with drifts averaging seven feet deep, and when the attack started snow flurrying down so hard that a further six inches had fallen between the time the attack started and daybreak, by which time "A" company of the 18th had taken 3,000 yards of territory, the village of Hepscheid, and 40 of the most surprised men in the whole German army. They simply could not believe that anyone would attack at such a time in such conditions. As one prisoner said, "We knew Yanks were crazy, but never thought them that crazy."

The going was so hard that it was necessary to change the lead man every 75 yards. On the plan the attack was to be supported by tanks. They set out but were still being dug out of drifts when this correspondent followed the bulldozing snow plough in past them (walking because her jeep was stuck too) around noon.

Yardage may sound poor rolling against the Russian miles. You would not think so watching men press on through this canyon country waist-high in snow, exquisite feather light as thistledown, but more awkward to negotiate than the heavy surf of a beach landing, and even more uncomfortable.

Every man carried two half pound blocks of T.N.T. to blow out the only place he has to live in. It is impossible to hew foxholes in this frozen ground, so, after scooping snow away, the only way to dig in, is by exploding the charge and then digging fast . . . mighty fast, because any kind of explosive charge draws attention in territory already getting more than enough of it anyway.

All these men have been fighting without cessation for thirteen days and nights. They have captured thirteen towns in that time and averaged a hundred and twenty prisoners a day.

All thirteen fights have started at night. This division likes night attack. They have improved some night attack tactics they learned in Africa and adapted sand to snow warfare in a way which puts a new shiver in your reaction to that oft-communiqued phrase 'grim fighting.'

In their words there has been more bayonet fighting than Americans have used in any other sector since D-Day. Our troops attack at a different time each night in white camouflage sheets. Without artillery preparation to break surprise or moonlit hush, they creep in to Bosche dug positions to kill, or prise the enemy out at knife point. It is a stealthy business of man hunting man from tree trunk to tree trunk . . . eerie, horrible, and against the austere, aloof beauty of the pines under which all this is happening, utterly incongruous.

Men are standing up to fighting in these conditions better than machines as is evidenced by the story given to me today of six men who had frostbitten feet and were trying to massage them back to feeling. When the order came to advance, their feet had swollen so they could not get their boots back on so went on without them. You cannot put spirit like that in machines.

Today the men who spearheaded this new drive had been fighting with no more than two eight day rest periods in eight months. One battery of gunners have been out of the line for only one day since D-Day.

Even weazels bringing up food and supplies are unable to muzzle through the drifts, but carrying all it takes to win out. Joe is wading on. If he has to hammer back through that Seigfried Line with nothing to support him but his weary legs and his Goddam guts, he'll get there and a long way beyond faster than anyone has any right to expect of him in country and conditions like these. End message."

Wonderful G.I.'s! They honored other insignias besides the Red One. But, like Sergeant Ehlers, never mind how the going might be, if they had to kill somebody so they could get on with the job, then they killed him and that was all there was to it. That was the way all soldiering was through the Ardennes campaign . . . tough. God it was tough! And magnificent!

CHAPTER IX

BONN AND REMAGEN

(February 8 to April 7, 1945)

The Situation

On February 8, 1945, the First Infantry Division was attached to the XVIII Corps. This Corps took over the north sector of the front line south of Krezau, from the VII Corps. Its disposition established the First Infantry Division on the north and the 82nd Airborne Division on the south, the boundary between the two divisions passing near and slightly north of the junction of the Kall with the Roer River.

On February 12, 1945, the First Infantry Division was attached to the III Corps. The Division finally crossed the Roer River on February 25, 1945.

From the Roer River, the Division rolled like a steamroller to the Rhine. The Rhine River was within shelling distance on March 7, 1945, when Bruhl, Berzdorf, Bornheim and Alfter fell into the Division's hands, and the big question was whether the Germans would blow up the Bonn Bridge. This, the Germans succeeded in doing on the evening of March 8th as the 16th Infantry drove down hot upon this strategic objective.

On March 16, 1945, the First Division crossed the Rhine for the second time in its history, and the next day went into action in Remagen. German artillery came into Remagen by the carload, and the Germans made counterattack after counterattack to recover lost ground.

The climax came on March 24-25, when action centered around

Geisbach in the north and Uckerath in the middle. The Germans were scheduled to counterattack on March 24th, but the First Division beat them to it, against three Panzer Divisions and a self-propelled gun brigade.

On March 27th, the race was on. The Division swung to the east and northeast, after smashing German armor, then cut to the north around Haiger and Dillenberg. The mission of the First Division was to expand and consolidate the corridor leading north, at the same time permanently hemming in the large German forces in the Ruhr.

On Easter Sunday, April 1, 1945, the Division undertook the longest tactical march in its history—from positions east of Siegen into the Buren area. Prisoners and German equipment were being swept up at a satisfying rate—airplanes, railroad guns, ammunition dumps, motor pools—all were overrun and absorbed.

With the closing of the Ruhr, the First Division took positions facing west. On April 8th, the Division turned east again, and took off for Berlin, crossing the Weser River.

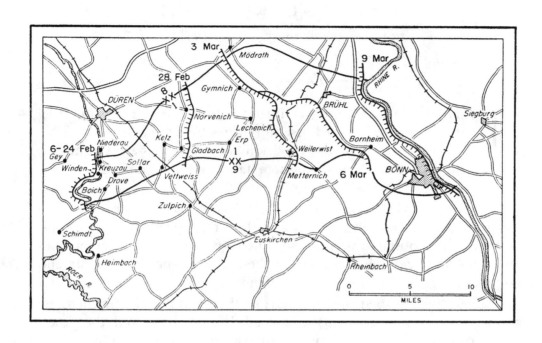

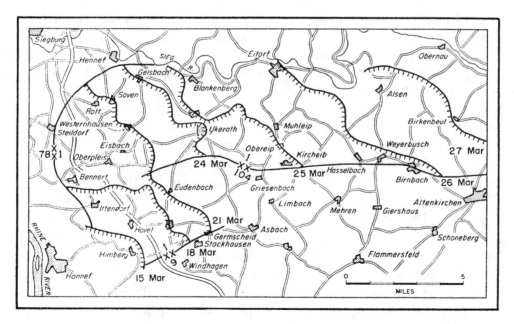

BONN AND REMAGEN
(February 8 to April 7, 1945)

The Record

THE FIRST Infantry Division (less Combat Team 16), moved to the forward assembly area February 8, 1945. The Command Post of the Division was at Grosshau, Germany. The mission of the Division was to take over the defense of the sector—Untermaubach-Bergstein-Grosshau.

When the Allies reached the Roer River (December 1944), or the terrain commanding the Roer, the river presented a serious obstacle. The obstacle was not so much geographic—the river was an imposing stream only because of the artificial speed of its current—it was a terrain feature bitterly defended.

The Division spent the best part of the month in this immediate sector. The prolonged rains added additional mud, and the Roer River rose rapidly, and continued to rise—higher and higher.

The Division finally crossed the Roer River on February 25, 1945. The situation had changed rapidly, in the meanwhile. Between the Division's advance to the high ground commanding the Roer, east of Langerwehe on December 8, 1944, and the final crossing on February 26, 1945, the all-important German offensive of December 16, 1944, had occurred, as well as the complete collapse of the eastern front and the advance of the Russians to the doorstep of Berlin. These two events had eliminated the 6th Panzer Army as an enemy potential. The 12th SS Panzer Division was badly battered by the First Division at Butgenbach. The collapse and disorganization of the offensive had left the German supply and materiel position in a precarious state. Top-grade troops had been largely drained off and the replacements were inferior troops of security and static level. Materiel was bad, and there was no gasoline. Despite this deterioration, the enemy opposed the crossing of the Roer River as bitterly as he might have been expected to do in his better days.

The initial assault across the Roer River took place on February

25th, to the north of the First Division sector, against sharp local resistance, and concentrated artillery fire. The Germans, however, apparently expected each unit facing him across the river to make a frontal attack. At any rate on February 26th, when the Division crossed the bridges of the 8th (U. S.) Infantry Division, and attacked south along the far side of the Roer, the Germans were taken completely by surprise.

The First Division attack was launched by the 16th Infantry at noon, February 25th. From Niedrau the 16th Infantry fanned southward to take Kreusau by mid-afternoon. Pushing on to the high ground west of Stockheim, the attack continued to the southeast where stubborn resistance was met from self-propelled guns and infantry in log and earth bunkers. The advance continued after dark, the first in a series of blacked-out moves that eventually "leap-frogged" the First Division to the Rhine.

These night attacks planned meticulously and detailed in organization were the exasperation of the Germans. Their previous reliance on being unmolested after dark to allow reorganization of new defenses, was gone.

On February 26th, the first enemy reaction to the Division attack took place. A company of German parachutists of the 8th Panzer Regiment supported by four assault guns, launched an attack from Thum towards Dove, only to meet intense artillery fire from the Division Artillery, and well directed small arms fire from the Division infantry elements.

Two of the German assault guns were knocked out, and the attack was dispersed. The attack had no effect on the progress of the Division troops. The assault continued and Boich was taken. Other Division units swept around to take Soller, the wooded area south of Stockheim, Schlagstein and Rath, while the Germans backed up into Vettweiss, Jakobwullsheim and Kalz. The next day this line was overrun, and a bridgehead was established over the Neffel Creek in the Norvenich Woods, east of Ober Bolheim.

On February 28th, Norvenich, Hochkirchen, Luxheim and Gladbach were cleared of Germans, and the Neffel Creek no longer existed as an effective barrier to the Division's advance.

The Division continued the attack rolling through the Rhine-land like a steamroller, and brought back recollections of the race through France. The Germans fell back on defending the towns in the built-up areas in the First Division zone of advance. Tanks could cut loose on clear cut and well defined targets, at will.

The fighting in the towns was often severe. The Germans were by no means going to quit. However the Division continued to over-run the rear installations of the Germans. On February 28th the 18th Infantry captured an entire battery of artillery because the battery's prime movers were out of gasoline. The Germans had not expected to see any American troops for another week or so.

The towns of Gymnich, Libar, Trippelsdorf, Metternich, Weiler-swist were captured in rapid-fire order, but the resistance was getting stiffer and stiffer. The Division ran into well-established and well-trained anti-aircraft units equipped with 20-mm machineguns. These flak troops had been outguards posted across the Rhine plain in the defense of the Ruhr, with the mission of defending the Ruhr and Western Germany. When the First Division advanced towards the Rhine these flak troops were used as Infantry.

The first full-scale defense of a town by the enemy was staged in Erp. The Division elements attacked Erp at 6:00 P.M., March 1, 1945, and ran into a heavy concentration of 88-mm's, self-propelled guns and automatic weapons. By midnight the Division had taken over half of the town of Erp, and a considerable bag of prisoners.

On March 22nd, Division troops took Gymnich, Memmerhofe, Poll and Ahren. The rest of the town of Erp was cleared of Germans. A small but bitter fire fight developed in the taking of Mellerhofe, and Division elements pushed on to Gymnich where a bitter fight of somewhat larger proportions developed. The Germans were without the necessary heavy weapons to hold off the Division thrust of tanks, and German tanks and the city itself fell, providing a bag of 100 prisoners as well.

Erp was the toughest nut of the day, but shortly after dawn March 3rd, the town fell and Division positions were consolidated. The night of March 2-3 the advance against the town of Lechnich continued, and by 3:00 A.M., March 3rd, the town was secure.

The attack to the east and to the Rhine River continued in the First Division sector, with the 16th Infantry securing the town of Weilerwist, and the 26th Infantry secured Bleisheim, Ober Liblar and vicinity, and the bridgehead across the River Erft. During the early morning hours, the 3rd Battalion, 18th Infantry was relieved by elements of the 18th Cavalry Squadron, and then moved to an assembly area in the vicinity of Norvenich, and with the remainder of the 18th Infantry, passed to First Division Reserve.

Shortly after midnight March 3rd, the 1st Battalion, 16th Infantry relieved elements of the 310th Infantry, in the town of Weilerwist. The 1st Battalion, 26th Infantry jumped off at 2:40 A.M. from Ahren, to secure the town of Bliesheim and a bridgehead across the Erft River. The 1st Battalion, 16th Infantry spent the entire day of March 4th cleaning out mines and booby traps in the town of Weilerwist.

On March 5th, the Division continued to attack to the east, with objectives on the high ground overlooking the Rhine River. The town of Metternich was cleared and the towns of Metren, Rosberg and Wallerberg were reached.

The reduction of Dersdorf on March 6th caused a bit of trouble, since it was defended by a stubborn group of Flak Troops, well equipped with 20-mm guns. Eventually at 9:00 P.M., the town was reported cleared, but even after Division troops had occupied the town, harrassing 20-mm fire from the vicinity of Rolsdorf and the wooded and high ground to the southeast continued to come in. While Dersdorf was being taken, other elements of the Division were pushing through Trenich, Balkhausen, Bruggen, Trippelsdorf, Gardorf, Waldorf and Ullekoven. These villages could hardly be said to have been taken by storm, although considerable resistance was put up by the Germans in Trippelsdorf.

The 16th Infantry reported that by 4:05 A.M., March 7th, Botzdorf had been taken, and later in the morning the town of Bornheim was reported clear of Germans. In the meanwhile the 2nd Battalion, 26th Infantry attacked at 6:00 A.M. with their objective the town of Bruhl and by 9:30 A.M., had taken that town.

During the early afternoon of March 7th, the 3rd Battalion,

16th Infantry passed through the 2nd Battalion to attack and secure both Roisdorf and Alfter, and, after clearing these towns, sent patrols as far east as Gransdorf.

The 2nd Battalion, 26th Infantry continued to push east, with Company F jumping off for Berzdorf at 3:15 P.M. Shortly afterwards a report came in that Company K, 26th Infantry was in the town of Sechtem. From Berzdorf the 2nd Battalion, 26th Infantry patrolled to the east reaching points a few hundred yards from the Rhine River.

By 9:15 P.M. the 18th Infantry was preparing to move on Bonn, having closed in an assembly area in the 9th Infantry Division sector. During this period the 16th Infantry and the 26th Infantry advanced to take limited objectives against moderate small arms and self-propelled gun fire, captured a total of 340 prisoners and meanwhile prepared for the attack on the city of Bonn.

On the 387th day of combat for the First Division, as a unit, the Division Artillery and attached units fired 139 missions in support of the advance.

Enemy positions on the east bank of the Rhine River were taken under fire by mortars of the 26th Infantry. Prisoners continued to flow through the Division cage at a high rate. On March 7th, seven hundred and twenty-six prisoners were processed through the First Division, among them the 60,000th prisoner taken by the First Infantry Division in World War II.

On March 8th, the 16th Infantry continued their attack to the east towards the Rhine River, jumping off from the vicinity of Roisdorf at 4:00 A.M., and reaching the Rhine by 7:00 A.M. After reaching the Rhine River line the 3rd Battalion, 16th Infantry consolidated its position and commenced pushing south along the river bank. At the same time elements of the 1st Battalion, 16th Infantry jumped off from Alfter maintaining contact with the 3rd Battalion, 16th Infantry and elements of the 18th Infantry on the south. At 4:00 A.M. the 1st Battalion, 18th Infantry attacked to capture Duisdorf, and then Lengsdorf. After a stiff fight these towns fell into Division hands.

In the late afternoon of March 8th, the 26th Infantry was relieved in their sector by the 14th Cavalry Group. The 1st Battalion, 26th Infantry moved from Bleisheim at 4:30 P.M., and then closed in an assembly area in the vicinity of Alfter by 7:30 P.M. The 2nd and 3rd Battalions of the 26th Infantry attacked from Duisdorf, the 1st Battalion taking Endenich, and then both the 2nd and 3rd Battalions of the 26th Infantry moved into the City of Bonn proper.

During this period the 2nd Battalion, 16th Infantry protected the left flank of the 1st and 3rd Battalions of the Regiment, and cleaned up any elements of scattered resistance, bypassed by their other battalions. Elements of the 3rd Battalion, 18th Infantry, cleared the town of Ollekoven, and also attacked into Bonn. The 1st Reconnaissance Troop, after cleaning out the towns of Lessenich and Messdorf, maintained contact between the 16th and 18th Infantry on its north. The Division Artillery and attached units supported the advance by firing 130 missions during this period.

On this day, March 8th, the First Division had continued attacking to the east, with its main objective the capture of the City of Bonn. At the end of the day, elements of the 16th and 18th Infantry were fighting in the streets of Bonn. Stiff resistance was encountered both on the outskirts and in the city, and over 1,000 prisoners were taken. Contact was maintained between the First Infantry Division and the 8th Infantry Division on the north, by the 14th Cavalry Group. At 8:30 P.M. the 3rd Armored Division joined the First Infantry Division and assembled in the vicinity of Liblar.

The Bonn Bridge, the only exit for the Germans, was a touch and go affair. Several German prisoners reported that they had seen the bridge prepared for demolition, and most of them were surprised that the bridge had not been blown already. The Bonn Bridge was blown at 9:15 P.M., March 8, 1945, by a Captain of the 6th (German) Engineer Regiment (later captured by the First Division), who had not slept for three days worrying over whether he would be able to blow the bridge at precisely the right moment. He succeeded admirably.

With the Bonn Bridge blown, resistance in the city decreased appreciably, and came to an official end at 3:10 P.M., March 9, 1945.

Some trouble was experienced with remnants of the 365th (German) Battalion, and a handful of misguided Volkssturmers, but the chief problem faced by the First Division was rounding up the large number of prisoners wandering around Bonn, some still in uniform, and others in civilian clothes.

With the city of Bonn quiet once more, except for enemy artillery shelling, cellars all over the town began giving up their yield of Landsers, some of whom had been hiding out for over a month. More than 200 deserters were flushed out of basements of civilian houses. Most of them had arrived in the area on furlough, and had simply decided to wait the arrival of the Americans, and the end of the war, instead of returning to their units. All during the race across the Rhineland, it was found that a large number of deserters could be expected as soon as the First Division troops reached towns and built-up areas where the German soldiers could get away from their noncommissioned and commissioned officers, without being missed.

Coincident with the appearance of the struggling Wermacht soldiery was an unprecedented number of civilians. During previous First Division operations in Germany, the number of civilians encountered was almost negligible, with the exception of the capture of Aachen. After the penetration of the 1st defense zone, east of the Roer River, however, the number of civilians encountered in the towns and villages exceeded the most optimistic Chamber of Commerce figures.

Hundreds of refugees from towns west of the Roer River had flooded back and others had come in from the heavy bomb targets of the cities of Cologne and Bonn. The screening and processing of these civilians presented enormous problems to the Military Government Detachments. In all, somewhere in the neighborhood of 150,000 civilians were estimated to be in the First Division Zone during the operation—55,000 in the City of Bonn, 20,000 in Bruhl, and 2,500 in Liblar.

The close of the period March 10, 1945 marked the completion of Phase No. 1 of the First Infantry Division's activity for the month of March, 1945. This was a continuation of the operation which started with the crossing of the Roer River, and ended with the clearing of all enemy territory west of the Rhine River within the First Division Sector, and the capture of the City of Bonn.

In the advance across the Cologne plain, the Germans put up a determined rear guard action, and as each town was attacked, moderate to heavy resistance was encountered in the advance. For the most part, the terrain up to the Erft River and the canal was extremely flat, but on crossing those obstacles a more rugged country was met, and the advance was slowed up as a result. Since the terrain afforded no natural barrier, and no defense system comparable to that of the Siegfried Line, the advance went faster than was anticipated, and a large number of prisoners of war passed into the First Division cage.

On reaching the outskirts of the City of Bonn, and in the clearing of that city, the enemy did not make the mistake that was made at Remagen, but managed to get a large percentage of his troops across to the east side of the Rhine River, and he destroyed his bridges behind him. However, the main objective of the First Division was to destroy all enemy bridges west of the Rhine River, and capture the City of Bonn, and that mission had been successfully accomplished.

For the period March 11 to 13, 1945, the First Division consolidated and held positions taken along the west bank of the Rhine River, adjacent to and in the City of Bonn. Orders were received whereby the First Division was to be relieved in position on the west bank of the Rhine River by the 8th Infantry Division, and then assemble in areas preparatory to movement across the Rhine River into the Remagen bridgehead.

At the close of March 16th, all units of the First Division were in assembly areas preliminary to the attack scheduled for March 17, 1945.

At 6:00 A.M., March 17, 1945, the 3rd Battalion, 18th Infantry attacked for limited objectives, and by 9:50 A.M. had secured these objectives in the vicinity of Frafenhohn and the hill to the southeast thereof. In the late afternoon the 3rd Battalion repulsed an enemy counterattack made by tanks and infantry.

At 6:00 A.M., March 17th, the 1st Battalion, 26th Infantry also jumped off to secure the crossroad in front of their position and reported "secure" about 4:00 P.M., in the face of heavy artillery fire. In the early afternoon of March 17th, the enemy counterattacked but was beaten off, losing five tanks in the hectic fight.

Division Artillery and attached units fired 73 missions during this period, in support of the attacks by the 18th and 26th Infantry Regiments. The First Division completed its 397th day of combat, as a unit, by attacking with the 18th and 26th Infantry Combat Teams. As the Division advanced toward the Cologne-Frankford Autobahn, it captured 230 prisoners.

During the first day's fighting, March 17th, the main units which the enemy had committed to block the expansion of the bridgehead were identified. Most of these prisoners were taken from Training Battalions (recently brought down from Denmark). During this day, the Germans were driven from the woods to the south. The villages of Grafenhorn and Huscheid were taken, but during the afternoon a company of German Infantry attacked First Division positions in these two villages. They were driven back to Nonnenberg. The most bitter fighting of the day took place south of Orscheid, along the Autobahn. The quality of the German Infantry did not prevent him from mounting frequent and ambitious counterattacks, driven home in desperation.

The Division attack continued and on March 18th, the high ground west of Eudenbach, the towns of Quirrenbach, Rostingen, Orscheid, Gratzfeld, Wullescheid and Stockhausen were cleared of Germans. The 2nd Battalion, 29th Panzer Grenadier Regiment counterattacked from the northeast in an effort to recapture Huscheid. A force of about 100 German Parachutists from the 5th Parachute Regiment kicked from behind by the terrible-tempered Colonel Becker, tried to retake Brungsberg from Quirrenbach. After rough and tough fighting the two attacks were beaten off. Shortly after 6:00 P.M., still another counterattack was launched down the Stockhausen-Himberg road, with four enemy tanks in support. It was repulsed with heavy fire, and Division troops pushed forward to occupy Stockhausen. During the day, enemy artillery fire grew in intensity with more than 4,500 rounds being recorded.

The towns of Nonnenberg and Eudenbach fell to the First Division on March 19th, after heavy fighting, and in the face of even heavier artillery concentrations, to which was added a sizeable portion of rocket fire. At 8:45 P.M., after a heavy rocket and artillery barrage on First Division positions in Eudenbach, the Germans attacked the town in strength from the northeast, east and southeast, with tanks and infantry. The attack achieved some success, an infiltration into Eudenbach.

Division artillery laid down heavy concentrations on the attacking force and compelled German follow-up troops to withdraw, pounding them heavily all the way.

At 11:00 A.M. the Germans started a series of strong counterattacks to recapture Gratzfeld from the east—four counterattacks in all—by a straggler Battalion of about 250 men. These attacks were repulsed and 200 prisoners were taken. Many enemy dead were left in the streets.

On March 20, 1945, the First Division published orders to the effect that: "The First Infantry Division (to which Combat Command R, 3rd Armored Division is attached), will continue to attack to expand the Remagen bridgehead; to destroy all enemy in its zone of action; seize and hold objectives assigned and execute reconnaissance to the reconnaissance line.

"The 26th Infantry protects the south flank and will maintain liaison with the 9th Infantry Division. The 18th Infantry will attack in its zone of action, maintaining contact with the 26th Infantry on the right and the 16th Infantry on the left. Combat Command R will maintain contact with the 78th Infantry Division on the left."

The First Division advanced 3,000 yards on March 20th, in the north, and 2,000 yards in the center of the Division Zone. Over 20 inhabited localities were taken by the First Division, of which the larger towns were Stieldorfhohn, Oberpleis, Herresbach and Berghausen. German resistance continued to be stubborn, supported by ever-increasing artillery, mortar and rocket fire.

The attack toward Stieldorfhohn and Oberpleis started shortly after midnight and proceeded well except for stubborn resistance in Boseroth. In the center the Germans were driven out of Berghausen.

The seriousness with which the Germans regarded the First Division's advance was indicated by the identification on March 21st of two regiments of the 363rd Infantry Division (German) which relieved what was left of the 3rd Panzer Grenadier Division the night of March 20-21, 1945. Two other important and troublesome identifications were those of the 244th and 902nd Assault Gun Brigades who brought with them a heavy support of self-propelled guns. In spite of these changes and reinforcements, however, the Germans were unable to halt the advance of the First Infantry Division. By dawn, March 21st, the general line Bockeroth-Uthweiler-Pleiserholm-Rubhausen was held.

Shortly after daylight, March 21st, the Germans began a strong series of counterattacks against the Division lines, especially on the right flank where the first attack was made with 200 infantry and five tanks. This first assault was broken, but the German infantry continued to apply pressure in an effort to retake the high ground. By 6:00 P.M., Rott, Soven, Westerhausen and Kurscheid were cleared, although the advance was contested by ten self-propelled guns operating between Soven and Westerhausen. Three guns were destroyed in Soven, and the First Division's move into Germscheid, on the right flank, was counterattacked by one hundred infantry and four self-propelled guns. Both Soven and Westerhausen were cleared on March 22nd, and the build-up areas in the eastern part of Hennef and the vicinity of Weiderschall were reconnoitered.

The 24-hour period of March 23, 1945, marked the 402nd day of combat for the First Infantry Division as a unit, and was spent relieving certain elements of the Division, and regrouping others for further attacks on the enemy. Units of the 104th Infantry Division were used as the relief of First Division elements. At the same time the attack was continued to the Hanf River by two battalions of the 16th Infantry, and quite a number of towns and locations were seized and occupied. The Division relentlessly drove the Germans back toward the east and northeast, from the Rhine River. During the late hours of the night, the town of Wellesburg and key ground within the First Division Sector, was taken by the 18th Infantry.

On March 24th, the attack by the Division continued. A change of orders stated that:—"Spearheaded by the 3rd Armored Division, the VII Corps would attack to the east, followed by the First Infantry Division on the left, and the 104th Infantry Division on the right." This was a part of the major attack to destroy all enemy in the VII Corps Zone, south of the Sieg River.

During the fighting of March 24, 1945, it was obvious that the Germans had indeed been planning a large and powerful operation. The day's fighting was as gruelling and hard-fought as any in the First Division's campaigns in Europe. At the end of the battle, however, Division troops had succeeded in driving 1,500 yards to the east to take the high ground east of the Hunf Creek, as well as the town of Uckerath. During this day, fourteen German counterattacks were reported, in addition to many smaller thrusts. Enemy mortar, artillery and rocket fire reached a peak of intensity, with more than 5,500 rounds coming in on the First Division Zone. It appeared that the Division, moving out to the east, had "jumped the gun" on the German offensive. During the morning—before dawn—Seisbach, Hennef and Lichtenberg were taken by the Division. Division units in Geisbach area were counterattacked beginning about 9:00 A.M., by self-propelled guns, tanks and infantry, in a continuous action which went on until 1:00 P.M., at which time the Germans managed to penetrate the town.

By liberal use of Division artillery and fighter-bombers of Allied Air Forces, on follow-up troops of the Germans, in the Greuelsiefen area, the Germans were prevented from exploiting their success and First Division elements were able to push German armor and infantry northeastward out of the town of Geisbach by 5:50 P.M.

Division troops which had reached the road near Streifen, shortly after dawn had bypassed an enemy force, and as soon as they reached the positions they were strongly counterattacked from both front and rear. The Division troops held on, however, and by noon the attack from the west had been eliminated.

Possibly the most severe fighting, however, took place in and around Uckerath, which appeared to be the main enemy stronghold in the sector. However, by the end of the day the town of Uckerath was in First Division hands.

The German prisoners taken in Uckerath were from the 62nd Volksgrenadier and 363rd Divisions. These regiments were due in Uckerath the day after the First Division attacked. The Division had cut off the enemy's plans by attacking one day too soon.

On March 25th, the fighting went on with equal intensity, supported by the appearance of all the major elements of the 130th Panzer Lehr Division, which had moved into this area on the night of March 24-25, 1945.

The major battles of March 24-25 seemed to mark a climax to the German's opposition to the First Division breakthrough. Though there was still stiff fighting to be done before the breakthrough was complete, and the armor could drive out, on March 24-25 the Germans had committed their major units, brought up to the greatest strength possible. At the end of March, the First Division had taken 4,319 prisoners, since beginning operation in the Remagen bridgehead. During the same eight days, the Division destroyed more than fifty tanks, and self-propelled guns, and ground up a total of five German Divisions—three Armored (9th and 130th Panzer and 3rd Panzer Grenadier) Divisions, and two Infantry (62nd and 363rd Volksgrenadier) Divisions.

The fighting continued with severity in some places, although for the most part the Germans were bending every effort to get their main force north of the Sieg River.

On March 26th, the advance of the First Division was continued to the north and east by all three infantry regiments, supported by Division Artillery and attached units. Elements of the 78th Infantry Division relieved elements of the First Infantry Division in some parts of the line.

On April 1, 1945, the First Infantry Division was given the mission of preventing all enemy movement from the west and southwest attempting to break out of the "ROSE" pocket in the Geseke-Buren-Ruthen Sector.

The "ROSE" pocket was formed by the union of the First and Ninth Armies north of Paderborn, April 1, 1945, and was named in honor of Major General Maurice Rose who commanded the 3rd Armored Division which spearheaded the attack of the First Army at the time of his death. General Rose was killed in the vicinity of Paderborn while with the forward elements of his Division.

At 7:00 A.M., April 1st, the 26th Infantry (less the 1st Battalion moving by motor), crossed their initial point and arrived in their new area. The 3rd Battalion, 26th Infantry, took the town of Ruthen. The 2nd Battalion took the town of Hammern.

During the afternoon elements of the 1st Battalion, 16th Infantry reported stiff resistance in the town of Steinhausen, but by late afternoon that town was cleared of the enemy. The 18th Infantry was relieved by the 3rd Battalion, 13th Infantry, 8th Infantry Division, and moved out to assembly areas, establishing road blocks to the west and to the south.

The 16th Infantry captured 20 locomotives, and 100 railroad cars in the vicinity of Steinhausen, and relieved elements of the 3rd Armored Division, near Buren.

Division Artillery and attached units, under control of their respective Combat Teams, moved to new positions, now under control of First Infantry Division Command.

On the 412th day of combat for the First Infantry Division, elements of the Division moved to the north to close the gap between the First and Ninth U. S. Armies, and captured the towns of Ruthen, Hammen, Geseke, and Steinhauser, meeting stiff resistance in every town.

On April 2, 1945, First Division Orders assigned the 16th Infantry to the job of securing objectives, blocking enemy movement from the west and northwest in its zone and to maintain contact with the 3rd Armored Division on its right.

The 26th Infantry (less its 1st Battalion), was to secure assigned objectives, also block enemy movement from the south and southwest and maintain contact with the 16th Infantry on the north.

The 18th Infantry (less its 2nd Battalion), plus Reconnaissance Troop and Company A, 86th Chemical Battalion (attached), was to block all enemy movement from the west and southwest, maintain contact with the 26th Infantry on its right, and hold one battalion in mobile reserve.

Many small towns and villages were taken by elements of the

First Division, but the Division was, for the most part, consolidating its positions—"marking time"—but with ears to the ground. It was rumored that another move was in the offing, and so . . . here it is:— "The VII Corps will advance to the east. The 3rd Armored Division on the left (north) and the 104th Infantry Division on the right (south). The First Infantry Division will pass through the 3rd Armored Division and continue the advance in conjunction with the 104th Division on Corps Order."

The Division being pinched out of its position by the 8th Division, assembled and prepared to move north and east. The 16th Infantry (reinforced), assembled and prepared to move out on orders.

On April 8, 1945, with the First Infantry Division in position, its mission was announced. This phase of operations was "Crossing the Weser River and then pushing on to the east to Osterode, western edge of the Harz Mountains.

Thus—in keeping with the reputation of the Division—"The First Division continues to spearhead any advance—anywhere—at any time."

◆　◆　◆

BONN AND REMAGEN

As I Saw It

By

COLONEL R. ERNEST DUPUY

THE road to Remagen began for me, oddly enough, south of the Loire, 380 miles away. Wintry sun, glinting through the windows of the warm farmhouse this smiling morning of 23 February, 1945, fell full on the sharp features of the French Colonel. He squinted, the while shaking his head.

"Alas, no," he pontificated. "It is too late now. *Les Canadiens,*"—he meant the First Canadian Army now bucking slowly into the Maas-Rhine nose southeast of Nijmegen—*"les Canadiens* have their hands full. As for the Americans, my dear Ernest, the unfortunate affair of the Ardennes has taken all initiative from your forces. We shall see no real assumption of offensive until summer. Our poor France must wait."

The old farmer and his wife, hanging on his words, nodded sorrowful assent. But we all drank a *coup* of good Anjou wine to the future and problematical success of the Allies. And I almost choked as I drank.

For I knew that on this fine morning the Ninth and First U. S. Armies were due to strike across the Roer River. I glanced at my watch; almost 0900. Yes, the big offensive would have been on for several hours now; the initial phase lines reached. The Ninth was assaulting as part of the 21st Army Group into the Cologne Plain; the First, protecting its right flank, was aiming toward Cologne itself.

I wished that I could have sprung this bombshell now, among my friends, but my lips were sealed. I was on the last leg of a quick trip down to the St. Nazaire pocket, swinging over on the return trip to visit my cousins near the quaint little walled city of Richelieu. The French officer, on liaison duty with SHAEF, who had accompanied me, knew nothing, of course, of our projected offensive.

Back that night to the madhouse of the Hotel Scribe, in Paris, our press center, I rushed for the war room, the little secret cubby hole of SHAEF Public Relations Division, where by phone daily we oriented ourselves over our private network with the armies. Sure enough, they were over the Roer. The big push was on!

What would happen next? The Big Red One had presented the A.E.F. with Aachen, gateway to the Cologne Plain, ages ago—before the dreary episode of the German counteroffensive and the Battle of the Bulge. Since that time Fritz had barred advance, thanks to the rushing Roer and the dams controlling it, as well as to his own rushed but efficient terrain exploitation beyond the river bank.

How far and how fast could First Army drive, with Patton's Third on the right hitting into the Eifel, with the Ninth on the left pointing for Dusseldorf? Cologne was dead ahead, but in front of it lay another potential barrier, one over which we had argued and sweated at SHAEF many times.

We were going to the Rhine, of course; to the Rhine and, God willing, over it, with the Combined Chiefs of Staff's clearly stated directive before us—to "strike into the heart of Germany." To do that we must first destroy the enemy west of the Rhine, then bridge the river itself.

First Army was aimed at Cologne. But before it now lay the shallow but wide Erft River network of canal and paralleling creeks, a muddy strip draining northward from the Eifel. The Erft and its canal swing in protective arc west of Cologne from Eustkirchen up to Dusseldorf, with behind it, from Bruhl to Bergheim, the low partly wooded hills of the Vorgebirge. Along those hillocks, according to intelligence reports, and particularly aerial reconnaissance, forced labor had been active for months, preparing defensive positions.

In fact, the potential defenses of the Vorgebirge had weighted the calculations of the G-2 people long ago—had clouded perceptions of enemy intentions during November and early December, before the Ardennes flamed in German assault.

For, given a good defensive position along the Erft, to delay Allied advance when once we were across the Roer, a heavy armored force debouching from the Eifel in northward stroke on our right flank might have played hob with us. This force the enemy had, in those days, and it was thus, considered many staff people, that he would play his cards. They had thought too much along those erroneous lines, unfortunately; they had convinced themselves.

Now the defensive position along the Erft still lay before us, but thanks to the debacle of the Bulge, there were no German armored reserves available; the remnants of Hitler's panzer divisions squandered in the Ardennes were either on the Russian front or up north trying to stop the Canadians.

The offensive went on for 2 days before we picked up the First Division on our war room map, moving over the 8th Infantry Division bridges across the Roer. It was striking south, according to the sitreps, against a surprised enemy, from Niedrau to Kreuzau, and up onto the high wooded ground east of the Roer near Stockheim.

The Big Red One was bucking the line with a vengeance, in

continued night attacks. The enemy 8th Para Regiment was putting up some defense now, but it wasn't enough. Breaking out of the woods, Soler, directly to the east, fell. Boich and Rath, to the south, were taken, giving breathing space along the east Roer bank, and the direction of attack shifted generally eastward.

Now the Division was going to town. By the end of 27 February, Vettweis was taken on the right, Jakobswullesheim and Kelz were overrun in the center, and on the left the Big Red One had reached northeast to snatch a bridgehead over Neffel Brook in the dense Norvenicher Wald, east of the hamlet of Ober Bolheim.

By next day the Division was astride 2 highways leading into Cologne—the Duren-Norvenich-Lechnich and Gladbach-Erp-Lechnich roads. The Neffel stream-line was in its hands from Gladbach north through Luxheim, Hochkirchen and Norvenich to the woods.

As an old 7th Field Artilleryman I was naturally interested in following the Division's fortunes, and Lieutenant Colonel James F. Hughes, my chief briefing officer, a former First Division man himself, fairly hung on the map as he posted information gleaned from sitreps and our telephone net to the armies.

First full-scale enemy resistance in the Division zone was struck next day, as elements of the German 353rd Infantry Division stood their ground stubbornly in Erp on the right of the advance. But north of that village Dorweiler, Pingsheim and Rath (another Rath, this) were cleared, and from Rath the plugging doughboys plunged on into Wisserheim. Elements of the 12th Volksgrenadier Division were identified opposing us, as well as the 353rd.

First Army was approaching the Erft line. Would that line hold at all, we questioned ourselves back at SHAEF? Could anything stop the tide now scouring the Cologne Plain? And what, in particular, would the Big Red One do? We soon found out.

On 2 March Erp was cleared of its stubborn defenders, which now included some paratroopers. From Ahrem up to Gymnich the Division was on the outer fringe of the Erft belt. Early next morning (0300) a night attack had pressed through Lechnich; the Division was astride the Zulpich-Cologne highway.

Blessem fell and we were over the Erft Canal itself. Then into

Liblar and our question was finally answered. The Big Red One was over the Cologne moat and biting into the Vorgebirge—those supposed defenses had turned out to be a hollow sham. Fritz was really paying through the nose now for his squandering of force in the Ardennes.

First Army was pushing through everywhere; troops to the north of the Division were entering the outskirts of Cologne city. Correspondents at SHAEF, in fine frenzy, were asking all sorts of questions as to what was happening.

On the northern edge of the Cologne Plain First Canadian Army was closing down, with Ninth U. S. Army romping on a wide end run from the south to wind the German First Para and Fifteenth Armies, respectively, back on one another into an ever-shrinking bridgehead west of Wesel. South of First Army, the Third was driving down both sides of the Moselle River towards the Rhine.

Cologne fell on 5 March, its last 2 bridges blown in methodical German style as our troops raced toward the waterfront. The First Division turning south below Bruhl, pushed toward Bonn where the bridge across the Rhine was still standing, cluttered by a stream of retreating German traffic. Rear guards were putting up a fight along the Bruhl-Bonn highway, but the Big Red One overrode opposition handsomely, taking Dersdorf, 6 miles from Bonn on 6 March, after stiff resistance had been encountered.

By this time armored elements of First Army were beginning to probe north and south toward the Rhine bank. And the First Division itself deployed for the taking of Bonn on 7 March, unknowing that the finger of Fate was pointing at a spot upriver, just 12 miles away.

Back at SHAEF everyone was wondering what would occur on the Rhine itself. There was no doubt about what was happening to the German armies west of the river. The meticulous Montgomery had for some time now been building up his resources for the full-dress river-crossing which 21st Army Group would make after the west bank in its zone had been "tidied up," to us a Montgomeryism.

Fritz, we knew, would do his best to hold open such bridges as had not already been destroyed by air bombing, until his bridgeheads were wiped out. Then demolitions would rip the strands away in the face of our advance. On the other hand, the outfits pushing back that last screen of German defense all had in the back of their minds the dream that perhaps someone would make a mistake, would cling to a bridge just too long. It had happened before in war.

That was what was in the minds of the wearers of the Big Red One as they pushed toward Bonn, over roads now jammed with civilian refugee traffic fleeing panic-stricken for safety. And that was what was in the minds of the leading elements of Combat Command B, 9th Armored Division, as they drove east from Eustkirchen, far on the south flank of the First Division.

It was 1630 on the afternoon of 7 March when the armored troops caught their first glimpse of the Rhine. They had smacked through Rheinbach and Stadt-Meckenheim, left Ahrweiler and its wooded hills behind them to their right rear as they opened the Ahr River valley at Bad Neuenahr. They swung around the nose of Hill 187 where the highway curves on the flat Ahr delta below Remagen.

Across the brownish Rhine, dead ahead, a gaunt steel skeleton stretched into the steep hills of the east bank. The Hindenburg Bridge, still standing! Throttle down, the lead vehicles plunged at it like hunters at a fence.

Over the bridge the armored elements raced, killing or capturing the few startled defenders who tried—too late—to plunge the handles of their demolition switches. They swept in the dusk through panic-stricken Erpel nestling below the crags, swung up the steep road to the high ground beyond.

First Army was across the Rhine! General Bradley telephoned the Supreme Commander that evening, catching him at dinner, to give him the great news. Exploitation of the bridgehead, the shifting of 5 divisions down to make it good, were immediately ordered.

Eisenhower, it is true, called up Field Marshal Montgomery, to pass the word and, as he later stated to our correspondents, to confer with him on the exploitation of the bridgehead. It was apparently a contingency not specifically provided for by the Combined

Chiefs of Staff in their plan, which called for Montgomery to make
the main effort across the Rhine.

But Bradley had his bridgehead, God-given to 12th Army
Group, as such things are to those who help themselves. Here was
the great opportunity. Full speed ahead was indicated. What was
definitely decided upon from the beginning, it seems, was that since
another tremendous prize might be dangling before us, the exploitation should not be northward, but rather to the east and south.

There were good reasons for this. If Fritz knew that Monty
was to make the main effort, and it is doubtful indeed that he did
not know the tremendous river-crossing was in the making, he would
look for the obvious—a northward push from First Army's bridgehead at Remagen down the right bank of the Rhine to assist in the
coming assault up Dusseldorf way and the Ruhr.

But there was in fact a bigger goal in sight. Monty was scheduled to drive over and skirt the northern edge of the Ruhr. A drive
by 12th Army Group's First Army, in concert with Montgomery's
21st Army Group (the Second British and Ninth U. S. Armies),
out of the Remagen bridgehead south and east, could lead to double
envelopment of the enemy forces between the Main and Ruhr Rivers
—something to make the military mind gasp.

But first that bridgehead had to be made strong and safe. The
only reserves the enemy could scrape up now would be from the
north anyway, so the initial exploitation would be gradually to the
south, the area of least resistance, while at the same time covering
hostile reaction from the north.

So it was that the Big Red One, only 10 miles away from
Remagen now, was one of the units tagged to move at once across
the Rhine.

The news of Remagen reached the Division next day, 8 March,
as it fought its way into Bonn, hoping against hope that it might
snatch that bridge. But it was not to be. The Krauts sent the iron
road and tramway structure toppling into the river while their rear
guards were still fighting in the town, leaving them and the thousands of civilian refugees cluttering the streets. Street fighting continued in Bonn all the next day and night before resistance ceased.

It was then that orders arrived sending the First Division into Germany once again, as part of the Remagen bridgehead force.

Back at SHAEF the official flash on Remagen did not come in until 1900 hours in the evening, Paris time, 8 March; early afternoon in New York, breakfast time in San Francisco. And as frenzied correspondents moved their bulletins the tickers began clattering across the United States. By wire and radio the good news spread to an American people just recovering from the setback of the Bulge, a people in a "show-me" frame of mind and still just a little bit suspicious of our capabilities.

The military "experts" at home—and abroad, too, for that matter—had been hanging on a wailing wall ever since the Ardennes. Hitler had put something over; our plans had been disrupted, set back for 6 months or more. Now they threw their crying towels in a corner, grabbed their "I-told-you-so" caps and went to town. American troops were over the Rhine; it was in the bag. It was all very American, very fine.

It was in the bag, too; but that bag would not be snapped shut until some mighty good troop leadership and mighty good fighting men had accomplished a lot more hard work.

The Big Red One assembled and moved toward Remagen, to make the second Rhine crossing in its history. The First Division had gone across for the first time 13 December, 1918, as part of the IV Corps, Third U. S. Army, moving down the Moselle valley that time, over into Coblenz and on to Montabaur to make part of the perimeter of our then bridgehead.

This time it was going over via Remagen, pathway of the 2nd Infantry Division back in 1918; and it would be fighting not so far from its stamping ground of 26 years and 3 months previous. Old names would be in the news, old places traversed by a new generation of fighting men bearing the badge of the Big Red One.

As a matter of background assistance, I had gotten up for our correspondents a march table of the Third Army of 1918, and left it on my desk overnight. Slugged "Third Army Occupying Germany," the paper caught the eye of my duty officer, making his nightly check to see that secret documents were properly disposed of.

Patton's Third Army was romping wild now Rhineward down the Moselle and crisscrossing in the Palatinate. The shocked duty officer read the caption, leaped on the paper and brought it reproachfully to me.

I commended him for his assiduity, pointed to the date—"12 December, 1918," and—he bought the drinks.

The Division moved over the rickety Hindenburg Bridge 16 March. Fritz was putting down long-range artillery fire now, hoping to smash the structure. The Luftwaffe was making occasional half-hearted passes at it too, through dense ack-ack. And First Army Engineers were working like Trojans to span the rushing river with pontoons, just downstream. They completed their work, in fact, before the tired and damaged bridge folded, too late to interrupt the movement of reinforcements and supply.

This time the Big Red One was going into battle some 20 miles north of its World War I headquarters in Germany—Montabaur. Resistance flared along the overpass across the autobahn back from the cliffs—that autobahn from Limberg to Cologne which had been Hitler's pride. It was nasty fighting there in the West Wald, with quickening artillery fire coming down. Elements of 3rd Para and 3rd Volksgrenadier Divisions were trying to hold, and not doing so badly at that, for although the overpass was cleared and Grafenhorn and Ruscheid taken, a counterattack supported by tanks rocked the Division back to Nonenberg. They were fighting at Orsheid, too, along the autobahn.

It was not until 18 March, the second day after they had crossed the river, that the Division took and held the high ground west of Eudenbach, drove the defenders from Gratzfeld, Wullescheid and Stockhausen.

Fritz was groping in the bottom of the barrel now, hunting for reinforcements, hurling in fragments of the dilapidated Fifth Panzer Army. They followed the pattern of German defense, in succession of vicious counterattacks from the northeast by 5th Panzer and 29th Panzer Grenadier Regiments.

Next day the Division finally took Nonenberg and Eudenbach, restoring the entire position after another violent counterattack.

On 20 March, the Big Red One had pushed eastward again, taking Steldorferhorn, Oberpleis, Herresbach and Berghausen. Elements of the 9th Panzer Division were now reinforcing the original defenders, and for 2 more days occurred a succession of small, vicious counterattacks as the Kraut sparred desperately for time, dragged in bits and pieces to bolster his line. And he had put the only large elements he could spare—130th Panzer Lehr and 11th Panzer Divisions,—on the move slowly from east of Cologne.

Now, while we watched the Remagen bridgehead slowly grow, its lines moving eastward from the river on the map, while we waited for the opening of Monty's great assault, Georgie Patton did it. "Without air or artillery preparation," as the official flash from 12th Army Group read, Patton had pushed Third Army elements by assault boat across the Rhine far above the Remagen area—at Oppenheim, midway between Mainz and Worms.

It happened 22 March, on the very eve of Monty's assault, and the bare fact for the moment blanketed the news from Remagen, took the keen edge off recital of the really magnificent move of Second British and Ninth U. S. Armies in their Rhine crossings in the north.

Let Monty cross the Rhine, with roar of massed artillery support, with fighter-bombers screaming overhead, with paratroopers and gliders sliding in from the sky, with Royal and U. S. Navy detachments helping on the water. So what? Patton stroked his ivory-handled shooting-irons and chuckled. He was there. And of bridgeheads now, totting up the score, the AEF had 3.

Locally, at Remagen, the enemy was still desperately trying to dam the flood. The Big Red One was meeting heavy opposition from Krauts clinging to the ridge line from Hammef to Ockerath, which Fritz hoped vainly to hold long enough to enable Panzer Lehr and 11th Panzer Division to assemble.

The Division was hammering at that ridge. It would keep on hammering until 25 March, when Adscheid, Blankenberg and Suchlerscheid fell. That crowned it—the Remagen bridgehead was secured once and for all now. The Hindenburg Bridge had gone, of course, by this time, but the wide pontoon bridges were emplaced, the enemy driven out of range, First Army pouring over.

Forty-eight hours later the Remagen bridgehead burst outward in offensive movement. First Army's left jutted in great arc toward Lippstadt. The greatest double envelopment in all the history of war—the iron ring around the Ruhr and some 300,000 German soldiers—was being forged as Ninth Army skirted the northeastern edge of Germany's great industrial area to meet the southern prong.

Armored spearheads shot from First Army's southern bridge-head zone to link with Third Army. And from the center spouted another avalanche of men and steel, bound due east. The Big Red One and its sister divisions were headed for the Harz Mountains in the final drive which would end in Czechoslovakia.

In our war room we began hastily shifting maps. On the air the Armed Forces Radio began to swing: "I'm Heading for the Last Round-Up." Walpurgis Night had come for Hitler and his gang.

CHAPTER **X**

THE LAST KILOMETER.
HARZ MOUNTAINS TO CZECHOSLOVAKIA.
(April 8 to May 8, 1945)

The Situation

The operations of April 8, 1945, in the VII Corps advanced the First Division to the line of Weser River at Lauenforde to support future advances to the east.

On April 9th, the First and Ninth American Armies were ordered to resume the advance to the east on the following day.

VII Corps consisting of the 1st Infantry Division, the 104th Infantry Division and the 3rd Armored Division, was directed to advance rapidly in its zone and seize the line Einbeck-Northeim-Duderstadt about April 10th; to continue this advance as far as the Elbe River. It was also to by-pass but contain any resistance in the Harz Mountains.

Both the VII Corps and the V Corps were authorized to exploit any opportunity to seize a bridgehead over the Elbe River, and to be prepared to make contact with Soviet Forces.

By April 11th, the First Division with the 4th Cavalry Group attached, had advanced to the western slope of the Harz Mountains against increased resistance which included road blocks, blown bridges, tanks, small arms and bazooka fire.

It was apparent that the last hope of the Germans was to pull back as many men as possible, as well as the greater part of his armor into the Harz Mountains where the terrain, if nothing else, would give him time to regroup his forces into some sort of order.

The rout began on April 18th and the First Division pushed into the rear areas of the enemy's Harz front and continued on April 19th when the high ground overlooking Blankberg and Thale was taken.

The payoff of the entire operation came on April 20th when all enemy forces in the First Division zone capable of resistance, had been destroyed.

With the wind up in the Harz Mountains, the war was over. The only people who would not admit it was over—were the Germans.

When the First Division moved down to Czechoslovakia and began adjusting the line, the Germans put up a stiff resistance in spots and elsewhere sat and waited the arrival of the Americans.

Along the main road from Cheb to Falkenau 88-mm guns were deployed in depth and each one had to be eliminated individually by the infantry before the tanks could move. Klinghart, Plesna Sneky, Minchov and Kynsperk were all cleared of Germans during May 6, 1945, but German artillery was still coming in.

At 8:15 A.M., May 7, 1945, the 1st Infantry Division received an order "Cease Firing"—the long-awaited order for which the Division had fought since November 8, 1942, from Oran through Tunisia, through Sicily, through France, through Belgium, through the Ardennes, through Germany to its final operation in Czechoslovakia.

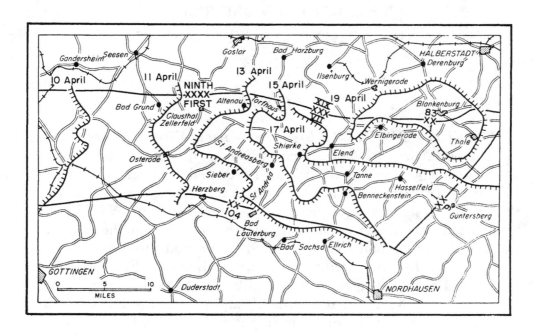

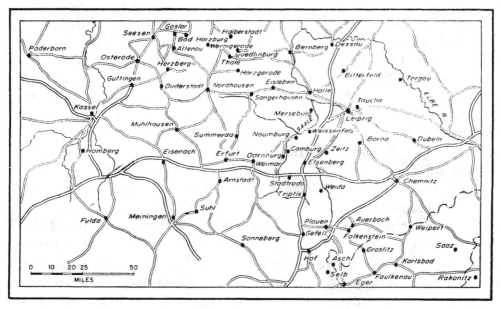

THE LAST KILOMETER.
(HARZ MOUNTAINS TO CZECHOSLOVAKIA)
April 8 to May 8, 1945.

The Record.

FIELD ORDER NO. 61, Headquarters First Infantry Division, April 8, 1945, stated: "VII Corps attacks to seize a bridgehead across the Weser River and exploits to the east. The First Infantry Division will attack to secure crossing of the Weser River, seize the bridgehead and expand it to the VII Corps bridgehead line prepared to continue the advance to the east on Corps order in conjunction with the 3rd Armored Division.

The 16th Infantry (reinforced), upon seizing the First Division bridgehead within its zone will establish and maintain contact with elements of the XIX Corps on the left and protect the left flank of the Division. Likewise the 18th Infantry (reinforced), will seize the bridgehead within its sector, maintaining contact with the 104th Infantry Division on the right. The 26th Infantry (reinforced), less one battalion, on return to Division control, to be Division Reserve prepared to advance through either one of the other regiments."

Until April 8, 1945, the First Division's contact with the enemy consisted of little more than corraling the bands of stragglers (the best part of them in civilian clothes) who were still trying to beat their way through the legendary Lippstadt-Paderborn gap.

On April 8, however, the Division crossed the Weser River. The Weser was a considerable barrier, and in their better days the enemy could have made it far more difficult and costly than the Roer River. Scratch units such as the enemy 6th Observation Battalion, and various engineer units first appeared to deny the crossing of the Weser. The structure of the German 6th Corps (formerly Wehrkreis VI) began to emerge and became even clearer with the capture of General Goerbig, one of the Corps' subordinate commanders, along with his brief case. When the Remagen bridgehead exploded and the Wehrkreis switched functions, orders were received to furnish a certain number of reserve divisions to be used as props and supports to stem the advance of Allied troops. Under the existing German manpower shortage, furnishing so much as a squad was squeezing blood from a stone, but the order remained and General Karst, abandoning all hope of retaining a replacement training system, ordered all the battalions in the area, both cadre and trainees, into the command. The resultant melange was known as the 466th Reserve Battalion. Quite a few other well-known SS organizations were recognized from the long line of prisoners that came into Allied hands.

In spite of this array of talent, the initial crossing of the Weser, by the First Division was made against light to moderate resistance in the vicinity of Beverungen, where a strongpoint manned by SS troops was encountered and cleared only after a short and bitter fight. Prisoners taken were again in high percentage from replacement units, encountered in such variety because they were in the area in the first place. The Paderborn-Weser-Harz region was the central training ground of the German Army.

On April 9th, the First Division deepened and reinforced its bridgehead across the Weser, and light to moderate resistance was encountered chiefly at road blocks and built-up areas. Gains of fifty to twenty kilometers were reported and approximately seven villages were cleared of Germans.

The 4th Cavalry Group was attached to the First Division on April 9th. Mission of this Group was to protect the north flank of VII Corps.

For the period April 9-10, the Division continued across the open terrain leading to the Harz Mountains, crossing the Leine River against feeble resistance and seizing the towns of Dassel, Northeim, and Einbeck. Apparently the last hope of the Germans was to pull back as many men as possible, as well as the greater part of his armor into the Harz Mountains where the terrain, if nothing else, would give him time to regroup his forces into some kind of an integrated unit.

That the Harz Mountains were the refuge of more than the 6th (Wehrkreis) Corps was not immediately apparent to the First

Division, as the Division pushed on rapidly to overrun the first line of outposts in front of the hills and forest.   Later in the fighting, from the variety of units encountered, both of the divisional and unit status, it became evident that the Harz Mountains were defended by four German Corps instead of one.

The terrain which the enemy could use for his defense was about as forbidding to an attacker as could be found.   It was more favorable to the enemy than the Ardennes because the road net was more limited.   It was tougher than the Hurtgen Forest because the woods were thicker and the ground more broken by ravines, hills and draws.   The roads were capable of carrying heavy traffic, and were easy to roadblock.   The number of trees that could be felled across the roads at critical points were only limited by the amount of explosive on hand and the number of men available to handle saws.   The roads which wound around the sides of the hills could be cratered at a moment's notice.

If the enemy had had better communications and had been in a better state of organization at the time he pulled back into the Harz Mountains, he could have made the mountains a major obstacle to the American's continued drive to the east.   The Germans had plenty of men, probably close to 100,000 and they did have supporting weapons in strength which gave them equality with the attacking forces, if not superiority, except in artillery.   True, there was little possibility that the Harz Mountains could hold out forever surrounded on all sides, but there was always hope that some sort of delay could be imposed on the Americans which would grant more time to the High Command of the Germans—time to do what was never clear.

On April 10th, the First Division, with the 4th Cavalry Group, continued its mission, protecting the left flank of the VII Corps. The 26th and 18th Combat Teams continued to push forward towards the east, working in close conjunction with the 4th Cavalry Group.   Further mission was to maintain contact with the 83rd Infantry Division and the 104th Infantry Division, respectively.

During the day, the 16th Infantry continued to mop up in its zone.   During this time the 16th Infantry was in Division Reserve.

The 18th Infantry in its movement to the east captured all of its assigned objectives, and by the close of the day the First Battalion held Sudheim and Hillerse; the 2nd Battalion secured Northeim; the 3rd Battalion was holding the towns of Lagershausen, Weibrechtsh and Fredelsloh.

The 26th Infantry continued its movement meeting numerous roadblocks and small pockets of resistance which were eliminated and by 3:00 P.M. the First and 2nd Battalions were in Eindeck and the 3rd Battalion had secured the towns of Oldendorf and Dassel.

On the 424th combat day as a unit, the Command Post of the First Division opened in Uslar at 2:00 P.M., April 10, 1945.

During April 11th the Division, driving hard on the enemy's heels, cleared Osterode, Bad Grund and Badenhausen. The fighting was considerably more intense than during the previous gallop from the Weser River, indicating that the Germans had begun their serious defense of the region. Osterode, the location of the tank repair shops of the 507th Heavy Tank Battalion, was the site of relatively severe fighting. Several German tanks opposed the seizure of the town, and pulled out only under pressure. Five enemy tanks were destroyed during the day. General Major Goerbig, commander of a battle group under the 6th (German) Corps, was captured in Bad Grund. From the general's testimony at the prisoner-of-war cage, it appeared that the overall command of the troops in the Harz Mountains was invested in the 11th Panzer Army, a unit whose antecedents were not very clear. It was evidently only a headquarters transferred from the eastern front, and was responsible to no one but Marshal Kesselring. There was no Army involved.

On April 12th, elements of the 18th Infantry relieved Task Force "LAUNDON" (104th Infantry Division) in the town of Herzberg. The 18th Infantry continued to mop up all enemy elements in its zone, and before the day was over the 3rd Battalion cleared the towns of Osterode and Freheit. The 26th Infantry continued to mop up in the towns of Clausthal, Zellerfeid and Badenhausen, fighting stiff resistance.

The First Division Artillery and attached units continued to support the advance. Considerable enemy resistance was encountered in terrain which was highly suitable for defense and during this period, 750 prisoners were taken. The Division Command Post opened at Osterode at 1:40 P.M.

During the day of April 12th, enemy resistance increased and reports indicated that organization of enemy units facing the First Division had improved considerably. Roadblocks continued to form the German's major means of delay, obstacles which were considerably increased in effectiveness by strong tank and self-propelled guns covering fire.

The second phase of the First Division's operations, during April, 1945 roughly covered the terrain from the Weser River in the vicinity of Lauenforde and Furstenberg on the river east to Clausthal-Zellersfeld, Osterode and Herzberg.

The Germans continued to defend this rat's nest of road blocks stubbornly during April 13th. In all cases advancing division units encountered heavy small arms fire and in several cases intense tank and mortar fire. The Division attacked to the east from Clausthal-Zellerfeld and succeeded in clearing Altenau during the evening in spite of the best efforts of a stubborn strongpoint on the high ground east of the town.

The mission of the First Division was to eliminate all enemy resistance within its zone of responsibility in the Harz Mountains, and to maintain contact with the 83rd Infantry Division on the north and the 104th Infantry Division on the south. This mission was accomplished.

On April 14th, the 16th Infantry continued to push on. The 2nd Battalion was cleaning up the town of St. Andreasberg by nightfall. The 26th Infantry continued to advance and its 2nd Battalion reached the town of Torfhaus and continued to mop up. The 18th Infantry moved on and its 2nd Battalion reached Lerbach and vicinity.

Division Artillery and attached units continued to support the advance made by the Division, and fired 71 missions with a total expenditure of 1,723 rounds of ammunition against personnel and tanks and also counter-battery missions. The First Engineers assisted in the advances by the construction of bridges, maintenance of roads, and removal of road blocks. Approximately 950 prisoners were taken on this day.

On April 15th, the daily quota of one new major unit in the prisoner's cage was supplied by the 15th German Parachute Regiment of their 5th Parachute Division. This outfit had drifted up to the Harz Mountains for refuge from the fighting in the south.

During the day the heaviest fighting centered around the approaches to Torfhaus, where the battle swung back and forth until late in the afternoon and included at least one German counterattack.

Other elements of the Division continued neutralizing enemy strongpoints on the high ground west and northwest of St. Andreasberg, where the enemy resisted again with tanks, self-propelled guns and dug-in infantry to protect key terrain features. During this time, St. Andreasberg, Benneckenstein and Hohegeiss were cleared.

Tanks and self-propelled guns continued to oppose the First Division advance to the outskirts of Braunlage and artillery fire increased. The toll of enemy tanks and equipment knocked out was growing in sizeable proportions. Since the beginning of the Division's operations in the Harz Mountains the bag included five 20-MM flak guns, eight 40-MM flak guns, six 88-MM guns and four 105-MM guns. Braunlage was finally cleared on April 17th against bitter resistance, which included the most severe artillery fire yet received in the Harz Mountains. Tanne was also cleared in heavy fighting, and more than 1,300 prisoners were taken during the day.

On April 19th the rout began as the First Division pushed into the rear areas of the enemy's Harz Mountain front. More than 3,000 prisoners were taken, including representatives of the 85th German Infantry Division "Potsdam" which was encountered on the right of the First Division. This German Division—"Potsdam" —was one of three hastily assembled units which were to hold the American advance and, according to the inflated propoganda spoon-fed to the German troops, was to counterattack to recapture the Ruhr.

This flag waving had little effect on the depressed spirits of the personnel of the "Potsdam" Division who realized they were being sent into a hopeless situation. During the day, Rubeland, Elend, Konigshof, Schierke and Rothehutte were taken and at the end of the day the enemy had been driven back something over 3,000 yards.

On April 19th, the 3rd Battalion, 16th Infantry had secured the town of Elbingerode by 7:30 A.M. after a sharp attack. The 2nd Battalion 18th Infantry cut off a sizeable enemy column south from Huttenrode, which had been driven south by the 16th Infantry. The 26th Infantry was mopping up in its area. At the close of this day, the 3rd Battalion, 26th Infantry took Hill 1142, the dominating terrain feature of the Harz Mountains. The 3rd Battalion 18th Infantry took the town of Thale.

During the day First Division Artillery and attached units fired 61 missions for an expenditure of 1,543 rounds of ammunition. The First Engineers, with the 238th Combat Engineer Battalion in direct support, removed road blocks, filled craters and repaired roads within the First Division zone.

The payoff of the entire operation came on April 20th, when more than 1,000 prisoners were taken by the First Division, and the Harz Mountains were reduced for all practical purposes. At the close of the day all enemy forces in the First Division zone capable of organized resistance had been destroyed. Of the 10,000 odd prisoners, nearly 8,000 were captured by the 18th Infantry in the Thale-Timmenrode area. This was the biggest haul of prisoners in the history of the First Division, and outdid any one day's operations in the Mons pocket. The prisoner-of-war cage was a tumultuous babel of crowds and confusion. Prisoners came streaming in all day and night, some of them under guard, some of them under their own power. Included in the bag were two generals and a comfortable representation of field officers. The Harz Mountains pocket and refuge for the Wehrmacht was all through.

The most unexpected result of the operation in the Harz Mountains however, was the surprising number of prisoners taken, an indication of just what force the four (German) Corps hemmed up in the pocket, had available. The First Division alone took 30,343 prisoners between April 1 and April 25, 1945, when the pocket was finally sponged up. Adjacent units walling up on the other side of the trap, brought the final total to 73,490 prisoners. Recaptured Allied prisoners, mainly French and Belgian, were recaptured and joined in the hunt, dragging dank Landsers out of the woods. But among the hordes of prisoners was the 100,000th prisoner captured by the First Infantry Division in World War II. He was at least significant if not productive of information. Seventeen generals showed up in the prisoner-of-war cage, among them ten taken by the Division.

On April 22nd, Operations Instructions Number 77, First Division Headquarters was issued, stating in brief that the Division would move April 22-23, 1945, from its zone to an assembly area in the vicinity of Blankenheim and would maintain order and prevent sabotage of important installations in the new assembly area. The 8th Armored (U.S.) Division would take over the responsibility of the Division area prior to noon of April 22, 1945.

On May 1, 1945, the Germans were all through. The political leaders and the Party boys were still grabbing at straws, but the Wehrmacht and the ordinary civilians were through. There was no big picture enemy situation because there was no enemy except in Czechoslovakia, which, of course, is where the First Division happened to be. The only question at hand was whether the enemy would fall over of his own weight or whether he would have to be pushed. In the end he had to be pushed.

For the first four days—May 1 to 4, 1945, the enemy reaction to the First Division's minor shiftings and improvements in the line was variable. In some cases the enemy put up stiff fighting at isolated road blocks and strongpoints, and in others Division patrols found towns completely clear of the enemy. The enemy force now facing the First Division seemed to be comprised of various units under the command of a General Benicke and called "Division Benicke". Many of the soldiers were, oddly enough, some of the best quality troops encountered by the Division in quite a while. These men were from an officer candidate school at the large training center of Milowitz in Czechoslovakia.

Although the enemy was down, he was still twitching. The enemy needed one more poling to stretch him out completely. The First Division with Combat Command "A" of the 9th Armored (U.S.) Division attached, delivered the blow on May 5, 1945.

Spread out on a 48-kilometer front, the division attacked again to the east. The advance encountered moderate resistance, a matter of surprise only to those experts who started predicting six months previously that the Germans had only one gasp left. The enemy defended strategic road junctions and village strongpoints bitterly, making good use of small arms and automatic weapon fire. Artillery fire was light, scattered and confined to the southern part of the Division zone.

At Drenice, the enemy held out in positions on a hill just north of the town, and the area was not cleared until late in the day, when Division tanks were able to move in and clear up the situation.

The First Division had been part of the V Corps since May 1st, 1945.

The advance continued on May 6th, against lighter and more scattered resistance as the Division pushed on ten to twenty kilometers in the northern and southern sectors. In the center, however, the Germans held out as though they had all Germany behind them. Along the main road from Cheb to Falkenov, 88-mm, anti-tank guns were deployed in depth, and each one had to be destroyed by the infantry before the tanks could budge. In the vicinity of Eubabrunn the enemy, although lacking the necessary artillery support, put up a tough fight. Klinghart, Plesna, Sneky, Mnichov, Sangerberg and Kynsperk were all cleared of enemy during the day, and five anti-tank guns were destroyed.

At 8:15 A.M., May 8, 1945, the First Division received orders to "CEASE FIRING", an order for which they had been fighting since November 8, 1942.

The first product of the cessation of offensive action was the surrender of General Major Fritz Benicke, commanding "Division

Benicke", and his staff. Later in the day several staff officers from the 12th German Army Corps entered the First Division lines to arrange a meeting between their commander, General Osterkamp, and a representative of the American forces. The 12th Corps commanded the sector between Chemnitz and Marienbad and numbered about 18,000 troops.

The meeting took place shortly after 9:00 A.M., May 8, 1945, in the Ross Inn at Elbogen. General Osterkamp and his party arrived in a fleet of Mercedes-Benz touring cars and proceeded immediately to business at hand. The general, a small dapper man, pressed and shined and be-medalled to within an inch of his life, attempted, with absolutely no success, to effect various small compromises in the terms, apparently trying to rescue some vestige of German "honor" from the affair. His major effort was to have the details of the surrender document read "Elbogen, Sudetenland". Brigadier General George A. Taylor, Assistant Commanding General of the First Infantry (U.S.) Division, and representative of the Commanding General, Third (U.S.) Army said: "There is no Sudetenland. You are in Czechoslovakia." In its final form the document read: "Elbogen, Czechoslovakia."

At the time of the German surrender, the 16th, 18th and 26th Infantry Regimental Combat Teams, in conjunction with Combat Command "A", 9th Armored (U.S.) Division were attacking progressively against moderate to light scattered resistance toward Karlsbad. At 8:15 A.M., May 7, 1945, the following message was received from V Corps: "All troops to halt in place and maintain defensive positions. Effective at once. Details to follow. CG V Corps." This message was transmitted to the three Combat Teams, via telephone.

The 8th of May, 1945, marked the last and 443rd combat day for the First Infantry Division (U.S.), as a unit in World War II. Thus ended the last aggressive action by the Division against the German Army which started for this unit on November 8, 1942, on the beaches at Oran, Algeria, continuing through the Tunisian Campaign and Sicily, with the final phase beginning on the Normandy Beaches, just eleven months and one day before the final shot was fired.

Unnumbered Operations Memorandum, dated May 7, 1945, Headquarters First Infantry Division was the last issued, and quoted the following telegram received through channels from Supreme Headquarters, Allied Expeditionary Forces, signed "EISEN-HOWER."

"1.   A representative of the German High Command signed the unconditional surrender of all German land, sea and air forces in Europe to the Allied Expeditionary Force and simultaneously to the Soviet High Command at 1:41 A.M., Central European Time, May 7, 1945, under which all forces will cease operations at one minute after midnight of May 8, 1945, (the first minute of May 9, 1945).

2.   Effective immediately all offensive operations by Allied Expeditionary Force will cease and troops will remain in present positions.   Moves involved in occupational duties will continue. Due to difficulties of communication there may be some delay in similar orders reaching enemy troops so full defensive precautions will be taken.

3.   All informed down to and including Divisions, Tactical Air Commands and Groups, Base Sections, and equivalent.   No release will be made to the press pending an announcement by the heads of the three governments.   SIGNED EISENHOWER."

*   *   *   *

That which follows is factual—it is still "The Record."

On the other hand, this, then, is the History of the First Infantry Division, United States Army, World War II.

"The Record" speaks for itself.

"As I saw it", is in the words of famed American War Correspondents who were present at "Danger Forward", and thus wrote of what they saw.

It has been written:—"The First Division is the United States Army and millions of replacements".   This expression is high compliment to the United States Army.   The First Division was predestined to spearhead the landings in Algeria, Sicily and the Normandy Beaches; it was in the field ready to respond to the attack in Tunisia—thus becoming a proving ground for all who were privileged to serve under its banners.

From the experiences gained in battle, officers and enlisted personnel of the First Infantry Division were called on to serve with newly-formed combat units of the Army—some as instructors—others as leaders of units.   Senior Officers from the First Division—"Combat-Wise", gained promotion to higher ranks to command Combat Divisions. A notable instance is that of Major General Willard G. Wyman, former Assistant Division Commander, 1st Infantry Division—later Commanding General, 71st Infantry Division.

Another instance is that of Major General Terry de la M. Allen, First Division Commanding General in the initial landings in Africa, later Sicily—who returned to the United States, formed, trained and led into battle the famed 104th Infantry Division.

Within the First Division the spirit was akin to that gained from experiences on "friendly fields of strife"—the play-grounds of America. "TEAMWORK" quickly developed in the First Division, World War II, and individuals lost their identity as they worked with one purpose in mind—"ONE for all—ALL for ONE".

The effectiveness of the stream-lined division became pronounced as smaller units of command responded with alacrity and effectiveness as the entire division became speedily mobile.

The skilled use of newly-developed small arms, automatic weapons and artillery, was swiftly applied against a stubborn enemy, and the coordination of all separate units of the First Division was welded into a hard-hitting, swiftly-moving, compact TEAM.

It was in the fields of Logistics that the Special Troops of the First Infantry Division held the upper hand over an enemy within his own country.   Under conditions that tried the skill of specialists, and the limitations of their weapons of war, sometimes beyond human endurance, through sand and heat of the desert, over mountainous, narrow (roads in name only) defiles, in rain-blown, muddy, snow-drifted, ice-bound roads of France, Germany, Belgium and Czechoslovakia, that ammunition, food, medical supplies—and Mail

—were delivered to the front-line troops of the Division by these Special Troops of the Division—The Service of Supply.

Lines of Communication were kept open—How? Newly-developed methods of communication were superior to those of the enemy, but the wiles of Nature kept pace with modern invention, and snow-bound, ice-packed terrain just would not yield to reason—BUT—the WORD got through somehow.

The work of the "Medics"—"God Bless 'em" stands out as a beacon to men whose souls have been tried, seared and still remain unshaken.

To the "Men of Faith" the "Gentlemen of The Cloth"—The Chaplains—who walked hand in hand with the Division down through the Valleys of the Shadows of uncertainty—the Faith of Our Fathers remained with us still—"Lord God of Hosts—Be with us Yet—Lest we Forget—Lest we Forget."

And to each other—may we never forget. We were members of:

"THE TEAM"

It was the same old GAME—with a different name,
And the scores ran a great deal higher.
The TEAMS had grown to a size unknown—
With GOD as the GREAT UMPIRE.

*   *   *   *

THE LAST KILOMETER
HARZ MOUNTAINS TO CZECHOSLOVAKIA
April 8 to May 8, 1945

As I Saw It

By

DREW MIDDLETON

" . . . of battles long ago."

By DREW MIDDLETON

LONDON—All of this took place a long time ago and in places a long way from the gray streets and slanting rain of an autumn day in London. Those who read it will, I hope, treat it not as history or as biography of an infantry division but as a memoir. During the second World War my path crossed that of the First Division of infantry, United States Army, on several occasions. It is because of the warm memories that live within the shadow of that name that I have written what follows.

Some of you will remember how in the fall of 1942 we were pitchforked eastward into Tunisia from Algeria and Morocco after the landings there. That country was wilder than those to the east and the fighting was confused and bitter although, when we look at it now, on a very small scale. It was there, in a camp on a hillside in an olive grove that the First Division first assumed in my mind that stature of a great fighting division which it kept throughout the war.

Curiously it came not from personal observation but from the report of a very tired, very angry fighter pilot of the R.A.F. who had been shot down that day by his own anti-aircraft.

"Where's your First Division" he asked. I said I didn't know, that there were odd battalions and companies of two armies stretched up and down Tunisia and no one knew where anyone else was at a given moment.

"Well, you'd better go and see them," he said, "They're bloody good. Bloody good. I saw them at Oran. The French were damned smart to chuck it. Your chaps would have cut them to bits."

In those days there were no Public Relations Officers to get in the way, so the next morning I drove from Thibar over the rocky shoulder of the mountains to the town of Teboursouk. From there I was directed on until I encountered various units of the division scattered on the hills and on the dry, cold valley floors of that tumult of land.

In those days the First Division had not won the honors in battle it collected later in the war. But unlike many of the divisions that were to follow it into battle, it did not suffer from an inferiority complex on that account. There was a confidence that few other American outfits had at that time and to use an overworked word there was a "soldierly" bearing about the men in the rifle companies which you missed elsewhere.

That is a part of the war that has been overshadowed by the great events of 1943 and 1944. But I think that what was done over that broken terrain by men new to war if not new to the army was a finer tribute to our American way of life than many more widely publicized campaigns later.

The First Division went in and fought a great many actions at places whose very names are forgotten now like Sened. Its men fought with bravery and with increased canniness. Long after the war I asked Field Marshall Von Rundstedt what he thought was the one characteristic an infantryman should have. "To learn quickly" he answered.

The First Division learned quickly.

That was a long difficult winter made no brighter by the defeat at the Kasserine Pass. In common with the other American units there the First Division took a knock but unlike some others it bounced back hard and fast. There was a great deal of hard fighting on the plain between Faid and Kasserine and more when the Tenth Panzer division pushed through the pass and struck for Thala and Tebessa.

You remember now a little, gray faced corporal, who seemed to be carrying all the ammunition in the world, who asked for a drink in the early hours of the morning.

"Those bastards run all over us yesterday, the big bastards" he said. "But we still got our guns and if we can get some ———ing artillery we'll hold them. They can't do that to the First Division two days in a row."

They didn't and I don't suppose anyone ever did.

When the spring came in 1943 I went up from Thibar into the mountains that run south from the Mediterranean where the First Division with the Crest of II Corps had been put into line. The division was now the most war-wise and efficient of any American division in Africa. It was less anxious to show its confidence although I remember Ken Downes telling me of a half finished letter found on the body of one of the riflemen who had died around El Guettar.

"Dear Folks," it had said, "Well, we've stopped the best they have . . ."

Headquarters was in a narrow valley in the hills. There was to be an attack the next day and your people were pretty quiet. They sat around talking about big league ball and the funny way the Arabs built their houses and about the way you could hear the report of a gun bounce off the cliffs.

It was April and getting hot. In back of the forward positions men had taken off their shirts and toasted in the sunshine. They looked back at the cliff to the west and told how they had gone up it on all fours and killed the Germans at their machine guns.

In the morning when the cannons quieted you heard the scuffle of feet, the clink of a dislodged stone and the grunt of men shifting ammunition and canteens. For a long time there was no sound and then we heard the even tap of a machine gun and looking up saw the thin red streams of tracer in the darkness.

A few days later the Germans gave way having been broken on Hill 609 and Longstop Hill. The whole Allied line moved forward, the Americans into Bizerte and the British into Tunis.

A few days later I ran into an officer I knew who commanded

a battalion of Ghurkas, those hardy and terrible fighters. He was, like many of his kind, a most unsoldierly soldier, and only the D.S.O. and M.C. on his battledress, balanced his drooping figure, his air of extreme lassitude and his Piccadilly accent.

"I say, you know, those First Division chappies of yours. Bloody marvellous they are, frightfully good. Like them better than the Guards, really I do. Almost as good as our chaps, you know."

Which from an officer of the Ghurkas is praise indeed.

Away to the north in England that autumn it was strange how the deeds of the First Division intruded themselves.

At dinner one night in a pub in Liverpool I talked to a big Canadian about the Sicilian campaign which I had missed.

He had, he admitted, done a lot of hard fighting in that dry and dusty country but he admitted that the climax of the campaign had been the taking of Troina by the Americans. Who took it? I asked.

"The First Division," he said.

It seemed that in that winter of 1943-1944 when the preparations were being made for the operation across the Channel that everyone I met had some word of praise for the First Division.

I caught up with them again in the rolling country south of Salisbury.

It was the month of January, very clear for England and very cold. When you drove along the narrow roads it was well to proceed with care for every so often you met a platoon or a company of the division swinging along.

They looked very good. The rifle companies which had suffered heavily in Tunisia and Sicily were back up to strength and there was that mixture of battle-scarred veteran and eager newcomer which the old soldiers say is the best mixture of all for a combat division.

There were a few new officers, not so many as I had feared, for one becomes attached to old friends, and the officers generally were addicted to the phrase "this is a functional division" while the men were more profanely confident.

One of the things that impressed me about the Division in those days was that it was adult. That winter, waiting for God knows what on the other side of the Channel, was not an easy one for them. Nor was that winter, the fourth of the war, an easy one for the people they lived among.

"You can always tell when soldiers have done a lot of fighting," said a bar tender in one of the villages. "They're easy like, don't do a lot of loud talking and bragging. I reckon these fellows, now, they're just about as good as I've seen."

From June 6 of 1944 onward I had the privilege of watching the Division in action often: in Normandy, in the long drive north-east to the German frontier and finally in the fighting around Aachen.

A lot of memories come crowding back.

The day near Mortain when the Germans were attacking and the air was full of dust and smoke and steel and I watched a sergeant, who had a hole through his hand, handle his men and get them ready for whatever might be coming from the other side.

"Remember, you sons of bitches," he said, "this is the First Division. They never moved us yet and they ain't going to start now."

The Division it seemed was always on the move. You would say good-night to them in one town and the next morning find them twenty or thirty miles to the east.

Finally when the wind began to blow cold from the north the Division closed in on the city of Aachen.

There were, I noticed, a lot of new faces in the ranks and among the officers. But the spirit was the same.

One thing I always liked about the First Division was that it took care of itself. There were other outfits who boasted a sort of hairshirt austerity in battle but since the First Division was seldom out of battle or at least out of contact with the Germans it decided that there was no use killing itself with hardship. The Germans were doing all the killing necessary.

So when you went to company and battalion headquarters up around Aachen you found that their people were living well. I once complained, as a joke, to an old friend that his luncheon table contained no pate de foie gras.

Three days later he opened a can with great ceremony remarking that this pate was the gift of a German officer some time dead.

"When the wind shifts, you can tell where he is," he remarked.

Aachen was a great battle. For it was the first German city to be taken by an invading army in over a hundred years and the effects of this blow to German pride were widespread and important. For battles are great not because of the numbers engaged or their duration but because of their effect on the contestants.

The best history of a war would be a record of what went on in the minds of the opposing commanders.

If such a history were to be written of World War II I am sure we would find that the capture of Aachen by the First Division ranked high among the defeats which convinced the high command of the German Army it had lost the war.

The battle was unique in two other respects; it was fought and won almost entirely by the First Division and at that time the Division having been in action almost continuously since June 6 was very tired.

Despite this it fought with more precision, skill and more surely, I think, than ever before.

If you remember, it was a difficult job. Aachen had to be taken room by room, house by house, and street by street, while at the same time the determined and desperate attacks of the Germans to break in from the east and relieve the garrison had to be halted.

So there were really two battles fought by the First Division; the slow painful fight in the city itself and the defense along Verlautenheide ridge to keep the Germans out.

It was a long process, or so it seemed then. Minor factors assumed a huge importance: the 88 which used to fire down the Adelbertstrasse whenever there was movement, the mortar which used to shell a street corner that you had to pass.

Then one day it was all over. I stood on the road near Brand and watched the refugees stream out of Aachen. Four and a half years before, a hundred miles to the east, I had seen Belgian refugees leave Louvain. The wheel of history had come full circle.

That night it rained heavily. I went into the silent town and said goodbye to some friends and then started south. When I passed the barracks in Brand, where the refugees were quartered, some men were unloading supplies from a truck.

I asked an M. P. what went on.

"Well, you gotta feed the Heinies, you know", he said.

As I drove south toward Aachen I thought that the First was one of the few divisions which would have fought the Germans so long and so bitterly and then made meticulous arrangements for the feeding and care of German refugees.

There is little more to say. I have tried to avoid that extravagant praise which other less notable divisions craved because I know that the First Division does not need it. And I have tried to show how wide was the First Division's influence on our Allies and, as I learned later, among the Germans.

A Captain Lachner, late of the German General Staff, told me that they always knew that "where the First Division was, there we would have trouble."

There is not much a civilian can really say about the bravery and ability of the Division, first because as a correspondent he had nothing to do with it and second because that is a part of the history of our country.

The End

SUPPLEMENT
NOTE:

This section of "Danger Forward" was compiled from all material available at this writing.

Full and complete reports for the European Theater of Operation have not yet been completed by the Department of the Army.

This History is "The Record" of the First Infantry Division as gleaned from the reports of its highly-coordinated and efficient Staff who administered and recorded as the Division swept through North Africa, Sicily, France, Belgium, Germany and Czechoslovakia.

It is hoped that accuracy has prevailed, and that no incident of service has passed by without recording—that all attached organizations have been duly credited with service under the Command of the First Infantry Division, United States Army, World War II.

HISTORY
FIRST INFANTRY DIVISION, UNITED STATES ARMY

The First Infantry Division, United States Army, was organized May 24, 1917, first as "The First Expeditionary Division"—later designated "First Division." The leading components of the First Division sailed for France, from Hoboken, New Jersey, and New York City, June 14, 1917. The Division arrived at St. Nazaire, France, June 21, 1917, and the reorganization of the Division was completed on French soil.

The following units composed the First Infantry Division, World War I:

FIRST BRIGADE: 16th Infantry, 18th Infantry, 2nd Machine-gun Battalion.

SECOND BRIGADE: 26th Infantry, 28th Infantry, 3rd Machine-gun Battalion.

FIRST ARTILLERY BRIGADE: 5th Field Artillery (155's), 6th Field Artillery (75's), 7th Field Artillery (75's), 1st Trench Mortar Battery.

DIVISION TROOPS: 1st Machine-gun Battalion, 1st Engineers, 2nd Field Signal Battalion, Headquarters Troop.

TRAINS: 1st Train Headquarters and Military Police, 1st Ammunition Train, 1st Supply Train, 1st Engineer Train, 1st Sanitary Train (Ambulance Companies and Field Hospitals Nos. 2, 3, 12 and 13).

The strength of the First Division in World War I was approximately 28,000; in World War II approximately 15,000.

Several organizations of the First Division can trace their service back to Revolutionary War days.

Battery D, 5th Field Artillery Regiment—"Alexander Hamilton's Battery," dates back to 1776.

Battery D, 6th Field Artillery Regiment—"Captain John McClelland's Company, Corps of Artillery," dates back to 1794.

The 16th U. S. Infantry dates back to May 4, 1861, and is an outshoot of the 11th U. S. Infantry.

The 18th U. S. Infantry, by Act of Congress, July 29, 1861, was organized as a three-battalion regiment.

The 26th and 28th U. S. Infantry Regiments date from February 2, 1901.

The 1st Quartermaster Regiment is of 1918 origin.

The 1st Engineers date back to 1846, through a service lineage that saw many reorganizations.

The 5th Field Artillery saw service in the Revolutionary War, the Philippine Insurrection, World War I and World War II.

The 6th Field Artillery went on from Revolutionary War days to the Indian Wars; then on to the War with Mexico; the Civil War; the Spanish-American War, World War I and World War II.

The 1st Engineers went through the major portion of the battle engagements of the Civil War, the Spanish-American War, World War I and World War II.

The 16th U. S. Infantry served in the Civil War, participating in practically all the major battles; served in the Spanish-American War, and also in the Philippine Insurrection; served in World War I and World War II.

The 18th U. S. Infantry served right along with the 16th, and participated in practically all the big battles of the Civil War; then served in the Spanish-American War and the Philippine Insurrection; was present at the Fall of Manila; served in World War I, and World War II.

The 26th and 28th U. S. Infantry Regiments served in the Philippine Insurrection; then served in World War I and World War II.

The first Commanding General of the First Division was Major General William L. Sibert.

The First Division became known as "Pershing's Own," as the Division accompanied General John J. Pershing to France, in World War I. Since that time, the rolls of the Division are as star-spangled with names of famous Generals who have served under its flags, as are the Division flags themselves.

One of the Commanding Generals of the First Division—now Lieutenant General Clarence R. Huebner, served with the First Division in World War I as an enlisted man, and at the end of World War I commanded an Infantry Regiment. In World War II, General Huebner commanded the First Division in combat, from August 7, 1943 to December 10, 1944. General Huebner held every grade in the First Division except Brigadier General.

BATTLE STREAMERS

The Battle Streamers on "The Colors" of the First Infantry Division are:

World War I

Lorraine, Aisne-Marne, Picardy, Montdidier-Noyone, St. Mihiel, Meuse-Argonne.

World War II

Algeria-French Morocco, Tunisia, Sicily, Normandy, Northern France, Ardennes-Alsace, Rhineland, Central Europe.

BATTLE STREAMERS (Foreign Decorations)

1. In colors of the French Croix de Guerre (with Palm), for Kasserine;
2. In colors of the French Croix de Guerre (with Palm), for Normandy;
3. In colors of the Belgian Croix de Guerre, for Mons;
4. In colors of the Belgian Croix de Guerre, for Eupen-Malmedy.

FOURRAGERES

1. French Fourragers in the colors of the French Croix de Guerre.
2. Belgian Fourragere in the the colors of the Belgian Croix de Guerre.

The First Division was reorganized in 1939, and "streamlined," with the 16th, 18th and 26th Infantry Regiments as components. Each regiment thus became a "Combat Team" in the newly-created "Triangular" Division, with an approximate strength of 3300 Infantrymen, with accompanying Medical, Engineer, Artillery, Signal, Ordnance, Quartermaster and Reconnaissance Troops.

With the Artillery Regiments—5th, 6th and 7th Field Artillery, the new order incorporated all three regiments into "First Division Artillery," designating the units as battalions. Out of the 6th Field Artillery Regiment, the 32nd and 33rd Field Artillery Battalions were created, and First Division Artillery was then composed of the 5th, 7th, 32nd and 33rd Field Artillery Battalions.

As the "streamlined" Infantry Regiment now carried an approximate strength of 3300, the Artillery Battalion strength was fixed at approximately 550. The 1st Engineers were so designated, and additional troops became "Service Troops." The overall strength of the First Division, World War II, was approximately 15,000.

In 1939, the Headquarters of the First Infantry Division was at Fort Hamilton, N. Y. It was not until 1940, during the Louisiana Maneuvers that the First Division really functioned afield as a Division. The 3rd Battalion, 18th Infantry, and the 3rd Battalion, 16th Infantry went through Amphibious Training at Culebra, Puerto Rico, in 1940. The First Division maneuvered with the First Marine Division at New River, North Carolina, August 1941.

Headquarters of the First Division on December 7, 1941, was at Fort Devens, Massachusetts. The Division went through Amphibious Maneuvers at Virginia Beach, Virginia, January, 1942; were at Camp Blanding, Florida, spring of 1942; thence to Fort Benning, Georgia for Air-Ground tests and demonstrations; thence to Indiantown Gap, Pennsylvania for staging overseas.

The advance detail of the First Division, consisting of the 2nd Battalion, 16th Infantry, and Advance Detachment Headquarters, sailed from Brooklyn, N. Y., July 1, 1942, for England.

The entire Division (less Advance Detachment), embarked on board the

H. M. S. Queen Mary, at Pier No. 90, New York City, sailing at 10:45 A.M., August 2, 1942, and arrived at Gourock, Scotland, August 8, 1942.

The Division disembarked at Gourock, Scotland, and proceeded to Tidworth Barracks in the south of England. From then on practically all the time was spent in Amphibious Training, while the Division remained in the United Kingdom.

It is significant that but a few days after the appointment of General Dwight D. Eisenhower as Allied Commander-in-Chief, the First Division was alerted for service overseas, as had been the First Division of World War I, when General John J. Pershing became Commander-in-Chief of the American Expeditionary Forces, in France.

The First Division is still serving overseas, with its Headquarters at Bad Tolz, Germany, in the Army of Occupation.

First to leave for combat in World War II, the First Division is again the last Division to come home, as was the case in World War I, when, under the Command of General John J. Pershing, the Division returned to the United States and paraded in New York City, September 10, 1919, with a final review in Washington, D. C., before the President of the United States, September 17, 1919.

FIRST INFANTRY DIVISION
WORLD WAR II
(November 8, 1942 to May 8, 1945)

STATISTICS
(Authorized strength of First Infantry Division—14,037)
World War II

Strength (November 8, 1942) 14,851
Replacements (to May 8, 1945) 28,892
GRAND TOTAL 43,743

Total days in Combat—443.

FIRST INFANTRY DIVISION
WORLD WAR II

BATTLE CASUALTIES

Killed in action 4,325
Missing in action 1,241
Wounded in action 15,457

TOTAL CASUALTIES 21,023

FIRST INFANTRY DIVISION
WORLD WAR II

MEDALS AND DECORATIONS

Decorations and medals represent more than the Nation's grateful acknowledgement of fidelity. They are a constant incentive to performance of outstanding deeds.

War's changing styles, introducing new weapons and tactics, have created new symbols of courage, achievement, and proficiency. The recipient of a medal has clearly demonstrated the strength of mind and spirit to encounter danger with fortitude, firmness and courage.

Sixteen members of the First Infantry Division were awarded the Congressional Medal of Honor for "Conspicuous gallantry and intrepidity involving risk of life above and beyond the call of duty in action with the enemy." The Roll of Honor:

    Barrett, Carlton W., Private;
    Brown, Bobbie E., Captain;
  * Defranzo, Arthur F., Sergeant;
    Ehlers, Walter D., Sergeant;
  * Henry, Robert T., Private;
    Lindsey, James W., Technical Sergeant;
  * McGraw, Francis X., Private First Class;
    Merli, Gino J., Private First Class;
  * Monteith, Jimmie W. Jr., 2nd Lieutenant;
  * Peterson, George, Staff Sergeant;
  * Pinder, John J., T/5
  * Reese, James N., Private;
    Shaefer, Joseph E., Staff Sergeant;
    Thompson, Max, Sergeant;
  * Warner, Henry, Corporal;
  * Will, Walter J., 1st Lieutenant.

* (Posthumous Award).

TOTAL AWARDS

Congressional Medal of Honor	16
Distinguished Service Cross	161
Distinguished Service Medal	4
Silver Star	6,116
Legion of Merit	79
Bronze Star Medal	14,138
Soldiers Medal	162
Air Medal	76
TOTAL AWARDS	20,752

FIRST INFANTRY DIVISION
UNITED STATES ARMY
COMMAND AND STAFF
(August 1942 to July 1945)

Division Commanders:

    Major General Terry de la M. Allen (2 Aug. 42 to 6 Aug. 43).
    Major General Clarence R. Huebner (7 Aug. 43 to 10 Dec. 44).
    Major General Clift Andrus (11 Dec. 44 to 1 July 45).

Assistant Division Commanders:
  Brigadier General Theodore Roosevelt, Jr. (2 Aug. 42 to 6 Aug. 43).
  Brigadier General Willard G. Wyman (7 Aug. 43 to 6 Oct. 44).
  Brigadier General George A. Taylor (7 Oct. 44 to 1 July 45).

Chief of Staff:
  Colonel Norman D. Cota (2 Aug. 42 to 29 Jan. 43).
  Colonel Stanhope B. Mason (30 Jan. 43 to 13 Dec. 44).
  Lieutenant Colonel Clarence E. Beck (14 Dec. 44 to 6 Jan. 45).
  Colonel Verdi B. Barnes (7 Jan. 45 to 1 July 45).

Assistant Chief of Staff (G-1):
  Major Paul Revere (2 Aug. 42 to 7 Dec. 42).
  Lt. Colonel Charles S. Ware (8 Dec. 42 to 1 July 45).

Assistant Chief of Staff (G-2):
  Lt. Colonel Robert W. Porter, Jr. (2 Aug. 42 to Aug. 43).
  Lieutenant Colonel James C. Curtis (23 Aug. 43 to 23 Sept. 43).
  Major Robert F. Evans (24 Sept. 43 to 8 Nov. 43).
  Lieutenant Colonel Verdi B. Barnes (9 Nov. 43 to 26 Nov. 43).
  Lieutenant Colonel Robert F. Evans (27 Nov. 43 to 8 April 45).
  Major John H. Lauten (9 April 45 to 1 July 45).

Assistant Chief of Staff (G-3):
  Lt. Colonel Stanhope B. Mason (2 Aug. 42 to 29 Jan. 43).
  Lieutenant Colonel Frederick W. Gibb (30 Jan. 43 to 15 July 44).
  Lieutenant Colonel Clarence E. Beck (14 Dec. 44 to 6 Jan. 45).
  Major Kenneth B. Lord (14 Dec. 44 to 6 Jan. 45).
  Lieutenant Colonel Clarence E. Beck (7 Jan. 45 to 1 July 45).

Assistant Chief of Staff (G-4):
  Lieutenant Colonel Clarence M. Eymer (2 Aug. 42 to 13 Dec. 44).
  Lieutenant Colonel Donald McB. Curtis (14 Dec. 44 to 11 June 45).
  Major William G. Ohme (12 June 45 to 21 June 45).
  Lieutenant Colonel Shelby F. Williams (22 June 45 to 1 July 45).

ORGANIZATION COMMANDERS:
ALGIERS
November 8 to November 10, 1942

FIRST DIVISION ARTILLERY

Commander:
  Brigadier General Clift Andrus.
  5th F.A. Battalion: Lieutenant Colonel Warren C. Stout.
  7th F.A. Battalion: Lieutenant Colonel Leroy C. Davis.
  32nd F.A. Battalion: Lieutenant Colonel Percy W. Thompson.
  33rd F.A. Battalion: Lieutenant Colonel Verdi Barnes.

16TH INFANTRY

Regimental Commander:
Colonel Henry B. Cheadle.
1st Battalion: Major William A. Cunningham.
2nd Battalion: Major Joseph B. Crawford.
3rd Battalion: Lieutenant Colonel Frederick W. Gibb.

18TH INFANTRY

Regimental Commander:
Colonel Frank U. Greer.
1st Battalion: Major Richard Parker; Major Robert H. York.
2nd Battalion: Major Ben Sternberg; Major John L. Powers.
3rd Battalion: Lieutenant Colonel Courtney P. Brown.

26TH INFANTRY

Regimental Commander:
Colonel Alexander N. Stark, Jr.
1st Battalion: Major Robert E. Tucker.
2nd Battalion: Major Leonard C. Godfray.
3rd Battalion: Lieutenant Colonel John W. Bowen.

SPECIAL TROOPS

1st Engineer Combat Battalion: Major Henry C. Rowland, Jr.
1st Medical Battalion: Lieutenant Colonel Samuel Bleichfeld.
1st Reconnaissance Troop: Captain Francis W. Adams.
1st Quartermaster Company: Lieutenant Colonel Norman P. Williams.
1st Ordnance (LM) Company: 1st Lieutenant Clarence P. Bartow.
1st Signal Company: Captain Glen S. Waterman.
Military Police Platoon: Captain Thomas F. Lancer.
Headquarters Company: Major Mitchell A. Mahardy.

ORGANIZATION COMMANDERS
TUNISIA
November 20, 1942 to May 8, 1943

1ST DIVISION ARTILLERY

Commander:
Brigadier General Clift Andrus.
5th F.A. Battalion: Lieutenant Colonel Robert N. Tyson; Lieutenant Colonel Warren C. Stout.
7th F.A. Battalion: Lieutenant Colonel Leroy C. Davis; Lieutenant Colonel George W. Gibb.
32nd F.A. Battalion: Lieutenant Colonel Percy W. Thompson.
33rd F.A. Battalion: Lieutenant Colonel Verdi B. Barnes.

16TH INFANTRY

Regimental Commander:

Colonel Henry B. Cheadle.

Colonel d'Alary Fechet.

1st Battalion: Lieutenant Colonel William A. Cunningham; Lieutenant Colonel Charles J. Denholm.

2nd Battalion: Lieutenant Colonel Joseph B. Crawford.

3rd Battalion: Lieutenant Colonel John H. Mathews; Lieutenant Colonel Charles P. Stone.

18TH INFANTRY

Regimental Commander:

Colonel Frank U. Greer.

1st Battalion: Lieutenant Colonel Robert H. York.

2nd Battalion: Lieutenant Colonel Ben Sternberg.

3rd Battalion: Lieutenant Colonel Courtney P. Brown.

26TH INFANTRY

Regimental Commander:

Colonel Alexander N. Stark, Jr.

Colonel George A. Taylor.

1st Battalion: Lieutenant Colonel Gerald C. Kelleher.

2nd Battalion: Lieutenant Colonel Clarence E. Beck; Lieutenant Colonel Derrill M. Daniel.

3rd Battalion: Lieutenant Colonel John W. Bowen; Lieutenant Colonel John T. Corley.

SPECIAL TROOPS

1st Engineer Combat Battalion: Lieutenant Colonel Henry C. Rowland, Jr.

1st Medical Battalion: Lieutenant Colonel Samuel Bleichfeld.

1st Reconnaissance Troop: Major Francis W. Adams.

1st Quartermaster Company: Captain John J. King.

1st Ordnance (LM) Company: Captain Charles P. Bartow.

1st Signal Company: Captain Henry F. Sander.

Military Police Platoon: Captain Thomas F. Lancer.

Headquarters Company: Major Mitchell A. Mabardy; Captain L. T. Peters.

ORGANIZATION COMMANDERS
SICILY
July 10 to August 16, 1943

1ST DIVISION ARTILLERY

Commander:

Brigadier General Clift Andrus.

5th F.A. Battalion: Lieutenant Colonel Robert N. Tyson.

7th F.A. Battalion: Lieutenant Colonel George W. Gibb.
32nd F.A. Battalion: Lieutenant Colonel Edmund S. Bechtold.
33rd F.A. Battalion: Lieutenant Colonel Walter J. Bryde.

16TH INFANTRY

Regimental Commander:
Colonel George A. Taylor.
1st Battalion: Lieutenant Colonel Charles J. Denholm; Major Edmund F. Driscoll.
2nd Battalion: Lieutenant Colonel Joseph B. Crawford; Lieutenant Colonel John H. Mathews.
3rd Battalion: Captain Bryce F. Denno; Lieutenant Colonel Charles T. Horner, Jr.

18TH INFANTRY

Regimental Commander:
Colonel George A. Smith, Jr.
1st Battalion: Lieutenant Colonel Robert H. York.
2nd Battalion: Lieutenant Colonel Ben Sternberg.
3rd Battalion: Major Joseph W. Sisson, Jr.

26TH INFANTRY

Regimental Commander:
Colonel John W. Bowen.
1st Battalion: Lieutenant Colonel Walter H. Grant.
2nd Battalion: Lieutenant Colonel Derrill M. Daniel.
3rd Battalion: Lieutenant Colonel John T. Corley.

SPECIAL TROOPS

1st Engineer Combat Battalion: Major William B. Gara.
1st Medical Battalion: Lieutenant Colonel Samuel Bleichfeld.
1st Reconnaissance Troop: Major Francis W. Adams; Captain William L. Blake.
1st Quartermaster Company: Captain John J. King.
1st Ordnance Company (LM) Captain Charles P. Bartow.
1st Signal Company: Captain Henry F. Sander.
Military Police Platoon: Major Thomas F. Lancer.
Headquarters Company: Major L. T. Peters.

ORGANIZATION COMMANDERS
NORMANDY
(June 6 to July 25, 1944)

1ST DIVISION ARTILLERY

Commander:
Brigadier General Clift Andrus.
5th F.A. Battalion: Lieutenant Colonel Robert N. Tyson.

7th F.A. Battalion: Lieutenant Colonel George W. Gibb.
32nd F.A. Battalion: Lieutenant Colonel Edward S. Bechtold.
33rd F.A. Battalion: Lieutenant Colonel Walter J. Bryde.

16TH INFANTRY

Regimental Commander:
Colonel George A. Taylor.
Colonel Frederick W. Gibb.
1st Battalion: Lieutenant Colonel Edmund F. Driscoll.
2nd Battalion: Lieutenant Colonel Herbert C. Hicks, Jr.
3rd Battalion: Lieutenant Colonel Charles T. Horner, Jr.

18TH INFANTRY

Regimental Commander:
Colonel George A. Smith, Jr.
1st Battalion: Lieutenant Colonel Robert H. York.
2nd Battalion: Lieutenant Colonel John Williamson.
3rd Battalion: Lieutenant Colonel Joseph W. Sisson, Jr.; Major Elisha O. Peckham.

26TH INFANTRY

Regimental Commander:
Colonel John F. R. Seitz.
1st Battalion: Lieutenant Colonel Francis J. Murdoch, Jr.
2nd Battalion: Lieutenant Colonel Derrill M. Daniel.
3rd Battalion: Lieutenant Colonel John T. Corley.

SPECIAL TROOPS

Commanding Officer:
Lt. Colonel Walter H. Grant.
1st Engineer Combat Battalion: Lieutenant Colonel William B. Gara.
1st Medical Battalion: Lieutenant Colonel Samuel Bleichfeld.
1st Reconnaissance Troop: Captain William L. Blake.
1st Quartermaster Company: Captain John J. King.
701st (LM) Ordnance Company: Captain Raymond C. Huntoon.
Military Police Platoon: Major Thomas F. Lancer.
Headquarters Company: Major Leonard T. Peters.

ORGANIZATION COMMANDERS
ST. LO AND MORTAIN
(July 26 to August 24, 1944)

1ST DIVISION ARTILLERY

Artillery Commander:
Brigadier General Clift Andrus.
5th F.A. Battalion: Lieutenant Colonel Robert N. Tyson.

7th F.A. Battalion: Lieutenant Colonel George W. Gibb; Major Donald A. Heath.

32nd F.A. Battalion: Lieutenant Colonel Edward S. Bechtold.

33rd F.A. Battalion: Lieutenant Colonel Walter J. Bryde.

16TH INFANTRY

Regimental Commander:

Colonel George A. Taylor.

Colonel Frederick W. Gibb.

1st Battalion: Lieutenant Colonel Edmund F. Driscoll.

2nd Battalion: Lieutenant Colonel Herbert C. Hicks, Jr.

3rd Battalion: Lieutenant Colonel Charles T. Horner, Jr.

18TH INFANTRY

Regimental Commander:

Colonel George A. Smith, Jr.

1st Battalion: Lieutenant Colonel Robert H. York.

2nd Battalion: Lieutenant Colonel Ben Sternberg.

3rd Battalion: Lieutenant Colonel Elisha O. Peckham.

26TH INFANTRY

Regimental Commander:

Colonel John F. R. Seitz.

1st Battalion: Lieutenant Colonel Francis J. Murdoch, Jr.

2nd Battalion: Lieutenant Colonel Derrill M. Daniel.

3rd Battalion: Lieutenant Colonel John T. Corley.

SPECIAL TROOPS

Commanding Officer:

Major Leonard T. Peters.

1st Engineer Combat Battalion: Lieutenant Colonel William B. Gara.

1st Medical Battalion: Lieutenant Colonel Samuel Bleichfeld.

1st Reconnaissance Troop: Captain William L. Blake.

1st Quartermaster Company: Captain John J. King.

701st (LM) Ordnance Company: Captain Raymond C. Huntoon.

1st Signal Company: Captain Herbert H. Wiggins.

Military Police Platoon: Captain Raymond R. Regan; Major Thomas F. Lancer.

Headquarters Company: Major Leonard T. Peters.

ORGANIZATION COMMANDERS
MONS AND AACHEN
(August 25 to November 9, 1944)

1ST DIVISION ARTILLERY

Commander:

Brigadier General Clift Andrus.

5th F.A. Battalion: Lieutenant Colonel Robert N. Tyson.

7th F.A. Battalion: Major Donald A. Heath.

32nd F.A. Battalion: Lieutenant Colonel Edward S. Bechtold.

33rd F.A. Battalion: Lieutenant Colonel Walter J. Bryde.

16TH INFANTRY

Regimental Commander:

Colonel Frederick W. Gibb.

1st Battalion: Lieutenant Colonel Edmund F. Driscoll.

2nd Battalion: Lieutenant Colonel Herbert C. Hicks, Jr.; Lieutenant Colonel Walter H. Grant.

3rd Battalion: Lieutenant Colonel Charles T. Horner, Jr.

18TH INFANTRY

Regimental Commander:

Colonel George A. Smith, Jr.

1st Battalion: Lieutenant Colonel Henry G. Learnard, Jr.

2nd Battalion: Lieutenant Colonel John Williamson.

3rd Battalion: Lieutenant Colonel Elisha O. Peckham.

26TH INFANTRY

Regimental Commander:

Colonel John F. R. Seitz.

1st Battalion: Major Francis W. Adams.

2nd Battalion: Lieutenant Colonel Derrill M. Daniel.

3rd Battalion: Lieutenant Colonel John T. Corley.

SPECIAL TROOPS

Commanding Officer:

Lieutenant Colonel Walter H. Grant.

Lieutenant Colonel Herbert C. Hicks, Jr.

1st Engineer Combat Battalion: Lieutenant Colonel William B. Gara.

1st Medical Battalion: Lieutenant Colonel Samuel Bleichfeld.

1st Reconnaissance Troop: Captain William L. Blake.

701st (LM) Ordnance Company: Captain Raymond C. Huntoon.

1st Signal Company: Captain Herbert H. Wiggins.

Military Police Platoon: Major Raymond R. Regan.

Headquarters Company: Major Leonard T. Peters.

ORGANIZATION COMMANDERS
HURTGEN FOREST
(November 10 to December 8, 1944)
1ST DIVISION ARTILLERY

Commander:

Brigadier General Clift Andrus.

5th F.A. Battalion: Lieutenant Colonel Robert N. Tyson.

7th F.A. Battalion: Major Donald A. Heath.
32nd F.A. Battalion: Lieutenant Colonel Edward S. Bechtold.
33rd F.A. Battalion: Lieutenant Colonel Walter J. Bryde.

16TH INFANTRY

Regimental Commander:
Colonel Frederick W. Gibb.
1st Battalion: Lieutenant Colonel Edmund F. Driscoll.
2nd Battalion: Lieutenant Colonel Walter H. Grant.
3rd Battalion: Lieutenant Colonel Charles T. Horner, Jr.

18TH INFANTRY

Regimental Commander:
Colonel George A. Smith.
1st Battalion: Lieutenant Colonel Henry G. Learnard, Jr.
2nd Battalion: Lieutenant Colonel John Williamson.
3rd Battalion: Lieutenant Colonel Elisha O. Peckham.

26TH INFANTRY

Regimental Commander:
Colonel John F. R. Seitz.
1st Battalion: Major J. K. Rippert.
2nd Battalion: Lieutenant Colonel Derrill M. Daniel.
3rd Battalion: Lieutenant Colonel John T. Corley.

SPECIAL TROOPS

Commanding Officer:
Lieutenant Colonel Herbert C. Hicks, Jr.
1st Engineer Combat Battalion: Lieutenant Colonel William B. Gara.
1st Medical Battalion: Lieutenant Colonel Samuel Bleichfeld.
1st Reconnaissance Troop: Captain William L. Blake.
1st Quartermaster Company: Captain John J. King.
701st (LM) Ordnance Company: Captain Raymond C. Huntoon.
1st Signal Company: Captain Herbert H. Wiggins.
Military Police Platoon: Major Raymond R. Regan.
Headquarters Company: Major Leonard T. Peters.

ORGANIZATION COMMANDERS
THE ARDENNES
(December 17, 1944 to February 6, 1945)

1ST DIVISION ARTILLERY

Artillery Commander:
Colonel William E. Waters.
5th F.A. Battalion: Major Vernon R. Rawie.

7th F.A. Battalion: Major Donald A. Heath.
32nd F.A. Battalion: Lieutenant Colonel Edward S. Bechtold.
33rd F.A. Battalion: Lieutenant Colonel Walter J. Bryde.

16TH INFANTRY

Regimental Commander:
Colonel Frederick W. Gibb.
1st Battalion: Lieutenant Colonel Edmund F. Driscoll.
2nd Battalion: Lieutenant Colonel Walter H. Grant.
3rd Battalion: Lieutenant Colonel Charles T. Horner, Jr.

18TH INFANTRY

Regimental Commander:
Colonel George Smith, Jr.
Colonel John Williamson.
1st Battalion: Lieutenant Colonel Henry G. Learnard, Jr.
2nd Battalion: Lieutenant Colonel John Williamson.
3rd Battalion: Lieutenant Colonel Elisha P. Peckham.

26TH INFANTRY

Regimental Commander:
Colonel John F. R. Seitz.
1st Battalion: Major J. K. Rippert.
2nd Battalion: Lieutenant Colonel Derrill M. Daniel.
3rd Battalion: Lieutenant Colonel John T. Corley; Lieutenant Colonel Francis J. Murdoch, Jr.

SPECIAL TROOPS

Commanding Officer:
Lieutenant Colonel Herbert C. Hicks, Jr.
1st Engineer Combat Battalion: Lieutenant Colonel William B. Gara.
1st Medical Battalion: Lieutenant Colonel Samuel Bleichfeld.
1st Reconnaissance Troop: Captain William L. Blake.
1st Quartermaster Company: Captain John J. King.
701st (LM) Ordnance Company: Captain Raymond C. Huntoon.
1st Signal Company: 1st Lieutenant Charles R. Alexander.
Military Police Platoon: Major Raymond R. Regan.
Headquarters Company: Major Leonard T. Peters.

ORGANIZATION COMMANDERS
BONN AND REMAGEN
(February 8 to April 7, 1945)

1ST DIVISION ARTILLERY

Artillery Commander:
Brigadier General William E. Waters.

5th F.A. Battalion: Lieutenant Colonel Vernon R. Rawie.
7th F.A. Battalion: Major Donald A. Heath.
32nd F.A. Battalion: Lieutenant Colonel Edward S. Bechtold.
33rd F.A. Battalion: Lieutenant Colonel Walter J. Bryde.

16TH INFANTRY

Regimental Commander:
Colonel Frederick W. Gibb.
1st Battalion: Lieutenant Colonel Edmund F. Driscoll.
2nd Battalion: Lieutenant Colonel Walter H. Grant.
3rd Battalion: Lieutenant Colonel Charles T. Horner, Jr.

18TH INFANTRY

Regimental Commander:
Colonel John Williamson.
1st Battalion: Lieutenant Colonel Henry G. Learnard, Jr.
2nd Battalion: Major Henry V. Middleworth.
3rd Battalion: Lieutenant Colonel Elisha O. Peckham.

26TH INFANTRY

Regimental Commander:
Colonel John F. R. Seitz.
1st Battalion: Lieutenant Colonel Jacob K. Rippert.
2nd Battalion: Lieutenant Colonel Derrill M. Daniel.
3rd Battalion: Lieutenant Colonel Francis J. Murdoch, Jr.

SPECIAL TROOPS

Commanding Officer:
Lieutenant Colonel Herbert C. Hicks, Jr.
1st Engineer Combat Battalion: Lieutenant Colonel William B. Gara.
1st Medical Battalion: Lieutenant Colonel Samuel Bleichfeld.
1st Reconnaissance Troop: Captain William L. Blake.
1st Quartermaster Company: Captain John J. King.
701st (LM) Ordnance Company: Captain Raymond C. Huntoon.
1st Signal Company: Captain Herbert H. Wiggins.
Military Police Platoon: Major Raymond R. Regan.
Headquarters Company: Captain George V. Visel.

ORGANIZATION COMMANDERS
"The Last Kilometer"
HARZ MOUNTAINS TO CZECHOSLOVAKIA
(April 8 to May 8, 1945)

1ST DIVISION ARTILLERY

Artillery Commander:
Brigadier General William E. Waters.

5th F.A. Battalion: Lieutenant Colonel Vernon R. Rawie.
7th F.A. Battalion: Major Donald A. Heath.
32nd F.A. Battalion: Lieutenant Colonel Edward S. Bechtold.
33rd F.A. Battalion: Lieutenant Colonel Walter J. Bryde.

16TH INFANTRY

Regimental Commander:
Colonel Frederick W. Gibb.
1st Battalion: Lieutenant Colonel Edmund F. Driscoll.
2nd Battalion: Lieutenant Colonel Walter H. Grant.
3rd Battalion: Lieutenant Colonel Charles T. Horner, Jr.

18TH INFANTRY

Regimental Commander:
Colonel John Williamson.
1st Battalion: Lieutenant Colonel Henry G. Learnard, Jr.
2nd Battalion: Major Henry V. Middleworth.
3rd Battalion: Lieutenant Colonel Elisha O. Peckham.

26TH INFANTRY

Regimental Commander:
Colonel John F. R. Seitz.
Colonel Francis J. Murdoch, Jr.
1st Battalion: Lieutenant Colonel Frank Dulligan.
2nd Battalion: Lieutenant Colonel Derrill M. Daniel.
3rd Battalion: Lieutenant Colonel Francis J. Murdoch, Jr.

SPECIAL TROOPS

Commanding Officer:
Lieutenant Colonel Herbert C. Hicks, Jr.
1st Engineer Combat Battalion: Lieutenant Colonel William B. Gara.
1st Medical Battalion: Lieutenant Colonel Samuel Bleichfeld.
1st Reconnaissance Troop: Captain William L. Blake.
1st Quartermaster Company: Captain John J. King.
701st (LM) Ordnance Company: 1st Lieutenant John R. Groves.
1st Signal Company: Captain Herbert H. Wiggins.
Military Police Platoon: Major Raymond R. Regan.
Headquarters Company: Captain George V. Visel.

FIRST INFANTRY DIVISION
ASSIGNMENT AND ATTACHMENT
TO HIGHER UNITS

8 Nov. 42, II Corps; 20 Nov. 42, II Corps, XIX (French); 10 July 43, II Corps, Seventh Army; 1 Nov. 43, ETOUSA; 6 Nov. 43, VII Corps, First Army; 2 Feb. 44, V Corps, First Army; 14 July 44, First Army; 15 July 44, VII Corps, First Army;

1 Aug. 44, II Corps, First Army; 16 Dec. 44, V Corps, First Army; 20 Dec. 44,
V Corps, First Army, BR-21st Army Group; 18 Jan. 45, V Corps, First Army, 12th;
26 Jan. 45 XVIII Corps (Airborne), First Army; 12 Feb. 45, III Corps, First Army;
8 Mar. 45, VII Corps, First Army; 27 Apr. 45, VIII Army, First Army; 30 Apr. 45,
V Corps, First Army; 6 May 45, Third Army.

FIRST INFANTRY DIVISION
RECORD OF EVENTS

(June 30, 1942 to May 8, 1945)

June 30, 1942, Command post at Indiantown Gap, Pennsylvania, U.S.A.

June 30, 1942, Advance Detail departed Indiantown Gap, Pennsylvania, U.S.A.

July 1, 1942, Advance detail departed New York, U.S.A.

July 14, 1942, Advance detail arrived Liverpool, England

July 30-Aug. 1, 1942, Division troops departed Indiantown Gap, Pennsylvania, U.S.A.

Aug. 2, 1942, Division troops departed (on board *H.M.S. Queen Mary*) New York, U.S.A.

Aug. 7, 1942, *H.M.S. Queen Mary* arrived Firth of Forth, Scotland

Aug. 8, 1942, Division troops debarked Gourock, Scotland

Aug. 9, 1942, Division troops arrived Tidworth Barracks, England

Aug. 10, 1942, Division Maneuvers, Inverrary, Scotland

Oct. 22, 1942, Division departed Glasgow, Fw. CP SS Reina del Pacifico, Rr. CP SS Warwick Castle, Firth of Clyde, Scotland

Nov. 8, 1942, Division arrived North Africa, Arzew, Algeria

Nov. 8, 1942, CP Tourville, Algeria, North Africa

Nov. 10, 1942, CP Assi Bou Nif, Algeria, North Africa

Nov. 11, 1942, CP Ste. Jean Baptiste, Algeria, North Africa

Nov. 12, 1942, CP Fme De Raoux-Ste. Barbe du Tlelat, Algeria, North Africa

Jan. 1, 1943, CP Fme. De Raoux-Ste. Barbe du Tlelat, Algeria, North Africa

Jan. 28, 1943, CP arrived Maktar, Tunisia, North Africa

Jan. 29, 1943, CP (advance) near Ousseltia, Tunisia, North Africa

Jan. 30, 1943, CP (advance) Kesra, CP (rear) at Maktar, Tunisia, North Africa

Feb. 21, 1943, CP (advance) 4 miles north of Bou Chebka on Bou Chebka-Tebessa Road, Tunisia, North Africa

Feb. 28, 1943, CP (forward echelon) Bou Kadra, Tunisia, North Africa

Mar. 12, 1943, CP (advance) 5 miles east of Bou Kadra on Bou Chebka-Ferina Road, Tunisia, North Africa

Mar. 18, 1943, CP (advance) at Lala, Tunisia, North Africa

Mar. 19, 1943, CP (advance) at Gafsa, Tunisia, North Africa

Mar. 21, 1943, CP (advance) at El Guettar, Tunisia, North Africa

Apr. 10, Apr. 16, 1943, CP (forward echelon) at Bou Kadra, Tunisia, North Africa

Apr. 17, Apr. 18, 1943, CP (advance) at Roumes Souk (Beja), Tunisia, North Africa

Apr. 18, Apr. 25, 1943, CP (advance) at Muncha, Tunisia, North Africa

May 3, May 4, 1943, CP (advance) at Djebel Badjar, Tunisia, North Africa

May 4, May 5, 1943, CP (advance) at Djebel Touta, Tunisia, North Africa

May 5, May 8, 1943, CP (advance) at Djebel Guenba, Tunisia, North Africa

May 11, 1943, CP (advance) at Sidi Chami, Tunisia, North Africa

May 13, May 19, 1943, CP (all elements) at Sidi Chami, Algeria, North Africa

June 8, July 5, 1943, Division concentration Staoueli, Planning Headquarters at Sidi Ferruch, Algeria, North Africa

July 5, 1943, CP (advance) on board U.S.S. Chase. CP (alternate) on board U.S.S. Barnett, Algiers, North Africa

July 6, 1943, Convoy in outer harbor, Algiers, North Africa

July 8, 1943, Convoy moved to sea joining DIME and CENT forces off Tunisia, North Africa

July 9, 1943, Division aboard convoy off Gela, Sicily

July 10, July 13, 1943, CP ashore near Gela, Sicily

July 14, July 15, 1943, CP (advance) opened near Ponte Olivo Airport near Gela, Sicily

July 16, 1943, CP (advance) opened at Mazzarino, Sicily

July 17, July 19, 1943, CP (advance) opened at Barrafranca, Sicily

July 20, July 21, 1943, CP (advance) opened at Villarosa, Sicily

July 22, July 23, 1943, CP (advance) opened at Alimena, Sicily

July 24, 1943, CP (advance) opened at Petralia, Sicily

July 25, July 28, 1943, CP (advance) opened at Gangi, Sicily

July 29, Aug. 2, 1943, CP (advance) opened at Sperlinga, Sperlinga, Sicily

Aug. 3, Aug. 13, 1943, CP (both advance and rear), opened at Cerami, Sicily. Major General Clarence R. Huebner assumed command of Division Aug. 6.

Aug. 13, Aug. 27, 1943, CP (advance) west of Randazzo, Sicily

Aug. 28, Oct. 13, 1943, CP (advance) at Palma di Montechiaro, Sicily

Oct. 14, Oct. 22, 1943, CP (advance) at Augusta, Sicily

Oct. 23, 1943, Entire Division departed Augusta, Sicily

Oct. 25, 1943, Entire Division arrived Algiers, Algeria, North Africa (did not debark)

Nov. 8, 1943, Entire Division arrived Liverpool, England

Nov. 9, Dec. 31, 1943, Entire Division Headquarters at Blandford, England

Jan. 1, June 2, 1944, Entire Division Headquarters at Blandford, England

June 3, 1944, Entire Division arrived CP (advanced) U.S.S. ANCON, CP (alternate) U.S.S. Chase, Portland, England

June 5, 1944, Division cleared Portland, England

June 6, 1944, CP (advance) Omaha Beach (Easy Red Beach) Calvados, France

June 7, 1944, CP (advance) Colleville-sur-Mer, Calvados, France

June 8, 1944, CP (advance) Russy, Calvados, France

June 10, 1944, CP (advance) Court Elay (1 kil s), Calvados, France
June 11, 1944, CP (advance) Sur-Le-Chemin-du-Gril, Calvados, France
June 12, 1944, CP (advance) Balleroy, Calvados, France
July 14, 1944, CP (advance) Colombieres, Calvados, France
July 20, 1944, CP (advance) St. Jean-de-Daye, Manche, France
July 25, 1944, CP (advance) Bois du Hommat, Manche, France
July 28, 1944, CP (advance) La Chapelle, Manche, France
July 28, 1944, CP (advance) Marigny, Manche, France
July 30, 1944, CP (advance) St. Denis-du-Gast, Manche, France
Aug. 1, 1944, CP (advance) Brecey, Manche, France
Aug. 3, 1944, CP (advance) Juvigny, Manche, France
Aug. 4, 1944, CP (advance) Logis de la Bocage, Manche, France
Aug. 7, 1944, CP (advance) Logis de la Bocage, Manche, France
Aug. 13, 1944, CP (advance) Ambrieres le Grand, Mayenne, France
Aug. 13, 1944, CP (advance) La Ferte Mace, Orne, France
Aug. 14, 1944, CP (advance) Couterne, Orne, France
Aug. 15, 1944, CP (advance) Bagnoles de l'Orne, Orne, France
Aug. 24, 1944, CP Le Thieulin, Eure-et-Loir, France
Aug. 25, 1944, CP (advance) Lardy, Seine-et-Oise, France
Aug. 27, 1944, CP (advance) Etiolles, Seine-et-Oise, France
Aug. 27, 1944, CP (advance) Servon, Seine-et-Oise, France
Aug. 28, 1944, CP (advance) House of Rothschild (Ferrieres), Seine-et-Marne,
     France
Aug. 28, 1944, CP (advance) Quincy Voisins, Seine-et-Oise, France
Aug. 29, 1944, CP (advance) Crouy, Seine-et-Marne, France
Aug. 30, 1944, CP (advance) Soissons, Aisne, France
Aug. 31, 1944, CP (advance) Chevrigny, Aisne, France
Sept. 1, 1944, CP (advance) Le Novion, Aisne, France
Sept. 3, 1944, CP (advance) Ecuelin, Nord, France
Sept. 4, 1944, CP (advance) Mons, Hainut, Belgium
Sept. 6, 1944, CP (advance) Roux (Charleroi), Hainut, Belgium
Sept. 7, 1944, CP (advance) Namur, Namur, Belgium
Sept. 8, 1944, CP (advance) Stockay, Namur, Belgium
Sept. 11, 1944, CP (advance) Lalouxe, Namur, Belgium
Sept. 14, 1944, CP (advance) Henri Chapelle (1½ km n), Liege, Belgium
Sept. 15, 1944, CP (advance) Hauset (vic 7 km s of Aachen), Liege, Belgium
Nov. 10, 1944, CP (advance) Vicht, Rhineland, Germany
Dec. 8, 1944, CP (advance) Hauset (7 km s of Aachen), Liege, Belgium
Dec. 17, 1944, CP (advance) Sourbrodt, Liege, Belgium
Jan. 27, 1945, CP (advance) Weverce, Liege, Belgium
Feb. 1, 1945, CP (advance) Hunningen, Liege, Belgium
Feb. 6, 1945, CP (advance) Aywaile, Liege, Belgium

Feb. 8, 1945, CP (advance) Groshau, Rhineland, Germany
Feb. 28, 1945, CP (advance) Drove, Rhineland, Germany
Mar. 2, 1945, CP (advance) Kelz, Rhineland, Germany
Mar. 6, 1945, CP (advance) Friesham, Rhineland, Germany
Mar. 7, 1945, CP (advance) Metternich, Rhineland, Germany
Mar. 15, 1945, CP (advance) Unkel, Rhineland, Germany
Mar. 21, 1945, CP (advance) Ittenbach, Rhineland, Germany
Mar. 24, 1945, CP (advance) Oberpleis, Rhineland, Germany
Mar. 27, 1945, CP (advance) Obereip, Rhineland, Germany
Mar. 28, 1945, CP (advance) Eichelhardt, Rhineland, Germany
Mar. 29, 1945, CP (advance) Allendorf, Nassau, Germany
Mar. 31, 1945, CP (advance) Bidenkopf, Nassau, Germany
Apr. 1, 1945, CP (advance) Wunnenberg, Westphalia, Germany
Apr. 7, 1945, CP (advance) Peckelsheim, Westphalia, Germany
Apr. 9, 1945, CP (advance) Lauemforde, Hanover, Germany
Apr. 10, 1945, CP (advance) Uslar, Hanover, Germany
Apr. 11, 1945, CP (advance Northeim, Hanover, Germany
Apr. 12, 1945, CP (advance) Osterode, Hanover, Germany
Apr. 17, 1945, CP (advance) St. Andreasberg, Hanover, Germany
Apr. 19, 1945, CP (advance) Benneckenstein, Brunswick, Germany
Apr. 24, 1945, CP (advance) Blankenheim, Halle-Merseburg, Germany
Apr. 27, 1945, CP (advance) Markleuthen, Bavaria, Germany
May 6, 1945, CP (advance) Cheb, Sudetenland, Czechoslovakia

FIRST INFANTRY DIVISION
ATTACHMENTS AND DETACHMENTS
ORAN
(November 8 to 10, 1942)

Coast Artillery:

    105th CA Bn (AA) Less Batteries C and D (RED Force)
    431st CA Bn (AA) Batteries C and D (RED Force)
    105th CA Bn (AA) Batteries A and B (CT-16)
    431st CA Bn (AA) Batteries C and D (CT-18)
    105th CA Bn (AA) Batteries C and D (WHITE Force)

Engineers:

    531st Engr. Shore Regt. (less 2nd Bn) (RED Force)
    531st Engr. Shore Regt. (3rd Bn) (CT-16)
    531st Engr. Shore Regt. (1st Bn) (CT-18)
    531st Engr. Shore Regt. (2nd Bn) (WHITE Force)

Armored:

    1st Armored Division (Combat Command B less Beach clm X)

Signal:
    286th Amphib Co. (det) (RED Force)
    162nd Sig Photo Co. (det) (RED Force)
    286th Amphib Sig Co. (det) (CT-16)
    162nd Sig Photo Co. (det) (CT-18)
    286th Amphib Sig Co. (det) (WHITE Force)

Field Artillery:
    12th FA Bn Hqrs. Det. (RED Force)
    12th FA Bn (Det) (CT-18)
    12th FA Bn (Det) (WHITE Force)

Rangers:
    1st Ranger Battalion

TUNISIA
(November 20, 1942 to May 8, 1943)

Air Support Party:
    Personnel

Armored:
    1st Armored Division:
        6th Armored Regiment (1st Bn)
        13th Armored Regiment (1st Bn)

Coast Artillery:
    105th CA Bn (AA)

Rangers:
    1st Ranger Battalion

Reconnaissance:
    56th Reconn Regt. (British)—1 squadron

Signal:
    2624 Signal Service Battalion

Tank Destroyer:
    601 Tank Destroyer Battalion
    701 Tank Destroyer Battalion

SICILY
(July 10 to August 16, 1943)

Air Corps:
    RAF and AAF

Armored:
    67th Armd Regt (Med Tk) 2 Plats

Artillery:
    106th AA Group (Hd & Hd Batt)
    105th CA Bn (AA) (AW) (SP)

113th CA Bn (AA) (Mob) (Sep)
690th CA Bn (AA) (Sep)
691st CA Bn (AA) (Sep)
692nd CA Bn (AA) (Sep)
693rd CA Bn (AA) (Sep)
17th FA Regt
107th CA Bn (AA) (AW)—Batts A & B
36th FA Bn E Batt
215th CA Bn (AA) (Gun) (Mob) (Sep)
13th FA Bn Det Hqrs
62nd FA Bn det (amm)

Broadcasting:
Broadcasting detachment

Censorship:
Censorship detachment

Chemical:
12th Cml Co (Maint) (-det)
21st Cml Co (Decon) Plat
83rd Cml Wpons Bn (Motz)

Civil Affairs:
Civil Affairs Detail

C. I. C.:
C. I. C. Detachment

Engineers:
531st Engr Shore Regt plus attached
531st Engr Shore Regt
2657th Engrs (det)
462nd Engr Co (-det)
809th Engr Bn (Av)
39th Engr Regt (C)
2602 Engr Co (pipeline)
401st Engr Bn (WS)
437th Engr Bn (Dep Trk)
62nd Engr Co (Topo)
601st Engr Bn (AM) Plat Co B

Medical:
261st Med. Bn (Amphib) (-1 Co.)
11th Field Hospital (1 Plat.)
93rd Evacuation Hospital (400 beds)
15th Evacuation Hospital (400 beds)

36th Ambulance Co. Det. Co. A
2nd Medical Supply Depot Section Supply Plat.
51st Med. Bn. (Collecting Co.) plus clrl. det.
2nd Aux. Surgical Group (7 teams)
8580 JJ Veterinary Det. T

Military Police:
504th MP Bn (-Cos. A, B and C)
342nd MP Escort Guard Co.

Naval Forces:
Naval Shore Bn # 4 (-1 Co.)
Naval Personnel

Observation Battalion:
1st Ob. Bn. (Det.)

Ordnance:
68th Ord. Co. (Amm.)
3407th Ord. Co. (MM)
63rd Ord. Bn. (Hq. & Hq. Det.)
43rd Ord. Bn. (Hq. & Hq. Det.)
3406th Ord. Co. (MM) (Q)
83rd Ord. Co. (HM) (Tk)
330th Ord. Co. (MTS) (-½ Co.)
79th Ord. Co. (Dep.) (-½ Co.)
262nd Ord. Co. (MM) (AA)
235th Ord. Co. (Bomb Disp.)—3rd Plat.

Port Battalions:
384th Port Bn.
382nd Port Bn. (Cos. C and D)

Public Relations:
Public Relations Detail

P. W. Proclamation Teams:
Personnel

Quartermaster:
86th QM Co. (Rhd.)
2637th QM Bn. (Trk.) (DUKWS)
46th QM Co. (GR) 2 Plats.
249th QM Bn. (TRK)
249th QM Bn (-Cos. E and F)
184th QM Co. (Sep. Sup.)
205th QM Bn. (GS) Co. A
47th QM Regt. (TRK) (-Cos. E and F) 2 Bn.

Rangers:

    1st Ranger Battalion

    4th Ranger Battalion

Reconnaissance:

    91st Rec. Squad.

Signal:

    286th Sig. Co. (2nd Plat.) 1 Regtl. Team

    72nd Sig. Bn. (Det.)

    163rd Sig. Photo Co. (Det.)

    206th Sig. Co. (Det.) S & I Sec.

    177th Sig. Co. 2 Rad. Secs.; 1 Tel. Sec.

Tanks:

    70th Tank Bn.

OMAHA BEACH TO CZECHOSLOVAKIA
(June 6, 1944 to May 8, 1945)

Antiaircraft Artillery:

    103rd Bn. (AA) (Mob.) (AW) Bty. B, 12 June 44 to 15 June 44

    461st Bn. (AA) (Mob.) (AW) Bty. D, 15 June 44 to 28 June 44

    103rd Bn. (AA) (Mob.) (AW) 16 June 44 to 7 Feb. 45

    461st Bn. (AA) (Mob.) (AW) Btys. B & D, 26 June 44 to 28 June 44

    639th Bn. (AA) (Mob.) (AW), 18 Dec. 44 to 31 Dec. 44

    460th Bn. (AA) (Mob.) (AW) Bty. A, 1 Jan. 45 to 1 Jan. 45

    103rd Bn. (AA) (Mob.) (AW) 24 Feb. 45 to 8 May 45

Armored:

    745th Tank Battalion, 6 June 44 to 8 May 45

    747th Tank Battalion, 7 June 44 to 15 June 44

    741st Tank Battalion, 7 June 44 to 15 June 44

    743rd Tank Battalion, 11 June 44 to 13 June 44

    635th Tank Destroyer Bn. . . . .

3rd Armored Group:

    3rd Armd. Div., 6 July 44 to 30 July 44

Combat Command B: 3rd Armd. Div., 6 July 44 to 30 July 44

    33rd Armd. Regt., 6 July 44 to 30 July 44

    36th Armd. Regt. (-3rd Bn.), 6 July 44 to 30 July 44

    391st Armd. FA Bn, 6 July 44 to 30 July 44

    83rd Armd. Rec. Bn., 6 July 44 to 30 July 44

    23rd Armd. Eng. Bn. (Cos. B & D), 6 July 44 to 30 July 44

    87th FA Bn (Armd.), 6 July 44 to 30 July 44

    703rd TD Bn (Cos. B & C) (-3rd Plat.), 6 July 44 to 30 July 44

    486th Bn (AA) (AW) (SP) Btys. A & D, 6 July 44 to 30 July 44

413th Bn. (AA) (Gun) (Mob.) Batt. B, 6 July 44 to 30 July 44

Combat Command A:

32nd Armd. Regt., 31 July 44 to 11 Aug. 44

36th Armd. Regt. (3rd Bn.), 31 July 44 to 11 Aug. 44

54th FA Bn, 31 July 44 to 11 Aug. 44

67th FA Bn, 31 July 44 to 11 Aug. 44

23rd Armd. Engr. Bn. (Cos. A & C), 31 July 44 to 11 Aug. 44

58th FA Bn, 31 July 44 to 11 Aug. 44

703rd TD Bn (SP) (Co. A & 3 Plats.), 31 July 44 to 11 Aug. 44

413th AA Bn (Gun) (Mob.) Bty. A, 31 July 44 to 11 Aug. 44

Combat Command R:

32nd Armd. Regt. (3rd Bn.), 8 Mar. 45 to 17 Mar. 45

33rd Armd. Regt. (2nd Bn.), 8 Mar. 45 to 17 Mar. 45

36th Armd. Inf. (3rd Bn.), 8 Mar. 45 to 17 Mar. 45

23rd Armd. Engr. Bn. (Co. C), 8 Mar. 45 to 17 Mar. 45

13th Armd. Regt. (8th Div.) (3rd Bn.), 8 Mar. 45 to 17 Mar. 45

703rd TD Bn (Co. C), 8 Mar. 45 to 17 Mar. 45

32nd Armd. Regt. (3rd Bn.), 20 Mar. 45 to 21 Mar. 45

33rd Armd. Regt. (2nd Bn.), 20 Mar. 45 to 21 Mar. 45

36th Armd. Regt. (3rd Bn.), 20 Mar. 45 to 21 Mar. 45

23rd Armd. Engr. Bn. (Co. C), 20 Mar. 45 to 21 Mar. 45

13th Armd. Inf. (8th Div.) (3rd Bn.), 20 Mar. 45 to 21 Mar. 45

703rd TD. Bn. (SP.) (Co. C), 20 Mar. 45 to 21 Mar. 45

COMBAT COMMAND A (9th Div.) (Armd.), 4 May 45 to 8 May 45

Cavalry:

102nd Cav. Rec. Squad, 11 June 44 to 13 June 44

38th Cav. Rec. Squad, 12 June 44 to 31 July 44

4th Cavalry Group, 1 Aug. 44 to 7 Aug. 44

24th Cav. Rec. Squad, 2 Aug. 44 to 17 Aug. 44

4th Cavalry Group (-4th Cav. Rec. Sq.), 12 Aug. 44 to 17 Aug. 44

4th Cav. Rec. Squad, 14 Aug. 44 to 17 Aug. 44

4th Cav. Group (-24th Cav. Rec. Sq.), 11 Nov. 44 to 30 Nov. 44

32nd Cav. Rec. Squad, 1 Mar. 45 to 10 Mar. 45

4th Cavalry Group, 9 Apr. 45 to 17 Apr. 45

Chemical:

81st Chem. Mort. Bn. (-Cos. B & D), 7 June 44 to 9 June 44

81st Chem. Mort. Bn. (-Cos. B & D), 9 June 44 to 9 June 44

81st Chem. Mort. Bn. (Cos. B & D), 1 July 44 to 30 Sept. 44

87th Chem. Mort. Bn. (Co. A), 1 Sept. 44 to 30 Sept. 44

87th Chem. Mort. Bn. (Cos. A & D), 1 Sept. 44 to 30 Sept. 44

87th Chem. Mort. Bn. (Cos. A & B), 1 Oct. 44 to 17 Dec. 44

86th Chem. Mort. Bn. (Co. C), 13 Jan. 45 to 23 Jan. 45
87th Chem. Mort. Bn. (Co. B), 24 Jan. 45 to 7 Feb. 45
90th Chem. Mort. Bn. (Co. A), 24 Feb. 45 to 10 Mar. 45
90th Chem. Mort. Bn. (Co. B), 30 Mar. 45 to 31 Mar. 45
86th Chem. Mort. Bn. (Co. A), 1 Apr. 45 to 12 Apr. 45
87th Chem. Mort. Bn. (Cos. C & D), 1 Apr. 45 to 12 Apr. 45

Engineers:

20th Engr. Combat Bn., 8 June 44 to 11 June 44
1106th Engr. Combat Group, 1 Oct. 44 to 31 Oct. 44
238th Engr. Combat Bn., 1 Oct. 44 to 31 Oct. 44
257th Engr. Combat Bn., 1 Oct. 44 to 31 Oct. 44
2nd Engr. Combat Bn. (2nd Div.) (Co. B), 14 Jan. 45 to 24 Jan. 45
299th Engr. Combat Bn., 24 Feb. 45 to 10 Mar. 45
994th Engr. Treadway Bridge Co. (1 Plat.), 24 Feb. 45 to 10 Mar. 45
276th Engr. Combat Bat. (1 light Equip. Plat.), 24 Feb. 45 to 10 Mar. 45
72nd Engr. Light Pon. Co., 24 Feb. 45 to 10 Mar. 45

MAJOR GEN. HENRY ALLEN

COMBAT COMMANDERS

MAJOR GENERAL C. R. HUEBNER

MAJOR GENERAL CLIFT ANDRUS

Looking across La Senia
airport toward Oran.
Note Djebel Murdjadjo
in background.

The Beaches of Arzeu.
November 1942.

Les Andalouses
December 1942

Typical Tunisian Arab.

North African transportation.

Kasserine Pass. (Looking Eastward) The Red One successfully counterattacks Rommel's breakthrough in February 1943.

The Red One closes in on Gafsa.

A chow line near El Guettar. 4 April 1943.

PW's.

American II Corps and Monty's British 8th Army effect juncture in Tunisian desert. 7 April 1943.

The shock of battle comes early to a small Sicilian town.

View toward Oran from Mers El Kebir. June 1943.

After Tunisia—en route to Oran.

Tunisian terrain. Rugged!

Half-track loses encounter with Teller Mine. Tunisia 1943.

Sicily Convoy.

Off Sicily the water was rough.

Admiral J. L. Hall, US Navy—who ably took the Red One into Sicily and into Normandy.

The USS Ancon. Headquarters ship.

The Convoy en route to Sicily.

Gela Sicily July 1943. Support across the beaches.

Gela Beaches.

Col. Gibb, C. O. 16th Infantry with Brig. Gen. Wyman at 16th Infantry CP—August 1944.

Omaha Beach after the fighting had moved inland 14 June.

1st Division patrol nearing a flanked German machine-gun position, Sicily 1943.

Patrol from 1st Division flanking a German machine-gun position in Sicily. The leader has called down our own artillery on the enemy position.

1st Division infantry moving to the attack in Sicily, 1943.

Barafrance. The tank trap and dragons teeth failed to stop the advancing infantry.

Rugged terrain surrounded Enna, key German communication center.

From Nicosia, the infantry continues the advance on Troina.

An artillery OP of the Division directs fire on Troina.

Entering the outskirts of "beat-up" Troina, advancing infantry keeps alert for snipers.

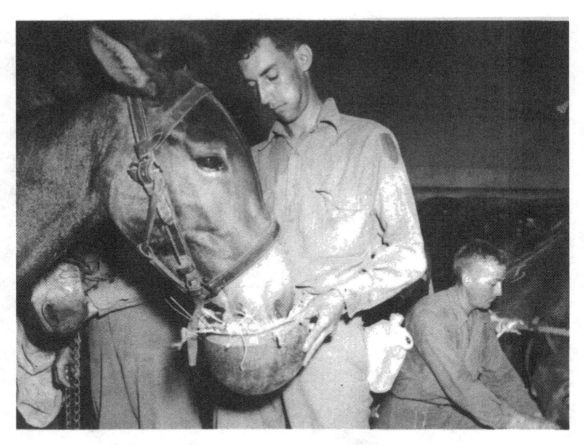

Rugged terrain around Troina necessitates pack trains for supply.

Artillery ammunition for the fight at Troina arrives by pack train.

Maj. Gen. Huebner, Division commander, makes a pre-invasion talk to part of the command.

Some pre-invasion planning over a relief map.

Aboard ship awaiting the cross channel invasion.

Fully loaded LST 51 in Portland Harbor, South England, awaiting the "go signal" for the invasion of Normandy.

Landing craft forming for the assault on Omaha Beach.

Assault waves start shoreward. Omaha Beach.

Omaha Beach as it appeared to assault landing craft on "D" day—6 June 1944.

Closer in, shell fire on the beach becomes discernible.

Follow up waves on Omaha Beach work their way to the shore line through the wreckage of previous waves.

Assault Infantry on Omaha Beach.

These obstacles on Omaha Beach failed to stop the Division.

"Easy Red," where the Division first broke through the shore defenses.

Omaha Beach was rough going all day the 6th of June.

Typical German defensive position on Omaha Beach.

This German gun position on Omaha Beach wasn't rugged enough.

The Rangers crossed this shale—and—

assaulted the height of these cliffs at Point der Hoe.

The 3rd Bn. 16th Inf. on Omaha Beach—D-day.

Les Andalouses. November 1942.

One way traffic off the beach.

Winning a beachhead has its costs.

Easy Red Beach from the defenders viewpoint.

ERNIE PYLE

Gen. Eisenhower visits the 1st Div. CP near Baleroi to present DSC's. In remarking on the accomplishments of the Division, Gen. Eisenhower said, "I know your record from the day you landed in Africa, then Sicily. I am beginning to think that the First Division is a sort of Praetorian Guard."

Gen. Teddy Roosevelt. Died of heart attack 12 July 1944. Buried St. Mere Eglise, Normandy, France.

Col. Seitz and Brig. Gen. Wyman observing the attack on Caumont.

Caumont, Normandy, France.

Col. Seitz, C. O. 26th Infantry at his CP near Caumont, talks to the Division Commander Gen. Huebner, and the Ass't. Div. Commander Gen. Wyman.

Coutances, France. 28 July 1944.

Division Commander Gen. Huebner, Ass't Div. Commander Brig. Gen. Wyman and Chief of Staff Col. Mason at Division CP at Mavenne. France, August 1944. Capt. Bennett (in window) joins Col. Mason in watching anti-aircraft fire on German planes.

Division crossing the Seine River vicinity Melun-Corbeil (just south of Paris) August 1944.

La Ferte-Mace, where the Falaise pocket was almost closed.

Gen. Huebner, Division Commander, Brig. Gen. Wyman, Assistant Division Commander and officers of the staff looking over the monument erected by the World War I First Division to commemorate their battle. In World War II the Division zone of advance again went through Soissons.

Near Stolberg, Germany, dragon's teeth in the Siegfried Line provides shelter for advancing infantry.

Aachen being bombed by P-38's after refusal of its commander to surrender the city and thereby avoid destruction.

Aachen undergoing destruction.

Belgian civilians line streets to cheer the Division through their town.

Tenacious Nazis continue to hold out in Aachen.

More destruction in Aachen.

Results of Aachen's defiance.

Into the dismal Hurtgen Forest.

The First Division moves into the Battle of the Bulge. January 1945.

Snow in the Butgenbach sector in January 1945. (Battle of the Bulge.)

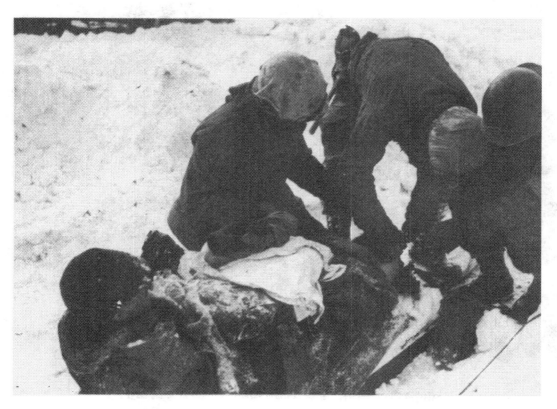

A German mine caused this casualty near Bullingen January 1945. (Battle of the Bulge.)

German snipers hide in the snow-covered ruins of Muringen January 1945. (Battle of the Bulge.)

Engineers repair a bridge near Moderscheid January 1945. (Battle of the Bulge.)

Near Geyer, Germany. First Division Engineers make road repairs to speed up the counter-attack against the Bulge.

First Division Engineers near Langendroich, Germany. Spring rains and melting snows have turned the roads into bottomless quagmires.

More road repairs to support the offensive toward the Roer River.

More bad road near Langendroich, Germany, in February 1945.

Gen. Clift Andrus, commanding the First Infantry Division after promotion of Gen. Huebner to the command of V Corps, escorts Lt. Gen. Omar Bradley to the Division CP in the Hurtgen Forest. February 1945.

Crossing the Roer River.

First Division Infantrymen near Lendersdorf, Germany, (east of the Roer River). February 1945.

Near Soller, Germany, the latter part of February 1945.

The flag which was carried across the Rhine at Coblenz December 13, 1918, in World War I by the 5th F. A. Battalion is presented to the Division so that the 5th F. A. may again take it across the Rhine.

Near Gladbach, Germany. The First Engineer Battalion has erected a Treadway bridge over the Neffel River.
March 1945.

First Division Infantrymen cross the Erft River near Bliesheim, Germany. March 1945.

Near Weilerswist, Germany, mortar men of the 80th Chemical Battalion, (attached to the First Division) set up
their guns to support the attack toward Metternich. March 1945.

Fighting in Bonn.

In Bonn, Division Infantrymen at last see the bridge across the Rhine.

Near Scheuren men of the 26th Infantry ferry across the Rhine.

Crossing the Weser River in an attack on Furstenberg. April 1945.

The attack on Neuhaus, Germany, April 1945.

At Saint Andreasburg, Germany, snipers again cause trouble. April 1945.

This distinguished prisoner was captured in the Hartz Mountain area. April 1945.

Brig. Gen. George A. Taylor, Ass't. Div. Commander, receives the surrender of Lt. Gen. Fritz Benicke and all troops under his command in the vicinity of Elbogen, Czechslovakia. May 7, 1945.

OPERATION "OCCUPATION"

The 1st Battalion 16th Infantry provides a soldierly Guard of Honor in Vienna.

Redeployment strikes again. A large contingent of homeward-bound "Spaders" hears the "all aboard" at Nurnberg Hauptbahnhof.

Anti-Tank Company augments the security around the Palace of Justice in Nurnberg for announcement of the verdicts and sentences of the top Nazi war criminals.

A VE Day ceremony in Eger, Czechoslovakia.

War crimes trials.

Division MP's continue to perform invaluable services for the Division.

Gen. Lucius D. Clay inspecting.

Retreat Formation—Landshut.

The 3rd Bn. 16th Inf. relieves the 3rd Infantry Regiment in Berlin.

On Dec. 28, 1945, Leon Mundeleer, Belgian Minister of National Defense, decorates the First Division colors with the Belgian Fourragere.

May his calls ever ring loud and clear!